I9P$12.00

Perspectives on Tort Law

P9-DIJ-326

Editorial Advisory Board

Little, Brown
and Company
Law Book Division

A. James Casner, Chairman
Austin Wakeman Scott Professor of Law, Emeritus, Harvard
  University

Francis A. Allen
Edson R. Sunderland Professor of Law, University of Michigan

Clark Byse
Byrne Professor of Administrative Law, Harvard University

Thomas Ehrlich
Provost and Professor of Law, University of Pennsylvania

Geoffrey C. Hazard, Jr.
John A. Garver Professor of Law, Yale University

Willis L. M. Reese
Charles Evans Hughes Professor of Law, Emeritus, Columbia
  University

Bernard Wolfman
Fessenden Professor of Law, Harvard University

Perspectives on Tort Law

Second Edition

Robert L. Rabin

Professor of Law, Stanford Law School

Little, Brown and Company   Boston and Toronto

Copyright © 1983, by Robert L. Rabin

All rights reserved. No part of this book may be reproduced in any form or by any electronic or mechanical means including information storage and retrieval systems without permission in writing from the publisher, except by a reviewer who may quote brief passages in a review.

Library of Congress Catalog Card No. 82-082847

ISBN 0-316-73003-3

Second Edition

Sixth Printing

EB

Published simultaneously in Canada
by Little, Brown & Company (Canada) Limited

Printed in the United States of America

To Yemima

Contents

Preface

Like generations of earlier torts professors, I begin the introductory course with discussion of assigned cases from a casebook, moving slowly at first, exploring the facts, issues, procedural framework and rationale for decision. During the semester, the pace will quicken and the issues will vary. At times we will discuss the practical aspects of settling tort cases and at other times we will explore the economic justification for liability rules. But as we move through negligence, strict liability and intentional torts, we will never stray too far from the cases. Whether our focus is on defective products or auto accidents, an understanding of the rules of liability will emerge gradually as we build, case by case and issue by issue, an edifice that houses the relevant legal principles — however ambiguous or imprecise. By the end of the semester, if the course has been handled satisfactorily, the students should have a sense of the doctrinal framework of tort law, some skill in legal reasoning, and a nascent understanding of the dynamics of the judicial process.

The course that does accomplish these pedagogical objectives has done well by the first-semester law student. Because the nature of the judicial process is largely unexplored territory outside of the professional school, case analysis is a new intellectual discipline for most entering students. The language of the law, as well as its procedure, is a mystery that takes time to unravel. It is small wonder, then, that the first-year student — whatever his or her reaction to law school — rarely is moved to reflect on dimensions of the curricular offerings that might have been slighted. When such questions do begin to arise, in the second or third year, it is usually because the repetition of the case analysis process has led to a sense of boredom, or because the concentration on appellate decisions has created a sense of unease about whether the student is really learning enough "real world" lawyering techniques.

Seven years ago, when I prepared the first edition of this book, many legal educators were engaged in self-criticism and a reexamination of goals precisely because law schools had concentrated too exclusively on what they do best: analyzing issues and exploring the subtleties of doctrine within the confines of a comprehensive collection of appellate court opinions. I see only limited evidence that basic approaches have changed in the intervening years. Without downgrading the traditional enterprise in the least, as with an excellent meal or a curative drug, one can react against too much of a good thing.

In collecting, editing, and commenting on the essays in this second edition, I have been guided by a continuing conviction that legal education is seriously slighting a critical dimension of the training of lawyers: a conception of professional education that includes exposure to the intellectual heritage of major disciplines.[1] The case method is particularly inapt for thorough exploration of the historical and ideological underpinnings of a system of legal rules. Particularly in the first year, a casebook channels the student's intellectual energy into exhaustive analysis of a series of conflicts and into elaborate synthesis of the general rules or principles that can be drawn from the discrete occurrences. This enterprise is curiously unidimensional; in a sense, rules of law are treated as if they have the same self-contained quality as those governing basketball or chess. The social, political, and economic factors that influence the development of doctrine are considered — if at all — through snippets from law review articles and notes interspersed between cases.

Missing from the traditional torts course, then, as from the curriculum more generally, is a concern about the historical, moral, and economic values that inform liability rules. Over the years an important literature on the intellectual foundations of tort law has been produced — much of which is familiar to virtually every torts teacher. Yet, in the past, we have not been willing to say that the classic questions about the nature of tort liability are sufficiently important to warrant independent analysis of the original sources, rather than merely tangential treatment within the confines of case analysis.

The essays in this book are intended to be representative of the major scholarly writing that has been done over the past century on

1. I would emphasize that I do not regard this dimension as the only element of legal education that has been slighted in the traditional curriculum. Claims can be made for more clinical training, directed research, specialized interdisciplinary courses, and a variety of other programmatic efforts to diversify and enrich the curriculum. Indeed, I would regard it as highly desirable if legal education were to move towards introducing a mix of curricular offerings that would allow the student to combine wholly disparate learning experiences, such as exploring the theoretical underpinnngs of tort law in one course and simulating the handling of a malpractice case in another.

the development and rationale of the tort system in the United States.[2] The organization of the materials follows the course of historical development. The era of rapid industrial growth beginning after the Civil War marks our point of departure. Along with unparalleled expansion of commercial activity and avenues of transportation came an unprecedented rise in the injury toll. As a consequence, tort law came of age. For the first time, liability rules were required that possessed sufficient breadth and scope to serve as a decision-making framework for cases involving victims of a staggering array of unintended harms. The result, of course, was the negligence system.

The first four chapters of the book deal with the law of negligence from a variety of perspectives. In the opening chapter, essays by Oliver Wendell Holmes and Richard Posner focus on an issue that remains central to tort law today: the justification for fault liability in cases of unintended harm. After this initial exploration of the meaning of the fault principle, Chapter Two attempts to assess the significance of the principle from a historical perspective. The essays by Charles Gregory and Gary Schwartz, along with my own contribution, explore the role of negligence from the preindustrial era to the present. Questions of equal import arise about the function of the system past and present. The Holmes and Wex Malone readings in Chapter Three explore the recurrent practical issue of the allocation between judge and jury of the power to decide. In the same chapter, James Henderson's essay focuses more broadly on the institutional capacity of courts to administer effectively a generalized duty of due care. Still another side of the system in action is examined in Chapter Four, in which Richard Pierce and H. Laurence Ross discuss aspects of the behavioral impact of tort liability rules.

Whether or not negligence law once ruled supreme, it is clear that we are now in a period of reexamining the principles of tort liability. Changing attitudes towards compensation, new forms of insurance, and a variety of other considerations have had a dramatic impact on tort law, creating a constant impetus towards nonfault reparation. But the negligence system has demonstrated the remarkable toughness — resilience, as well as resistance — in the face of pressure for reform. The literature of tort law has benefited greatly

---

2. The scope of the book is limited primarily to consideration of liability for unintentional physical harm. Consequently, the coverage includes negligence, strict liability, and no-fault compensation systems. At the same time, the scope of the book is broad enough to include analysis of foreign systems — whether the system be English case law or the New Zealand accident compensation plan — when a comparative view seems illuminating.

from the consequent tension between fault and nonfault systems. Academics, as well as courts and legislatures, have been forced to reexamine established principles of liability.

Chapters Five through Seven focus on this continuing process of reevaluation and change. Guido Calabresi, Jon Hirschoff and Calabresi, Posner, Walter Blum and Harry Kalven, and Steven Shavell bring to the debate an economic perspective, analyzing the competing systems of liability rules from the standpoint of economic efficiency. In Chapter Six, George Fletcher and Richard Epstein eschew economics in favor of distinctive schemes of corrective justice, focused on considerations of interpersonal equity. Finally, in the last chapter theory merges with practice as Henderson, and Blum and Kalven, respectively discuss social insurance plans and auto compensation — legislative alternatives for accomplishing, in varying degrees, compensation irrespective of fault and outside the tort system.

The readings were selected, edited, and organized with the classroom in mind. This book is designed for use in either of two ways: it can serve as a supplementary volume in an introductory torts course, or it can be used as the primary text for an advanced course or seminar. In conjunction with an introductory course the readings, with accompanying notes and questions, can readily be keyed to the subject matter covered in torts casebooks since virtually all of the essays can be inserted into the sequence of a typical introductory course. In some instances — such as the Fletcher and Epstein articles on theories of corrective justice and the Henderson piece on the New Zealand social insurance system — the volume actually takes up issues that might otherwise be ignored in such a course. In still other instances, the instructor might want to substitute an excerpt from this volume for the more detailed treatment in a casebook; for example, the Blum and Kalven piece on auto compensation plans might accomplish this end.

The volume was prepared, however, with the recognition that many torts teachers are severely constrained by the limited hours allocated to the introductory course. With this in mind, I have designed — and have myself taught — the volume as a text that stands on its own in a torts seminar. The excerpts are deliberately of a length sufficient for thorough analysis, and the notes and questions are specifically meant to serve as a basis for class discussion. The chronological, historical organization should satisfy the fundamental pedagogical tenet that the materials for a seminar demonstrate a coherent approach to a clearly delineated subject matter.

The volume is intended, then, as an exploration of the ideological roots of tort law. Torts teachers have been well served by treatise and text writers, as well as by a long tradition of law review scholarship analyzing tort doctrine. That literature provides an excellent supplement for the student who seeks missing pieces of the doctrinal puzzle or, perhaps, simply wants confirmation that all of the pieces are properly in place. It has not been my purpose to duplicate that effort. Rather, I have tried to present a variety of perspectives on tort law from scholars who have been stimulated by the intellectual challenge of timeless questions about allocating liability for personal harm.

Acknowledgments

I would like to express my appreciation to a number of people who made important contributions to this book. My colleagues Marc Franklin, Tom Grey, and Mark Kelman offered helpful suggestions on content and provided valuable criticism of the introductions, notes, and questions. I benefited greatly from the work of Jean Castle in preparation of the manuscript. I would also like to thank the authors and copyright holders of the following works, who permitted their inclusion in this book:

Richard A. Posner, A Theory of Negligence, 1 Journal of Legal Studies 29-34, 36-48 (1972). Reprinted by permission.

Charles O. Gregory, Trespass to Negligence to Absolute Liability, 37 Virginia Law Review 359, 361-370 (1951). Reprinted by permission of The Virginia Law Review and Fred B. Rothman & Company.

Gary T. Schwartz, The Vitality of Negligence and the Ethics of Strict Liability, 15 Georgia Law Review 963, 963-977 (1981). This article was originally published in the cited volume and is reprinted by permission. I similarly express appreciation to the Georgia Law Review for permission to reprint my essay, The Historical Development of the Fault Principle: A Reinterpretation, 15 Georgia Law Review 925, 927-961 (1981).

Wex S. Malone, Ruminations on Cause in Fact, 9 Stanford Law Review 60-70, 71-75, 81-85, 97-99 (1956). Copyright © 1956 by the Board of Trustees of Leland Stanford Junior University. Reprinted by permission.

James A. Henderson, Jr., Expanding the Negligence Concept: Retreat from the Rule of Law, 51 Indiana Law Journal 467, 468-482 (1976). Reprinted with permission from the Indiana Law Journal and Fred B. Rothman & Co.

Richard J. Pierce, Jr., Encouraging Safety: The Limits of Tort Law and Government Regulation, 33 Vanderbilt Law Review 1281, 1288-1307 (1980). Copyright © 1980 Vanderbilt Law Review. Reprinted by permission.

Reprinted by permission from H. Laurence Ross, Settled out of Court (Chicago: Aldine Publishing Company); copyright © 1970 by H. Laurence Ross.

Bombaugh, The Department of Transportation's Auto Insurance Study and Auto Accident Compensation Reform, Table 3, copyright © 1982 by the Directors of the Columbia Law Review Association, Inc. All rights reserved. This article originally appeared at 71 Colum. L. Rev. 207 (1971). Reprinted by permission.

Guido Calabresi, The Costs of Accidents 17-21, 26-29, 68-75, 135-138, 139-141, 143-152, 160-161 (1970). Reprinted by permission of the Yale University Press from the Costs of Accidents, by Guido Calabresi. Copyright © 1970 by Yale University.

Walter J. Blum and Harry Kalven, Jr., The Empty Cabinet of Dr. Calabresi: Auto Accidents and General Deterrence, 34 University of Chicago Law Review 239, 246-259, 261-263, 264-266 (1967). Reprinted by permission.

Guido Calabresi and Jon T. Hirschoff, Toward a Test for Strict Liability in Tort, 81 Yale Law Journal 1055, 1056-1078, 1082-1084 (1972). Reprinted by permission of The Yale Law Journal Company and Fred B. Rothman & Company from The Yale Law Journal, Vol. 81, pp. 1056-1078, 1082-1084.

Richard A. Posner, Strict Liability: A Comment, 2 Journal of Legal Studies 205-212, 213-215 (1973). Reprinted by permission.

Steven Shavell, Strict Liability versus Negligence, 9 Journal of Legal Studies 1, 1-9, 22-25 (1980). Copyright © 1980 by the University of Chicago Law School. Reprinted with permission of the author and the University of Chicago as publisher.

George P. Fletcher, Fairness and Utility in Tort Theory, 85 Harvard Law Review 537, 543-560, 569-573 (1972). Copyright © 1972 by the Harvard Law Review Association. Reprinted by permission.

Richard A. Epstein, A Theory of Strict Liability, 2 Journal of Legal Studies 151 (1973). Reprinted by permission.

Walter J. Blum and Harry Kalven, Jr., Ceilings, Costs and Compulsion in Auto Compensation Legislation, 1973 Utah Law Review 341, 343-355, 356-357, 359-370, 376-377. Reprinted by permission of the Utah Law Review.

James A. Henderson, Jr., The New Zealand Accident Compensation Reform, 48 University of Chicago Law Review 781, 782-801 (1981). Copyright © The University of Chicago Law Review. Reprinted by permission.

Perspectives on Tort Law

Chapter 1

The Search for a Rationale for Fault Liability

For more than a century, three theories of redress have provided the framework for constructing a comprehensive basis of liability for unintended harm: negligence, strict liability, and no-fault recovery. Clearly, the dominant theory during most of this period has been negligence. Leading cases are filled with resounding affirmations, such as that of Commissioner Earl in Losee v. Buchanan: "...the rule is, at least in this country, a universal one, which, so far as I can discern, has no exceptions or limitations, that no one can be made liable for injuries to the person or property of another without some fault or negligence on his part."[1] Similarly, treatises, texts, and casebooks on the tort law place major emphasis on the doctrinal foundations of negligence law: duty, breach, proximate cause, cause in fact, and the various defenses (with particular attention to contributory and comparative negligence).[2]

As might be expected, given the central role of negligence law, a great deal of attention has been devoted to exploring the rationale for liability based on fault. Some commentators, linking the rise of negligence to the industrial revolution, have argued that the fault principle—as a less expensive theory than strict liability—was a

---

1. Losee v. Buchanan, 51 N.Y. 476 (1873).
2. Questions of duty, proximate cause, cause in fact, and such defenses as assumed risk do not arise exclusively in negligence cases; nonetheless, they are usually given classroom and scholarly attention in the context of determining fault liability— the negligence case.

means of protecting youthful industries from inordinate liability.[3] We will return to this theme in the next chapter, which focuses on the historical development of the fault principle.

The two essays in this section, written nearly a century apart, suggest the range of justifications that can be offered for a system of liability based on fault. Oliver Wendell Holmes wrote The Common Law during the latter half of the nineteenth century, which is generally regarded as the golden age of the law of negligence. His statement of the ethical basis for fault liability is recognized as the classic rationale for the principle in its ascendancy. A contemporary commentator, Richard Posner, defends the negligence doctrine, now under attack, as a system for the efficient allocation of economic resources. Taken together, these essays lay the foundation for a comprehensive examination of the rationale for the fault principle.

The Common Law*

Oliver Wendell Holmes

Lecture III

Torts — Trespass and Negligence

The object of the next two Lectures is to discover whether there is any common ground at the bottom of all liability in tort, and if so, what that ground is. Supposing the attempt to succeed, it will reveal the general principle of civil liability at common law. The liabilities incurred by way of contract are more or less expressly fixed by the agreement of the parties concerned, but those arising from a tort are independent of any previous consent of the wrong-doer to bear the loss occasioned by his act. If A fails to pay a certain sum on a certain day, or to deliver a lecture on a certain night, after having made a binding promise to do so, the damages which he has to pay are recovered in accordance with his consent that some or all of the harms which may be caused by his failure shall fall upon him. But when A assaults or slanders his neighbor, or converts his neighbor's property, he does a harm which he has never consented to bear, and if the law makes him pay for it, the reason for doing so must be found in

---

3. See Gregory, Trespass to Negligence to Strict Liability, pp. 35-42, *infra,* and references in Note 5, p. 43.
*Source: 77-80, 81-84, 88-99, 107-110 (1881).

some general view of the conduct which every one may fairly expect and demand from every other, whether that other has agreed to it or not.

Such a general view is very hard to find. The law did not begin with a theory. It has never worked one out. The point from which it started and that at which I shall try to show that it has arrived, are on different planes. In the progress from one to the other, it is to be expected that its course should not be straight and its direction not always visible. All that can be done is to point out a tendency, and to justify it. The tendency, which is our main concern, is a matter of fact to be gathered from the cases. But the difficulty of showing it is much enhanced by the circumstance that, until lately, the substantive law has been approached only through the categories of the forms of action. Discussions of legislative principle have been darkened by arguments on the limits between trespass and case, or on the scope of a general issue. In place of a theory of tort, we have a theory of trespass. And even within that narrower limit, precedents of the time of the assize and jurata have been applied without a thought of their connection with a long forgotten procedure.

Since the ancient forms of action have disappeared, a broader treatment of the subject ought to be possible. Ignorance is the best of law reformers. People are glad to discuss a question on general principles, when they have forgotten the special knowledge necessary for technical reasoning. But the present willingness to generalize is founded on more than merely negative grounds. The philosophical habit of the day, the frequency of legislation, and the ease with which the law may be changed to meet the opinions and wishes of the public, all make it natural and unavoidable that judges as well as others should openly discuss the legislative principles upon which their decisions must always rest in the end, and should base their judgments upon broad considerations of policy to which the traditions of the bench would hardly have tolerated a reference fifty years ago.

The business of the law of torts is to fix the dividing lines between those cases in which a man is liable for harm which he has done, and those in which he is not. But it cannot enable him to predict with certainty whether a given act under given circumstances will make him liable, because an act will rarely have that effect unless followed by damage, and for the most part, if not always, the consequences of an act are not known, but only guessed at as more or less probable. All the rules that the law can lay down beforehand are rules for determining the conduct which will be followed by liability if it is followed by harm, — that is, the conduct which a man pursues at his peril. The only guide for the future to be drawn from a decision against a defendant in an action of tort is that similar acts, under circumstances which cannot be distinguished except by the result from those of the defendant, are done at the peril of the actor; that if he escapes liability, it is simply because by good fortune no harm comes of his conduct in the particular event.

If, therefore, there is any common ground for all liability in tort, we shall best find it by eliminating the event as it actually turns out, and by considering only the principles on which the peril of his conduct is thrown upon the actor. We are to ask what are the elements, on the defendant's side, which must all be present before liability is possible, and the presence of which will commonly make him liable if damage follows.

The law of torts abounds in moral phraseology. It has much to say of wrongs, of malice, fraud, intent, and negligence. Hence it may naturally be supposed that the risk of a man's conduct is thrown upon him as the result of some moral short-coming. But while this notion has been entertained, the extreme opposite will be found to have been a far more popular opinion; — I mean the notion that a man is answerable for all the consequences of his acts, or, in other words, that he acts at his peril always, and wholly irrespective of the state of his consciousness upon the matter....

As has just been hinted, there are two theories of the common-law liability for unintentional harm. Both of them seem to receive the implied assent of popular text-books, and neither of them is wanting in plausibility and the semblance of authority.

The first is that of Austin, which is essentially the theory of a criminalist. According to him, the characteristic feature of law, properly so called, is a sanction or detriment threatened and imposed by the sovereign for disobedience to the sovereign's commands. As the greater part of the law only makes a man civilly answerable for breaking it, Austin is compelled to regard the liability to an action as a sanction, or, in other words, as a penalty for disobedience. It follows from this, according to the prevailing views of penal law, that such liability ought only to be based upon personal fault; and Austin accepts that conclusion, with its corollaries, one of which is that negligence means a state of the party's mind. These doctrines will be referred to later, so far as necessary.

The other theory is directly opposed to the foregoing. It seems to be adopted by some of the greatest common-law authorities, and requires serious discussion before it can be set aside in favor of any third opinion which may be maintained. According to this view, broadly stated, under the common law a man *acts* at his peril. It may be held as a sort of set-off, that he is never liable for omissions except in consequence of some duty voluntarily undertaken. But the whole and sufficient ground for such liabilities as he does incur outside the last class is supposed to be that he has voluntarily acted, and that damage has ensued. If the act was voluntary, it is totally immaterial that the detriment which followed from it was neither intended nor due to the negligence of the actor.

In order to do justice to this way of looking at the subject, we must remember that the abolition of the common-law forms of pleading has not changed the rules of substantive law. Hence, although pleaders now generally allege intent or negligence, anything which would formerly have been sufficient to charge a defendant in trespass is still sufficient, notwithstanding the fact that the ancient form of action and declaration has disappeared.

In the first place, it is said, consider generally the protection given by the law to property, both within and outside the limits of the last-named action. If a man crosses his neighbor's boundary by however innocent a mistake, or if his cattle escape into his neighbor's field, he is said to be liable in trespass quare clausum fregit. If an auctioneer in the most perfect good faith, and in the regular course of his business, sells goods sent to his rooms for the purpose of being sold, he may be compelled to pay their full value if a third person turns out to be the owner, although he has paid over the proceeds, and has no means of obtaining indemnity.

Now suppose that, instead of a dealing with the plaintiff's property, the case is that force has proceeded directly from the defendant's body to the plaintiff's body, it is urged that, as the law cannot be less careful of the persons than of the property of its subjects, the only defences possible are similar to those which would have been open to an alleged trespass on land. You may show that there was no trespass by showing that the defendant did no act; as where he was thrown from his horse upon the plaintiff, or where a third person took his hand and struck the plaintiff with it. In such cases the defendant's body is the passive instrument of an external force, and the bodily motion relied on by the plaintiff is not his act at all. So you may show a justification or excuse in the conduct of the plaintiff himself. But if no such excuse is shown, and the defendant has voluntarily acted, he must answer for the consequences, however little intended and however unforeseen. If, for instance, being assaulted by a third person, the defendant lifted his stick and accidentally hit the plaintiff, who was standing behind him, according to this view he is liable, irrespective of any negligence toward the party injured.

The arguments for the doctrine under consideration are, for the most part, drawn from precedent, but it is sometimes supposed to be defensible as theoretically sound. Every man, it is said, has an absolute right to his person, and so forth, free from detriment at the hands of his neighbors. In the cases put, the plaintiff has done nothing; the defendant, on the other hand, has chosen to act. As between the two, the party whose voluntary conduct has caused the damage should suffer, rather than one who has had no share in producing it. . . .

[Holmes discusses a number of early English precedents that appear to have based liability on defendant's voluntary injurious act without reference to fault.]

In spite, however, of all the arguments which may be urged for the rule that a man acts at his peril, it has been rejected by very eminent courts, even under the old forms of action. In view of this fact, and of the further circumstance that, since the old forms have been abolished, the allegation of negligence has spread from the action on the case to all ordinary declarations in tort which do not allege intent, probably many lawyers would be surprised that any one should think it worth while to go into the present discussion. Such is the natural impression to be derived from daily practice. But even if the doctrine under consideration had no longer any followers, which is not the case, it would be well to have something more than daily practice to sustain our views upon so fundamental a question; as it seems to me at least, the true principle is far from being articulately grasped by all who are interested in it, and can only be arrived at after a careful analysis of what has been thought hitherto. It might be thought enough to cite the decisions opposed to the rule of absolute responsibility, and to show that such a rule is inconsistent with admitted doctrines and sound policy. But we may go further with profit, and inquire whether there are not strong grounds for thinking that the common law has never known such a rule, unless in that period of dry precedent which is so often to be found midway between a creative epoch and a period of solvent philosophical reaction. Conciliating the attention of those who, contrary to most modern practitioners, still adhere to the strict doctrine, by reminding them once more that there are weighty decisions to be cited adverse to it, and that, if they have involved an innovation, the fact that it has been made by such magistrates as Chief Justice Shaw goes far to prove that the change was politic, I think I may assert that a little reflection will show that it was required not only by policy, but by consistency. I will begin with the latter. . . .

. . . So long, at least, as only physical or irresponsible agencies, however unforeseen, co-operated with the act complained of to produce the result, the argument which would resolve the case of accidentally striking the plaintiff, when lifting a stick in necessary self-defense, adversely to the defendant, would require a decision against him in every case where his act was a factor in the result complained of. The distinction between a direct application of force, and causing damage indirectly, or as a more remote consequence of one's act, although it may determine whether the form of action should be trespass or case, does not touch the theory of responsibility, if that theory be that a man acts at his peril. As was said at the outset, if the strict liability is to be maintained at all, it must be maintained throughout. A principle cannot be stated which would retain the strict liability in trespass while abandoning it in case. It cannot be said that trespass is for acts alone, and case for consequences of those acts. All actions of trespass are for consequences of acts, not for the acts themselves. And some actions of trespass are for consequences more remote from the defendant's act than in other instances where the remedy would be case.

An act is always a voluntary muscular contraction, and nothing else. The chain of physical sequences which it sets in motion or directs to the plaintiff's harm is no part of it, and very generally a long train of such sequences intervenes. An example or two will make this extremely clear.

When a man commits an assault and battery with a pistol, his only act is to contract the muscles of his arm and forefinger in a certain way, but it is the delight of elementary writers to point out what a vast series of physical changes must take place before the harm is done. Suppose that, instead of firing a pistol, he takes up a hose which is discharging water on the sidewalk, and directs it at the plaintiff, he does not even set in motion the physical causes which must co-operate with his act to make a battery. Not only natural causes, but a living being, may intervene between the act and its effect. Gibbons v. Pepper, which decided that there was no battery when a man's horse was frightened by accident or a third person and ran away with him, and ran over the plaintiff, takes the distinction that, if the rider by spurring is the cause of the accident, then he is guilty. In Scott v. Shepherd, . . . trespass was maintained against one who had thrown a squib into a crowd, where it was tossed from hand to hand in self-defence until it burst and injured the plaintiff. Here even human agencies were a part of a chain between the defendant's act and the result, although they were treated as more or less nearly automatic, in order to arrive at the decision.

Now I repeat, that, if principle requires us to charge a man in trespass when his act has brought force to bear on another through a comparatively short train of intervening causes, in spite of his having used all possible care, it requires the same liability, however numerous and unexpected the events between the act and the result. If running a man down is a trespass when the accident can be referred to the rider's act of spurring, why is it not a tort in every case, as was argued in Vincent v. Stinehour, seeing that it can always be referred more remotely to his act of mounting and taking the horse out?

Why is a man not responsible for the consequences of an act innocent in its direct and obvious effects, when those consequences would not have followed but for the intervention of a series of extraordinary, although natural, events? The reason is, that, if the intervening events are of such a kind that no foresight could have been expected to look out for them, the defendant is not to blame for having failed to do so. It seems to be admitted by the English judges that, even on the question whether the acts of leaving dry trimmings in hot weather by the side of a railroad, and then sending an engine over the track, are negligent, — that is, are a ground of liability, — the consequences which might reasonably be anticipated are material. Yet these are acts which, under the circumstances, can hardly be called innocent in their natural and obvious effects. The same doctrine has been applied to acts in violation of statute which could not reasonably have been expected to lead to the result complained of.

But there is no difference in principle between the case where a natural cause or physical factor intervenes after the act in some way not to be foreseen, and turns what seemed innocent to harm, and the case where such a cause or factor intervenes, unknown, at the time; as, for the matter of that, it did in the English cases cited. If a man is excused in the one case because he is not to blame, he must be in the other. The difference taken in Gibbons v. Pepper, cited above, is not between results which are and those which are not the consequences of the defendant's acts: it is between consequences which he was bound as a reasonable man to contemplate, and those which he was not. Hard spurring is just so much more likely to lead to harm than merely riding a horse in the street, that the court thought that the defendant would be bound to look out for the consequences of the one, while it would not hold him liable for those resulting merely from the other; because the possibility of being run away with when riding quietly, though familiar, is comparatively slight. If, however, the horse had been unruly, and had been taken into a frequented place for the purpose of being broken, the owner might have been liable, because "it was his fault to bring a wild horse into a place where mischief might probably be done."

To return to the example of the accidental blow with a stick lifted in self-defence, there is no difference between hitting a person standing in one's rear and hitting one who was pushed by a horse within range of the stick just as it was lifted, provided that it was not possible, under the circumstances, in the one case to have known, in the other to have anticipated, the proximity. In either case there is wanting the only element which distinguishes voluntary acts from spasmodic muscular contractions as a ground of liability. In neither of them, that is to say, has there been an opportunity of choice with reference to the consequence complained of, — a chance to guard against the result which has come to pass. A choice which entails a concealed consequence is as to that consequence no choice.

The general principle of our law is that loss from accident must lie where it falls, and this principle is not affected by the fact that a human being is the instrument of misfortune. But relatively to a given human being anything is accident which he could not fairly have been expected to contemplate as possible, and therefore to avoid. In the language of the late Chief Justice Nelson of New York: "No case or principle can be found, or if found can be maintained, subjecting an individual to liability for an act done without fault on his part. . . . All the cases concede that an injury arising from inevitable accident, or, which in law or reason is the same thing, from an act that ordinary human care and foresight are unable to guard against, is but the misfortune of the sufferer, and lays no foundation for legal responsibility." If this were not so, any act would be sufficient, however remote, which set in motion or opened the door for a series of physical sequences ending in damage; such as riding the horse, in the case of the runaway, or even coming to a place where one is seized with a fit and strikes the plaintiff in an unconscious spasm. Nay, why need the defendant have acted at all, and why is it not enough that his existence has been at the expense of the plaintiff? The requirement of an act is the requirement that the defendant should have made a choice. But the only possible purpose of introducing this moral element is to make the power of avoiding the evil complained of a condition of liability. There is no such power where the evil cannot be foreseen. Here we reach the argument from policy. . . .

A man need not, it is true, do this or that act, — the term *act* implies a choice, — but he must act somehow. Furthermore, the public generally profits by individual activity. As action cannot be avoided, and tends to the public good, there is obviously no policy in throwing the hazard of what is at once desirable and inevitable upon the actor.

The state might conceivably make itself a mutual insurance company against accidents, and distribute the burden of its citizens' mishaps among all its members. There might be a pension for paralytics, and state aid for those who suffered in person or estate from tempest or wild beasts. As between individuals it might adopt the mutual insurance principle pro tanto, and divide damages when both were in fault, as in the rusticum judicium of the admiralty, or it might throw all loss upon the actor irrespective of fault. The state does none of these things, however, and the prevailing view is that its cumbrous and expensive machinery ought not to be set in motion unless some clear benefit is to be derived from disturbing the status quo. State interference is an evil, where it cannot be shown to be a good. Universal insurance, if desired, can be better and more cheaply accomplished by private enterprise. The undertaking to redistribute losses simply on the ground that they resulted from the defendant's act would not only be open to these objections, but, as it is hoped the preceding discussion has shown, to the still graver one of offending the sense of justice. Unless my act is of a nature to threaten others, unless under the circumstances a prudent man would have foreseen the possibility of harm, it is no more justifiable to make me indemnify my neighbor against the consequences, than to make me do the same thing if I had fallen upon him in a fit, or to compel me to insure him against lightning.

I must now recur to the conclusions drawn from innocent trespasses upon land, and conversions, and the supposed analogy of those cases to trespasses against the person, lest the law concerning the latter should be supposed to lie between two antinomies, each necessitating with equal cogency an opposite conclusion to the other.

Take first the case of trespass upon land attended by actual damage. When a man goes upon his neighbor's land, thinking it is his own, he intends the very act or consequence complained of. He means to intermeddle with a certain thing in a certain way, and it is just that intended intermeddling for which he is sued. Whereas, if he accidentally hits a stranger as he lifts his staff in self-defence, the fact, which is the gist of the action, — namely, the contact between the staff and his neighbor's head, — was not intended, and could not have been foreseen. It might be answered, to be sure, that it is not for intermeddling with the plaintiff's property, that a man is sued; and that in the supposed cases, just as much as in that of the accidental blow, the defendant is ignorant of one of the facts making up the total environment, and which must be present to make his action wrong. He is ignorant, that is to say, that the true owner either has or claims any interest in the property in question, and therefore he does not intend a wrongful act, because he does not mean to deal with his neighbor's property. But the answer to this is, that he does intend to do the damage complained of. One who diminishes the value of property by intentional damage knows it belongs to somebody. If he thinks it belongs to himself, he expects whatever harm he may do to come out of his own pocket. It would be odd if he were to get rid of the burden by discovering that it belonged to his neighbor. It is a very different thing to say that he who intentionally does harm must bear the loss, from saying that one from whose acts harm follows accidentally, as a consequence which could not have been foreseen, must bear it.

Next, suppose the act complained of is an exercise of dominion over the plaintiff's property, such as a merely technical trespass or a conversion. If the defendant thought that the property belonged to himself, there seems to be no abstract injustice in requiring him to know the limits of his own titles, or, if he thought that it belonged to another, in holding him bound to get proof of title before acting. Consider, too, what the defendant's liability amounts to, if the act, whether an entry upon land or a conversion of chattels, has been unattended by damage to the property, and the thing has come back to the hands of the true owner. The sum recovered is merely nominal, and the payment is nothing more than a formal acknowledgment of the owner's title; which, considering the effect of prescription and statutes of limitation upon repeated acts of dominion, is no more than right. All semblance of injustice disappears when the defendant is allowed to avoid the costs of an action by tender or otherwise.

But suppose the property has not come back to the hands of the true owner. If the thing remains in the hands of the defendant, it is clearly right that he should surrender it. And if instead of the thing itself he holds the proceeds of a sale, it is as reasonable to make him pay over its value in trover or assumpsit as it would have been to compel a surrender of the thing. But the question whether the defendant has subsequently paid over the proceeds of the sale of a chattel to a third person, cannot affect the rights of the true owner of the chattel. In the supposed case of an auctioneer, for instance, if he had paid the true owner, it would have been an answer to his bailor's claim. If he has paid his bailor instead, he has paid one whom he was not bound to pay, and no general principle requires that this should be held to divest the plaintiff's right.

Another consideration affecting the argument that the law as to trespasses upon property establishes a general principle, is that the defendant's knowledge or ignorance of the plaintiff's title is likely to lie wholly in his own breast, and therefore hardly admits of satisfactory proof. Indeed, in many cases it cannot have been open to evidence at all at the time when the law was settled, before parties were permitted to testify. . . .

Supposing it now to be conceded that the general notion upon which liability to an action is founded is fault or blameworthiness in some sense, the question arises, whether it is so in the sense of personal moral short-coming, as would practically result from Austin's teaching. The language of Rede, J., . . . gives a sufficient answer. "In trespass the intent" (we may say more broadly, the defendant's state of mind) "cannot be construed." Suppose that a defendant were allowed to testify that, before acting, he considered carefully what would be the conduct of a prudent man under the circumstances, and, having formed the best judgment he could, acted accordingly. If the story was believed, it would be conclusive against the defendant's negligence judged by a moral standard which would take his personal characteristics into account. But supposing any such evidence to have got before the jury, it is very clear that the court would say, Gentlemen, the question is not whether the defendant thought his conduct was that of a prudent man, but whether you think it was.

Some middle point must be found between the horns of this dilemma.

The standards of the law are standards of general application. The law takes no account of the infinite varieties of temperament, intellect, and education which make the internal character of a given act so different in different men. It does not attempt to see men as God sees them, for more than one sufficient reason. In the first place, the impossibility of nicely measuring a man's powers and limitations is far clearer than that of ascertaining his knowledge of law, which has been thought to account for what is called the presumption that every man knows the law. But a more satisfactory explanation is, that, when men live in society, a certain average of conduct, a sacrifice of individual peculiarities going beyond a certain point, is necessary to the general welfare. If, for instance, a man is born hasty and awkward, is always having accidents and hurting himself or his neighbors, no doubt his congenital defects will be allowed for in the courts of Heaven, but his slips are no less troublesome to his neighbors than if they sprang from guilty neglect. His neighbors accordingly require him, at his proper peril, to come up to their standard, and the courts which they establish decline to take his personal equation into account.

The rule that the law does, in general, determine liability by blameworthiness, is subject to the limitation that minute differences of character are not allowed for. The law considers, in other words, what would be blameworthy in the average man, the man of ordinary intelligence and prudence, and determines liability by that. If we fall below the level in those gifts, it is our misfortune; so much as that we must have at our peril, for the reasons just given. But he who is intelligent and prudent does not act at his peril, in theory of law. On the contrary, it is only when he fails to exercise the foresight of which he is capable, or exercises it with evil intent, that he is answerable for the consequences.

There are exceptions to the principle that every man is presumed to possess ordinary capacity to avoid harm to his neighbors, which illustrate the rule, and also the moral basis of liability in general. When a man has a distinct defect of such a nature that all can recognize it as making certain precautions impossible, he will not be held answerable for not taking them. A blind man is not required to see at his peril; and although he is, no doubt, bound to consider his infirmity in regulating his actions, yet if he properly finds himself in a certain situation, the neglect of precautions requiring eyesight would not prevent his recovering for an injury to himself, and, it may be presumed, would not make him liable for injuring another. So it is held that, in cases where he is the plaintiff, an infant of very tender years is only bound to take the precautions of which an infant is capable; the same principle may be cautiously applied where he is defendant. Insanity is a more difficult matter to deal with, and no general rule can be laid down about it. There is no doubt that in many cases a man may be insane, and yet perfectly capable of taking the precautions, and of being influenced by the motives, which the circumstances demand. But if insanity of a pronounced type exists, manifestly incapacitating the sufferer from complying with the rule which he has broken, good sense would require it to be admitted as an excuse.

Taking the qualification last established in connection with the general proposition previously laid down, it will now be assumed that, on the one hand, the law presumes or requires a man to possess ordinary capacity to avoid harming his neighbors, unless a clear and manifest incapacity be shown; but that, on the other, it does not in general hold him liable for unintentional injury, unless, possessing such capacity, he might and ought to have foreseen the danger, or, in other words, unless a man of ordinary intelligence and forethought would have been to blame for acting as he did....

Notwithstanding the fact that the grounds of legal liability are moral to the extent above explained, it must be borne in mind that law only works within the sphere of the senses. If the external phenomena, the manifest acts and omissions, are such as it requires, it is wholly indifferent to the internal phenomena of conscience. A man may have as bad a heart as he chooses, if his conduct is within the rules. In other words, the standards of the law are external standards, and, however much it may take moral considerations into account, it does so only for the purpose of drawing a line between such bodily motions and rests as it permits, and such as it does not. What the law really forbids, and the only thing it forbids, is the act on the wrong side of the line, be that act blameworthy or otherwise....

NOTES AND QUESTIONS

1. Is Holmes taking the position that some notion of personal fault always served as an underpinning for tortious liability?

2. The dogfight situation Holmes discusses is the famous case of

Brown v. Kendall, 6 Cush. (60 Mass.) 292 (1850). In attempting to separate two fighting dogs, defendant struck plaintiff—who had come up behind him—in the eye causing serious injury. Chief Justice Shaw, in a landmark opinion, held that the defendant's liability turned on whether he was at fault. Within two decades, on the other side of the Atlantic, another highly influential case in the formative era of modern tort law was decided: Rylands v. Fletcher, L. R. 3, H. L. 330 (1868). Interestingly, *Rylands* is generally accorded the same centrality as a linchpin of strict liability that has been granted Brown v. Kendall in the realm of fault liability. Yet, Holmes gives only cursory attention to *Rylands*. See The Common Law, pp. 116-117. In making the case for the fault principle, does Holmes actually present the strongest arguments that might have been made for strict liability at that time?

3. What exactly is the relationship that Holmes posits between freedom of choice, on the one hand, and the fault principle, as contrasted to strict liability, on the other?

4. How is the relationship between freedom of choice and the fault principle affected by the legal system's adopting an objective standard for determining liability? Does Holmes satisfactorily establish "a middle point" (p. 12, *supra*), forging a link between fault liability and an objective standard of judgment? Does he successfully explain the exceptions to the objective standard in cases where defendants are afflicted with serious personal defects?

5. Can an objective standard of fault liability be explained on a basis other than freedom of choice?

6. Does compensation for injury victims have a place in Holmes's scheme of moral values underlying fault liability?

7. For a stimulating essay on Holmes the man and the jurist, see Rogat, The Judge as Spectator, 31 U. Chi. L. Rev. 213 (1964). The standard biographical treatment of Holmes during the period under consideration is M. Howe, Justice Holmes: The Proving Years 1870-1882 (1963).

A Theory of Negligence*

Richard A. Posner

Negligence—the failure to exercise the care of an ordinarily prudent and careful man—has been the dominant standard of civil liability for accidents for the last 150 years or so, in this as in most

*Source: 1 J. Legal Stud. 29-34, 36-48 (1972).

countries of the world; and accident cases, mainly negligence cases, constitute the largest item of business on the civil side of the nation's trial courts. Yet we lack a theory to explain the social function of the negligence concept and of the fault system of accident liability that is built upon it. This article attempts to formulate and test such a theory, primarily through a sample of 1528 American appellate court decisions from the period 1875-1905.

I

There is an orthodox view of the negligence concept to which I believe most legal scholars and historians would subscribe that runs as follows: Until the nineteenth century a man was liable for harm caused by his accidents whether or not he was at fault; he acted at his peril. The no-fault standard of liability was relaxed in the nineteenth century under the pressure of industrial expansion and an individualistic philosophy that could conceive of no justification for shifting losses from the victim of an accident unless the injurer was blameworthy (negligent) and the victim blameless (not contributorily negligent). The result, however, was that accident costs were "externalized" from the enterprises that caused them to workers and other individuals injured as a byproduct of their activities. Justification for the shift, in the orthodox view, can perhaps be found in a desire to subsidize the infant industries of the period but any occasion for subsidization has long passed, laying bare the inadequacy of the negligence standard as a system for compensating accident victims. The need for compensation is unaffected by whether the participants in the accident were careless or careful and we have outgrown a morality that would condition the right to compensation upon a showing that the plaintiff was blameless and the defendant blameworthy.

There are three essential points here. The first, that the adoption of the negligence standard was a subsidy to the expanding industries of the nineteenth century, is highly ambiguous. It is true that if you move from a regime where (say) railroads are strictly liable for injuries inflicted in crossing accidents to one where they are liable only if negligent, the costs to the railroads of crossing accidents will be lower, and the output of railroad services probably greater as a consequence. But it does not follow that any subsidy is involved — unless it is proper usage to say that an industry is being subsidized whenever a tax levied upon it is reduced or removed. As we shall see, a negligence standard of liability, properly administered, is broadly consistent with an optimum investment in accident prevention by the enterprises subject to the standard. Since it does not connote, as the orthodox view implies, an underinvestment in safety, its adoption cannot be equated with subsidization in any useful sense of that term. We shall also see that many accident cases do not involve strangers to the enterprise (such as a traveler at a crossing), but rather customers, employees, or other contracting parties, and that a change in the. formal law governing accidents is unlikely to have more than a transient effect on the number of their accidents. Finally, whether the period before the advent of the negligence standard is properly characterized as one of liability without fault remains, so far as I am aware, an unresolved historical puzzle.

The second major point implicit in the orthodox view is that the dominant purpose of civil liability for accidents is to compensate the victim for the medical expenses, loss of earnings, suffering, and other costs of the accident. Hence, if it is a bad compensation system, it is a bad system. Yet Holmes, in his authoritative essay on the fault system, had rejected a compensation rationale as alien to the system. People, he reasoned, could insure themselves against uncompensated accidents, and there was accordingly no occasion for a state accident-compensation scheme. Holmes left unclear what he conceived the dominant purpose of the fault system to be, if it was not to compensate. The successful plaintiff does recover damages from the defendant. Why? Suppose a major function of the negligence system is to regulate safety. We are apt to think of regulation as the action of executive and administrative agencies. But the creation of private rights of action can also be a means of regulation. The rules are made by the judges aided by the parties. The burdens of investigation and of presenting evidence are also shouldered by the parties. The direct governmental role is thus minimized — a result highly congenial to the thinking of the nineteenth century. Such a system cannot function unless the damages assessed against the defendant are paid over to the plaintiff. That is the necessary inducement for the plaintiff to play his regulatory role of identifying violations of the applicable judge-made rule, proving them, and when appropriate pressing for changes in the rule.

The third essential point in the orthodox view is that negligence is a moral concept — and, in the setting of today, a moralistic one. The orthodox view does not explore the moral roots of fault, but contents itself with asserting that such moral judgments as can be made in the usual accident case are an anachronistic, even frivolous, basis for determining whether to grant or withhold redress. The rejection of moral criteria as a basis for liability follows easily from the conception of the fault system as a compensation scheme and nothing more: it would be odd to deny welfare benefits on the ground that the recipient's misfortune was not the product of someone's wrongful conduct.

Characterization of the negligence standard as moral or moralistic does not advance analysis. The morality of the fault system is very different from that of everyday life. Negligence is an objective standard. A man may be adjudged negligent though he did his best to avoid an accident and just happens to be clumsier than average. In addition, a number of the established rules of negligence liability are hard to square with a moral approach. Insane people are liable for negligent conduct though incapable of behaving carefully. Employers are broadly responsible for the negligence of their employees. The latter example illustrates an immensely important principle. In less than four per cent of the cases in our sample was the defendant accused of actually being negligent. In all other cases the defendant was sued on the basis of the alleged negligence of employees or (in a few cases) children. The moral element in such cases is attenuated.

Moreover, to characterize the negligence concept as a moral one is only to push inquiry back a step. It is true that injury inflicted by carelessness arouses a different reaction from injury inflicted as the result of an unavoidable accident. We are indignant in the first case but not the second. The interesting question is why. What causes us to give the opprobrious label of careless to some human conduct but not other and to be indignant when we are hurt by it? The orthodox view gives no answer.

II

It is time to take a fresh look at the social function of liability for negligent acts. The essential clue, I believe, is provided by Judge Learned Hand's famous formulation of the negligence standard — one of the few attempts to give content to the deceptively simple concept of ordinary care. Although the formulation postdates the period of our primary interest, it never purported to be original but was an attempt to make explicit the standard that the courts had long applied. In a negligence case, Hand said, the judge (or jury) should attempt to measure three things: the magnitude of the loss if an accident occurs; the probability of the accident's occurring; and the burden of taking precautions that would avert it.[8] If the product of the

8. United States v. Carroll Towing Co., 159 F.2d 169 (2d Cir. 1947); Conway v. O'Brien, 111 F.2d 611 (2d Cir. 1940).

first two terms exceeds the burden of precautions, the failure to take those precautions is negligence. Hand was adumbrating, perhaps unwittingly, an economic meaning of negligence. Discounting (multiplying) the cost of an accident if it occurs by the probability of occurrence yields a measure of the economic benefit to be anticipated from incurring the costs necessary to prevent the accident. The cost of prevention is what Hand meant by the burden of taking precautions against the accident. It may be the cost of installing safety equipment or otherwise making the activity safer, or the benefit forgone by curtailing or eliminating the activity. If the cost of safety measures or of curtailment — whichever cost is lower — exceeds the benefit in accident avoidance to be gained by incurring that cost, society would be better off, in economic terms, to forgo accident prevention. A rule making the enterprise liable for the accidents that occur in such cases cannot be justified on the ground that it will induce the enterprise to increase the safety of its operations. When the cost of accidents is less than the cost of prevention, a rational profit-maximizing enterprise will pay tort judgments to the accident victims rather than incur the larger cost of avoiding liability. Furthermore, overall economic value or welfare would be diminished rather then increased by incurring a higher accident-prevention cost in order to avoid a lower accident cost. If, on the other hand, the benefits in accident avoidance exceed the costs of prevention, society is better off if those costs are incurred and the accident averted, and so in this case the enterprise is made liable, in the expectation that self-interest will lead it to adopt the precautions in order to avoid a greater cost in tort judgments.

One misses any reference to accident avoidance by the victim. If the accident could be prevented by the installation of safety equipment or the curtailment or discontinuance of the underlying activity by the victim at lower cost than any measure taken by the injurer would involve, it would be uneconomical to adopt a rule of liability that placed the burden of accident prevention on the injurer. Although not an explicit part of the Hand formula this qualification, as we shall see, is implicit in the administration of the negligence standard.

Perhaps, then, the dominant function of the fault system is to generate rules of liability that if followed will bring about, at least approximately, the efficient — the cost-justified — level of accidents and safety. Under this view, damages are assessed against the defendant as a way of measuring the costs of accidents, and the damages so assessed are paid over to the plaintiff (to be divided with his lawyer) as the price of enlisting their participation in the operation of the system. Because we do not like to see resources squandered, a judgment of negligence has inescapable overtones of moral disapproval, for it implies that there was a cheaper alternative to the accident. Conversely, there is no moral indignation in the case in which the cost of prevention would have exceeded the cost of the accident. Where the measures necessary to avert the accident would have consumed excessive resources, there is no occasion to condemn the defendant for not having taken them.

If indignation has its roots in inefficiency, we do not have to decide whether regulation, or compensation, or retribution, or some mixture of these best describes the dominant purpose of negligence law. In any case, the judgment of liability depends ultimately on a weighing of costs and benefits. . . .

We begin by looking at the broad institutional and doctrinal framework of the negligence system as revealed by the appellate cases. Both in this and the next part (specific rules of liability) I have tried to report the information revealed by the sample as fully as possible rather than simply mine it for examples, although I have excluded a certain amount of redundant or peripheral material.

It will be helpful to make an initial distinction between two broad categories of accident: accidents to strangers (for example, a streetcar running down a pedestrian), and accidents to parties in a contractual or other bargaining relationship (customers, employees, tenants, and the like). Of the 1494 cases in the sample for which the requisite information is available, 54 per cent involve accidents between strangers, 30 per cent involve accidents to employees, 12 per cent involve accidents to passengers (mostly railroad and streetcar passengers), and 4 per cent involve accidents to other customers and other contracting parties, mostly tenants. The regulatory function of negligence liability is evident in cases involving accidents to strangers. Where the costs of transacting are high, an unregulated market will not bring about an optimum level of accidents and safety. More than 90 per cent of the cases in this group involve types of accidents in which the costs of transaction are probably very high — mainly cases involving railroad and streetcar crossing accidents, railroad collisions with trespassing people and cattle, accidents to pedestrians and other travelers involving defects in the sidewalk or street, other road accidents, ship collisions, and dog bites. In such chance-encounter accidents it is unrealistic to expect much bargaining between the parties in advance over the level of safety and the economic function of liability is evident: it is to bring about the level of accidents and safety that the market would bring about if transactions were feasible — the efficient level. In the second group of cases, the parties already have a contractual relationship and the impact of liability rules on accidents and safety is more problematic. The parties are normally free to rearrange by contract whatever liabilities are imposed by the law: the stagecoach company can contract with its passengers for a lower or higher standard of care.

Even here, the costs of explicit agreement on safety may not be negligible. Many transactions take place without a formal written contract. The costs associated with specifying in detail the perform- ance contracted for are too high. When buying a train ticket, one doesn't receive a contract spelling out the railroad's undertaking with respect to safety appliances and to the careful selection and supervi- sion of engineers, firemen, conductors, and dispatchers. It is left to the courts to decide, should the need arise, what safety precautions the parties would have agreed upon if negotiations had taken place, and this is doubtless on the whole a cheaper way of proceeding. The level of safety that the parties would have negotiated would presum- ably have been the efficient level, in the sense that the passenger would have demanded and the company supplied that quantum of safety precautions at which the cost of preventing an additional accident (in a higher price for the ticket, in less comfort, more delay, etc.) would have just exceeded the cost of the accident, if it occurred, discounted by the probability of its occurrence. In the event of an accident and a consequent suit by the injured passenger, it is the court's job to determine whether the company lived up to its bargain—whether, that is, it supplied the optimum amount of safety. The inquiry is thus the same as in the case of an accident to a stranger and this, together with the similarity in the type of injury that results, may explain why the courts treat both stranger and contracting-party cases mostly without distinction under the negli- gence standard. They make some distinctions, however, with respect to cases involving accidents to employees, and in discussing the elements of the doctrinal framework of the negligence system we will therefore treat those cases separately.

Breach of the Defendant's Duty. The general rule is that the defendant owes to those whom he might chance upon and injure a duty to exercise due care—the care of an ordinarily prudent and careful man. The breach of that duty is actionable negligence. However, a higher duty—the duty of the highest practicable care, the duty to avoid the slightest negligence—is owed by a common carrier (usually, in our period, a railroad) to its passengers while they are on board. As an approximation to the likely understanding of the parties to the contract of carriage, the exception seems a reasonable one. Strictly speaking, it is nonsense to speak of a standard of care higher than that of due care. An enterprise will not spend $100 in safety appliances to avert a $90 accident when it can satisfy its legal obligations by paying a $90 judgment. The rule that common carriers owe a higher duty to their passengers signifies that passengers expect (and are willing to pay for) a high level of safety—because the railroad has a comparative advantage in accident prevention (indeed, passengers are normally helpless to avert an accident) and because a collision or derailment (like a plane crash today) is likely to kill or seriously injure them. These factors are absent or attenuated in the case of a passenger injured on the station grounds—say by a loose board in the platform—or a passenger injured in a private vehicle, and, as we would predict, the standard of highest practicable care is not applied in those cases.

The second major exception to the ordinary-care standard concerns the liability of land occupiers, in our period usually railroads, to uninvited entrants, usually trespassers using the track as a path. Here the duty (with some exceptions discussed later) is a lesser one: not to use due care, but only to avoid a knowing injury. The rule is a corollary of a system of property law that is designed to protect rights of exclusive possession. Since it is often difficult to exclude trespassers, the imposition of a duty to look out for their safety would interfere with the landowner's use of his property. The rule of no liability may also rest on a judgment that the utility of trespassing, in general, is less than the cost that would have to be incurred to prevent injury to trespassers along railroad rights of way and in other areas that the general public is not invited to enter.

It is difficult to particularize the standard of ordinary care without discussing particular types of accident, a later inquiry, but there are two general principles relating to its implementation that are significant. The first is that the violation of a statute prescribing a duty of care is negligence per se as to a member of the class intended to be protected by the statute who is injured as a result of the violation. The theoretical interest of this principle is that it potentially displaces a good deal of the judicial function in negligence cases, including the Hand formula. If the legislature fixes a speed limit of 10 miles per hour for trains at crossings, it is no longer open to the court to decide, by a balancing of costs and benefits, what speed under what conditions will optimize railroad crossing accidents. It would be comforting for the economic theory of negligence liability to think that legislatures, too, used a Hand-type formula in fixing statutory duties of care but as we shall see the theoretical basis for expecting them to do so is much weaker than in the case of courts.

Another critical element in applying the standard of due care is the weight assigned customary practices. Can a plaintiff argue that the failure to have air brakes is negligence, at a time when no railroad has them? Or is it a defense that the railroad has the same safety appliances as every other railroad or as the average railroad of its class? If compliance with the average or customary practice in the trade automatically discharged the defendant's duty of due care, there would be cases where the negligence system failed to optimize safety. Suppose the only benefit of a safety appliance is to a stranger to the industry in our earlier sense—someone with whom the enterprise has no contractual relationship and will not enter into one because of transaction costs. No firm in the industry will have an incentive to install the appliance, for it will not be able to recover its cost by charging a higher price to customers or setting a lower wage to employees (notice, however, that air brakes are not that kind of appliance). Thus, the market will not induce the adoption of such an appliance even if its benefits in accident prevention exceed its costs — and neither would the negligence system if compliance with industry custom were a defense. It is therefore interesting, in terms of principle, to observe that the courts in our period held that custom was not a defense, although, as we shall see, in practice a plaintiff faced an uphill struggle to convince a court that failure to adopt an appliance nowhere in use in an industry exhibited a want of ordinary care.

Contributory Negligence. Another fundamental principle of the common law of negligence is that if the victim of the accident failed to exercise due care, and his breach contributed to the accident, he is barred from recovery even though the defendant was negligent. That the plaintiff has a duty of care flows directly from our exegesis of the Hand formula. There are cases where the cheapest accident preventer is the prospective victim himself and so should be liable. But the principle of contributory negligence, as the name implies, is commonly applied in cases where the defendant is also negligent and the question arises, why bar recovery in those cases too? The answer, I suggest, is that it is impossible, in general, to show that permitting recovery in cases where either party could have avoided the accident (if the plaintiff was negligent but the accident would have happened anyway the defense of contributory negligence fails) would bring the level of safety and accidents closer to the optimum point. If we make the defendant always liable in such a case, defendants as a class will have more incentive to take safety precautions than if they are never liable, since in the latter instance the cost of accidents to them would be lower. But correspondingly plaintiffs as a class would have less incentive to take safety precautions in the first case than in the second, because the accident cost to them would be higher in the second—more of their accidents would be uncompensated. If the effects are thus symmetrical, there is no economic basis for attempting to shift the loss from injured to injurer.

This analysis ignores, however, the case where, although either party, victim or injurer, could have prevented the accident at a lower cost than the accident cost discounted by the probability of its occurrence, the cost of prevention to the injurer would have been lower than the cost of prevention to the victim. The correct economizing rule here is to make the injurer liable, even though the victim may be said to have been contributorily negligent. This refinement is nowhere explicit in the cases, but it may have been implicit. Glancing ahead for a moment at the specific rules of contributory negligence discussed in the next part, one finds only rare instances where the sacrifice required of the victim by the law to avert an accident is disproportionate to that required of the injurer.

Causation. The courts require proof of a causal connection between the breach of duty, either defendant's or plaintiff's, and the injury. Dispense with such proof, and you are no longer talking about the costs of accidents. If the defendant was negligent but the accident would have occurred anyway, it would be incorrect to view the costs of the accident as the consequence of his negligence since they would not have been avoided by the exercise of due care. Yet the defendant was negligent: would not an award of damages serve a useful purpose, therefore, by punishing him for his breach of duty, thereby encouraging him to comply in the future with the requirements of efficiency? This I question. Where the standard of care applied to a particular activity is economically correct there will be incentive enough for firms to comply. If they do not they face a judgment bill (for accidents occasioned by their failure to comply with the standard) larger than the cost of taking the precautions required by the standard. Punishment — an exaction that exceeds the costs to society (here, accident costs) imposed by the particular violation being punished — is necessary where the violator is frequently not apprehended, because a rational lawbreaker will discount the gravity of any legal sanction by the probability that it will be imposed. There are hit-and-run accidents, and if they are a more serious problem in the age of the automobile, there must have been cases in the period covered by this study in which the injurer was not apprehended, especially when trains killed livestock or lone walkers on the track or engine sparks ignited crops or buildings. But such cases must have been exceptional and it is unlikely that most victims of negligent injuries failed to assert their claims because they couldn't identify the injurer. It is, in contrast, quite likely that most price-fixing conspiracies (for example) are never brought to bar, due to their covert character. One is therefore not surprised to find that punitive damages are normally disallowed in negligence cases and allowed in price-fixing cases. Moreover, an appropriate punishment component is built into the negligence system. If an injurer attempts to conceal his identity and is sued, his efforts at concealment may be considered evidence of willfulness justifying the imposition of punitive damages (however, the sample contains no such cases).

Punishment for negligence would close an important safety valve in the negligence system. A standard of care is necessarily a crude approximation to optimality. Allowing enterprises a choice whether to comply or pay the social costs of violation may permit a closer approximation. Suppose there is a rule that a dam owner is responsible for flood damage unless his dam is at least 16 feet high. Presumably the rule reflects a judgment that the cost of raising the dam is less than the cost of the floods that a lower dam would fail to contain. One owner thinks the rule is incorrect. He estimates that the only flood likely to occur is one that would swamp a 16-foot dam and therefore that he can save money by violating the rule. Courts are not infallible and we give maximum play to individual judgment if we let the dam owner act on his estimate. If he is wrong, he will have to pay a judgment, but if he is correct an unnecessary expenditure on dam building will have been saved. One can reply that it is just as likely that a standard of care will be too lax as too strict; and if the former a punitive sanction will tend to compensate for the laxity. But this leads to the same stand-off as in our earlier discussion of contributory negligence, and with the same implications. If the only recognized basis for invoking legal processes to shift an accident loss from the victim to another party is the expectation of improving the efficiency of resource use, then before we can recognize a right of action (in this case a right to sue for injuries that would have occurred anyway) we must be able to say that the shift will improve efficiency; and we cannot.

Foreseeability.   Courts invoke the doctrine of "proximate" cause to excuse defendants from liability for unforeseeable consequences of negligence. A train stops at a crossing and a group of rowdy passengers debark. A lady driving a carriage waiting at the crossing for the train to move on is frightened. After a delay the passengers reembark and the train moves on but the lady is now late, it is growing dark, her driving is erratic because of fright and anxiety, she drives into a ditch and is injured. The railroad may have been negligent in permitting the train to be delayed at the crossing and the rowdy passengers to debark but the courts do not view its negligence as the "proximate cause" of her accident. Such a result follows from the economic standard of negligence. If negligence is a failure to take precautions against a type of accident whose cost, discounted by the frequency of its occurrence, exceeds the cost of the precautions, it makes sense to require no precautions against accidents that occur so rarely that the benefit of accident prevention approaches zero. The truly freak accident isn't worth spending money to prevent.

Moreover, estimation of the benefits of accident prevention implies foreseeability.

Respondeat Superior. As mentioned earlier, in few cases in the period covered by the sample was the defendant accused of being personally negligent. Most suits are based on the doctrine of respondeat superior, which makes an employer liable to third parties for the torts of his employees committed in furtherance of their employment. The doctrine at first glance seems inconsistent with the economic theory of negligence. A careless workman is like a defective machine. A company should devote resources to screening out careless workmen just as it should devote resources to inspecting its machinery for defects but there comes a point where a further expenditure on supervision of employees or on inspection of machinery would exceed the accident costs that the expenditure would save. The law recognizes this quite clearly with respect to machinery. A firm was liable (in the period covered by the sample at any rate) only for those defects that a reasonable inspection would have discovered. But the law seemingly takes an inconsistent position with respect to the careless workman. The employer is liable regardless of his care in attempting to prevent carelessness.

The inconsistency is more apparent than real. A machine is inanimate and undeterrable. A workman is not. But liability for negligence will not deter a workman who has no money to pay for the accidents he causes. This greatly complicates the formulation of an appropriate standard of care for the employer. Suppose that a railroad in hiring locomotive engineers makes a reasonable effort to screen out clumsy, irresponsible, accident-prone individuals. A serious problem would remain. An engineer—let him be as prudent and skillful as you want—is running behind schedule, so he opens the throttle. The resulting speed is dangerous to pedestrians at crossings but if the engineer is a coldly rational man the danger will not inhibit him. Being judgment-proof, he is not answerable for the consequences to pedestrians. Thus, a railroad not only must exercise care in hiring workers; it must impose sanctions on them for carelessness, because tort law cannot deter the judgment-proof. By making the railroad strictly liable for the torts of its employees in the scope of their employment, which is the effect of respondeat superior, the law creates a mechanism by which the railroad can decide for itself how much to invest in preventing its workers from being careless. It will invest until the last cent of its investment in worker safety saves one cent in accident costs. There will be cases where no reasonable expenditure would have averted the accident and where, therefore, the effect of respondeat superior is to shift losses without affecting the level of safety. But the only alternative would have been for the courts to regulate in great detail the company's methods of selecting, supervising, and disciplining employees.

Our interpretation of respondeat superior derives additional support from the distinction that the courts of the period made between employees and independent contractors. If you hired a contractor to do a job and left the manner of work entirely up to him, you were not liable for injuries caused by his negligence or the negligence of his employees. But if you supervised the details of his work you were liable. These distinctions are economically defensible. If there is no supervision of the work in which the accident occurs, there is no basis for anticipating that the work will be done more safely if the principal is liable. Nor is there a presumption that an independent contractor is insolvent and therefore undeterrable by the threat of tort liability from behaving, or permitting his employees to behave, carelessly. But the principal has a duty to select a competent contractor and if the work involves large risks to safety, such as bridge construction, this duty cannot be discharged, the courts held, by perfunctory inquiry.

The principle of respondeat superior was not applied to the family. Parents were liable for the torts of their children only if negligent in supervising them. Perhaps the reason for treating employers and parents differently is that employers in fact have greater control over the behavior of their employees on the job than do parents over their children. The employer can select his employees, discharge them, and prescribe rewards and punishments to which rational beings will respond. Children tend to be ungovernable; natural parents do not choose their children; children cannot be fired for having been careless. A rule of strict parental liability would have little regulatory effect—and would thus violate what we have tentatively identified as the basic character of the negligence system—because in most cases parents would be incapable at reasonable cost of preventing careless behavior of their children.

Industrial-Accident Doctrine. In cases where the accident victim is a worker suing his employer, the courts in our period applied a number of special doctrines. The most fundamental was that respondeat superior was inapplicable: with important exceptions to be noted, an employer was not liable to his employees for injuries inflicted by their fellow employees. A comparison between this principle and the contrary principle in the case of accidents to strangers brings out clearly the essential economic logic of the negligence system. A pedestrian at a crossing doesn't know the engineer or fireman of any of the trains that pass and is in no position to play a role in preventing accidents by identifying careless workers. In contrast, a fellow employee is in the best position to identify a careless worker, at least if they work in reasonable proximity. The fellow-servant rule, as the exception to respondeat superior is known, provides, in principle at least, a powerful instrument for industrial safety when combined with the rule making the employer liable for injuries inflicted on an employee through the negligence of a fellow employee if the employer was on notice of the fellow employee's habitual neglect or incompetence. The effect of the two rules is to give employees a strong incentive to report careless fellow workers to their supervisors. Some incentive would exist anyway because people generally don't like to be injured, but it is reinforced when an employee knows that if he does not report his fellow's negligence and is injured he will have no right to compensation from his employer. Any rational human being, but perhaps especially a worker lacking assets or adequate insurance, private or social, fears an uncompensated accident even more than a compensated accident. The fellow-servant rule was evidently designed to direct that fear into constructive channels.

The major question in implementing the rule is what criteria to use in deciding whether one employee of a company is a fellow of another. To deem all the workers of a company fellow servants would carry well beyond the rationale of the rule, because an employee doesn't have the opportunity to observe and evaluate the work habits of all the other employees of a large firm. Several tests competed for judicial favor in our period. We shall examine them later. For now it is enough to note the major limitation on the scope of the rule: it did not immunize the employer from liability for the negligence of those employees responsible for the conditions in which the injured employees worked. The brakeman may be barred from recovery if injured through the negligence of a locomotive engineer, but not if the negligence is an employee's whose duty was to inspect the car for defective hand holds or clear the roadbed or repair the automatic couplers or install a block system. Such work is not done in proximity to the operating employees and the latter will neither know who the responsible workers are or have any basis for evaluating the care with which they have worked until an accident occurs.

The rule of contributory negligence applied in cases where an employee was suing his employer. A distinct although related doctrine, assumption of risk, also applied and figures in many of the cases. Under this doctrine an employee was barred from recovering damages where the accident was the result of hazards known by or obvious to him. If a brakeman is employed on a train that is not equipped with the standard safety appliances, he knows this, and he is injured in an accident that would not have occurred had it been so equipped, the employer is not liable, even if the cost of the appliances is less than the discounted accident cost. This result is supported by economic logic. Attitudes toward risk are not distributed uniformly among the population. Some people will pay a good deal more than $1 for a lottery ticket that gives the holder a chance of 1 in 1000 to win $1000; others won't pay anything. The former have a preference for risk, the latter an aversion to it. Suppose in our train example that the cost of the standard appliances would be $10 per worker per year and they would produce a $15 saving in accident costs by reducing the likelihood that the worker would sustain a $1000 injury from 1/50 to 1/200. Since the brakeman knew that the train was not equipped with the standard appliances, and therefore that his chances of injury were higher than normal, why was he willing to continue working? Presumably he was paid to take the risk. We can draw the further inference that he was a risk preferrer. Had he been risk neutral, and the going wage for brakemen on trains equipped with the standard appliances was (say) $500 a year, the railroad would have had to pay him $515 to compensate him for the increased risk; but it would not have done so since it could have employed him at a lower net cost ($510) by installing the devices. If a brakeman is willing to work for less than $510, as our example assumes, the efficient (cost-minimizing) solution is for the railroad to hire him and not install the safety appliances. This solution would be frustrated if assumption of risk were not a defense, because then the railroad would have to install the safety appliances in order to avoid a judgment bill larger than their cost.

The assumption of risk doctrine enables the risk preferrer to market his taste for risk, but it also allows the risk averse to exploit their aversion. Let the wage for a locomotive engineer be $750 a year with a 1/1000 chance of sustaining a $3000 injury in the course of the year, and let the cost of reducing that chance to 1/2000 be $2 per engineer per year in additional safety appliances. Since the cost of the additional appliances exceeds the benefits, the railroad would not be guilty of negligence if it failed to install them. But suppose that enough locomotive engineers to staff the company's trains are highly risk averse. They are so eager to minimize the likelihood of an accident that if the company will install the appliances they will accept a wage reduction from $750 to $745 a year. The company will install the appliances and save $3 a year per engineer. If the company later removes the appliances without informing the engineers and one of them is injured in an accident that would have been prevented by the appliances, the company will be liable to him for the costs of the accident under the rule that a company is liable to an employee for breach of its customary safety standards.

Damages. For the Hand formula to optimize safety, the rules for determining damages once the defendant's liability has been established must measure with reasonable accuracy the social costs of accidents. In cases involving bodily injury short of death, an accident victim's economic loss has the following components: (1) any damage to property; (2) any medical and hospital expenses and other outlays necessitated by the accident; (3) the present value of all earnings lost or likely in the future to be lost as a result of any temporary or permanent disability caused by the accident; and (4) any suffering to the victim, his family, and in some cases perhaps others, resulting from pain, disfigurement and impairment of ability to enjoy life. In general the rules of damages during the period embraced by the sample track the elements of economic loss. Damage to property is fully recoverable, as are any outlays for medical or other expenses incurred in consequence of the accident. Lost earnings, past and future, are compensable. Damages for "pain and suffering," a category nearly coterminous with item (4) above, are also allowable although the only one whose suffering may be considered is the victim himself. In two respects the courts evidenced some economic sophistication. They allowed compensation for loss of nonpecuniary but real earnings, such as a housewife's; and by providing for compensation in a lump sum paid at the time of judgment rather than in periodic payments during the period of disability they avoided the disincentive effects of tying continued compensation to continued inability to work and economized on administrative and policing costs.

The measurement of damages in death cases presents special problems. It is difficult to discover the value that an individual places on his life. If you ask someone how much money he would demand in exchange for giving up his life on the spot, he is likely to reply that no price would be high enough—his price is infinite. But that is because he would have only an infinitesimal amount of time in which to enjoy the proceeds of his sale. Judging from how people risk their lives constantly for small gains in convenience, the average individual will, and in effect does, sell years of his life quite cheaply so long as he expects to have some time in which to enjoy the gains from the sales. The solution of the courts of our period was to allow no damages to the victim's estate for the death itself (there might, of course, be pain or suffering before death and they would be compensable), but to compensate the pecuniary loss suffered by the victim's family. They measured this loss not by the amount of earnings that the victim lost by his death but by the amount of contribution from his earnings to the family's support that the family lost by his death, which is the correct economic measure.

No damages were allowed for the survivors' grief. Since this is a real cost, its exclusion seems economically unsound, even if we assume that the family in working-class homes of the nineteenth century was a less romantic institution than the family of today (we shall see that the working class were the main victims of accidents). Cases involving the death or disability of children may seem especially anomalous in their exclusion of sentimental factors. The basic measure of damages was the child's contribution to his parents' income, which had two components: the child's earnings until he reached his majority, which by law belonged to the parents, minus the expenses of his upkeep; and the likely support that the child would contribute in the parents' old age. This is correct so far as it goes, and perhaps in an era of large families, high infant mortality, little knowledge of contraception, and no social security, a child of working-class parents was sometimes viewed by them as an income-producing asset whose destruction could be compensated for in much the same way as the destruction of property. That would be consistent with a notable study of working-class families of the period. The modern view of children is different and the basis on which damages are computed in children's death cases has changed greatly since the period with which we are concerned.

A seemingly peculiar feature of the law of damages is that the defendant is liable to the full extent of the victim's injuries, even if the extent could not have been foreseen. A team accidentally runs down a man with a preternaturally thin skull and kills him. A normal man would not have been injured seriously. The driver is nonetheless fully liable for the death if the accident resulted from his negligence. The result seems at first glance inconsistent with the principle discussed earlier that one is not liable for the unforeseeable consequences of negligence. However, there is a good reason for distinguishing in this regard between the fact of injury and its extent. We want the total liability of negligent injurers to equal the total cost of their accidents. If instead of attempting to determine damages in each case on an individual basis, we used an average figure (the injury a man of average strength and health would have sustained in an accident of the same type), then we would be overcompensating some (those who are stronger or healthier than average) as well as undercompensating the weaker. But overcompensating for injuries may cause the accident rate to rise. Insurance companies will not insure a building against fire for more than it is worth lest arson be encouraged. Nor should the law of negligence encourage the strong to court injury by overcompensating them when an injury occurs. But then the weak must not be undercompensated, lest the total liability of negligent injurers fall short of the total cost of their accidents.

We have considered the major substantive doctrines of the negligence system as revealed by the sample. It remains to consider the institutional framework of the system. The essence of the system in its institutional or procedural aspect is that it is adversary, decentralized, and nonpolitical in a sense that I shall explain. The motive force of the system is supplied by the economic self-interest of the participants in accidents. If the victim of an accident has a colorable legal claim to damages, it pays him to take steps to investigate the circumstances surrounding the accident; if the investigation suggests liability, to submit a claim to the party who injured him or the party's insurance company; if an amicable settlement cannot be reached, to press his claim in a lawsuit, if necessary to the highest appellate level. The other party has a similar incentive to discover the circumstances of the accident, to attempt a reasonable settlement, and, failing that, to defend the action in court. By creating economic incentives for private individuals and firms to investigate accidents and bring them to the attention of the courts, the system enables society to dispense with the elaborate governmental apparatus that would be necessary for gathering information about the extent and causes of accidents had the parties no incentive to report and investigate them exhaustively. The parties, of course, are not disinterested, but competition between them to persuade a judge can be expected to produce a reasonable approximation to the underlying reality....

NOTES AND QUESTIONS

1. Posner claims that negligent injury arouses a sense of indignation that is not associated with an "unavoidable" accident. Is he correct? He further suggests that the orthodox view of negligence is unable to explain the supposedly sharper reaction to negligently caused harm. Is his own explanation persuasive?

2. Posner suggests that the Learned Hand formula "was an attempt to make explicit the standard that the courts had long applied." This speaks, of course, only to the venerable character of *appellate* court approximation of the economic efficiency test. Does it matter that jury instructions on the breach of duty question usually only made reference to a general standard of reasonable care under the circumstances?

3. Has Posner satisfactorily reconciled contributory negligence as an absolute bar to plaintiff's recovery with the principle of optimizing economic efficiency? Is he remiss in failing to discuss comparative negligence? What about the situation in which the cheapest way of avoiding the accident involves joint activity by injurer and victim? See generally Schwartz, Contributory and Comparative Negligence: A Reappraisal, 87 Yale L. J. 697 (1978).

4. Referring to the extensive use of respondeat superior as a basis of liability, Posner concludes that "the moral element in [negligence] cases is attenuated." Do you agree?

5. Try to articulate the assumptions about behavior underlying the discussion of the assumed-risk defense in industrial injury cases. Do they seem plausible?

6. Posner contends that the fellow-servant rule was a "powerful instrument for industrial safety." In the absence of the rule, would the Hand formula have served the cause of industrial safety less well? Again, what are the underlying behavioral assumptions?

7. Do Holmes and Posner take distinctly different positions on the justification for the negligence system? Assuming they do, would it nonetheless be possible to find that they both offer convincing justifications for the application of fault principles in unintentional injury cases? Whatever may be the case, they clearly share one characteristic: each treats the law of negligence as a comprehensive system that applies fault principles to the resolution of virtually all unintentional injury cases. This would seem to suggest that the judicial system in fact considers highway injury cases as inter-changeable with industrial injury claims. Is it possible to view the proliferation of specialized doctrines in certain categories of accident cases as in fact indicating a more selective commitment to the fault principle? See Rabin, The Historical Development of the Fault Principle, 15 Ga. L. Rev. 925 (1981), excerpted at pp. 44-70, *infra*.

8. Posner has applied economic analysis to a wide variety of other legal fields. See generally Posner, Economic Analysis of Law (2d ed. 1977). His economic efficiency rationale for the fault principle is reiterated in Landes & Posner, The Positive Economic Theory of Tort Law, 15 Ga. L. Rev. 851 (1981). For a wide-ranging critique of his views on efficiency, utilitarianism, and the legal system — with considerable attention given to his tort theory — see Symposium on Efficiency as a Legal Concern, 8 Hofstra L. Rev. 485-771, 811-973 (1980). The economic perspective on tort liability rules is considered in greater detail in Chapter 5 of this volume.

Chapter 2

The Role of Fault Liability: Historical Perspectives

In exploring different justifications for the fault principle, we took for granted its central role during the past century in providing a framework of rules for redressing unintended harm. Clearly, a correspondence exists between the emergence of tort law as a distinct field in the latter half of the nineteenth century and the rise of liability based on negligence. From a historical standpoint, however, these parallel developments raise a number of important questions about the changing character of tort law.

To begin with, how did the law respond to claims for redress of personal harm before tort law crystallized into a distinct system of rights and obligations? And after a common-law doctrinal framework developed, what were its precise contours — was negligence, in fact, a comprehensive principle of liability after the mid-nineteenth century, or was the system characterized by competing, and to some extent conflicting, theories of redress? Finally, how stable was the set of liability rules that eventually emerged? Is the fault principle as significant today as it was at the beginning of this century?

Before turning our attention to the modern era (dating roughly from a century ago), the scattered evidence of earlier approaches to the redress of personal harm deserves brief examination. In medieval England, redress for injury appears to have served the function of ameliorating the desire for revenge.[1] The kinsfolk of an injured person were "rewarded" for abstaining from clan warfare by receiving damages according to the station of the victim. Concomitantly, forfeiture of the animate or inanimate instrument of harm was an accepted obligation in such a case. Civil and criminal remedies were indivisible, and the procedure for securing justice was a far cry from the modern adversary model. The alleged wrongdoer was subjected to trial by oath and ordeal, two processes that placed considerable reliance on religious stricture and revelation in determining guilt. There seems to have been no presentation of evidence about the defendant's actual course of conduct in order to determine blameworthiness. Thus, neither the process nor the substance of the law appears to have been designed to facilitate a determination of "fault" in the modern sense.

In the mid-thirteenth century, as part of the development of the forms of action, the writ of trespass appeared on the scene and established the first clear benchmark for the history of tort as an independent branch of law. Trial by oath and ordeal disappeared as part of a general secularization of the judicial process. Substantive liability in trespass turned on whether the victim could establish that the defendant injured him through a "direct" act. The first essay in this section, by Charles Gregory, ventures into the historical maze at this point, discussing the rise and fall of the forms of action and tracing developments down to the advent of the industrial era.

In the essay that follows Gregory's, I raise questions both about the traditional account of liability in the preindustrial era and about the generally accepted view that the industrial era was in fact characterized by a comprehensive fault principle. Focusing on the supposed golden age of negligence, roughly the period from the Civil War to World War I, I argue that close contextual scrutiny of major contemporaneous categories of injury claims raises serious doubt about the pervasiveness of liability based on fault.

Finally, Gary Schwartz brings the account up to the present in an essay that explores tort law developments in the last two decades. He concludes that a consolidation of liability rules has occurred that relies more than ever on the fault principle.

1. For a more detailed account of the origins of Anglo-American tort liability, see Malone, Ruminations on the Role of Fault in the History of the Common Law of Torts, 31 La. L. Rev. 1 (1970). His discussion draws heavily on the classic treatment of the English antecedents to contemporary tort law in F. Pollock & F. Maitland, History of the English Law (1895). An excellent later study of the English experience, beginning with the development of the writ system, is S. Milsom, Historical Foundations of the Common Law (2d ed. 1981), chaps. 11 and 13. An interesting cross-cultural survey discussing tortious liability in preliterate societies is McLaren, The Origins of Tortious Liability: Insights from Contemporary Tribal Societies, 25 U. Toronto L.J. 42 (1975).

Trespass to Negligence to Absolute Liability*

Charles O. Gregory

Civil liability in the common law was originally based on a fairly simple concept — trespass. The King's Court in early England issued the writ of trespass to any litigant who could show that he had sustained a physical contact on his person or property, due to the activity of another. If this litigant-plaintiff could then convince the court that the defendant had intentionally brought about this contact, he had judgment for damages because of the trespass — unless the defendant could justify his act. But if the plaintiff could not establish intent, then in order to recover he had to go ahead and show that he had sustained some actual damage — at least as far as trespass to his person was concerned. Theoretically this was also true of unintended trespass to land, although the courts were always inclined to *presume* some damage to land in such situations. For convenience, therefore, let us confine the discussion to trespass against the person, until otherwise indicated. And before proceeding, it should be noted that this ancient concept of trespass had reference to any contact achieved as the consequence of one's conduct against the interest of another, no matter under what circumstances it occurred, as long as the defendant's causative conduct was his voluntary act.

In the early days of the King's Court, the only available writ was that of trespass. Plaintiffs who sustained harm under non-trespassory circumstances were not able to bring suit in the King's Court. Thus, suppose the defendant in a particular instance was building a house adjacent to the highway. As he was carrying a beam along a scaffold, he stumbled and unintentionally dropped the beam on the sidewalk, so that it hit a passerby named White on the head, causing him severe harm. White could easily procure a writ of trespass and recover damages. It was immaterial that the defendant dropped the beam unintentionally; and it made no difference whether or not the defendant was negligent or otherwise at fault. This was a trespass under the early law; and this primitive conception of trespass implied all the fault that was necessary for liability.

Shortly thereafter, let us assume, Black came walking along and stumbled over the beam, falling so that his head hit the beam, with the result that he sustained identically the same harm as that suffered by White. Suppose that the defendant had not had time to remove the beam from the sidewalk nor to post warnings; and also assume that Black neither saw the beam as he walked along nor was careless

*Source: 37 Va. L. Rev. 359, 361-370 (1951).

in having failed to see it. When Black sought a writ entitling him to sue the defendant, there was none available which was appropriate for his case; and he was unable to recover damages. That was because there was no trespass by the defendant against him, since the force initiated by the defendant had come to rest before Black was hurt. Indeed, the only force involved in Black's case was that supplied by Black himself when he came walking along and stumbled.

Poor Black never could understand why White was allowed recovery and he was denied it. Each had sustained the same hurt from the same unintended conduct of the same defendant — the dropping of the beam. The only difference Black could perceive was that White was "lucky" enough to get hit by the beam, so that he was allowed to recover with no questions asked. In the meantime, there were people who were accidentally hit by arrows shot at targets and by limbs cut off trees — all of whom were allowed to recover; while others who were hurt "consequentially" — that is, on whose person there had been no direct contact resulting from unexpended forces initiated by others — were denied recovery. This apparent unbalance of justice was no doubt responsible for the creation of a new writ, to be issued in situations where harm had occurred otherwise than by a "direct" or trespassory contact. The new writ was called "trespass in a similar case" — a misnomer, because it was intended to function in the absence of trespassory contact. Lawyers, however, soon came to refer to this new writ as the action on the case and nicknamed it "case," in contradistinction to trespass.

This development occurred in the thirteenth and fourteenth centuries. Thereafter, people in Black's position were enabled to bring their suits before the King's Court. But that did not mean that they were necessarily entitled to recover. Since they could not show a trespassory contact, they had to supply some other element justifying the imposition of liability on the people who had been instrumental in causing their harm. For by this time even an unintended trespassory contact was regarded as tantamount to *a trespass;* and a trespass of any kind was accepted as a wrong in itself, without inquiry into the circumstances leading up to it. Those who sued in case, therefore, because they could not show a trespassory contact, had to submit some item of illegality or fault to take the place of the missing element of trespass in order to establish liability. In actions on the case for inadvertently caused harm to person or property, this new item of illegality or fault ultimately became what we now speak of as negligence. For negligence, as it has operated during the past century or so to afford a basis of liability, is a fairly modern concept. Certainly its modern significance was completely unknown at the time when the action on the case was developing. But something of the sort no doubt operated to furnish the basis for liability during these early times in the absence of the trespassory contact.

At any rate, as the centuries rolled around, it became apparent that Black's descendants in the law were not much better off than they had been when only the writ of trespass was available — certainly in comparison with litigants who fell into White's category. For plaintiffs like White found trespassory contacts so easy to prove; and legal fault or the early counterpart of negligence was not at all easy to establish. To illustrate, let us return to the instance of the defendant who dropped the beam which hit White and over which Black stumbled. Whatever the circumstances were which governed the defendant's dropping of the beam, they were by hypothesis identically the same as far as the two hurt litigants were concerned. Yet all White has to do under this new development is still merely to show contact and damages, while Black has to undertake the burden of proving fault, at the risk of losing his suit if he cannot do so. If we assume that there was some explanation of the incident showing that defendant's conduct was reasonable and not due to his fault, then if Black cannot offer convincing evidence to the contrary, defendant will get the judgment in his case. But White, on the other hand, will still recover damages.

The frequent recurrence of this state of affairs was bound to irritate litigants in Black's position — not so much because they failed to recover as that White *did* recover without any real showing of fault. And they were not satisfied with the explanation that the unintended contact was trespassory and that such trespass implied fault in itself. To them the courts seemed to be maintaining a double standard for determining liability to govern unintentionally caused harm — that of fault or social inadequacy in cases like Black's and absolute liability without fault in cases like White's.

Moreover, defendants themselves began to notice this double standard and to complain bitterly about it. Builders whose non-negligently dropped beams hit plaintiffs before they came to rest on the ground felt themselves unfairly treated under a system of alleged justice which excused other builders from liability for harm caused after their beams had reached the ground. Such a capricious and one-sided administration of civil liability might even become a factor tending to discourage them from enterprise and investment!

This very consideration began to worry American judges during the first half of the nineteenth century. They disliked the imposition of liability without fault and reacted against any manifestation of this notion. It is true that we inherited the English common law when the original colonies became independent states; and it formed the basis of our legal system. But many of our judges believed that the development of this young country under a system of private enterprise would be hindered and delayed as long as the element of chance exposed enterprisers to liability for the consequences of pure accident, without fault of some sort. And this point of view became manifest in several state court decisions a little more than a century ago. . . .

Chief Justice Lemuel Shaw, of the Massachusetts Supreme Court, gets most of the credit for the establishment of a consistent theory of liability for unintentionally caused harm. The case in which he marked the departure from the past was Brown v. Kendall,[6] decided in 1850. There it appeared that two dogs, belonging respectively to the plaintiff and defendant, were engaged in mortal combat. Defendant undertook to separate the dogs by beating them with a stick. Of course, the dogs moved about a good deal as they fought; and both plaintiff and defendant anxiously followed them around. At a certain point defendant raised his stick over his shoulder to strike the dogs, and the end of the stick then happened to hit the plaintiff in the eye while he was standing behind the defendant, causing him serious damage. These are the bare essential facts of the case. It does not appear from the report that either the defendant or the plaintiff was in any way negligent, although such negligence or its absence were matters for the jury to pass on.

The plaintiff sued the defendant in trespass for damages. After all, he had been hit in the eye by a stick set in motion by the defendant—a clear case of direct contact. He thought that this contact or, as he called it, this trespass, entitled him to recover damages for the resulting harm, without showing anything else. Such a theory of liability, he claimed, was historically traditional and was based on defendant's commission of the tort of trespass.

But the Massachusetts Supreme Court turned the plaintiff down cold. Shaw denied that the contact between defendant's stick and plaintiff's eye had any substantive significance at all. Certainly he did not believe that this unintended contact amounted to the tort of trespass, on which liability could be established. He admitted that the contact had procedural significance, enabling the plaintiff to bring his suit under the action of trespass rather than in case. And he declared that all of the old precedents cited by the plaintiff, in which it appeared that unintentionally caused direct physical contacts amounted to trespass, meant no more than that. They did not imply that any such contact was a trespass in the sense that it was a tort, in itself. Apparently that would be true only if the contact were intentionally inflicted. He then stated as a general principle that when harm occurs as the consequence of an unintended contact, it is

6. 60 Mass. (6 Cush.) 292 (1850).

actionable only on the basis of negligence, just as if there had been no contact at all in the causing of the harm. Thus, according to Shaw's principle, White and Black in the hypothetical case discussed above, would henceforth be treated exactly the same and White would have no advantage over Black merely because he sustained his harm by a direct hit while Black suffered consequentially.

Now Shaw, of course, had indicated in his opinion that White and Black had always been treated the same — that one who had been hurt by an unintended contact had never enjoyed any advantage over others whose unintentionally caused harm had not resulted from a direct hit. The available evidence, however, indicates that this was not so. To be sure, Shaw was correct in pointing out that many of the cases decided during the preceding century involved merely the question of whether or not the plaintiff had properly sued in trespass or in case as a purely procedural matter. But he did not mention the older precedents which indicated that an unintended but harmful contact on another's interest was an actionable trespass in itself.

As an alternative basis of liability in the absence of available evidence of negligence, the plaintiff in this dog fight case sought a ruling to the effect that one who sustained harm as the consequence of an unintended direct hit resulting from another's conduct, was entitled to a sort of presumption that such other was negligent and that the burden of disproving negligence was on such other. Thus, he wanted to have the jury instructed that, in view of the direct contact resulting from the defendant's act, even though it was not intended, the defendant must offer convincing evidence that he was not negligent in order to escape liability and that otherwise he would be liable. But Shaw and his court refused to compromise their new principle in this way. They said that the burden of proving negligence in a case of this type always lay on the plaintiff and that it never shifted, leaving the defendant free to sit tight and wait for the plaintiff to show that he had been negligent. For if the burden of disproving negligence were placed on the defendant, simply because of the chance that plaintiff's harm had occurred as the result of a direct hit, then the courts would be lending the element of contact or "trespass" a substantive significance similar to that which they had already denied. Whenever the defendant in such a case was unable to convince the jury of his due care or lack of negligence, liability would be imposed on him in the absence of any proof of fault. He would thus have lost the benefit of the doubt which was still accorded to the defendant whose conduct allegedly harms another, but not under the circumstances of a direct hit. Such a result would go far to cancel out the consistency in theory of liability which the Massachusetts court was endeavoring to establish.

Brown v. Kendall, the dog-fight case, quickly became a landmark in the law of torts. Such was the prestige of the Massachusetts court and its Chief Justice that this case established the view that an unintentional contact on one's interest, achieved through the conduct of another, was not a trespass at all in the sense that it was a tort, even if damage ensued. In other words, under this new principle the tort of trespass could occur *only* when there was an intentional invasion of one's interest. The only significance of an unintentional contact was that the person whose interest was directly hit might bring his suit in the form of trespass if he wished to do so—a matter of purely procedural significance which was fast becoming of no importance with the advent of the codes abolishing the forms of action. If he wanted to win thereafter, a plaintiff hurt by an unintended contact would have to prove the commission of a tort based on negligence, just as if there had been no trespassory contact at all. And with this consistency of theory came another basic notion: no longer was there any theory of absolute liability without fault in our common law to govern the disposition of cases where one sustained harm unintentionally inflicted as the result of another's conduct.

While it is pure speculation, one of Chief Justice Shaw's motives underlying his opinion appears to have been a desire to make risk-creating enterprise less hazardous to investors and entrepreneurs than it had been previously at common law. Certainly that interpretation is consistent with his having furthered the establishment of the fellow servant doctrine and the expansion of the assumption-of-risk defense in actions arising out of industrial injuries. Judicial subsidies of this sort to youthful enterprise removed pressure from the pocketbooks of investors and gave incipient industry a chance to experiment on low-cost operations without the risk of losing its reserve in actions by injured employees. Such a policy no doubt seems ruthless; but in a small way it probably helped to establish industry, which in turn was essential to the good society as Shaw envisaged it. And, of course, he also had in mind the obvious advantages of consistency in legal theory.

Seven years earlier, in 1843, the highest New York court had enunciated a principle similar to that promulgated in Massachusetts.[8] There it appeared that a six-year-old defendant had thrown a stone at random and it had struck the plaintiff's five-year-old daughter in the eye, causing serious damage. The evidence indicated, however, that the young defendant was not at fault, which presumably meant that he did not intend to hit the little girl and was not to be held negligent in having done so. In any event, the jury seems to have found it to be

8. Harvey v. Dunlop, 39 N.Y.C.L. Rep. 193 (Hill & Dennio Supp. 1843).

a case of inevitable accident: and following the instructions of the trial court, it gave the verdict to the defendant. In his appeal the plaintiff assigned error in these instructions. After all, he contended, the defendant had thrown the stone, which had hit his daughter's eye. And while a child of six could hardly be held for negligence, at least he could be made liable at common law for his trespasses.

But the highest New York court affirmed the judgment for defendant, the Chief Judge declaring: "No case or principle can be found, or if found can be maintained, subjecting an individual to liability for an act done without fault on his part." He then went on to say, however, that where harm is inflicted by the defendant, "it should be presumed to have been done wrongfully or carelessly," the burden of proving the contrary to be placed on him. This notion was urged upon the Massachusetts court seven years later in the dog-fight case; but Shaw rejected it as bad law because of the advantage it gave a plaintiff who happened to be hurt through the purely fortuitous circumstance of contact.

A somewhat similar instance, illustrating the difficulty with which a few of our state courts made the break from the past, occurred in 1835.[9] The Vermont Supreme Court then declared the law to be that a plaintiff who was run down by a horse and buggy driven by the defendant, could not recover damages if this occurrence was the "result of unavoidable accident" and if "there was no want of prudence or care on the part of the defendant." But then the court went on to say something inconsistent with this statement. "Therefore," its Chief Justice observed, "where a person is doing a voluntary act, which he is under no obligation to do, he is held answerable for any injury which may happen to another, either by carelessness or accident." Now much the same idea was later expressed, in a slightly different way, in the trial court's instructions to the jury in Brown v. Kendall, the Massachusetts dog-fight case. There the trial court said that if what the defendant did "was not a necessary act, and [he] was not in duty bound to part the dogs, but might with propriety interfere or not as he chose, [he] was responsible for the consequences of the blow, unless it appeared that he was in the exercise of extraordinary care, so that the accident was inevitable, using the word not in a strict but a popular sense."

The meaning of this kind of language is hard to grasp. But whatever it means, it runs counter to the main principle that Shaw ultimately stated in the dog-fight case. Certainly Shaw recognized it as drivel, since its validity depended upon drawing a distinction between human contact which was "necessary," or performed

9. Vincent v. Stinehour, 7 Vt. 62 (1835).

pursuant to some duty, on the one hand, and that which the defendant merely had a right to engage in, on the other hand. Naturally the defendant in Brown v. Kendall didn't have to separate the fighting dogs. It was not a necessary act, in the sense that there was any compulsion on him to perform it. Shaw said, rather, that it "was a lawful and proper act, which he might do by proper and safe means." And he then made it clear that his new principle applied to all human conduct lawfully embarked upon, whether it was driving a horse for pleasure or profit, shooting at targets, building houses or anything else. The only test was to be whether or not such lawful conduct was carefully or negligently performed. Otherwise his new principle would not mean very much, since most human conduct is not compulsory or necessary but is undertaken either for economic gain, for personal value ends, including recreation, or just for something to do.

Perhaps judges using the kind of language which Shaw disapproved were somewhat uncertain about the relatively new concept of negligence. After all, that concept did not then have a very long tradition; and its career in the modern sense was entirely in the future. It is fairly apparent from the examples cited by these judges in their opinions that they were confusing so-called unnecessary conduct with what clearer-headed judges like Shaw would have called conduct from which a jury might be permitted to infer negligence. Again, it is barely possible that they were in this fashion attempting to explain away some of the older precedents which Shaw had preferred simply to ignore — that is, the earlier English decisions in which liability for unintentionally caused harm resulting from direct contacts was based on trespass regardless of the absence of negligence.

NOTES AND QUESTIONS

1. Whether recovery in trespass could be based entirely on the harm resulting from a "direct" act without reference to considerations of personal fault, as Gregory suggests, has been a hotly debated issue. Reconsider the question in Note 1, p. 13, *supra*, about Holmes's view. Like Gregory, Dean Wigmore argued that the early common law recognized strict liability in tort for harm caused to person or property. See Wigmore, Responsibility for Tortious Acts: Its History, 7 Harv. L. Rev. 315, 382, 491 (1894). Identifying Holmes with an opposing view, Nathan Isaacs attempted to establish a conciliatory position by arguing that the law moved cyclically through

alternating periods of fault and strict liability. Isaacs, Fault and Liability, 31 Harv. L. Rev. 954 (1918).

Scholarly opinion continues to be deeply divided. Gary Schwartz criticizes both Gregory and M. Horwitz, The Transformation of American Law, 1780-1860, at 63-108 (1977), arguing that both the English and American precedents are inconclusive on a strict liability principle prior to the industrial era. His discussion provides an excellent bibliographical essay on recent Anglo-American historical scholarship dealing with the evolution of tort law to the advent of the Industrial Revolution. See Schwartz, Tort Law and the Economy in Nineteenth-Century America: A Reinterpretation, 90 Yale L.J. 1717, 1722-1734 (1981). Similar skepticism about whether tort law possessed any well-defined principle of liability prior to the mid-1800s is expressed in L. Friedman, A History of American Law, 261-262, 409-410 (1973), and G. White, Tort Law in America: An Intellectual History 13-15 (1980). Is Gregory's position on the principle of strict liability central to his thesis about the impact of industrialization?

2. What role does Gregory assign the negligence principle in the industrial era? Does the landmark opinion in Brown v. Kendall, which is central to his analysis, in fact lend support to his thesis? Is it important that the case arose in the context of a dogfight where one neighbor unintentionally injured another?

3. The second landmark case discussed by Gregory, Harvey v. Dunlop, again involved an injury among neighbors, resulting from a stone-throwing incident. How does the case bear on Gregory's negligence thesis? Compare the landmark English cases establishing the basic framework of negligence law — cases generally involving highway injuries among strangers. See, e.g., the discussion in Rabin, Some Thoughts on Tort Law from a Sociopolitical Perspective, 1969 Wisc. L. Rev. 51, 57-60. Do these cases suggest that considerations other than protection of industry might have been motivating the judges in the early negligence era?

4. In any event, in what sense was it a "judicial subsidy" to industrial enterprises, as Gregory suggests, to base liability on negligence?

5. The thesis that protection of industry was a central purpose of the development of the negligence principle has been endorsed by tort historians whose reading of the past diverges on many other points. Along with Gregory, consider L. Friedman, A History of American Law 409-427 (1973), and M. Horwitz, The Transformation of American Law, 1780-1860, at 67-108 (1977). For a critical view of this scholarship, see Schwartz, Tort Law and the Economy in Nineteenth Century America: A Reinterpretation, 90 Yale L.J. 1717 (1981). Even wider agreement seems to exist that negligence con-

stituted a comprehensive principle of liability in the industrial era. In addition to the references above (including Schwartz), see G. White, Tort Law in America: An Intellectual History 12-19, 60-62 (1980). On this point, as well as the debate over the liability principle in the preindustrial era discussed above in Note 1, consider the essay that follows.

The Historical Development of the Fault Principle: A Reinterpretation*

Robert L. Rabin

The purpose of this essay is to raise some fundamental questions about the historical account of the rise of negligence. I regard the view that the industrial era was dominated by a comprehensive theory of fault liability for unintended harm as largely a myth. I also think that there is limited historical evidence to support a long-standing "tension" in the common law between strict liability and negligence. Along similar lines, I view it as a serious mistake to characterize the pre-industrial era as one of strict liability. In short, I believe that the historical record needs to be reassessed in its entirety.

Where does one begin? In this essay I can be suggestive only. The groundwork, however, was laid many years ago. At the height of the Legal Realism movement, Leon Green asserted, but failed to articulate satisfactorily, the view that tort law consisted largely of a patchwork of various "functional" or "relational" interests. Green thought that there were sharp distinctions between the judicial treatment of unintended harms arising in contexts as different as land occupancy and manufacturing. I consider this insight a starting point. Some of the recurring kinds of harm—arising out of "functional" relationships, such as worker-employer or land occupier-entrant— were long dominated by a contract perspective, others by fixed notions of property rights, and still others by ethical presuppositions that were translated into "no duty" classifications. Modern tort conceptions of generalized duties were late arrivals.

From a functional perspective, the focus on a dominant tension between strict liability and fault seems misplaced. To the contrary, I will argue that fault liability emerged out of a world-view dominated largely by no-liability thinking. That world-view provides the key to understanding why the efforts to establish the early vitality of a

*Source: 15 Ga. L. Rev. 925, 927-961 (1981).

comprehensive fault principle are seriously flawed. In pointing out why the existing historical account is unpersuasive, I hope to suggest more concretely the contours of a more accurate rendition of liability in tort for unintended harm in the decades following the Civil War.[12]

II. The Fault Thesis: Four Fallacies

Many voices attest to the comprehensive theory of fault liability that emerged in the second half of the nineteenth century. Before questioning the validity of the role assigned to the fault principle, however, we need to look briefly at the rationale for basing liability on fault. If we are to explore the territory falling outside the principle, it is essential at the outset to have some sense of the inner domain of fault.

When one probes a bit, however, the precise character of the fault principle becomes problematic. It was no less eminent a figure than Oliver Wendell Holmes who, in The Common Law, sought to provide an "argument from policy" for the fault system. Holmes felt certain that the times required that liability be restricted in scope to negligent acts. But when he came to supporting his position with reasoned elaboration, the rationale proved rather elusive:

> A man need not, it is true, do this or that act — the term *act* implies a choice — but he must act somehow. Furthermore, the public generally profits by individual activity. As action cannot be avoided, and tends to the public good, there is obviously no policy in throwing the hazard of what is at once desirable and inevitable upon the actor.

That strict liability, the *bête noire* of the piece, would work greater restrictions on freedom of action than would negligence is treated as self-evident. It is not, of course.[15] Thus, the "policy" basis for negligence does not clearly emerge.

To complicate matters further, Holmes goes on to argue forcefully for an *objective* standard of due care — one that would measure

12. Throughout this essay, when I refer to the early industrial era or the purported era of comprehensive fault liability, I have in mind the period stretching roughly from 1870 to 1915....

15. From an economic perspective, whether an actor is strictly responsible or liable only for her negligent acts, she will be deterred only when the marginal cost of harm resulting from further activity exceeds the marginal cost of avoiding the injury. Under strict liability, the injurer will bear the cost of "unavoidable injuries," whereas those costs are borne by the injured party in a negligence system. But this distinction only goes to the initial allocation of injury costs; in theory, at least, the total resource activity is unaffected....

A caveat is in order. The concepts of market deterrence and efficiency propounded by latter-day law and economics thinkers may be far-removed from what Holmes had in mind when he referred to the goal of promoting individual activity....

the negligence of any particular actor against what "a prudent man" might have done under the circumstances, rather than against the subjective capacity of the individual himself. Clearly, this requirement is likely to discourage "individual activity" by the hapless fellow who ventures forth, doing his best, but nonetheless injures others through his subpar motor skills. In a sense, as Holmes admits, an objective standard smacks of strict liability. He eschews consistency, in part, because of the exigencies of administrative convenience. But in advocating an objective standard, more than administrative feasibility seems to have been at stake for him. He also suggests that "when men live in society, a certain average of conduct, a sacrifice of individual peculiarities going beyond a certain point, is necessary to the general welfare."

This theme of holding the actor responsible to the standards of expected behavior in the community is resorted to repeatedly in the literature seeking both to establish the character of "the reasonable man" and to provide an explanation for putting the question of "due care" to a jury. It suggests a moral basis for the fault principle, bound up in an organic sense of custom, community, and individual responsibility.

Writing a century later, Richard Posner posits an economic justification for the fault principle. Drawing on the often cited Learned Hand formula,[21] Posner suggests that the common law courts intuitively relied upon economic efficiency considerations in fashioning the negligence principle. The thesis is that the common law judges, at some level of consciousness, were convinced that one should be held at fault only when the costs of avoiding injurious conduct were less than the harm imposed on the victims of the activity.

Is the economic rationale for the fault principle distinct from the moral justification? Referring to the Master, Landes and Posner find "prefigurings of the economic approach" in The Common Law. I remain dubious. Contemporaneous judicial opinions, as well as most of the early torts scholarship—including Holmes—seem to link the due care standard to community expectations of *reasonable* behavior, rather than to the economist's perception of *rational* behavior. Although the two often would correspond, I see no necessary linkage. As Terry, another of Posner's early champions, put it, "mere

---

21. See United States v. Carroll Towing Co., 159 F.2d 169, 173 (2d Cir. 1947), where Judge Hand put the negligence calculus in mathematical terms: "[I]f the probability [of injury] be called P; the injury L; and the burden [of protection] B; liability depends upon whether B is less than L multiplied by P," i.e., whether $B < PL$.

error of judgment is not negligence" because — he asserted — reasonable men sometimes make mistakes, too.[25]

For present purposes, however, it is sufficient to note the ambiguity surrounding the fault rationale. Because my basic contention is that neither the moral nor the economic conception of fault comes close to capturing the complexity of the liability system that existed in the early "negligence" era, there is no need to seek a precision of meaning that almost certainly distorts reality in any event.

In fact, the distortion in the historical record — the exaggerated sense of the pervasiveness of the fault principle — has virtually nothing to do with imprecision about the meaning of "fault." Rather, the fundamental problem is an ambiguity in the doctrinal concept of *negligence*, which appears consistently in the literature on the fault principle.

The problem arises because, as a matter of usage, "negligence" is employed in two distinct ways. When an actor breaches a duty of due care, we speak of the violation — the breach itself — as negligence. In this sense, negligence is synonymous with lack of due care. However, as every first-year law student soon learns, the question of liability is not always so easily resolved. For "negligence," *as a cause of action*, consists of a number of additional elements — the issue of duty itself, the matter of cause-in-fact, the question of proximate cause, and, of course, the requirement of damages. It is only when all of these elements are present that "negligence," in the second sense, is established.

The great failure of tort historians has been the tendency to ignore this fundamental distinction.[26] The same can be said for many of the early landmark cases proclaiming a single-minded commitment

---

25. ...Of course, errors of judgment and mistakes could be treated as situations where the cost of acquiring adequate information to avoid the harm exceeded the risk of injury, and, as a consequence, did not suggest lack of due care. There is no reason to think that the early torts scholars entertained this narrow conception of "the reasonable man." To the contrary, the overall portrait is one of a person sometimes reacting passionately and instinctively in extraordinary situations.

26. Clearly, the elements of negligence doctrine cannot be taken uncritically as the definition of fault liability without further analysis. Otherwise, the assertion that the fault principle supplied a comprehensive basis for redressing unintentional harms would be tautological: the fault principle would be simply the label attached to the sum of negligence doctrine.

Nonetheless, all cases of redress for unintended harm have been lumped together by torts scholars under the rubric "negligence." Thus, for example, landowner liability cases have been treated as part of "the negligence system" even though they traditionally were decided with reference to categories bearing an attenuated relationship to the fault principle....

to the fault principle. When tort scholars survey the post-Civil War period and remark on the comprehensive principle of fault liability, they virtually always fail to distinguish between the two meanings of negligence. The fault principle is thus robbed of any sensible meaning, because key elements in a negligence case having nothing to do with breach of due care—particularly, the duty question—frequently are determinative of major categories of injury claims.[28]

By developing this line of argument, I hope to demonstrate why the fault principle was far from dominant during the supposed heyday of fault. I will try to do so by examining some systematic distortions—one might say methodological flaws—in the construction of the historical record that have led tort scholars either to understate or ignore the wide array of unintended harms that were not governed by fault principles.

A. Dealing with Doctrine

I begin by discussing three important classes of cases where negligence, in the narrow sense of lack of due care, played a relatively limited role in allocating losses for unintended harm. At the outset, consider the case of landowner's liability. It is familiar legal lore that the landowner's obligations in tort traditionally were derived from his status *vis-à-vis* the injured entrant. If the victim was a trespasser, well-established doctrine barred recovery unless the landowner could be charged with willful misconduct. In the case of a "licensee"—one who entered for purposes other than the business benefit of the occupier—a landowner was liable solely for known, hidden dangers about which he failed to provide a warning. Only in the case of an "invitee" did the courts regard landowners as owing a duty of due care.

These categories had very little to do with nineteenth-century notions of fault liability. Consider, for example, the court's approach in the leading case of Humphrey v. Twin State Gas & Electric,[30] where the question was whether the defendant-utility company, which was licensed to run a power line over the land of another, could claim that landowner's rights against a trespasser who had been injured by

28. As will be evident, I am only referring to cases where reliance on elements other than breach of duty indicates an *inconsistency* with the fault principle. Thus, a finding that defendant was not the cause in fact of plaintiff's injury is not inconsistent with a comprehensive fault basis of liability because fault liability assumes a causal nexus. But a finding that a particular category of defendants owes no duty to injury victims, even when lack of due care is established, is directly at odds with the claim that fault is a comprehensive liability principle. Such a claim assumes a *general* duty of due care.

30. 100 Vt. 414, 139 A. 440 (1927).

exposure to the utility company's transmission wire. In rejecting the defendant's effort to capitalize on the status of another, the court noted:

> [T]he rule exempting a landowner from liability to a trespasser injured through the condition of the premises, is found to have originated in an overzealous desire to safeguard the right of ownership as it was regarded under a system of landed estates, long since abandoned— under which the law ascribed a peculiar sanctity to rights therein.... The object of the law being to safeguard and protect the various rights in land, it is obviously going quite far enough to limit the immunity to one whose rights have been invaded.[31]

The landowner cases are filled with such historical assertions. Indeed, it was this same high regard for the sanctity of land that dictated the carving out of the peculiar category of "licensees" from the general mass of land users who legitimately beat a path across Blackacre for one purpose or another.

I do not mean to suggest that the law of landowner's liability was entirely insensitive to developing notions of fault. To the contrary, the painstaking development of new categories affording greater protection to hapless entrants, such as "discovered trespassers" and "implied invitees," attests to a growing restiveness about the traditional protections extended to landowners. But the persistence of the categories throughout the supposed heyday of fault liability, in an increasingly urbanized society where injuries to social guests were rife, indicates that status concerns—born of another age—did not die easily.

Indeed, when the California Supreme Court took the rather bold step of abolishing the categories in Rowland v. Christian,[34] almost a century had passed since the era of pervasive fault liability had been ushered in—according to the commentators. Moreover, *Rowland* itself nicely demonstrates the nonfault conceptions underlying the traditional approach. Plaintiff was badly cut by a cracked bathroom faucet handle in his friend's apartment. He sued her on the ground that she failed to mention the danger to him, despite having demonstrated her awareness of the defect by notifying her landlord of it. Unless the crack in the porcelain was clearly evident, there can be little doubt that the occupier was in a better position than the guest to avoid the injury. Typically, notice is relatively costless in this kind of case, and often a risk-minimizing repair effort itself involves very little expense. In economic terms, then, the limited duty to social

31. Id. at 418, 139 A. at 442.
34. 69 Cal. 2d 108, 443 P.2d 561, 70 Cal. Rptr. 97 (1968).

guests frequently leads to a different result than the fault principle would dictate.

The same is true if we employ instead a moral basis for fault grounded in community expectations of due care. At first blush, one might be tempted to define "fault" with reference to the status of the party injured. But then the fault principle becomes circular: the duty issue is swallowed up in the determination of due care. Putting status considerations aside, we can test the outcome that the fault principle would dictate by treating the plaintiff in *Rowland* as a business invitee. Clearly, "fault" unfettered by contextual constraints—i.e., duty limitations—would point to liability. In the landowner liability cases, then, we encounter an initial indication that the fault principle was less than all-embracing.

The crux of the matter here was one of status. Shortly, we will see status playing an equally dominant role in two strikingly different contexts. Before moving on, however, it is worth examining the occupier-entrant relationship from another perspective. In focusing on the common law classifications of entrants, one finds a categorical impulse to deny or limit liability. But where the landowner is victim rather than culprit, the rationale for limited liability—the primacy of land occupancy—is sufficiently powerful to embrace the counter-principle of strict liability as well.

In this regard, many of the early land-related categories of strict liability can be viewed as "reverse no-liability" situations. If landowners owed virtually no duty of care to entrants on their land, conversely those who in fact entered without permission and proceeded to cause physical damage, or interfered in some substantial way with the owner's unfettered enjoyment of his homestead, owed an absolute obligation to compensate for harm done. On this basis, a cluster of disparate cases, apparent anomalies in the fault era—wild animal, blasting, and nuisance actions, for instance, as well as the doctrine of Rylands v. Fletcher—share a common heritage. To put it simply, virtually unlimited enjoyment of one's own land was a two-sided coin, at once supporting a conditional freedom to maintain land as one wished, and, at the same time, promoting a conditional freedom affirmatively to enjoy one's land without interference. The critical point is that in neither case did the emergence of the fault principle supersede the dominant system of privileged status afforded to land occupancy.

Consider next a very different context. Early products liability cases also were decisively influenced by status considerations. Once again, the consequence was to introduce doctrinal barriers that served to vitiate the fault principle until the New York Court of

Appeals decided MacPherson v. Buick Motor Co.[39] at the very end of the supposed heyday of negligence.

The era was ushered in by the famous, or infamous, case of Winterbottom v. Wright.[40] Plaintiff was the driver of a mailcoach supplied to the Postmaster General by the defendant, who agreed to maintain the coach in a safe condition. Plaintiff was hurt when the coach broke down due to a defect that might fairly be assigned to the defendant's negligence. In an often-cited opinion, Lord Abinger expressed his distaste for products liability in no uncertain terms:

> There is no privity of contract between these parties; and if the plaintiff can sue, every passenger, or even any person passing along the road, who was injured by the upsetting of the coach, might bring similar action. Unless we confine the operation of such contracts as this to the parties who entered into them, the most absurd and outrageous consequences, to which I can see no limit would ensue.[41]

Earlier in the opinion, Lord Abinger had stressed the point that appears repeatedly in roughly contemporaneous decisions imposing a regime of no-liability for unintentional harm: that the case is one of first impression in which no precedent exists for such an action.[42] This is wholly at odds, of course, with the frequent assertions in the literature that liability in tort was strict at the dawn of the negligence era. The disagreement, however, is more apparent than real. It is largely a matter of emphasis. Looking only at the earlier cases where responsibility for harm was recognized — "direct" personal injuries and early trespassory invasions of property — liability can indeed be interpreted to be strict. But wild beasts on the rampage were not a ubiquitous feature of the industrial era. If one searches for reasonably close antecedents to the new classes of injuries spawned by an industrializing society, a very different perspective emerges.

The judges in these early industrial-era cases generally were called upon to resolve unintentional injury claims that seemed quite novel. Their response was very frequently — as in the defective products context — to view the cases as totally unprecedented *from a tort perspective*. When Lord Abinger and his colleagues confronted such a case, the rather original idea of tort liability had an unfamiliar ring; contextually, the more familiar characterization for dealing with defective product claims was contract, and, quite naturally, the

---

39. 217 N.Y. 382, 111 N.E. 1050 (1916).
40. 10 M & W. 109, 152 Eng. Rep. 402 (Ex. 1842).
41. Id. at 114.
42. Id. at 113. See also Russell v. Men of Devon, 100 Eng. Rep. 359, 2 Term Rep. 667 (K.B. 1788) (establishing municipal immunity); Farwell v. Boston & W.R.R., 45 Mass. (4 Met.) 49 (1842) (establishing fellow-servant rule).

doctrinal structure suggested by that system of rules — no liability without privity of contract — prevailed.

As the exceptions to the privity limitation developed, so artfully manipulated by Judge Cardozo in *MacPherson*, the fault principle gradually overcame limitations based on contract. Thus, liability based on a fault principle eventually prevailed. It did so, however, against a contrapuntal theme of no-liability, not strict liability. In fact, throughout the heyday of the negligence era, the fault principle fashioned a series of ever-widening crevasses in a terrain still dominated by nonliability as far as defective product claims were concerned. Fault simply was not the dominant principle in allocating losses.[46]

A particularly instructive instance of the central role of context in shaping doctrine is found in a well-known early pair of New York cases.[47] These cases are especially interesting for present purposes because they deal with the same injury claim — first in a landowner suit and then in a products liability action. A steam boiler owned by a paper mill exploded and was propelled onto the property of the plaintiff where it destroyed buildings and personal property he owned. Plaintiff sued the paper mill, but could not establish negligence on its part. As a consequence, plaintiff relied on Rylands v. Fletcher and other cases where strict liability had been recognized.[48] In an opinion often cited as a landmark in the recognition of the comprehensive theory of fault, the court rejected the application of *Rylands* and proceeded at length to stress the rule, "a universal one," that fault must be shown before one is held responsible for unintended injury.[49] Clearly, the "reverse no-liability" principle of protecting landowners — strict liability in support of the sanctity of land — was on the wane.

---

46. But did this class of injuries really amount to much in the period from *Winterbottom* to *MacPherson*? This is, of course, an empirical question, requiring careful research on the rise of third-party commercial dealings in various lines of risk-generating products. As far as I know, there is no reliable source of statistical information on the incidence of household and industrial injuries caused by manufactured products in the hands of third-party users.

Nonetheless, in my view the tort literature is seriously misguided. Relying on court records, particularly appellate opinions, is likely to be highly misleading. There is no reason to think that even a small fraction of the workers, passengers, pedestrians, and householders injured by the crude and rough-hewn products of the day would have pursued tort claims under the early regime of "negligence" law. Indeed, the historical record suggests some grounds for thinking that in transport and industry a very considerable injury toll was generated by machinery and parts supplied by outside manufacturers. See, e.g., Burke, Bursting Boilers and the Federal Power. 7 Tech. & Culture 1 (1966).

47. Losee v. Clute, 51 N.Y. 494 (1873); Losee v. Buchanan, 51 N.Y. 476 (1873).

48. Losee v. Buchanan, 51 N.Y. 476, 479 (1873).

49. Id. at 491.

But the remarkable feature of the litigation is that in the companion case brought against the *manufacturer* of the boiler, who was conceded to have been negligent, the court again held that the hapless victim had no remedy. Here, the "universal rule of fault" turns out to be somewhat less than all-embracing because:

> [The manufacturer] contracted with the [paper] company, and did what was done by them for it and to its satisfaction, and when the boiler was accepted they ceased to have any further control over it or its management, and all responsibility for what was subsequently done with it devolved upon the [paper] company.... [The manufacturer] owed [plaintiff] no *duty* whatever at the time of the explosion either growing out of contract or imposed by law.[50]

A clearer statement that fault principles were entirely inapplicable to the case would be hard to imagine. There is not a trace here of concern about the economic efficiency of the outcome, or of moral justification for the manufacturer's careless conduct. Apart from a handful of still-exceptional cases, the domain of tort simply had not yet extended to this particular category of unintended harms — product defects due to the negligence of an unrelated party. Because the harm was caused by a product failure, contract thinking dominated — a bitter irony to the victim, of course, who had not even the most attenuated commercial relationship with his injurer.

Contract was even more central in yet another context, the industrial injury, where once again a doctrinal overlay at odds with the fault principle dominated the disposition of unintentional harm cases. Here, the nonfault doctrines of assumed risk and fellow servant robbed the negligence principle of much of its vitality. Both doctrines would have been superfluous if the judicial system had been wholeheartedly committed to liability based on fault. The defense of assumed risk would have added nothing to case-by-case determinations of the injured worker's contributory negligence, and the fellow-servant rule would have given way to the normal inquiry into the employer's imputed negligence under the respondeat superior doctrine.[53]

The efforts made to salvage these two defenses, by establishing their consistency with an economic justification for the fault principle, are unconvincing. With regard to assumed risk, Posner has argued that the courts, by effecting a trade-off between higher wages and an injury premium, were giving explicit recognition to the worker's

---

50. Losee v. Clute, 51 N.Y. 494, 496-97 (1873).
53. Of course, the respondeat superior doctrine itself can be viewed as a nonfault principle, since negligence is imputed to the principal as a matter of law. For present purposes, though, I will overlook this rather significant departure and simply explore whether the imputed fault principle was applied consistently....

desire to market his taste for risk.[54] Resting this argument, as he does, on freedom of contract is obviously circular. The empirical question is whether workers in relatively dangerous occupations possessed the autonomy and mobility to effect trade-offs between safety and wages in their negotiations with employers, or whether they simply were impelled by circumstances to confront unwanted hazards. Posner offers no evidence on this score. As Gary Schwartz has indicated, there is some historical documentation to suggest the contrary.[55] In a similar vein, a leading contemporaneous authority on industrial injury law remarked:

> Upon the average man it is certain that the fear of the disagreeable, and it may be, frightful consequences which will almost certainly ensue from the failure to obtain work or from the loss of a position, must always operate as a very strong coercive influence, indeed. To speak of one whom that fear drives into or detains in a dangerous employment as being a voluntary agent is a mere trifling with words.[56]

Moreover, the history of workmen's compensation reform is singularly free of any reference to laborers protesting against the legislation on the grounds that a compulsory safety premium was likely to have a depressing effect on wages.[57] Where were the risk-preferring workers when their wage premiums were under siege? If the historical record is to be believed, they were unappreciatively on the side of unseating their judicial protectors.

Any trace of harmonization between the fault principle and assumed risk is further weakened when one examines the scope of the doctrine closely, for it was by no means limited to well-understood risks of the workplace. To the contrary, Labatt points out that the doctrine was applied to abnormal or transitory risks of the employment as well as "normal" hazards.[58] Moreover, Schwartz, in his study of New Hampshire cases, concludes that the risks assumed were not limited to those immediately apparent in the employment situation.[59]

---

54. ...It should be noted that Posner is in fact arguing that the assumed risk defense was economically justified for reasons having nothing to do with the fault principle. In essence, his position is that the risk-preferring worker was allowed to contract out of his right to recover for employer fault.

55. See Schwartz, Tort Law and the Economy in Nineteenth Century America: A Reinterpretation, 90 Yale L.J. 1717, 1769 & nn.389-90 (1981). See also E. Downey, History of Work Accident Indemnity in Iowa 67-77 (1912).

56. 3 C. Labatt, Master and Servant §963, at 2490 (1913).

57. See, e.g., E. Downey, Workmen's Compensation 14-15 (1924) (pointing out that organized labor had endorsed workmen's compensation); Hearings Before U.S. Employer's Liability and Workmen's Compensation Commn., S. Doc. No. 90, 62d Cong., 1st Sess. vol. I, part III.

58. See 3 C. Labatt, *supra* note 56, §955.

59. See Schwartz, *supra* note 55, at 1769-70 & nn.391-92.

The case for reading the other major bar to recovery, the fellow-servant rule, congruently with the fault principle is equally weak.[60] The main argument is that the rule, as a general policy, encouraged a worker to watch his fellow employees and report careless behavior to the common employer, who was not himself in a good position to monitor negligent conduct. This rationale builds on two assumptions, neither of which is particularly plausible.

First, the argument assumes that the employer, once notified, would have an incentive to sanction the careless employee. Obviously, such an incentive would exist only under one of two conditions: if the employer, once notified, was no longer insulated from tort liability; or, if the employer, whether insulated or not, systematically believed that careless employees were less productive workers. There appears to be no solid support for either conclusion.[62] Second, the argument assumes that the courts regarded an "informer rule" as likely to work. But there is no particular reason to think that an employee would be more concerned about his personal safety from a workplace accident than about physical threats of retaliation if he were to turn in a fellow worker.

Students of industrial injury law are aware, of course, of the numerous exceptions that were engrafted on the fellow-servant doctrine. In typical fashion, the courts created corrosive exceptions to a doctrine that was exceedingly harsh in practice; thus, the ban was lifted where the fellow servant was a "vice-principal," or when the co-workers were in "different departments," and in innumerable other arcane circumstances. The most that can be said for this bevy of exceptions, which varied considerably from one jurisdiction to another, is that they were mired in confusion.

Indeed, Posner seems oblivious to the inconsistencies in his own effort to make economic sense of the myriad exceptions:

> The combined effect of these rules was to limit the application of the fellow-servant rule to approximately those areas where the employee was reasonably competent to discover and report negligent conduct

60. At first blush, holding *only* the negligent fellow servant responsible — the party actually at fault — might appear to make the injury rules more closely reflect fault thinking. But this ignores the overriding judicial commitment to respondeat superior in virtually every other employee negligence situation. . . .

62. On the first point, Posner mentions in passing the rule that an employer who was notified of "habitual" neglect was subsequently liable for related harm. See Posner, [A Theory of Negligence, 1 J. Legal Stud. 29] at 44. But Schwartz's examination of California decisions indicates that in a dozen cases where the employer's negligent retention was raised, the claim was denied without exception. See Schwartz, *supra* note 55, at 1770 & n.395.

On the second point, speculation is useless. Intuition does not suggest whether workers who, at times, created risks to fellow employees would have been regarded as more or less productive than other workers.

endangering him. The pattern that emerged with respect to railroad collisions is illustrative. If a member of the operating crew is injured through the negligence of another operating employee, a brakeman, fireman, switchman, or engineer, whether on his train or another train of the employer on the same line, the employer is not liable.

Obviously, these railroad illustrations on their face do not support the argument that the doctrine was intended to encourage monitoring of fellow employees in close proximity. And, once again, Schwartz's study of the California cases indicates that proximity did not play a decisive role.[65] Clearly, some courts were troubled by the harshness of the fellow-servant rule, but the judicial impulse to reshape industrial injury law in accordance with fault principles was still in a haphazard state when the workmen's compensation movement swept the country.

Moreover, it should be noted that the assumption of risk doctrine was never limited to industrial injury cases. Even after the enactment of workmen's compensation legislation, assumption of risk retained a limited vitality in a distinct class of cases where victims knowingly participated in an activity that presented some degree of danger, although not a sufficient risk of harm to warrant a finding of contributory fault. Typical is Murphy v. Steeplechase Amusement Co.,[66] a Cardozo opinion where the claim of an injured plaintiff, victim of a fall in a funhouse, was dismissed with an epigram worthy of Holmes: "The timorous may stay at home." As has often been noted, this type of assumed risk case — frequently involving injuries at sporting events — is in fact a backhanded way of creating a no-duty category.

The baseball fan who comes home with a broken nose, victim of a screaming line drive, generally has had to bear the costs of his slow reflexes. But the ban on recovery has nothing to do with negligence in failing to anticipate the risk of a foul ball entering the stands. Nor is the ballpark insulated from liability on the grounds that the cost of screening the stadium would be excessive — a cost-benefit analysis that is virtually never undertaken in the opinions. Rather, a general duty of due care is suspended in these cases because of the widespread feeling that certain forms of entertainment are enhanced by a sense of open-air participation in the events taking place on the field.[69]

65. Schwartz, *supra* note 55, at 1770 & n.393.

66. 250 N.Y. 479, 166 N.E. 173 (1929).

69. The rebuttal that the courts simply are accommodating the taste of "risk preferrers" fails because the no-duty rule is general — the courts entertained a conclusive presumption of knowledge of the risks associated with the activity.

Nonetheless, it might be argued that these cases actually involve a determination

Long ago, Frances Bohlen argued that assumption of risk should not be viewed as an isolated doctrine limited to the employment relation. On the contrary, he asserted that as a historical matter the doctrine accurately expressed the fundamental attitude of tort law toward the victim of unintended injury:

> In the law of torts, at least, the idea of any obligation to protect others was abnormal. In time it came to be recognized that such duties might be forced upon persons who should engage in certain public pursuits. Upon carriers, innkeepers, and those engaged in the many trades and callings which mediaeval society regarded as services essential to the public well-being, was laid, as an inseparable incident, the duty not merely of refraining from injurious misconduct, from violence and fraud, but in addition the duty of the positive performance of careful service. In time many obligations of a somewhat similar sort were imposed upon certain classes of often occurring relation, thus eating into the original conception that a man had no cause of complaint if violence were not done to him and if he were not misled to his harm. But even to these new relation obligations the individualistic tendency of the law lent its color. When the obligations inherent in the various relations in which in civilized society the citizens are placed to one another came to be formulated, it was almost universally held that fair play was all that was required from one who was dealing without recompense with another.[70]

The fault principle is clearly at odds with the notion that "fair play," or good faith, is all we owe our neighbors in the way of care. But as I have argued, the fault principle emerged only gradually, in piecemeal fashion, as status considerations were eroded by the proliferation and homogenization of the notion of risk. Our vision of "the negligence era" has been clouded. We have failed to distinguish between that which was characteristically new — the developing concept of due care — and the insistent remnants of the past.

In this section, I have tried to put the doctrinal evidence of a complex, and in a sense contradictory, liability system in sharper focus. But the picture remains incomplete until the historical roots of the emergence of tort law are examined in somewhat greater detail.

---

of no breach of duty, rather than no duty owed — in other words, that they are *bona fide* fault cases. The argument would be that the courts are taking cognizance of the loss of utility resulting from the diminished sense of participation in the event, along with the material costs of fencing in, when they apply the risk-benefit calculus. Although the utility loss to the participant is clearly a social cost of screening, it is precisely the kind of loss that distinguishes the duty issue from the breach of duty issue. The Hand formula anticipates an assessment of the defendant's *direct* burden of adequate protection, rather than an accounting for every social cost associated with a rule of liability. Otherwise, the duty issue would be subsumed into virtually every breach of duty determination.

70. Bohlen, Voluntary Assumption of Risk, 20 Harv. L. Rev. 14, 14-15 (1906).

B. Remembering History

Traditionally, we are told that tort law developed out of the antecedent forms of action that governed compensation for personal harm—trespass and case. In a sense, this is true. Perusing the landmark cases like Brown v. Kendall, one finds that the ancestral bond between trespass and tort at the threshold of the negligence era is clear.

But the difference between kinship and family resemblance is considerable. The main flaw in the traditional account of the rise of negligence is the narrow focus on cases like Brown v. Kendall, usually involving interpersonal harms among strangers, which, in turn, relied upon a limited range of historical precedent—essentially, cases arising under the trespassory forms of action. Unfortunately, focusing on the immediate lineage of the fault principle diverted attention from a vast area of common law history that is of central concern to the development of liability for unintended harm.

Property and contract had developed considerably earlier. These venerable systems of legal rules tended to dominate the thinking of common law courts throughout the negligence era in situations where the line between characterization as "tort," on the one hand, and "property" or "contract," on the other, was indistinct. I have discussed three important instances of this overlap in the preceding section. My principal intention here is to reassess those classes of cases from a more distinctly historical vantage point. In particular, I want to elaborate on the relational context that was exceedingly influential in the early development of tort law.

Entrants on land were relegated to a singular system of rights and duties because they were regarded as functionally distinct from strangers injured on the highway. In the supposed heyday of the fault principle, there was in fact no abstract notion of a general duty of due care irrespective of time, place, and status—whatever courts and commentators might have loosely proclaimed to the contrary. The rights of trespassers and licensees were filtered through a system of limitations on the use of land which were grounded in long-established historical attitudes toward property ownership. Only slowly, over a period extending well beyond the supposed halcyon days of negligence, were these property-dominated principles subordinated to the tort system.

Similarly, a regime that competed vigorously with tort, the law of contract, dominated the judicial approach in cases of product defect and industrial injury. The powerful influence of contract in product injury cases, embodied in the privity doctrine, is particularly revealing. Unlike victims of industrial accidents, the injured party had no limiting contract with the manufacturer; indeed, in cases like Losee v.

Clute, the victim had not contracted with *anyone* regarding the dangerous product.[77] Yet, privity barred a right of action.

These product injury cases demonstrate the tenacity of established patterns of thought. The mere existence of a claim based on a defective product, rather than any actual bargaining involving the injured plaintiff, led the common law judge to draw on a contract analogue. The emerging tort system did not provide the dominant perspective, the "obvious" analogue, in these cases until the end of the "negligence era." Until then, it remained too weak to overcome the restrictive power of contract characterization.[78]

The primacy of contract law is most apparent in the industrial injury context. The injury scenario was viewed through the prism of the employment relation, rather than with reference to tort principles of trespass *cum* negligence. This is not to deny the modernizing influence of the industrial revolution. On the contrary, the judicial treatment of industrial injury cases indicates a deep ambivalence on the part of the courts; their ardent attachment to business prosperity apparently was tested severely by the massive injury toll. But the consequent erosion of harsh industrial injury liability rules reflected more confusion than consistency of approach until the workmen's compensation movement finally supplanted the tort system.

In short, the fault principle was a foreign element in the industrial injury context. As a result, principles of negligence and contributory negligence lived in uneasy community with the nonfault doctrines of assumed risk and fellow servant — doctrines grounded in assumptions about freedom of contract in the labor market having nothing to do with tort principles. Most likely, after a sufficiently long gestation period the fault principle would have assumed a dominant position in these cases, as it did in the other fields we have explored. But that dominance definitely was not established during the "heyday of negligence."

Now it is time to put my argument in proper historical perspective. If tort scholars have viewed the record of the past too narrowly, they nonetheless have read a portion of it accurately. Clearly, the fault principle played an important, even if not pervasive, role in shaping late nineteenth-century unintentional injury cases. Particu-

77. See Losee v. Clute, 51 N.Y. 494 (1873), where plaintiff's property was destroyed by a bursting boiler, made by defendant, which was catapulted onto his land from a neighboring mill. Consider also the class of cases where a worker is injured by unreasonably dangerous machinery supplied by his employer but negligently manufactured by another party, i.e., the third-party workplace injury claim, as distinguished from the classic industrial injury case. Here again, the plaintiff has not even indirectly purchased the defendant's unreasonably dangerous product.

78. Indeed, paralleling *Rowland* in the land occupiers context, the influence of contract has continued to be substantial in defective product cases until fairly recently. . . .

larly in cases involving strangers, whether on the highway, at grade-crossings, or in other public areas, pre-industrial status conceptions provided little direct guidance. Within a short period of time, the courts were confronted with recurrent injury situations having no close analogue in the earlier common law. Railroads and motor vehicles, for example, created a variety of risks to strangers that bore no obvious likeness to the harm caused by stampeding animals, stealthy poachers, or irresponsible innkeepers.

Here, our tort historian, whether wearing the hat of an economist or moral philosopher, stakes out a persuasive position. Unimpeded by the burden of a fixed conceptual approach, the courts could indulge the individualistic ethic of the day—discernible, as we have seen, in Holmes's classic disquisition on the virtues of encouraging individual freedom of action, The Common Law.

Interestingly, Holmes's encomium in support of the negligence principle is virtually oblivious to the characteristic kinds of harm arising in the industrialized world in which he lived. Repeatedly, he draws on illustrative cases that evoke a pastoral setting in which the past differs from the present only in the evolution of moral thought—from strict responsibility to the fault principle.[81] From all appearances, the author of The Common Law was unaware of novel categories of injuries that were in fact occurring on an everyday basis as he wrote. Ignoring the particulars of his own world, he set the tone for a narrow rendition of the historical record that markedly overemphasized the dominion of negligence.

C. Defining a Universe

Until now, I have focused on a set of status relationships where doctrinal contradictions raise serious questions about the fidelity of common law courts to the fault principle and invite a more searching view of the historical role of context in the development of liability for unintended harm. Next, I want to explore the classes of potential claims that fell victim to general prohibitory inclinations of the judiciary. Here again, there are serious grounds for questioning the pervasive character of fault liability. Yet, in defining the universe of unintended harms, these categories of potential claims usually are ignored by the students of early negligence law.

Twenty years ago, the New York Court of Appeals decided to abandon its intransigent stand against recognizing the tort of negligently caused emotional distress. Looking backwards, one might

---

81. It should be emphasized, however, that Holmes never espoused an unqualified acceptance of a past era of strict liability.

reasonably ask why the court adamantly had refused for so long to recognize recovery. Was there typically doubt about the defendant's negligence in this class of cases? Certainly not in the leading case of Mitchell v. Rochester Railway Co.,[83] where the defendant had driven his horses in an admittedly reckless fashion leading to the plaintiff's injury. Perhaps, then, the question of ascertaining damage itself was in doubt. Not in *Mitchell,* nor in a number of the early cases, where the victims were pregnant women who suffered miscarriages shortly after the incidents in question.[84]

What is the explanation, then, for the deep-seated reluctance of common law courts to grant redress for negligently caused emotional distress? The reasons given for denying recovery are familiar and seem to express genuine judicial concerns. Judges worried about detecting "pure" emotional distress in cases where the court had neither the hard evidence of a stillborn child nor righteous indignation against an intentional wrongdoer. Particularly in the former instance, they expressed a concomitant fear of unleashing a massive volume of cases. The specter of highly speculative jury verdicts probably also cast a pall.

For our purposes, however, the interesting point is that these claims reside in a relatively obscure corner of the history of fault liability. This untended area can be characterized more generally as the domain of no-duty. The fault theory maintains its pervasive character by largely ignoring the fact that a variety of prima facie negligent activities systematically were treated as outside the ambit of negligence law.

Thus, early emotional distress cases are either overlooked as an occasional aberration or "explained" by reference to that ever-popular rationale—the judicial sensitivity to excessive "transaction costs" in determining negligence. But on the latter score, the supposedly burdensome administrative costs in emotional distress cases went to the determination of causation and damages, *not* to lack of due care. As a result, the "transaction costs" argument establishes nothing more than that fault was not a key determinant of liability in this category of cases.

Transaction costs aside, however, why make much of a handful of "sport" cases? After all, very few claims for emotional distress can

83. 151 N.Y. 107, 45 N.E. 354 (1896).
84. Cases involving pregnant women appear, in fact, to have triggered the initial departure from the no-duty rule....
More generally, recovery for the consequences of emotional distress was hardly a novelty at common law. A variety of intentional torts, such as assault and false imprisonment, as well as the pain and suffering element in traditional negligence cases, attest to the willingness of common law judges to recognize the legitimacy of nonphysical harm.

be identified in the court records of the period. Here, however, a particularly salient methodological flaw in counting appellate cases is evident. It is not just that leather-bound volumes of higher court opinions are "unrepresentative" of the bread-and-butter tort cases of the time. More critically, the crux of the problem is that fault theorists disregard entire classes of injuries because the victims had not the slightest reason to think that they suffered compensable harm. The fact that generations of such victims bore the costs of the injuries without recourse to litigation provides no foundation for believing that the social cost of such accidents was immaterial.[87]

Again, for the present, consider only the instance of emotional distress. In 1961, when the New York Court of Appeals recognized a tort action in Battalla v. State,[88] it expanded the reach of negligence theory to encompass a new kind of claim. The tort theorist who surveyed the universe of recognized injury claims before *Battalla*, and purported to discover a comprehensive theory of fault liability, labeled classes of harms as "cases" that fell within the recognized ambit of the negligence system, and then concluded that fault liability provided an all-pervasive scheme of recovery for unintended injuries.

The question, of course, is how much was left out by this circularity in defining the universe. One can only speculate, but there is reason to think that the gaps are considerable. Pure economic harm caused by a negligent injurer is entirely ignored, for example. Bartender worked for Ludwig's Old Bavarian Ale House. Injurer, driving his vehicle carelessly, fatally injured Ludwig. Bartender was out of a job and without income for six months before he found another position. It would have been useless to sue; until recently, there was virtually no chance of recovering for economic harm resulting from physical injury to another, apart from special circumstances. Thus, Bartender absorbed the loss out of his own resources or became dependent on public assistance.

What is interesting here is not that any particular injury victim fails to recover. In a given instance, perhaps in many cases, there

87. Whether, for example, John and Jane Doe were immune to severe emotional distress from viewing the maiming of their child in the late 1800's is an empirical question. Posner's argument, in a related context, that children were viewed solely as income-producing assets, see Posner, [A Theory of Negligence, 1 J. Legal Stud. 29] at 47, is based on a single source, S. Thernstrom, Poverty and Progress—Social Mobility in a Nineteenth Century City 155 (1964), which does not support his reference. Thernstrom argues that the working-class families in his study did not have high educational aspirations for their children. It does not follow that they attached less emotional value to their relationships with their children than at present. Moreover, in emotional distress and other such categories where tort actions were infrequently brought, it may well have been the existence of a single, seemingly conclusive legal precedent, such as *Mitchell*, that dampened any incentive to litigate similar kinds of cases for a long period afterwards....

88. 10 N.Y.2d 237, 176 N.E.2d 729, 219 N.Y.S.2d 34 (1961).

might be general agreement that the Learned Hand calculus or customary notions of fault indicate that the victim should bear the loss. Once we recognize a flat no-duty rule in economic loss cases, however, we are no longer talking about an *instance* of negligence; instead, we are barring recovery by reference to a negligence *system*.

Recovery for pure economic loss actually bears a generic resemblance to recovery for the more frequent kind of emotional harm, "third-party" mental distress.[91] In both situations, a negligence system raises no truly distinctive issue. Whether these "interests," mental tranquility and economic security, should be protected raises a substantially similar policy issue under a system of strict liability or a no-fault scheme—indeed, even where the issue is recovery against an intentional wrongdoer. Under any system of liability, there is an overriding concern—which can be labeled "economic" or "moral"—about saddling an injurer with virtually unlimited responsibilities for compensation. This fundamental concern is extraneous to the theory of fault liability; yet, it is a concern which, under the rubric "no-duty," systematically limits the universality of the negligence principle.[92]

I am suggesting that we must shift our perspective if we are to understand the place of fault in the development of liability for unintended harm. We must take full account of the limitations as well as the reach of the system. Consider, for example, what we now regard as the "area" of professional malpractice. Although I have conducted no systematic survey, my impression is that these cases were brought infrequently during the purported heyday of negligence. Does this suggest that doctors and lawyers of the era were less prone to be careless than at present? Hardly, I think. While it is certainly true that the level of medical practice was less sophisticated in the last century, I would guess that, relatively speaking, about as many doctors were failing to meet customary standards of the day (in setting a broken limb, for example) as now.

Along the same lines, there is absolutely no reason to think that nineteenth-century attorneys were less likely to be careless, stupid, or venal than lawyers of today. With all due allowance for a less litigious society, I would argue that these professional malpractice cases were rarely brought principally because it was highly unlikely that they

91. That is, mental distress from witnessing an injury to another.
92. Obviously, the point can be carried to an extreme. I am not suggesting that a fault system that fails to protect against a stranger's "distress" from reading about a tort injury in the newspaper is departing in any meaningful way from adherence to the fault principle. Somewhere a line must be drawn. Whatever the de minimis principle might be, however, it seems clear to me that a system excluding virtually any recovery for mental distress and economic loss apart from a linkage to physical injury has limited substantially the principle of recovery for loss based on fault.

would succeed under the negligence system. Privileges, defenses, no-duty limitations, and evidentiary rules would have been utilized to bar recovery. Thus the claims were simply disregarded.

While certain categories of claims were virtually unthinkable, however, others presented recurrent situations where an injurer's fault was dismissed instead through recourse to one of a variety of immunities. Consider, for instance, the exclusions from negligence liability carved out for governmental entities, charitable institutions, and members of the injury victim's family. In each of these situations, the courts relied on a form of no-duty analysis to bar recovery on nonfault principles.

How is one to explain these apparent anomalies? None of the explanations that have been offered is entirely satisfying. Intrafamily tort immunity may have reflected an organic notion that the nuclear family was a unit, rather than a loose aggregation of autonomous individuals. Possibly, the charitable immunity derived from a barely suppressed sentiment that beggars cannot be choosers. And it may be that governmental immunity was simply one aspect of a broadly felt antipathy to socializing the cost of injuries.

Whatever may be the case, it seems quite clear that the immunities were inconsistent with the fault principle. They were, after all, *blanket* immunities. By definition, none of these categorical exclusions involved a case-by-case cost-benefit calculus. Nor is it apparent why economic efficiency considerations would have dictated category-wide exemptions from liability. If moral considerations entered into the foundation for the immunities, it was for reasons that bore no relationship to the fault principle. Rather, we again confront categories of cases, and much larger classes of forsaken claims, that are located outside the ambit of fault liability.

D. Telling a Story

The no-duty issue is not always confronted as squarely as the previous section might suggest. Often, courts fail to distinguish clearly between duty and breach, appearing to employ the fault principle to reach a result that might be as easily, or better, explained by reasons that are difficult or embarrassing to articulate. In such cases, doctrine frequently becomes an artifice, and we need to look elsewhere for clues to the weight we can attach to statements of principle.

At least since the legal realists, who may have made too much of a good insight, lawyers have been reminded that judges, as well as advocates, organize and emphasize "the facts" in a way that makes doctrinal analysis appear to follow logically from the circumstances giving rise to a legal dispute. Although this proposition has the ring of authenticity, we sometimes lose sight of its import.

In the present context, its relevance is this. If courts determine fault by invoking negligence doctrine where "the facts" of the case could as easily be reconstituted to suggest that due care was largely irrelevant to the decision, one would be hard-pressed to assert that fault considerations were actually determinative of the outcome. In those circumstances, asserting that liability turned on the fault principle would be no more than stating that breach of duty considerations governed whenever courts had the ingenuity to construct a factual scenario that fit nicely within the established doctrinal framework.

The circularity that I am suggesting is endemic to history written on the basis of appellate court decisions. Richard Posner, for example, has attempted to demonstrate the consistency of tort doctrine with the economic analysis of fault by reference to leading decisions and, at times, by analysis of entire categories of cases.[102] It would be an overwhelmingly time-consuming task, and a diversion from the central purpose of this essay, to engage in a detailed critique of the methodology of appellate case analysis. Instead, let me give a few illustrations that should suggest both the highly problematic nature of the enterprise and, more importantly, the potential distortion in the role of fault liability that it encourages.

Consider the well-known case of Adams v. Bullock,[104] where Landes and Posner find "as clear a statement as one might ask of the proposition that the optimal level of care is a function of its cost."[105] Indeed, Judge Cardozo asserted that plaintiff, who was electrocuted when a long wire he was carrying touched the defendant's uninsulated trolley line beneath an overpass, had failed to demonstrate negligence — because the injury was highly unlikely and the defendant would have been put to considerable expense abandoning the overhead system of electricity.

The difficulty, however, is that the analysis rests on a version of the facts that is entirely oblivious to the trivial cost of a warning sign at the overpass. The economic justification for the due-care determination depends on the circularity of taking the court's story of the case at face value.

---

102. See Landes & Posner, [The Positive Economic Theory of Tort Law, 15 Ga. L. Rev. 851,] at 893 [1981,] where the authors rely on leading cases. In Posner's earlier statement of his thesis [Posner, A Theory of Negligence, 1 J. Legal Stud. 29 (1972)], he analyzed a sample of appellate court decisions from the period 1875-1905.

104. 227 N.Y. 208, 125 N.E. 93 (1919).

105. Landes & Posner, [The Positive Economic Theory of Tort Law, 15 Ga. L. Rev. 851,] at 894 [1981].

Obviously, it would be intolerable to live in a world where we were confronted by warning signs at every corner. But the overpass in *Bullock* may have been one of very few in the community, and the presence of a sign indicating the uninsulated power wires would have guarded against a relatively hidden danger. The critical point is that the "calculus of risk" as employed in the case does not even take account of the realistic burden of adequate protection. In failing to do so, the court implicitly denies recovery on the ground of no duty to warn.

Thus, the case makes economic sense, and correspondingly supports a "fault" analysis, as long as we tell the story as Cardozo did, with emphasis on the cost of alternative means of supplying power to the trolleys. This analysis emphasizes one version of "the facts" — the capacity to protect the entire community from the risk of electrocution. But once we adopt a duty-to-warn version of the story, emphasizing the failure to incur the minimal outlay for a "Danger — Power Lines Below" sign rather than stressing the cost of underground transmission, the outcome of economic analysis becomes wholly problematic.[106]

Viewed in this way, a large category of cases — sharing the common characteristic that the injury which occurred might have been cheaply avoided through a warning — is treated as consistent with fault principles by organizing "the facts," in every instance, in a way that minimizes or ignores the cost-effectiveness of a warning. In more conventional terms, my point is that these cases appropriately might be viewed as "no-duty" situations, i.e., situations where judicial reluctance to acknowledge the existence, in the first instance, of a duty to warn substantially attenuates the discussion of due care.

The duty to warn issue is merely illustrative of the serious difficulties in knowing when to take the courts at their word. Consider the well-worn foreseeability doctrine. In discussing its economic rationality, Posner, as might be expected, raises the question why defendants should be responsible for low-probability risks where the expected accident cost will be near zero. As Judge Cardozo reasoned in the celebrated *Palsgraf* case, there should be no liability in a situation which Posner likens to "a truly freak accident."[108]

---

106. It is, of course, still possible to square the decision with the fault principle if the risk of harm was virtually nil. But refusing to acknowledge the possibility of a nearly costless warning obscures the calculus of risk. Moreover, it is interesting to note — with respect to the minimal risk of harm — that *Adams* involved the appeal of a verdict for the plaintiff which had been affirmed by the intermediate appellate court.

108. Palsgraf v. Long Island R.R., 248 N.Y. 339, 162 N.E. 99 (1928). Posner's discussion is in R. Posner, [Economic Analysis of Law] §6.8, at 130 [2d ed. 1977].

Again, the analysis rests on very shaky factual premises. *Palsgraf* does indeed involve "a freak accident" as long as we uncritically focus, along with Cardozo, on the oddity of a boarding passenger's package exploding and shattering a weighing scale some distance away—next to the unfortunate victim. Who could foresee such bizarre consequences from a porter's innocent efforts to assist a harried passenger?

Suppose, however, that the facts had been framed to focus on the weighing scale, rather than on the well-being of boarding passengers. And suppose further that the scale was mounted in such a way that any number of hazards on a heavily-used platform might have caused injury to a nearby victim—albeit few of such hazards were as unlikely as an exploding package. Does the injury in *Palsgraf* remain "unforeseeable"—a freak accident? Perhaps. But on the other hand, possibly the breach of duty calculus now suggests that the injury victim should recover.

In short, fault analysis provides a proper resolution in *Palsgraf* as long as we adopt an accommodating version of the facts. By another account, the court may have been saying that the railroad did in fact maintain the scale in a careless way but, after all, even railroads cannot be held responsible for everything they do wrong. Negligence has its limits, under this view, which perhaps are best left undefined by resort to a bit of doctrinal subterfuge.

Foreseeability analysis and its unruly big brother, the doctrine of proximate cause, provide innumerable examples of the potential for imaginative story-telling. Take the wildest set of circumstances. Thawing ice floes break loose and float down a river, smashing into ships and loosening them from their moorings, causing the vessels to crash into a bridge, which collapses forming—along with the ships—a dam that backs up the river and floods the vicinity.[110] Does the Learned Hand formula register a low-foreseeability determination of no negligence? Do customary standards of community behavior provide guidance in applying the fault principle? On reflection, one looks at the bizarre concatenation of events and highlights some circumstance or other—perhaps the failure to raise the bridge quickly, possibly the improbability of the flood, or conceivably the inadequate measures taken to secure the vessels. Depending on the emphasis, the "fault" of one set of actors or another becomes more apparent. It is a non sequitur to conclude that "fault" has determined the resolution of the case.

There is nothing very new in all of this. Entering law students

110. See In re Kinsman Transit Co., 338 F.2d 708 (2d Cir. 1964), *cert. denied,* 380 U.S. 944 (1965).

rather quickly develop a skill at what might be termed "purposive characterization." But perhaps in the manipulation of doctrine the deeper meaning is lost and a false sense of intellectual coherence is created. Although torts teachers treat proximate cause and duty to warn issues, among others, as aspects of "negligence doctrine," it does not follow necessarily that the underlying conflicts are always, or even usually, decided with reference to fault principles — as distinguished from fault *language*. It may be that the core meaning of the "fault" principle — whether it be based on economic efficiency or customary standards of behavior — is so sorely taxed in some kinds of cases that the courts fall back upon a purely formal doctrinal analysis through the artful crafting of stories that create the illusion of a coherent decisional framework.

III. The Role of Fault Revised: A Functional Perspective and Beyond

Is tort law in the process of coming full circle to the position that "a man acts at his peril"?[113] Has liability for unintended harm been dominated, over the course of two centuries, by a continuing struggle between comprehensive theories of fault and strict liability? To the contrary, I have argued that negligence law developed, in the nineteenth century, out of a continuing struggle with the principle of no-liability. Throughout the "heyday of negligence," the common law courts wrestled with issues that forced a choice between powerful no-liability principles and a fledgling doctrine of fault liability. Gradually the no-liability principles — immunities, privileges, and no-duty considerations imported from other conceptual systems (property, contract, and such)[114] — retreated, like a melting glacier in a hostile environment, before the successive onslaughts of fault and, later, strict liability rules.[115]

The principal burden that a comprehensive negligence approach had to surmount was the prevailing tendency to view unintentional harms contextually. Like injuries were *not* viewed in like fashion in the early negligence era. While courts paid lip-service to a general principle of fault liability, a victim of a defective product injury in fact

113. The phrase is used repeatedly in O. W. Holmes, [The Common Law,] with reference to strict liability.

114. Consider, as another instance, the variety of imputed contributory negligence rules that thrived for a time during the early development of the fault principle....

115. The chronology is not quite so neat. Consider, for example, the historical development of products liability rules. Strict liability emerged, in limited form, well before the fault principle began to be seriously questioned as a general proposition....

was subject to very different liability rules than was an injured social guest; an injured worker's case against his employer had little in common with an injured passenger's action against his carrier; a patient harmed by the incompetence of her doctor was not treated in parallel fashion to a pedestrian run over by an omnibus.

Putting aside the many claims that withered in the shadow of the formal law, and which almost certainly would accentuate these contextual differences, my argument is that functional considerations — derived by a conservative judiciary from traditional notions of class privilege, social custom, and commercial usage — were a dominant feature of the legal landscape, serving to dilute substantially the force of the fault principle.

What was the corresponding impact of industrial growth on tort law during the period that we are examining? The standard interpretation is that state-court judges, in sympathy with business growth, fashioned a *limiting* principle of negligence as a protective shield for "infant industry." To the contrary, I have argued that no-liability attitudes dominated many of the status relationships that were to ripen into injury categories in the industrial era. Thus, if there was protectionism, it was a natural consequence of deeply conservative, preexisting sentiments toward loss allocation, rather than a retreat from a more liberal compensation principle.

Admittedly, when Commissioner Earl adamantly refused to extend the strict liability principle of Rylands v. Fletcher to the exploding boiler in Losee v. Buchanan — indeed rejecting *Rylands* outright — he did so on the premise that fault was a more suitable basis for liability than "absolute" responsibility in a society committed to industrial expansion. But fault as a more generalized limiting principle is largely a function of the selectivity of torts casebook and treatise writers. On the contrary, in this period of rapid modernization, industrial growth and the fault principle typically worked in combination to *expand* liability rather than to limit it. Industrial growth generated an insistent pressure for compensation through a steadily rising mass of injury claims. At the same time, the fault principle gradually undermined the comparatively less generous no-liability tendencies of the common law through the corrosive influence of "exceptions" developed to the privity bar, the fellow-servant defense, and similar limitations.

Viewed against a parsimonious early common law, then, it is the steadily growing compensatory influence of the fault principle, rather than its insulating effect, that emerges as the notable characteristic of industrialization. Nonetheless, fault remained awash in a sea of contradictory principles during the early industrial era. The really dramatic consequences of industrialization came later, leading eventually to a substantially more robust fault principle.

In the long run, the "levelling" impact of industrialization played a central role in eroding the functional obstacles to an expansive negligence principle. Industrialization eventually created a new arrangement of social relations that highlighted the anachronistic nature of many of the existing no-duty categories in tort. As a consequence, various status relationships were sapped of their vitality.

In mid-twentieth-century America, the attempt to maintain distinctions between the various purposes for which one entered a store or visited a friend became increasingly strained. The effort to distinguish between consumer expectations on the basis of direct purchase from a manufacturer and commercial dealings through an intermediary met its demise even earlier, as did the colossal superstructure of industrial injury law. Liability insurance and risk-pooling considerations became critical determinants as long-standing immunities began to crumble.

Industrialization brought affluence that was comparatively widely shared. Affluence, in turn, opened the way to a collective generosity of spirit far exceeding that of the early negligence era, a receptivity to a fairly expansive compensation principle. Thus, eventually the field of debate shifted considerably: a genuine tension between strict liability and negligence did arise. The compartmentalization of tort law did not vanish; indeed, to some extent, the functional approach spilled over into the new arena where the comparative merits of strict responsibility and fault now were intensely debated. But that, as they say, is another story.

NOTES AND QUESTIONS

1. Reconsider this essay's discussion of Holmes and Posner on the rationale for the fault principle, pp. 45-47, *supra*, as well as Gregory's treatment of the rise of negligence in the preceding essay. How many bases for the fault principle can you identify? To what extent are they inconsistent with each other?

2. Reconsider Posner's analytical stance in light of this essay. Is Posner proposing a "positive" or "normative" theory of fault liability? What about Holmes? Which, if any, of the various justifications for the fault principle are inconsistent with the historical thesis in the last essay?

3. Do the land-occupier cases necessarily rest on nonfault principles derived from the status of land holding, as this essay suggests? Couldn't it be argued that the categories reflected economic efficiency

considerations in an era of large land-holding when any real degree of control over the premises was infeasible? In the succeeding era, could a similar efficiency argument be made regarding the difficulties faced by railroads in controlling access to their rights-of-way?

4. Consider the argument made at various points in the essay that the preindustrial era was characterized by no-liability rules rather than strict liability. Is it convincing?

5. This essay suggests that systems of legal rules traditionally labeled "contract" and "property" were the source of status relationships among individuals that created concomitantly limited duties and obligations, and that yet another system of rules, categorized as "tort," initially established a framework of liability rules governing relationships among strangers. How useful do you find this dichotomy? Does the essay argue that the dichotomy remained fixed during the supposed heyday of negligence, or does it suggest a continuous process of change?

6. Why does the essay conclude that only recently has "a genuine tension" between strict liability and negligence arisen?

7. The essay is critical of appellate case methodology as a basis for determining the role of negligence liability. Reassess the various reasons for the skeptical attitude expressed. Are they convincing? Doesn't the essay itself rely to a considerable extent on appellate case analysis in questioning the pervasiveness of the fault principle? Can you suggest another approach that would have been more convincing?

The Vitality of Negligence and the Ethics of Strict Liability*

Gary T. Schwartz

I. Introduction

It is a commonplace to observe that there has been an explosion of tort liability during the past quarter-century. The observation strikes me as entirely accurate. What has not been sufficiently observed, however, is the extent to which this explosion has quite explicitly been an explosion of negligence liability. Let "the negligence principle" be defined initially as the idea that when there is negligent conduct that causes harm, the negligent actor should be held

*Source: 15 Ga. L. Rev. 963, 963-977 (1981).

responsible. The last quarter-century has witnessed what can fairly be described as a vindication or unleashing of the negligence principle — the dismantling of obstacles that previously have impeded the achievement of that principle's full potential. To document these observations concerning the present vitality of the negligence principle is one of this essay's purposes. . . .

II.   The Vitality of Negligence in Contemporary Tort Law

A.   Negligence Progressions

Among the leading events within tort law during the past quarter-century has been the abrogation of a variety of immunities that intruded into tort law late in the nineteenth century and early in the twentieth. Thus, almost everywhere, the tort immunity of charitable institutions has been done away with. Intrafamilial immunities increasingly have been discarded, rendering spouses liable to each other, parents liable to their children, and vice versa. In addition, a broad, insensitive doctrine of governmental immunity generally has been replaced by a carefully selected set of particular immunity rules.

True enough, the abrogation of immunity exposes charities, family members, and governments to liability in general, not simply liability under a negligence theory. Nevertheless, almost all of the "abrogating" opinions that I have read have in fact involved claims based on the negligence principle. And given the general backdrop of existing tort liability rules, for all practical purposes the liability of charities, family members, and governments basically amounts to negligence liability. Moreover, it has not been unusual for an abrogating opinion explicitly to place emphasis on the negligence principle. "Since the early days of the common law, a cause of action in tort has been recognized to exist when the negligence of one person is the proximate cause of damage to another." "[W]hen there is negligence, the rule is liability, immunity is the exception." With immunities abrogated, the negligence principle is being pressed into intriguing — and perhaps vexing — new applications. We now know that a parent can be liable to his teenage child for negligently approving of that teenager's participation in a dangerous activity away from home, and that a husband can be liable to his wife for negligently failing to shovel the snow when his failure causes her to suffer a sidewalk injury. In California, decisions on highway and freeway design are increasingly subject to tort-law review. That state's statutory provisions on governmental liability for public property in a dangerous condition consist of a rather elaborate restatement of the variables of the magnitude of the risk and the cost of risk prevention, variables that have been significant to a negligence analysis at least since the Learned Hand opinion in *Carroll Towing*, espousing a formula for negligence that has been accepted by leading tort authorities.

If formal immunity doctrines have fallen, two doctrines possessing a partial immunity quality have given way as well. In many jurisdictions auto guest statutes or guest doctrines have been overturned, thereby subjecting motorists to full liability for their negligence. The opinions that have invalidated guest statutes on constitutional grounds have relied explicitly on the general rule of negligence liability as the factor rendering constitutionally suspect (because unequal) the nonliability of the negligent motorist. As for the tort liability of landowners, as recently as fourteen years ago this liability was determined by a labyrinth of specific rules that largely subordinated the negligence standard. Increasingly, that labyrinth has been repudiated, exposing landowners to liability pursuant to the general negligence principle, which renders the status of the plaintiff-entrant relevant only insofar as it pertains to what should count as negligence in the individual case.[20] The judicial opinions repudiating that labyrinth have repeatedly emphasized the negligence principle.

Other changes in the law likewise have expanded the scope of the negligence tort. The traditional rule of contributory negligence as a complete defense now has been superseded in a clear majority of states by a more modern rule of comparative negligence. This rule allows many more victims of negligent conduct to recover for their injuries (at least in part); also, in the views of many, the comparative negligence rule entails a proper refinement or clarification of basic negligence ideas. Additionally, judicial opinions recognizing new affirmative duties have set up new arenas for negligence arguments.[24] In many jurisdictions, a landlord is now liable if (but only if) he is negligent in failing to safeguard the tenants in his apartment building

20. The question of the relevance of status to negligence may be more difficult than the *Rowland* opinion [Rowland v. Christian, 69 Cal. 2d 108, 443 P.2d 561, 70 Cal. Rptr. 97 (1968)] makes it appear. As *Rowland* notes, "in many situations . . . the conduct necessary upon the defendant's part to meet the burden of exercising due care as to invitees will also meet his burden with respect to licensees and trespassers." Id. at 118, 443 P.2d at 567, 70 Cal. Rptr. at 103. But on other occasions, safeguarding the trespasser will in fact subject the landowner to a significant added burden. To what extent is tort law's respected "reasonable man" less willing to expend substantial sums to protect an unwanted trespasser than to protect his invited guest? What happens when a divergence opens up between the "reasonable person" approach to negligence and the Learned Hand risk-cost approach?

24. There is now a burgeoning body of case law on the various meanings of the negligence standard as applied to the quality of supervision provided by camp counselors to their youthful charges. . . .

against foreseeable criminal attacks. A psychotherapist is liable if he is negligent in failing to give a *Tarasoff* warning;[26] and the *Tarasoff* opinion contains an important expression of the contents of the negligence standard.[27]

Professional malpractice claims have soared during the past decade in ways that understandably have led to assessments of "crises." "Malpractice" basically signifies negligence in the professional setting. The increase in claims is largely due to changes both in the perceptions and attitudes of patients and in the advising and forensic abilities of trial lawyers. Patients, aided by counsel, are now more likely to recognize (and be offended by) malpractice where it has occurred, and lawyers have developed greater skills in demonstrating in the courtroom the facts of a malpractice case.[29] The bar's efforts have been abetted, however, by judicial abandonment of the locality rule and by the occasional judicial tendency to reduce the deference paid to the content of professional custom. For better or worse, ignoring local practice and reducing the controlling effect of custom releases malpractice arguments from previous constraints and permits courts to consider more fully the typical negligence variables of risk magnitude and risk prevention costs.

At least in the single (if conspicuous) state of California, there have been further and quite recent negligence developments of a dramatic sort. In J'Aire Corp. v. Gregory, the California Supreme

26. See Tarasoff v. Regents of Univ. of Cal., 17 Cal. 3d 425, 551 P.2d 334, 131 Cal. Rptr. 14 (1976).

27. "Obviously we do not require that the therapist...render a perfect performance; the therapist need only exercise 'that reasonable degree of skill, knowledge, and care ordinarily possessed and exercised by members of [that professional specialty] under similar circumstances.' Within the broad range of reasonable practice and treatment in which professional opinion and judgment may differ, the therapist is free to exercise his or her own best judgment without liability; proof, aided by hindsight, that he or she judged wrongly is insufficient to establish negligence." Id. at 438, 551 P.2d at 345, 131 Cal. Rptr. at 25.

29. Undoubtedly, enhancements in the claims sophistication of both victims and lawyers have served, in general, as a major (if nondoctrinal) force in the recent explosion of negligence suits. The sports pages provide examples of suits that would have been barely thinkable 25 years ago, even though the relevant law already was in place. Outfielder Ruppert Jones currently is suing the Oakland Coliseum for $6,000,000 for injuries he suffered when, as a visiting New York Yankee, he crashed into the Coliseum's outfield wall. His suit alleges negligence in the inadequacy of the warning track and the absence of padding on the wall itself. L.A. Times, April 12, 1981, §III, at 4, col. 1. Race driver Clay Regazzoni is suing the Long Beach Grand Prix Association for $20,000,000 for a car crash that left him a paraplegic; he claims negligence in allowing an escape route to become cluttered with disabled cars, causing him to strike into a barrier. L.A. Times, March 7, 1981, §III, at 6, col. 1.

It is possible that the defense of assumption of risk would have weighed more heavily on these claims in the 1950's than it does today. The judicially administered decline of this defense provides another example of doctrinal shift that has encouraged the assertion of negligence arguments.

Court recognized a new generic tort of the negligent infliction of economic loss, a tort that permits — at least to some extent — the ignoring of the complexities of the contract doctrine of intended third-party beneficiary. (In *J'Aire*, a restaurant tenant was allowed to recover against a general contractor who, through negligence, failed to perform fully on his contract with the tenant's landlord to renovate the landlord's building, thereby causing the tenant to lose business.) Moreover, in Molien v. Kaiser Foundation Hospital, the California court now has developed a general tort covering the negligent infliction of emotional stress, a tort that seemingly can be relied on even when the defendant's conduct contains nothing at all by way of a risk of physical injury. (In *Molien*, a doctor carelessly diagnosed the plaintiff's wife as syphilitic; the resulting arguments between the plaintiff and his wife broke up their marriage.) In *J'Aire* and *Molien*, the court concluded that the basic power of the negligence principle facilitates its escape from its traditional confinement to problems of personal injury and property damage.

In all of these ways, the tort liability explosion of the last quarter-century has been very closely tied to changes in the law that have increasingly enabled the negligence principle to expand to its full capacity. But a more complete account of the last quarter-century also requires a survey of the character of that period's strict liability developments. If it were true that the law was moving strongly in the direction of a general rule of automatic liability for all harm caused, then the judicial affirmation of the negligence principle of liability for harm negligently caused might well seem unmomentous, a mere matter of application.

B.   Strict Liability Developments

Our common-law tradition includes a limited number of strict liability rules. These include strict liability for trespassing cattle and strict liability for animals known to be dangerous. But in the contemporary world of tort, these animal rules are in and of themselves of trivial consequence, and in the recent literature they have not been relied on at all as precedents or analogies in proposals for additional strict liability rules. A common-law doctrine of strict liability for ultrahazardous activities was synthesized by the First Restatement from various sources, including the blasting cases and the melange of opinions in Rylands v. Fletcher. The Second Restatement, however, seeks to deprive this liability rule of much of its strictness by insisting that the appropriateness of the activity's location and "the value of the activity to the community" — considerations seemingly bearing on the activity's reasonableness or negligence—weigh heavily in the rule's application.[40] Moreover, given the hypothesis of the rule itself, one would expect claims under the rule to be abnormal and uncommon; and as a matter of the realities of litigation, ultrahazardous cases seem few and far between. In recent years, very few activities have been newly designated by the judiciary as ultrahazardous or abnormally dangerous; if anything, courts tend to reject ultrahazardous arguments in a rather perfunctory way.[44]

There *is* one common-law strict liability rule that has loomed enormously large in judicial opinions in recent years: the rule rendering manufacturers liable for defects in their products. As the dust begins to settle, however, it is now being suggested that this rule largely comprises merely an intelligent rounding off of the rights independently available under a mature negligence system.[45] After all, the rule requires the identification of some "defect" in the product; to say that a product is "defective" is to say that the product is "wrong" or "faulty" in some significant respect, and product fault is almost always associated with some negligence for which the manufacturer properly can be held responsible. An authentic rule of strict liability would be one holding manufacturers liable for all accidents caused by the use of their products; plausible though such a rule may be in light of supposedly basic products liability policies, it is one in which courts have displayed no more than trivial interest. The strictness of the existing "defect" rule—even if only at its margins— is subject to testing in the rare case in which a product defect has *not* been brought about by manufacturer negligence; in these cases, many courts have waffled on strict liability by recognizing a "defense" of unavoidability or unknowability.

The modern design-defect cases have attracted special attention. While the leading judicial opinions typically are written with strict liability phraseology, the liability test that most of them espouse requires the court to balance the risks of the product's design against

40. . . . It may well be . . . that the Restatement's concern for locational suitability is faithful to the *Rylands* notion of a "non-natural" land use. . . . If so, however, then the *Rylands* doctrine itself seems lacking in strictness.

44. See, e.g., Ramsey v. Marutamaya Ogatsu Fireworks Co., 72 Cal. App. 3d 516, 528 n.2, 140 Cal. Rptr. 247, 253 n.2 (1977) (fireworks display not ultrahazardous); Orser v. George, 252 Cal. App. 2d 660, 60 Cal. Rptr. 708 (1967) (use of firearms not ultrahazardous).

The Price-Anderson Act apparently creates strict liability for the harm caused by nuclear-power-plant disasters. See 42 U.S.C. §2210(n)(1) (1976). The Act is most controversial, however, for its liability ceiling: $560,000,000 per disaster. See Duke Power Co. v. Carolina Environmental Study Group, 438 U.S. 59 (1978) (upholding constitutionality). Overall, the Act was intended by Congress to "encourag[e] the private development of electric energy by atomic power." Id. at 86.

45. See, e.g., Schwartz, Foreword: Understanding Products Liability, 67 Calif. L. Rev. 435, 454-64 (1979).

that design's benefits. But what this test essentially consists of is an application of the Hand negligence formula in the products setting. It is hardly surprising, therefore, that so many design-defect opinions seem deeply concerned with traditional negligence considerations. To be sure, there are scholars who vehemently object to modern design-defect law. However, they generally make clear that what they object to is precisely the negligence principle in these ambitious modern applications. Their claim is that risk-benefit balancing, notwithstanding its negligence pedigree, is, in difficult cases, simply beyond the effective capacity of judge or jury. Ironically, then, these objections help verify that the modern design cases, despite their strict liability rhetoric, effectively involve not the repudiation of the negligence principle, but rather an effort to apply or extend that principle in what is assuredly a factually dramatic fashion.

The two leading categories of accidents in our society are highway accidents and on-the-job accidents. No-fault auto compensation proposals were given very serious attention during the early 1970's. For whatever reasons, however, since 1975 the no-fault movement has become stymied: there have been no no-fault adoptions, and one repeal (Nevada). In many no-fault states, moreover, the no-fault feature is a mere "add-on" that in no basic way disturbs the rights (and liabilities) established by the preexisting negligence system; in other states, a low "threshold" results in only a limited displacement of tort. In addition, all no-fault plans preserve the negligence action for the more serious highway accidents—a curious preservation, since the condemnation of the negligence system which typically accompanies no-fault proposals generally emphasizes that system's "undercompensation" of the most seriously injured. But whatever the auto no-fault "threshold" and "cap," no-fault—though certainly oriented around the goal of compensation—turns out to be surprisingly lacking in strict liability features. To the extent that no-fault does modify negligence law, what it primarily entails is not strict liability, but rather the abolition of tort liability, combined with compulsory first-party insurance. Under Keeton-O'Connell Basic Protection, the driver of one car injured in a two-car accident recovers solely from his own insurance company, regardless of the accident's causes; under the Uniform Motor Vehicle Accident Reparation Act, the guest in a car who is injured in a two-car collision collects from his own family's insurance company, rather than from the insurance company of either of the motorists.

Workers' compensation is not at all novel, of course; it has been an essential part of our personal-injury system for almost seventy years now. It is clear, however, that during the past quarter-century the scope of compensable injuries under workers' compensation has been expanded by the judiciary, which is evidently sympathetic to workers' compensation's strict liability principle. Indeed, workers' compensation does contain the most genuinely strict liability rule within all of personal injury law. Even that rule's strictness, however, is capable of overestimation. Workers' compensation consists, after all, of a combination of strict liability and no liability, inasmuch as the employer bears no responsibility for much of the employee's economic losses and none for his intangible losses. In any event, under workers' compensation the worker always has been free to sue any third party whose tort has contributed to his injury. And there has been a proliferation of such third-party suits in recent years; the injured employee is thus increasingly a major participant in the tort system. For purposes of these so-called third-party suits, what is noteworthy is the interest that many courts have displayed in the negligence of the victim's own employer—negligence that workers' compensation supposedly had rendered entirely immaterial. Courts have found, for example, that the defendant-employer committed its negligence while engaged in some "capacity" other than its capacity as an employer and is therefore directly vulnerable under the "dual-capacity doctrine" to the employee's third-party negligence claim. On the construction site, when the employee of a subcontractor suffers injury that is caused by the subcontractor's negligence, many courts have been willing to impute that negligence under some vicarious liability rule to the prime contractor, all of which allows the employee to recover in tort on account of his employer's negligence. Quite frequently, employee injuries occur because of the combination of the tort of some third party and the negligence of the employer. When in such circumstances the employee recovers full tort damages from the third-party tortfeasor, courts in leading states like New York and Illinois now allow the third party to sue the negligent employer for a proportionate contribution to the tort liability that the third party has been required to bear. In these jurisdictions, the employer's negligence thus exposes the employer to ultimate liability that can be well in excess of the supposed workers' compensation ceilings.

In recent years, various authorities, expressing their criticisms of the negligence standard, have invited courts to establish important new rules of strict liability. The courts have reacted, in turn, by barely acknowledging that these invitations have been tendered. In 1967, Justice Tobriner issued a trial-balloon concurring opinion recommending strict liability for the unexpected adverse results of medical treatment. Since then, no court—not even Justice Tobriner's own— has given this recommendation any serious consideration. Also in 1967, the California Supreme Court, in applying an "unreasonableness" liability test to an insurer that had refused to settle within a policy's limits, indicated in extended dictum a keen interest in a possible rule of insurer strict liability. In subsequent opinions, this dictum has been all but forgotten, with unreasonableness continuing as the governing liability standard. Half a dozen years ago, Professor Ursin, in a well-crafted article, proposed a rule of landowner strict liability for injuries caused by defects on commercial property.[65] Though this proposal has prompted interest among academics, it has been thoroughly ignored by the judiciary.

To sum up, then, one is hard-pressed to discern those gains in the case law that others seem to say strict liability has been registering. The doctrine of strict products liability seems little more than a reasonable and moderate adaptation of the basic negligence standard; the ultrahazardous rule has stagnated in the courts and retreated in the Second Restatement; auto no-fault has been waylaid, and hardly counts as strict liability anyway; the field of workers' injuries has been rendered notable by the return of the employee as a tort plaintiff and by the judicial absorption in the phenomenon of employer negligence; and the courts have responded with apathy to a number of respectable strict liability suggestions. These assessments of strict liability areas can be usefully contrasted to at least certain of the developments in negligence law. No one has suggested that therapists should be strictly liable for all harm done by their patients, or landlords strictly liable for all assaults suffered by their tenants; nor have there been any recommendations of strict liability for all forms of emotional distress. In these circumstances, the very idea of liability in tort seems tied to the assumption of liability founded on some fault related standard.

As indicated, the tort of negligence has prospered enormously in recent years; meanwhile, the tort (rather, the torts) of strict liability have not really blossomed in the way that the literature has seemed to suggest. As for the prosperity of negligence, a preliminary assessment is that judges have been strongly impressed by the ideas favoring the negligence principle and have undergone a loss of belief — whether wisely or not — in the host of reasons that have long been relied on to restrain that liability.

NOTES AND QUESTIONS

1. Schwartz catalogues an impressive number of areas where limitations on negligence liability have been eliminated in recent years. There appears to be a general erosion of limitations on

---

65. Ursin, Strict Liability for Defective Business Premises — One Step Beyond *Rowland* and *Greenman*, 22 U.C.L.A. L. Rev. 820 (1975).

professional liability, immunities based on status, and impediments to claims against land occupiers. What accounts for these developments? Is it the growth of liability insurance? Emerging patterns of industrialization and urbanization? Breakthroughs in technology and communications? Loss of confidence in experts? A combination of these factors and others?

2. Are these developments in tort law, abrogating particularized duty relationships, part of a broader movement in the legal order towards the diminution of status-based relationships? To put it another way, is there evidence in other legal areas of a movement towards the recognition of generalized duties owed to others—a recognition, perhaps, that we live in a world of strangers—as opposed to special, contextually defined obligations?

3. Schwartz mentions the protection now afforded to types of interests not previously afforded recognition in their own right, such as harm due to economic loss and emotional distress. Does the recognition of a more expansive duty of due care in these areas turn on the same kinds of considerations as the erosion of status limitations between the parties, mentioned above?

4. In a footnote (see p. 74, *supra*), Schwartz mentions heightened claims consciousness as "a major force in the recent explosion of negligence suits." Would you expect claims consciousness to be an important variable in accounting for "the expansion of the negligence principle"? Is claims consciousness likely to be shaped by social norms other than the likelihood of prevailing under the existing system of liability rules?

5. Assuming that Schwartz is correct in stating that recent decades have witnessed a marked expansion in the negligence principle, is this development likely to impose special burdens on the judicial process? On this question, see the readings in Chapter Three, particularly Henderson, pp. 109-122, *infra*. Is a broad-based fault liability principle socially desirable? On this issue, see the economic perspectives discussed in Chapter 5 and the moral theories presented in Chapter 6.

6. As Schwartz suggests, the most significant modern application of strict liability has been in the products liability area. Presumably, when leading state courts—most notably, perhaps, the California Supreme Court—began enunciating a doctrine of strict liability for defective products, they thought that something more than labels was at stake in choosing between strict liability and negligence (consider also the collective effort that yielded the Restatement of Torts (Second), §402A). Is Schwartz suggesting that modern products liability law is in fact just another application of the fault principle? For a fuller statement of his views on this issue, see

Schwartz, Foreword, Understanding Products Liability, 67 Cal. L. Rev. 435 (1979).

7. Is Schwartz arguing that negligence theory has been more influential than strict liability in recent years in shaping no-fault auto and workers' compensation? What is his position in each case? Is it persuasive?

8. Why has the movement towards more expansive liability been primarily to negligence rather than to a principle of liability without fault? Is it explained by characteristics of the judicial process? Note that the two areas in which the fault principle has been at least partially displaced, according to Schwartz, are workers' compensation and auto no-fault—two areas where legislative schemes have been enacted. What significance would you attach to this fact?

In a landmark article, Professor Jeremiah Smith predicted that once no-fault liability had become an established fact for workers' injuries it would spell the demise of the negligence system. See Smith, Sequel to Workmen's Compensation, 27 Harv. L. Rev. 235 (1912). Hindsight raises serious doubts about his prophetic powers. Does the historical development of negligence law provide clues to the tenacity of the fault principle?

Chapter 3

The Process of Adjudication in Negligence Cases

At the outset, the question of who will decide the key issues in a negligence case is for the trial judge to answer. Immediately, then, the doctrinal framework of the negligence system becomes a device for allocating power. And the role assumed by appellate courts in reviewing tort judgments has reinforced the primacy of allocational issues, for appellate courts have traditionally been largely concerned with whether judge and jury exercised discretion within their respective spheres.

Is the issue of who decides merely a routine matter of procedure, or does it mask underlying questions about how the negligence system allocates losses? Clearly, if juries are consistently more disposed that judges to exercise discretion in favor of compensating injury victims, then the locus of decision-making power has very real, substantive consequences. Most jurists, trial lawyers, and commentators have in fact assumed that such a tendency exists.

The pivotal issue in a negligence case is breach of duty. Here, the issue of who decides arises in the definition of the standard of care. Should the law simply ask whether the defendant exercised "due care" — i.e., acted as a reasonable person would — in the circumstances of the case, or should it define negligent conduct through precise rules? In the excerpt from The Common Law that follows, Oliver Wendell Holmes addresses this critical question. A negligence system based upon an elaborate behavioral code of conduct would confine decision-making discretion more closely than would a general standard of due care. Since the issue of due care has traditionally been viewed as a "question of fact" for the jury, the practical effect of precise rules would be to reduce the influence of the jury with its presumed bias in favor of compensation. In contrast, negligence law as it has actually developed has stated the standard of care in highly general terms, and consequently left to the jury a major role in determining the breach-of-duty issue. Holmes questions the wisdom of tolerating the unpredictability of outcome that results from a commitment of such broad discretion to the jury.

The allocation of power between judge and jury is an all-pervasive theme in negligence cases. Whenever a question of the scope of the defendant's duty, ordinarily considered to be exclusively within the judicial province, is reformulated as an issue of "proximate cause," the chief practical consequence is enhancement of the role of the jury in determining the resolution of the issue. Conversely, the causal relation issue, generally considered a question within the jury's fact-finding domain, sometimes is treated as a matter of law appropriate for the judge to decide. The essay by Wex Malone included in this section addresses the latter relationship: the role of judge and jury in deciding the causal relation issue. Read together, Holmes, Malone, and the accompanying notes are meant to provide a reasonably comprehensive view of how a negligence system allocates decision-making power between judge and jury.

Like Holmes, James Henderson is highly critical of a negligence system characterized by a generalized duty of due care, rather than by precise rules of conduct. But Henderson's concern goes beyond the allocation of decision-making power between judge and jury. Instead, he questions the very capacity of the adjudicatory process to resolve open-ended issues of "reasonable conduct" in a satisfactory fashion. As a consequence, he expresses strong reservations about recent trends in tort law that seem to dictate just such reliance on a general reasonableness formula in resolving a wide variety of increasingly "polycentric" issues.

From an even broader perspective, a discussion of the process of adjudication would be incomplete without reference to the relationship between court and legislature.[1] Traditionally, torts has been considered a common-law area, in which primary responsibility for formulation and development of the law has been left to the courts. Nevertheless, judges have often been reluctant to overrule well-established — but anachronistic — doctrines that involve issues of major policy.

1. For a detailed discussion of the comparative competence of court and legislature in making major policy changes in tort law, see R. Keeton, Creative Continuity in the Law of Torts, 75 Harv. L. Rev. 463 (1962).

In recent years, courts have on occasion self-consciously referred to considerations of institutional legitimacy in dealing with questions such as whether to replace the traditional contributory negligence rule with one of comparative negligence, or whether to abolish charitable, municipal, and intrafamily tort immunities. To test your own tolerance for judicial activism in the torts field, consider the possibility of judicial action substituting scheduled damages in cases of noneconomic harm for the existing general pain and suffering award. What would be the major objections to such a move? Can you generalize from those objections to a set of more fundamental limitations on judicial activism in reforming tort law?

The Common Law*

Oliver Wendell Holmes

... [A]ny legal standard must, in theory, be capable of being known. When a man has to pay damages, he is supposed to have broken the law, and he is further supposed to have known what the law was.

If, now, the ordinary liabilities in tort arise from failure to comply with fixed and uniform standards of external conduct, which every man is presumed and required to know, it is obvious that it ought to be possible, sooner or later, to formulate these standards at least to some extent, and that to do so must at last be the business of the court. It is equally clear that the featureless generality, that the defendant was bound to use such care as a prudent man would do under the circumstances, ought to be continually giving place to the specific one, that he was bound to use this or that precaution under these or those circumstances. The standard which the defendant was bound to come up to was a standard of specific acts or omissions, with reference to the specific circumstances in which he found himself. If in the whole department of unintentional wrongs the courts arrived at no further utterance than the question of negligence, and left every case, without rudder or compass, to the jury, they would simply confess their inability to state a very large part of the law which they required the defendant to know, and would assert, by implication, that nothing could be learned by experience....

The principles of substantive law which have been established by the courts are believed to have been somewhat obscured by having

*Source: 111-112, 120-127, 128-129 (1881).

presented themselves oftenest in the form of rulings upon the sufficiency of evidence. When a judge rules that there is no evidence of negligence, he does something more than is embraced in an ordinary ruling that there is no evidence of a fact. He rules that the acts or omissions proved or in question do not constitute a ground of legal liability, and in this way the law is gradually enriching itself from daily life, as it should. Thus, in Crafton v. Metropolitan Railway Co., the plaintiff slipped on the defendant's stairs and was severely hurt. The cause of his slipping was that the brass nosing of the stairs had been worn smooth by travel over it, and a builder testified that in his opinion the staircase was unsafe by reason of this circumstance and the absence of a hand-rail. There was nothing to contradict this except that great numbers of persons had passed over the stairs and that no accident had happened there, and the plaintiff had a verdict. The court set the verdict aside, and ordered a nonsuit. The ruling was in form that there was no evidence of negligence to go to the jury; but this was obviously equivalent to saying, and did in fact mean, that the railroad company had done all that it was bound to do in maintaining such a staircase as was proved by the plaintiff. A hundred other equally concrete instances will be found in the text-books.

On the other hand, if the court should rule that certain acts or omissions coupled with damage were conclusive evidence of negligence unless explained, it would, in substance and in truth, rule that such acts or omissions were a ground of liability, or prevented a recovery, as the case might be. Thus it is said to be an actionable negligence to let a house for a dwelling knowing it to be so infected with small-pox as to be dangerous to health, and concealing the knowledge. To explain the acts or omissions in such a case would be to prove different conduct from that ruled upon, or to show that they were not, juridically speaking, the cause of the damage complained of. The ruling assumes, for the purposes of the ruling, that the facts in evidence are all the facts.

The cases which have raised difficulties needing explanation are those in which the court has ruled that there was prima facie evidence of negligence, or some evidence of negligence to go to the jury.

Many have noticed the confusion of thought implied in speaking of such cases as presenting mixed questions of law and fact. No doubt, as has been said above, the averment that the defendant has been guilty of negligence is a complex one; first, that he has done or omitted certain things; second, that his alleged conduct does not come up to the legal standard. And so long as the controversy is simply on the first half, the whole complex averment is plain matter for the jury without special instructions, just as a question of ownership would be where the only dispute was as to the fact upon which the legal conclusion was founded. But when a controversy arises on the second half, the question whether the court or the jury ought to judge of the defendant's conduct is wholly unaffected by the accident, whether there is or is not also a dispute as to what that conduct was. If there is such a dispute, it is entirely possible to give a series of hypothetical instructions adapted to every state of facts which it is open to the jury to find. If there is no such dispute, the court may still take their opinion as to the standard. The problem is to explain the relative functions of court and jury with regard to the latter.

When a case arises in which the standard of conduct, pure and simple, is submitted to the jury, the explanation is plain. It is that the court, not entertaining any clear views of public policy applicable to the matter, derives the rule to be applied from daily experience, as it has been agreed that the great body of the law of tort has been derived. But the court further feels that it is not itself possessed of sufficient practical experience to lay down the rule intelligently. It conceives that twelve men taken from the practical part of the community can aid its judgment. Therefore it aids its conscience by taking the opinion of the jury.

But supposing a state of facts often repeated in practice, is it to be imagined that the court is to go on leaving the standard to the jury forever? Is it not manifest, on the contrary, that if the jury is, on the whole, as fair a tribunal as it is represented to be, the lesson which can be got from that source will be learned? Either the court will find that the fair teaching of experience is that the conduct complained of usually is or is not blameworthy, and therefore, unless explained, is or is not a ground of liability; or it will find the jury oscillating to and fro, and will see the necessity of making up its mind for itself. There is no reason why any other such question should not be settled, as well as that of liability for stairs with smooth strips of brass upon their edges. The exceptions would mainly be found where the standard was rapidly changing, as, for instance, in some questions of medical treatment.

If this be the proper conclusion in plain cases, further consequences ensue. Facts do not often exactly repeat themselves in practice; but cases with comparatively small variations from each other do. A judge who has long sat at nisi prius ought gradually to acquire a fund of experience which enables him to represent the common sense of the community in ordinary instances far better than an average jury. He should be able to lead and to instruct them in detail, even where he thinks it desirable, on the whole, to take their opinion. Furthermore, the sphere in which he is able to rule without taking their opinion at all should be continually growing.

It has often been said, that negligence is pure matter of fact, or that, after the court has declared the evidence to be such that negligence *may* be inferred from it, the jury are always to decide whether the inference shall be drawn. But it is believed that the courts, when they lay down this broad proposition, are thinking of cases where the conduct to be passed upon is not proved directly, and the main or only question is what that conduct was, not what standard shall be applied to it after it is established.

Most cases which go to the jury on a ruling that there is evidence from which they may find negligence, do not go to them principally on account of a doubt as to the standard, but of a doubt as to the conduct. Take the case where the fact in proof is an event such as the dropping of a brick from a railway bridge over a highway upon the plaintiff, the fact must be inferred that the dropping was due, not to a sudden operation of weather, but to a gradual falling out of repair which it was physically possible for the defendant to have prevented, before there can be any question as to the standard of conduct.

So, in the case of a barrel falling from a warehouse window, it must be found that the defendant or his servants were in charge of it, before any question of standard can arise. It will be seen that in each of these well-known cases the court assumed a rule which would make the defendant liable if his conduct was such as the evidence tended to prove. When there is no question as to the conduct established by the evidence, as in the case of a collision between two trains belonging to the same company, the jury have, sometimes at least, been told in effect that, if they believed the evidence, the defendant was liable.

The principal argument that is urged in favor of the view that a more extended function belongs to the jury as matter of right, is the necessity of continually conforming our standards to experience. No doubt the general foundation of legal liability in blameworthiness, as determined by the existing average standards of the community, should always be kept in mind, for the purpose of keeping such concrete rules as from time to time may be laid down conformable to daily life. No doubt this conformity is the practical justification for requiring a man to know the civil law, as the fact that crimes are also generally sins is one of the practical justifications for requiring a man to know the criminal law. But these considerations only lead to the conclusion that precedents should be overruled when they become inconsistent with present conditions; and this has generally happened, except with regard to the construction of deeds and wills. On the other hand, it is very desirable to know as nearly as we can the standard by which we shall be judged at a given moment, and, moreover, the standards for a very large part of human conduct do not vary from century to century.

The considerations urged in this Lecture are of peculiar importance in this country, or at least in States where the law is as it stands in Massachusetts. In England, the judges at nisi prius express their opinions freely on the value and weight of the evidence, and the judges in banc, by consent of parties, constantly draw inferences of fact. Hence nice distinctions as to the province of court and jury are not of the first necessity. But when judges are forbidden by statute to charge the jury with respect to matters of fact, and when the court in banc will never hear a case calling for inferences of fact, it becomes of vital importance to understand that, when standards of conduct are left to the jury, it is a temporary surrender of a judicial function which may be resumed at any moment in any case when the court feels competent to do so. Were this not so, the almost universal acceptance of the first proposition in this Lecture, that the general foundation of liability for unintentional wrongs is conduct different from that of a prudent man under the circumstances, would leave all our rights and duties throughout a great part of the law to the necessarily more or less accidental feelings of a jury.

It is perfectly consistent with the views maintained in this Lecture that the courts have been very slow to withdraw questions of negligence from the jury, without distinguishing nicely whether the doubt concerned the facts or the standard to be applied. Legal, like natural divisions, however clear in their general outline, will be found on exact scrutiny to end in a penumbra or debatable land. This is the region of the jury, and only cases falling on this doubtful border are likely to be carried far in court. Still, the tendency of the law must always be to narrow the field of uncertainty. That is what analogy, as well as the decisions on this very subject, would lead us to expect.

The growth of the law is very apt to take place in this way. Two widely different cases suggest a general distinction, which is a clear one when stated broadly. But as new cases cluster around the opposite poles, and begin to approach each other, the distinction becomes more difficult to trace; the determinations are made one way or the other on a very slight preponderance of feeling, rather than of articulate reason; and at last a mathematical line is arrived at by the contact of contrary decisions, which is so far arbitrary that it might equally well have been drawn a little farther to the one side or to the other, but which must have been drawn somewhere in the neighborhood of where it falls....

The same principle applies to negligence. If the whole evidence in the case was that a party, in full command of his senses and intellect, stood on a railway track, looking at an approaching engine until it ran him down, no judge would leave it to the jury to say whether the conduct was prudent. If the whole evidence was that he attempted to cross a level track, which was visible for half a mile each way, and on which no engine was in sight, no court would allow a jury to find negligence. Between these extremes are cases which would go to the jury. But it is obvious that the limit of safety in such cases, supposing no further elements present, could be determined almost to a foot by mathematical calculation.

The trouble with many cases of negligence is, that they are of a kind not frequently recurring, so as to enable any given judge to profit by long experience with juries to lay down rules, and that the elements are so complex that courts are glad to leave the whole matter in a lump for the jury's determination. . . .

NOTES AND QUESTIONS

1. Forty-six years after the publication of The Common Law, Holmes, sitting as a Justice on the Supreme Court, wrote the opinion in Baltimore & Ohio Railroad Co. v. Goodman, 275 U.S. 66 (1927). Goodman's administratrix had brought an action against defendant railroad, charging negligence in running down the decedent. In response, defendant argued that Goodman was contributorily negligent for failing to come to a complete stop at the fatal crossing. Whether stopping would have allowed Goodman to assess effectively his predicament was open to dispute. Justice Holmes, however, thought Goodman was contributorily negligent as a matter of law:

> . . . if a driver cannot be sure otherwise whether a train is dangerously near he must stop and get out of his vehicle, although obviously he will not often be required to do more than stop and look. . . . It is true . . . that the question of due care very generally is left to the jury. But we are dealing with a standard of conduct, and when the standard is clear it should be laid down once and for all by the Courts . . . . [at 70]

Seven years later Justice Cardozo, who had replaced Holmes on the Court, wrote the opinion in Pokora v. Wabash Railroad Co., 292 U.S. 98 (1934). Pokora was injured in a grade-crossing collision while driving his truck. There was evidence that his view was largely obstructed by a string of box cars on a side track. Plaintiff stopped and looked, but he did not get out of his vehicle before proceeding. On the authority of the *Goodman* case, the lower courts held him contributorily negligent as a matter of law. The Supreme Court reversed, "limiting Goodman accordingly." Cardozo constructed a variety of hypothetical grade-crossing scenarios, demonstrating that in some situations it is highly questionable whether Holmes's standard would, in fact, promote safety. He then concluded that:

> Illustrations such as these bear witness to the need for caution in framing standards of behavior that amount to rules of law . . . . Extraordinary situations may not wisely or fairly be subjected to tests or regulations that are fitting for the common-place or normal. In default of the guide of customary conduct, what is suitable for the traveler caught in a mesh where the ordinary safeguards fail him is for the judgment of a jury. [at 105-106]

Does the Goodman-Pokora episode undermine Holmes's argument in the excerpt from The Common Law?

2. Reconsider the opening paragraph of the preceding excerpt from The Common Law. Is predictability an important value in cases such as grade-crossing collisions? In tort cases generally?

3. What other values are promoted by limiting the range of jury discretion along the lines suggested by Holmes?

4. Is it possible to devise criteria that would translate Holmes's position into manageable guidelines for a trial court judge? In other words, how would you go about defining for such a judge the situations where he should avoid relying on the jury in deciding the negligence issue?

5. Is the logical extension of Holmes's position that *every* decision about whether particular conduct is considered negligent might be better decided by a judge? Is the logic of Cardozo's position that such decisions should always be left to the jury? Is it clear that either of these "extreme" positions is less defensible than the traditionally recognized allocation of power between judge and jury?

6. Holmes says that "when a judge rules that there is no evidence of negligence, he does something more than is embraced in an ordinary ruling that there is no evidence of a fact." What does he mean?

7. Compare other techniques by which the judge narrows the scope of jury discretion on the negligence issue, such as the use of relevant statutes and customary practices. Two articles by Professor Clarence Morris are instructive: The Role of Criminal Statutes in Negligence Actions, 49 Colum. L. Rev. 21 (1949), and Custom and Negligence, 42 Colum. L. Rev. 1147 (1942). A particularly interesting treatment of the role of presumptions and inferences as an allocational device is Jaffe, Res Ipsa Loquitur Vindicated, 1 Buffalo L. Rev. 1 (1951).

Ruminations on Cause in Fact *

Wex S. Malone

For nearly a century judges and writers have struggled to unravel the tangled skein of fact and policy. Even today the search is on for a judging and language technique that will enable courts to deal with these two components separately and effectively. In tort controversies the focal point for scrutiny in this respect has been the issue of causation. At the close of the last century courts used the term "cause" indiscriminately to express either their conclusion as to "what happened" or as a means of explaining what law "ought to do about it." As it became increasingly obvious that no single expression could fully support the burden of both inquiries without confusion, legal science began to recognize two separate notions — cause-in-fact, and "proximate" or "legal" cause. This was generally regarded as a major triumph of analysis. Writers of opinions undertook to explain in detail that the two types of cause perform entirely separate functions in the resolution of a tort dispute and that they are associated only by a vague common denominator — a confusing language similarity.

"Proximate" or "legal" cause has claimed the lion's share of attention, while cause-in-fact, or "simple" cause, is always regarded as though it raises only a question of fact. The judge, it is commonly said, can do no more than propound the inquiry on causation. It is wholly within the jury's province when it becomes an issue at all.

Certainly it is true in a sense that simple cause is a question of fact. The production of testimony, often in lavish and conflicting detail, is essential to the effort to establish or refute simple cause. Frequently it is necessary to know not only what happened, but what *might* have happened if the defendant's conduct had been other than what it actually was. Sometimes the services of experts must be enlisted for this purpose. Certainly, also, the issue of simple cause is for the consideration of the jury whenever the evidence affords ground for reasonable difference of opinion. Instructions on the weight of evidence must be given as in other factual disputes, and the power of the court to nonsuit or direct a verdict exists here as in other contests concerning facts.

The Process of Determining Cause-in-Fact

Nevertheless, I find that even with reference to this issue of simple cause the mysterious relationship between policy and fact is likely to

Source: 9 Stan. L. Rev. 60-70, 71-75, 81-85, 97-99 (1956).

be in the foreground. In this Article it will be demonstrated that policy may often be a factor when the issue of cause-in-fact is presented sharply for decision, much as it is when questions of proximate cause are before the court. The presence of policy factors is obscured by the accidental circumstance that the word "cause" is one that the law has borrowed from the layman's terminology, and this child of the street, unlike the artificial creatures of our professional vocabulary, simply will not behave. It refuses to submit to any effort at classification and it insists upon spilling itself throughout every area of the controversy.

A cause is not a fact in the sense that its existence can be established merely through the production of testimony. Although evidentiary data must supply the raw material upon which a finding of cause or no-cause will be based, yet something must first be done with this data by the trier, be he judge or juryman. He must refer the facts presented by the testimony to some judging capacity within himself before he can venture the conclusion that a cause exists. He must arrange the events established by the evidence into a relationship of some kind and he must satisfy himself that the relationship can properly be labeled "cause." The most that can be said is that the trier is making a deduction from evidentiary facts. This operation is not self-performing. It calls into play a variety of intellectual functions that are peculiar to the trier as an individual. It is these that play the decisive role in reaching an answer, and it is clear that they are no integral part of the raw fact data upon which the operation is being performed.

Doubtless the above observation holds true to some extent, not only for cause, but for the entire phenomenon of proof. Raw evidence requires interpretation. It must be referred to the experience of the trier before it can acquire meaning. The extent to which the past experience and the judging personality of the trier will be brought into play depends to a large extent upon what is being proved. Very little of a trier's experience background, for example, is required in order to induce him to agree that an automobile tire presented in evidence is "different" from other tires. Somewhat more is required to tell him that the tire is "old," and a goodly amount of his capacity to reach conclusions must be brought into play before he can announce that the tire is "bad," that it is "unfit for use" or that its presence on a vehicle indicates negligence on the part of a car owner. Furthermore, it is noteworthy that in passing from one of these determinations to another we have moved almost imperceptibly from matters of "fact" to matters of "judgment" or "evaluation."

Even more important, the evaluation which the trier will make of the new fact data will necessarily be affected by the purpose he is seeking to serve. This is particularly true of cause, which, as we have ✳

seen, is merely an acceptable deduction from evidential facts. All deductions are drawn purposively — that is to say, they are drawn for a reason. A moment's reflection will show that this is true. A car is being driven in haste by an irresponsible youngster along a road which has recently been covered with large loose gravel. A wheel picks up a piece of rock and hurls it into the face of a pedestrian. The comments that this incident may evoke from each of several by-standers will differ. A neighbor of the youthful driver may attribute the accident to the indifference of the child's parents, who ought not to allow him to drive. This, she will say, is the cause of the injury. A critical road engineer may see the cause of the accident in terms of improper road construction. A teacher of physics may be inspired to use the same incident as an illustration of the impact of a given speed upon an object of certain weight and dimensions. This, he observes, is the cause of the phenomenon. Each observer has put the term "cause" to the use that interests him. Each has drawn upon his own background in varying degrees and each has brought into play different parts of his judging capacity. No single one of these attributions of cause can be said to be more valid than any other, for each observer is using the term for his own purpose.

This same observation is applicable in the court room. Where a doctor and a judge both seek to answer the same question of simple cause, the answers given may be different because their respective interpretations of cause are colored by the purpose to which each puts that word. An elderly worker with a heart ailment of long standing happens to drop dead while engaged in some trivial task for his employer. A medical expert is likely to testify with assurance that the exertion was not *a* cause of the death. He may explain that the heart was spent and that there was nothing about the work being done that could account for the tragedy. He finds that the relation-ship between the two events is not sufficiently close to justify him in characterizing it as a cause and effect relationship.

However, it is important to bear in mind that the medical expert is not examining this phenomenon in the abstract, but rather in the light of his role as a physician. He cannot escape forming associations between events that will comport with the purposes of his profession, for this is the only way in which a causal relationship can be meaningful to him. His situation is somewhat analogous to that of the critical road engineer in the earlier illustration. The mission of the man of medicine is to diagnose, to cure if possible, or to suggest those preventive measures which medical science can offer for future reference. In passing judgment upon a coronary collapse, the physician will likely envision as causes only those factors with which he can deal in diagnosing, in curing or in seeking to forestall future occurrences of this kind for other persons. The trivial strain that occurs during the employment will form for the medical expert only an incident in a relatively neutral background. It will represent one of a series of commonplace recurrent events with which medical science is helpless to deal. To aggravate aggravation, to accelerate acceleration, to make the inevitable more inevitable are foreign to the expert in medicine. The medical facts relative to the previous condition of the heart are much more meaningful to him because they constitute a challenge to his profession.

If the opinion of the expert on the cause of the coronary collapse is being offered in a suit for compensation by the widow of the aged worker, the judge or other trier of fact must make the final determination on the causal relation between the exertion and the failure of the heart. Again, the judge, like the medical expert, does not examine the relationship in abstraction. He must weigh it in the terms of his professional calling—the administration of justice. He must determine those risks for which the employer should be held responsible and he must fix the proper point of contact between employment and death for this purpose. He has been furnished a mere policy outline in the form of a workmen's compensation statute whose interstices must be filled in through resort to his own notions on appropriateness. The inquiry before him is a complex one: Is the relationship between the trivial exertion and the collapse of the worker's heart sufficient to justify a court of law in taking affirmative action?

Those factors that have proved useful in the resolution of legal disputes, rather than for the purposes of medicine, will dominate the deliberations of the judge. He likely will be impressed by the law's desire to throw its protection around the susceptible and aged worker as well as the one who is in sound health. His judicial experience in other areas of compensation law has made him aware of the fact that the point of contact between job and injury need not be a close one for the purposes served by this statute. He appreciates the fact that workmen's compensation serves as a compromise vehicle which meets only in part the real needs of the worker or widow. Furthermore, he is aware of the traditional uncertainty of the mind of medical science, and he well knows that judges cannot escape the responsibility of taking prompt and final action upon such approximations of truth as can be made available in the courtroom. Much misunderstanding between lawyers and physicians could be obviated if members of both professions would realize that "simple" causation is not merely an abstract issue of fact and that the resolution of the cause problem depends largely upon the purpose for which cause is to be used. What is *a* cause for the judge need not be *a* cause for the physician. It is through the process of selecting what is to be regarded as a cause for the purpose of resolving a legal dispute that considerations of policy exert their influence in deciding an issue of cause-in-fact.

Cause and the "But-For" Test

It appropriately has been observed that "proof of what we call the relation of cause and effect...can be nothing more than 'the projection of our habit of expecting certain consequents to follow certain antecedents merely because we had observed these sequences on previous occasions.'" From this it is clear that the process is basically one of conjecture, for facts almost never represent themselves in identical patterns. All that can be said with any assurance is that the facts introduced in evidence call to mind or suggest sequences between events which have been previously observed, or that the facts in evidence bring into play generalities which we have derived from previous observations (such as fire causes burn) and which we regard as being more or less dependable.

Furthermore, even though the habit of expecting certain consequences to follow certain antecedents is projected toward a new situation, we are still not in a position to announce that a cause and effect relation has been established. Previous observations by a stargazer may enable him to say with absolute assurance that when a given constellation rises to the heavens another constellation will soon come into view over the horizon. Yet, no one in this modern world would assume that the rising of the first constellation is a *cause* of the appearance of the second. The inevitable character of the sequence as gained from past observations is not enough to establish the relation of cause and effect. Other portions of our knowledge are too likely to get in the way of such a conclusion. There must be some acceptable point of affinity between the new event and old experience that is satisfactory, and this point of satisfaction can be established only in terms of the purpose toward which the whole process of decision is being directed.

In an effort to lend some sense of definiteness and finality to the process described above, the courts have evolved several tests, the most frequently used of which is the "but-for" test. One fact or event, it is said, is a cause of another when the first fact or event is indispensable to the existence of the second. In the trial of controversies this means that a defendant should not be charged with responsibility for a plaintiff's harm unless he can conclude with some degree of assurance that the harm could not have occurred in the absence of the defendant's misconduct. It is noteworthy that this very announcement is a statement of legal policy. It marks an effort to point out the bare minimum requirement for imposing liability. Unless we can go this far, we must dismiss the claim without further ado. If we do reach this point, we are warranted in investigating further under the guise of determining proximate cause.

One might ask why the minimal relationship was established at this point, rather that at some other. Perhaps the answer is that the but-for test seems to be the best the law can do in its effort to offer an approximate expression of an accepted popular attitude toward responsibility. In passing homely judgments on everyday affairs we assume that we should not blame a person whose conduct "had nothing to do with" some unfortunate occurrence that followed. Some such attitude as this, however it may be expressed, is essential if we are to pass judgments at all, for if we were to adopt any other position we could never know whom to blame for what, or we would blame everybody for everything. If judgment is to be selective, if it is to have any salutary effect on future conduct, it must begin from some such point. Hence, we are willing to exonerate a suspected person whenever we decide that his conduct "had nothing to do with" the event in which we are interested.

Notice, however, that the man in the street does not ordinarily fix a minimal cause solely in terms of factual deduction and then proceed in a separate operation to determine whether this factual cause is one for which responsibility should be imposed. His inquiry is single. The bifurcated approach is one adopted by the law in an effort to separate that which to a large extent is inseparable, and in the process we lose much of the meaning of the very phenomenon we are investigating. For the layman cause and purpose are a single blend. His pronouncement on causation is pregnant with a purposive quality. In other words, it implies the idea that A's conduct is relevant to B's injury for the purpose the declarant has in mind. The but-for rule is hardly an adequate substitute for this homely blend of fact and policy that is so deep-rooted in our approach to everyday problems. It marks an attempt to poise the inquiry on a wholly abstract plane, stripped of all evaluative overtones. The essential weakness of the but-for test is the fact that it ignores the irresistible urge of the trier to pass judgment at the same time that he observes. It is an intellectual strait jacket to which the human mind will not willingly submit. The test was discredited even for philosophical usage by David Hume, its originator. It has been rejected by courts for many types of controversies because, as we shall see, it has often failed to afford even an approximate expression of the minimal requirement for imposing legal liability.

However this may be, the but-for test has a marked peculiarity which recommends it strongly for legal usage. Like other legal formulas, it is not self-executing. It calls upon the judge or juryman to determine what would have happened if the defendant had not been guilty of the conduct charged against him. At times this determination is made so automatically that the cause issue is little more than a bit of formalism in the trial. But at other times the same test demands the impossible. It challenges the imagination of the trier to probe into a purely fanciful and unknowable state of affairs. He is invited to make an estimate concerning facts that concededly never existed. The very uncertainty as to what *might* have happened opens the door wide for conjecture. But when conjecture is demanded it can be given a direction that is consistent with the policy considerations that underlie the controversy.

The permissible range for conjecture is unlimited. We can never be absolutely certain that our estimate is correct. The point at which we might be satisfied can be expressed in many ways, such as "barely possible," "possible," "not unlikely," "as possible as not," "probable," "highly probable" or "virtually certain." Language is very rich for this purpose and demands but a minimum of commitment on our part.

Since the issue of causation is commonly regarded as an issue of fact, it lends itself readily to the techniques that control the proof of factual matters. Cause is established by "probabilities" or by that even more noncommunicative phrase, "the weight of the evidence," or by conflicting testimony or inferences upon which reasonable minds may differ. Again, consistent with the analogy of establishing facts, courts retain the power to nonsuit or direct a verdict whenever they feel that the jury's conjecture with reference to the nonexistent state of affairs would not be acceptable to the law. Thus, the judge is vested with authority to conjecture upon the very process of conjecture itself. His own estimate, in turn, is subject to the check of the appellate court. Here, then, is a complex of machinery and formulas that affords the greatest possible latitude for the rendering of a judgment tailored to meet the needs of the occasion.

Judge's Power Over the Cause Issue

The judge enjoys an extensive power either to dismiss the plaintiff's claim because he has failed to make out a case on the issue of causation or to refer the question of cause freely to the jury for its consideration. There is language available that can make either decision sound thoroughly plausible. The formulas that he can enlist for this purpose are of the greatest conceivable variety, and the changes that can be rung upon subtle shades of meaning are nothing less than remarkable.

Whenever the judge has concluded that the showing on the issue of cause is not sufficient to warrant a submission to the jury, he is likely to emphasize that there is a sharp distinction between a "mere possibility" and a showing of "probability" or "reasonable probability." The evidence must do more than leave the matter "in equilibrio." The opinion may point with conviction to some factor other than defendant's misconduct that could plausibly account for the accident, and it will highlight the inferential and speculative character of the conclusion urged by the plaintiff.

> The plaintiff slipped upon the ice. That by itself was a sufficient, certain, and operating cause of the fall. No other explanation is needed to account for what happened. It is possible that the slope of the walk had something to do with it. . . . There is not a particle of proof that it did. To affirm it is a pure guess and an absolute speculation. Are we to send it to a jury for them to imagine what might have been?

Since cause itself is not a fact and must necessarily be an inference drawn from data furnished by the evidence, arguments such as those set forth above always sound formidable.

Sometimes a court in refusing to submit the issue of cause to the jury, will tighten the formula to such a point that it is difficult to avoid the impression that a criminal controversy is involved and that all elements of defendant's liability must be shown conclusively. Plaintiff, it is sometimes said, must produce "evidence of circumstances 'so strong as to preclude the possibility of injury in any other way and provide as the only reasonable inference'" that the injury or death was caused by the negligence of the defendant.

> The plaintiff must fail if the evidence does not show that the injury was the result of some cause for which the defendant is responsible, and where the proof is by circumstances, the circumstances themselves must be shown and not left to rest in conjecture, and when shown it must appear that the inference sought is the only one which can fairly and reasonably be drawn from the facts.
>
> As we have said, the burden is on the plaintiffs to persuade the trial court that their theory as to the cause of the fire is correct, and that burden is not satisfied by testimony which tends to show that the negligence of the defendant *may* have caused or even that it probably did cause the fire if it appears that the fire may have resulted from some other cause for which the defendant was not responsible.

On the other hand, whenever the court is willing to accept the judgment of the jury on the cause issue, it will not encounter the slightest difficulty in finding acceptable and convincing language to justify the refusal of a nonsuit. Instead of emphasizing the distinction between "possibilities" and "probabilities" the judge will likely call attention to the fact that no inference can be proved to a certainty. It is enough that it is "reasonable." The opinion may resort to new and intermediate expressions, such as "more than a possibility," or it may observe that if defendant had performed his duty, the victim "might" have been saved. "We cannot say that there was *no likelihood* that a rope three feet above the deck. . . would not have saved the seaman [who was washed overboard]. . . . [Emphasis added.]"

. . . In the mine run of cases the facts are so clear that the issue of causal relation need not even be submitted to the jury. Cause is not often a dispute over which the litigants earnestly cross swords. But the issue does become serious whenever the judicial process demands an answer to the unknowable, and it is in such instances that a wide range of language makes it possible for the judge to exclude the jury from participation or to enlist its full and conclusive service, just as he may see fit. There are no settled rules of law that demand the doing of one rather than the other in such instances. The often stated rule that an issue must be submitted to a jury if reasonable men may draw different conclusions from the evidentiary data is in fact only a formula and in no way impinges on or directs the court's judgment to submit or not submit the issue.

We are interested, therefore, in such factors as there may be that influence the exercise of this wide range of judicial discretion with reference to the nonsuiting process. Of course the judge's own sense of the possibilities and probabilities of the cause controversy are in themselves of tremendous importance, and often the court's convictions are overwhelming and determine the outcome of the issue without much ado. But such cases are seldom troublesome. The difficult ones are those that require the judge to select from among the various shades of likelihood the one that strikes him as being most appropriate for the particular controversy before him. This process of selection is not carried on in a vacuum by some philosopher meditating upon the niceties of etiology. For the judge the choice is purposeful, and his purpose is the administration of justice in the very special controversy before him.

Policy Factors That Influence the Outcome of the Cause Issue

At this point matters of policy and estimates of factual likelihood become hopelessly intervolved with each other. The ultimate question is one of liability and that question is reflected in every area of the controversy. We can now ask: How great must be the affinity of causal likelihood between the defendant's wrong and the plaintiff's injury in order to justify the judge submitting the cause issue to the jury? The answer is that the affinity must be sufficiently close in the opinion of the judge to bring into effective play the rule of law that would make the defendant's conduct wrongful.

Some rules of law are tremendously exacting and rest upon time-honored moral considerations. They are safeguards for well-established interests of others, and their mantle of protection embraces a large variety of risks. He who violates such a rule will be hèld responsible for any harm that can be causally associated in any plausible way with his wrongdoing. The court, for instance, will seldom hesitate to allow the jury a free range of speculation on the cause issue at the expense of an intentional wrongdoer who is charged with having physically injured another person.

Other rules of law rest on less secure foundations. They may have emerged only recently to afford some limited measure of protection against a narrow scope of risks. The conduct prohibited may fail to meet the requirements of permissible activity by only a narrow margin. The violator of such a rule may be entitled to expect that the judge should protect him against exposure to an adverse jury finding in all cases except where there is an overwhelming factual likelihood that he brought about the plaintiff's injury.

All rules of conduct, irrespective of whether they are the product of a legislature or are a part of the fabric of the court-made law of negligence, exist for purposes. They are designed to protect *some* persons under *some* circumstances against *some* risks. Seldom does a rule protect every victim against every risk that may befall him, merely because it is shown that the violation of the rule played a part in producing the injury. The task of defining the proper reach or thrust of a rule in its policy aspects is one that must be undertaken by the court in each case as it arises. How appropriate is the rule to the facts of this controversy? This is a question that the court cannot escape.

Some rules of conduct, particularly those that are extracted from the broad notion we call negligence, cover a vague, indefinite area of risk that escapes all efforts of advance charting. Other rules of conduct were designed for fairly narrow and definite purposes. The precise reasons for their existence can be fathomed without too much difficulty. Whenever it can be said with fair certainty that the rule of conduct relied upon by the plaintiff was designed to protect against the very type of risk to which the plaintiff was exposed, courts have shown very little patience with the efforts of defendant to question the sufficiency of the proof on cause. Such cases nearly always reach the jury if the plaintiff's contention on this issue has the slightest factual plausibility. Not infrequently an opinion will openly betray the operation of this influence:

> Where the jury had a right to find such actual negligence, followed by the existence of the very danger which might have been expected to arise therefrom, it cannot be said as a matter of law that the plaintiff is bound to go further and to exclude the operation of other possible causes to which conceivably the danger might have been due, instead of having been due to the actual negligence which has been shown.
>
> Considering that such lines were run for the express purpose, among others, of protecting seamen, we think it a question about which reasonable men might at least differ whether the intestate would not have been saved, had it [the line] been there.

In other opinions the interdependence of policy and factual likelihood is more subtly suggested in the language of the court. An interesting decision in this respect is Reynolds v. Texas and Pac. Ry. — a classic in torts casebooks. Plaintiff, a stout woman, was being urged down the stairs leading from defendant railroad's platform to its tracks. The negligence alleged was the failure of the defendant to provide adequate lighting. She fell, and later instituted suit for the resulting injuries. The railroad contended with considerable plausibility that a two-hundred-fifty-pound woman hurrying to descend a stairway under the insistent urging of her companions might well have fallen even if adequate lighting had been provided. The court, however, in supporting a finding of causal relation, observed: "[W]here the negligence of the defendant greatly multiplies the chance of accident...and is of a character naturally leading to its occurrence, the mere possibility that it might have happened without the negligence is not sufficient to break the chain of cause and effect...."

It is noteworthy that the court has neatly avoided all reference to the probabilities requirement. The rule violated by defendant was designed to protect hurrying stout passengers in the very predicament of this plaintiff. It is therefore enough that its wrongdoing enhanced the chance of accident, that it increased the risk in some appreciable measure. The competing causes urged by defendant all constituted risk factors against which protection was afforded by the very rule that was violated.

The processes of risk sorting and of estimating factual likelihood are sometimes only different facets of a single indivisible inquiry. An engineer fails to give the statutory crossing signal. If an accident follows, shall the railroad defendant be allowed to contend successfully that the person crossing the right of way would not have heard the whistle if it had been blown — can it set up the inattention of the traveler as a competing cause? "The purpose of the required signals is to attract and arrest attention. It assumes both the possibility and probability of inattention."

The question raised here is not easy. The statutory signal rule was not enacted to protect the utterly indifferent or foolhardy wayfarer. At the same time, however, its protection is not restricted to those whose ears are precisely attuned to the prospect of the whistle's sound. The question of factual likelihood must be tackled whenever the scope of protection afforded by the rule of law is before the court for determination. How, then, can the question of simple cause even be approached by the court until this vital matter of legislative policy has been resolved? And once the answer has been given and the limits of the rule's protection have been defined with some precision for the particular case, there is no meaningful cause-in-fact question left for the jury. Conversely, if the court has allowed the jury to impose liability on the railroad because there is "some likelihood" that the allegedly indifferent wayfarer would have heard the whistle, has not the judge, by the very submission of the issue, passed at least his tentative judgment upon the scope of protection afforded by the statute requiring the giving of the signal?...

Competing Causes—Accidental Shooting Cases

Every situation in which the cause issue is fairly in doubt opens the possibility of the existence of a competing cause or causes. In the seaman rescue cases, for instance, the causal inquiry can be posed so as to raise the question whether the failure to rescue was caused by the defendant's failure to supply an available life ring, or, on the other hand, was caused by the distance intervening between the boat and the struggling victim, the fast running of the sea or the inability of the sailor to swim, etc. Similarly, in the fire entrapment cases we can ask the question, was the death of the victim caused by the failure to provide a fire escape, or, on the other hand, was it caused by the intervention of a closed door or the presence of smoke or flame between the victim and the place where the fire escape should have been provided? In short, the cases in which the existence of a competing cause or causes is emphasized do not involve any new principle that is not present in other cases.

Whether or not the presence of a single or several competing causes will be urged by defendant is entirely a matter of effective presentation in the courtroom. In some instances a competing cause will stand out with bold dramatic vividness and will bring into arresting focus the weakness of the plaintiff's claim with reference to the factual likelihoods. When the defendant can argue the existence of a competing cause, he is in a position to avail himself of a powerful forensic weapon. We are accustomed to mathematical and syllogistic thinking, and where the chances are in even mathematical balance and there are only two plausible causal alternatives — either A or B — we are likely to insist on some positive assurance that A, not B, was the cause. In such cases our reaction is sharply tempered by our sense of contrast. The probabilities formula stares us boldly in the face, and there is no means of escape through resort to the subtle shades of factual likelihood. We are confined in a verbal strait jacket, and unless doubt can be cast upon the existence of the other cause, or upon its competitive character, we must either submit to the probabilities formula or else flout it openly.

The situation here will become difficult, if, in addition, the rule violated by defendant is one which has a commanding thrust policy-wise and which affords protection against even the *possibility* of injury. The dilemma presented in such cases demands all the ingenuity that the court can muster, and decisions that allow the jury to impose liability in the face of mechanically balanced probabilities are likely to be widely criticized. This is well illustrated by a group of cases in which an accidental shooting was inflicted by one of two or more gun handlers. The most recent and widely discussed of these controversies is Summers v. Tice. Plaintiff and the two defendants were hunting together. Each of the defendants used a twelve-gauge shotgun with number seven and one-half shot. The usual procedure is to maintain a straight line abreast. But plaintiff proceeded up a hill and went forward of the line formed by defendants, thus making a triangle, with the plaintiff on a plane above that of the defendants. One of the latter flushed a quail, which flew in a line that bisected the triangle formed by the parties. Both defendants fired at the bird, and a pellet lodged in the eye of the plaintiff. It was absolutely impossible from the evidence to say that the shot of one defendant, rather than the other, was the cause of injury. The Supreme Court of California affirmed the ruling of the trial court allowing the jury to impose joint liability on both defendants in the absence of affirmative proof by either one of them showing that the injury was more plausibly caused by the other.

Other courts had reached a similar conclusion by purporting to find a relationship sufficient to make the parties joint tortfeasors, even though the evidence did not show an orthodox relationship, such as conspiracy or joint venture, which would ground vicarious liability. But in the *Summers* case the California court proceeded more directly. It flatly rejected the dogma of proof by probabilities as applied to the facts before it. The court was faced with the problem of determining whether the shooting by either defendant bore a relationship to the wounding that was close enough to bring into play the very exacting rule which both of them had violated.

Two policy notions stand out boldly in this particular controversy. First, facing the court were two defendants, one or the other of whom undoubtedly wounded the victim. Can the judge afford to permit these two wrongdoers to pass the ball of legal responsibility back and forth between themselves while the outraged victim stands helplessly on the sideline? Such a prospect is, naturally, one from which a court will retreat whenever possible. But this alone is hardly enough to override the established requirement of proof by probabilities where two competing causes are balanced in equipoise. Most jurisdictions, including California, have held, for instance, that a collision of vehicles on the highway does not give rise to any inference of negligence against either driver in favor of a third person injured by the collision. But the important factor distinguishing Summers v. Tice is that both defendants were shown to be wrongdoers. Furthermore, both of them had violated one of the most exacting rules that courts are called upon to administer — the rule protecting against the accidental discharge of firearms.

The law has always dealt strictly with accidental shootings. Although it is commonly said today that liability here rests on negligence, the standard of care in these cases is hitched up to top notch. Until recently the gun handler who shot another was obliged to exonerate himself from liability by showing that the accident was utterly without his fault. The strict rules of trespass lingered on in this area of liability longer than in any other, and even at the present time the doctrine of res ipsa loquitur will inevitably carry such a case to the jury. Furthermore, where the misuse of firearms is involved, courts are willing to hold the defendant for almost any consequence, however attenuated it may be, that flows from his conduct. In such cases proximate cause doctrines have their greatest reach. In the firearms cases, where courts most readily extend protection and where the normal requirement of fault is paid little more than lip service, it is to be expected that the victim of an accidental shooting will be allowed access to the jury on the issue of cause whenever his contention in this respect is at all plausible. A strict attitude against the defendant in any particular type of litigation, such as this, will likely make itself felt in every area of the controversy. The issue of causation is no exception. If the situation in Summers v. Tice had not presented the equal balance of probabilities with such dramatic vividness, the court would have experienced no embarrassment in submitting the cause issue to the jury with reference to either defendant. Respectable statements previously observed could readily have been adapted to the facts of this case. The court could have stated with considerable plausibility that "we do not think the testimony left it so clear that the shot came from some source other than this defendant's gun that it would be proper to direct a verdict," or that "we cannot say that there was no likelihood that the shot found in the eye of the victim came from the shotgun in the possession of this defendant.". . .

Cause-in-Fact and Proximate Cause

Although policy considerations frequently exert their influence when we attempt to resolve a simple cause inquiry, it does not follow that we cannot draw a valid distinction between this inquiry and the puzzling phenomenon we call proximate cause. The difference between them, however, is a difference largely of degree, rather than of kind. Fact inquiries and questions of policy come before the courts in every conceivable blend. Sometimes the question as to what law should do stands out with relative boldness, even though the inquiry bears a transparent veneer of fact. At other times our convictions on policy make themselves felt only in urging us one way or another as we speculate on the factual likelihoods or estimate the quantitative part played by the defendant's wrongdoing. When policy can be recognized openly as the dominating factor, so that it can be dealt with directly, the problem can be meaningfully labeled as one of proximate cause, duty, risk, negligence, etc. On the other hand, when the attention of the trier is focused primarily on what happened and the usual techniques of factual inquiry can be effectively used, the issue is properly termed one of simple cause although policy impulses may assist materially in giving the proper turn to the judgment. Language has not yet furnished us with sharper tools than these. But this need not be a matter of concern so long as we understand the language devices we currently use.

The successful administration of tort disputes rests upon artistry and skill to a greater extent than we seem to be willing to admit. In our effort to regard legal administration purely as a rational science we have attempted to bound out certain areas which we define as pure policy, and we insist that these must be for the consideration of the court alone. We conceive of the jury's function as exclusively that of finders of fact. But we are indeed hard pressed to maintain this distinction except in the roughest terms. We must concede that it does not hold with respect to the issue of negligence. Under the guise of the "reasonable man" formula, juries regularly decide in one operation what the defendant *ought* to have done, and whether he *did* it. Both aspects of this operation are under the supervision of the judge whose mission is to keep the jury within proper bounds.

Similarly, the jury is frequently allowed to participate in the solution of proximate cause problems, even though the content here is almost entirely a matter of fixing policy. If the problem makes too great a demand on the ability of the jurymen to conform to legal notions of fairness, or if it relates to a matter which the judge feels should be formally and conclusively settled once and for all, he is vested with ample authority to rescue the power of conclusive judgment on the proximate cause question and to use it himself. The effort by writers, and occasionally by courts, to oust the issue of proximate cause from judicial usage and to reallocate the same inquiry within the judge's exclusive domain of declaring duties has not been successful except in those instances where the court has already become convinced that jury participation would be unwise. Most attempts to lay down a formula that would definitively assign to the judge and jury their respective functions in administering the proximate cause issue have become lost in the tangled undergrowth of the law. This, I believe, is as it should be.

What has been said above with reference to the issues of negligence and proximate cause holds true also for the issue of simple cause. The judge first fixes the proper area of estimation for the jury. He may refuse to allow them to have the issue. But if he brings the jurymen into operation he leaves them free to react toward the policy involved in the light of the special fact situation before them. Thus, he is in a position to utilize to the fullest extent the jurymen's talents on those matters toward which the law is relatively neutral and where the layman's sense of values is deemed to be as good as that of the judge. This leaves the judicial process free for tasks more worthy of the mettle of the court and it confirms to some extent the layman's belief that the jury has a role to play in the solution of tort controversies beyond that of merely fixing the facts. We expect judges to assign rational-sounding reasons for their decisions on policy matters. Theirs is the ponderous task of "declaring the law." They must make their decision in each case jibe with what has been authoritatively said in the past. Thus distinction is heaped upon distinction and law becomes increasingly and unnecessarily complex. Yet, in most instances the individual judgment passed on the controversy at hand has little or no value for future litigation, since the policy questions are too closely related to the factual issues to be segregated from them. Any effort to make a formal explanation of such policy decisions overtaxes the power of language and is productive only of confusion. Once the judge has denied a nonsuit, it is better that judgments of this kind should be handed down without explanation by the jury, which is then dissolved back into society.

NOTES AND QUESTIONS

1. Compare Malone's argument, at the end of the excerpt, for broadening the scope of jury power to decide the cause-in-fact issue with Holmes's view of the jury's role in deciding the negligence issue. Are the two positions fundamentally opposed? Is Malone's position the same as that taken by Cardozo in the *Pokora* case, at pp. 89-90, *supra*?

2. A passenger on a ship falls overboard in mid-ocean. Others aboard the ship cannot respond to her screams for help because no lifesaving equipment is available. Whether such equipment would have facilitated a rescue is hotly disputed at trial. In what sense is the judge's decision whether to send the case to the jury a "policy" issue? If the case is submitted, in what sense is the consequent jury determination a policy decision?

3. Is it Malone's thesis that *all* cause-in-fact determinations are policy issues? Is his use of the term "policy" inextricably bound up in his conception of the mental processes performed in drawing inferences from "raw facts"?

4. Do you agree that because Summers v. Tice was a "firearms case" it was appropriate to apply a more sweeping conception of causal relation than would have been called for if a more innocent instrument of harm were involved?

5. Suppose the defendant's identity is in question. Should a court be more disposed to send the case to the jury when the plaintiff was injured by a hit-and-run truck driver than when a like injury resulted from a hit-and-run bicyclist? Is your answer to the immediately preceding question on Summers v. Tice decisive?

6. When defendant's identity is in question, should the role of the judge on the causal relation issue be influenced by whether the injury was caused by intentional wrongdoing or negligent behavior? Reconsider Malone at pp. 100-102, *supra*.

7. The path-breaking work of Leon Green influenced virtually every subsequent torts scholar who addressed the question of the relationship between judge and jury. Emphasizing the same "purposive" or "instrumental" approach to judicial decision making that is evident in Malone, Green covered the entire range of issues that arise in a negligence case in his two early classics, Rationale of Proximate Cause (1927) and Judge and Jury (1930).

Expanding the Negligence Concept: Retreat from the Rule of Law*

James A. Henderson, Jr.

Introduction

That recent years have witnessed revolutionary reforms and developments in the common law of torts, and particularly in negligence, comes as no surprise to anyone teaching, studying, or practicing in this field. That these reforms and developments have been supported by a substantial majority of legal writers is equally obvious to anyone familiar with the literature on the subject. What may not be so obvious, and therefore what I have chosen to advance as the thesis of this article, is that these widely welcomed developments, taken together, seriously threaten the integrity and even the survival of the system of negligence-based liability toward the improvement of which they were originally advanced. Simply stated, we torts people, especially the torts teachers and scholars among us, are in serious trouble; and the sooner we wake up to what we are doing to ourselves and to our subject, the better.

The source of the difficulty, as I shall attempt to demonstrate in the following analysis, is the tendency in recent years to focus upon the substantive objectives of our liability system almost to the total exclusion of any shared concern for the realities and limitations of the processes by which those objectives are realized. The overlooked fact is that adjudication has limits which may be exceeded regularly only at great risk to the integrity of the judicial process. The most basic limit of adjudication is that it requires substantive rules of sufficient specificity to support orderly and rational argument on the question of liability. The reforms and changes in the law of negligence in recent years have, purportedly to advance identifiable social objectives, eliminated much of the specificity with which negligence principles traditionally have been formulated. We are rapidly approaching the day when liability will be determined routinely on a case by case, "under all the circumstances" basis, with decision makers (often juries) guided only by the broadest of general principles. When that day arrives, the retreat from the rule of law will be complete, principled decision will have been replaced with decision by whim, and the common law of negligence will have degenerated into an unjustifiably inefficient, thinly disguised lottery.

Specifically, my objectives in this article are: (1) to develop a basic

*Source: 51 Ind. L.J. 467, 468-482 (1976).

theory of adjudication which reveals both the limits of that process and the necessity for relatively specific rules of decision; (2) to explain the manner in which traditional negligence doctrines have served to render the liability issue adjudicable; (3) to describe recent substantive developments in the law of negligence in a way that will demonstrate the threat they pose to the integrity of our traditional common law liability system; and (4) to suggest steps which must be taken to reduce the threat and to help to assure the continued vitality of our torts system. In the course of my analysis, I shall have some unkind words for torts scholars and writers. Much of what has been published in recent years has been relatively indifferent to the problems raised here; some of it has been downright irresponsible. However, I do not intend to create the impression that I am alone in the concerns herein expressed. A number of torts writers have expressed concern over the workability of a system of tort liability guided only by general principles. It is in the hope of bringing others over to this point of view that the following analysis is offered.

I.   The Limits of Adjudication

Adjudication is a social process of decisionmaking in which the affected parties are guaranteed the opportunity of presenting proofs and arguments to an impartial tribunal[1] which is bound to find the relevant facts and to apply recognized rules to reach a reasoned result.[2] It is certainly not the only process of decision in which interested parties are afforded the opportunity to participate — elections call for participation through voting, and contracts involve participation through negotiation. But adjudication is unique in that each affected party's participation takes the form of a claim, supported by proof and argument, that established legal rules entitle him to a favorable result as a matter of right. The dominant mood with which a judicial tribunal approaches its task of decision is that of seeking, in accordance with applicable rules, the single right result in each case.[3]

1. The word "tribunal" is employed here to emphasize that I am not referring to the judge, as such, but to the judicial institution as a whole. I shall employ the word "court" in the same way — to refer to the institution, very often judge *and* jury, by which torts disputes are adjudicated.

2. See Fuller, Collective Bargaining and the Arbitrator, 1963 Wis. L. Rev. 3, 19. I am indebted to Professor Fuller for the basic principles regarding the nature and limits of adjudication. See also Henderson, Judicial Review of Manufacturers' Conscious Design Choices: The Limits of Adjudication, 73 Colum. L. Rev. 1531, 1534-39 (1973).

3. I am aware of the influence in recent years of the legal realists and the tendency for lawyers today to recognize that courts do, and must, exercise discretion in deciding cases. . . . However, I would insist that my statement, hedged with the notion of "dominant mood," is accurate and useful. . . .

It follows from this characterization of the nature of the litigants' participation in adjudication that only certain kinds of problems, or at least problems which are framed in a certain way, lend themselves to being solved rationally by the adjudicative process. Essentially, these are problems to which recognized rules of decision apply [,] sufficiently limiting the range of inquiry and isolating the issues presented so that each issue may be addressed by the parties in turn, to the temporary exclusion of the other issues. There may be a relatively large number of issues to be decided which may be, and usually are, related logically to one another. But as each is addressed in argument, the litigants may temporarily exclude consideration of the others and assume a favorable result with regard to them. The common law of contracts provides some of the clearest examples of problems framed in such a way as to lend themselves readily to adjudication. Potentially, at least, a contracts case involves the resolution of one of the most unadjudicable problems imaginable—the allocation of scarce resources in society. However, the case is rendered manageable by the legal rules, recognized by courts to govern liability in contract, which operate to present the issues in a way that supports meaningful participation by the affected parties. The parties argue over whether the elements of a contract are present, not over whether a particular allocation of resources is in the overall best interest of society.[4] A relatively large number of issues may be presented—e.g., offer, lapse, acceptance, breach, excuse, and measure of recovery; but the issues will have been arranged and ordered by the law of contracts so that the parties may address them in an orderly sequence. The participation of the parties in the decision of such a case will be meaningful in the sense that they will be able to rely upon established rules of decision and to argue as a matter of right for a judgment in their favor.[5]

---

4. To be sure, considerations of reasonableness and public policy play a part in the argument and decision of even technical contract issues. . . . But only in a limited and relatively formal way are the "interests of society" recognized as part of the actual criteria for decision. . . . On a philosophical plane, it is probably true that even the most formal rule may require that the interests of society be considered in its application. . . . However, practically speaking the formality of contract law reduces the necessity of such considerations to a workably minimal level.

5. I should emphasize that in speaking of recognized rules of decision as prerequisites to adjudication, I do not intend to imply that courts are incapable of playing a role in the creation and development of such rules. Obviously, courts have traditionally, and quite properly, participated in the common law process of formulating and refining rules of decision. See generally B. Cardozo, The Nature of the Judicial Process (1921); R. Keeton, Venturing to Do Justice (1969); K. Llewellyn, The Common Law Tradition (1960). Because my quarrel is not with judicial law reform, as such, but rather with the particular nature of recent reforms in tort law, an in-depth exploration of the methods by which courts create law is beyond the scope of this paper. Suffice it to say that the phenomenon which concerns me here—i.e., the abandonment of

Most of the problems which arise every day in our society are not the subject of relatively specific rules of decision, and therefore are unadjudicable. For example, solutions to problems such as "What shall I eat for lunch today?" or "What shall my family and I do with ourselves during our next vacation?" or "How shall our society react to the physical degradation of the environment?"[6] cannot sensibly be adjudicated because of the absence of recognized rules of decision narrowing and issue isolation which would permit these problems to be addressed rationally by the affected parties urging the tribunal to arrive at a single right result. Instead of being arranged in an essentially linear manner, as are the issues in a classically legal problem, the issues, or elements, in these problems are interrelated in such a way that sensible consideration of any issue, or element, requires the simultaneous consideration of most, or all, of the others. Because adjudication requires problems the various issues and elements of which may be taken up in an orderly sequence, it follows that adjudication is not suited to solving the problems last described, at least in the absence of rules of decision which serve to narrow and isolate the issues presented.

Of course, simply because these problems do not lend themselves to being solved by adjudication does not mean that they are incapable of intelligent solution. Processes of decision which do not depend upon recognized rules of decision are perfectly suited to addressing open-ended problems of the sort with which we are here concerned. Two such processes deserve special mention: contract negotiation and the exercise of managerial authority.[7] In contract negotiation, the affected parties work out a mutually acceptable solution through the give-and-take process of arm's length bargaining. Managerial authority is exercised when one person has the authority to impose his own, discretionary solution upon those affected thereby. Once again, the difference between adjudication and these other processes of decision rests not only upon the presence in the former of relatively specific rules of decision, but also upon the very different way in which the affected parties participate. Although the exercise of managerial authority may superficially resemble adjudication, in actuality the manager acts differently from a court. Thus, the persons affected by the manager's decision might

---

formality in the rules governing negligence-based liability — poses very different, and more serious, problems than does the phenomenon of courts engaging in the continuing process of rule creation, refinement, and reform.

6. The assumption here is that there are no applicable rules of decision. Stated in this fashion, these questions are clearly unadjudicable. . . .

7. See generally Fuller, Adjudication and the Rule of Law, 1960 Proc. Am. Socy. Intl. L. 1, 5.

be given the opportunity to plead for a favorable result, in the sense that they might be allowed to exercise their vocal chords or practice their typing. But without sufficiently specific rules of decision, their participation would not be the sort guaranteed at the outset. In the end, bound by no legal rule of decision, the manager would be left to decide the case largely on his own, employing common sense, or instinct, or intuition.

To appreciate more fully the way in which legal rules function in permitting litigants to participate meaningfully in adjudication, it will be helpful to consider a concrete example of what would happen if for some reason the rules of decision failed to perform their above-described function of limiting and isolating the issues presented. Let us consider the second hypothetical example of an unadjudicable problem advanced above—i.e., the problem of planning the family vacation. In most instances, of course, families are able to work out amicable solutions to this problem by means of a combination of negotiation and managerial authority. However, it is not difficult to imagine an otherwise happy family of four (husband, wife, and two teenage children) hopelessly fragmented over such a problem. What would happen if a court were to undertake to resolve the question of where the family should go, and what it should do, on its next vacation? One can easily envision each of the four affected family members being given the opportunity in court to plead, in turn, for a result favorable to him or her. Depending upon how it were handled, such a proceeding could certainly be made to resemble adjudication, at least superficially. However, assuming that economic circumstances permitted a fairly wide range of choice, and assuming there were no more specific guide to decision than "what is best for the family,"[11] or "the most reasonable compromise," would the parties be able effectively to participate as litigants in the decision process in accordance with the classic adjudicative model advanced earlier?

Most emphatically, "No." In the absence of recognized rules which might serve as the basis for making a principled decision, the permutations and combinations of considerations which would enter into the intelligent planning even of something as relatively mundane as a family vacation would inevitably frustrate the most skillful litigant and the most conscientious decisionmaker. The issues of monetary costs, alternative dates, modes of transportation, possible

---

11. Obviously, a court might look to family custom for a sufficiently specific rule with which to decide the case. Thus, if in a particular family it were customary to have vacation plans determined by a single family member each year, the members taking turns, the issue of "Which vacation?" could be transformed into the more manageable question of "Whose turn is it this year?" However, I am assuming no such custom is available.

destinations, durations of stay, types of accommodations, etc., are all interrelated in the non-linear manner described above, and a decision with regard to any one could intelligently be made only in relation to decisions with regard to most, or all, of the others. Even if the court were to choose a single issue — total cost, for example — upon which to focus initially, any resolution of that issue would only be tentative in that it would have to be reconsidered in rationally resolving the next issue — e.g., the mode (and hence the cost) of transportation. And then the first two issues would be "upset" once again when the third issue — e.g., alternative destinations — was reached; and the first three, when the fourth was reached; and so on.[13]

In the end, the attempted adjudication of such a problem would be transformed, perhaps subtly, into something other than a trial in which litigants "present proofs and arguments to an impartial tribunal bound to apply recognized rules to reach a reasoned result." Either the court would bring pressure upon the parties (in the extreme, perhaps, by threatening to deny them any vacation at all) to work out a compromise solution among themselves; or the court would appoint one family member to make the decision for the family; or the court would assume the role of a benevolent head of the household who, though willing to listen patiently to the entreatments of those affected by the decision, would be free to reach a solution by the exercise of managerial authority, bound only by the limits of common sense. If, as is likely, the latter course were followed, the shift from the adjudicative mode to the discretionary, managerial mode would not be lost on the participants, who could be expected correspondingly to shift their arguments away from the confusing details of the various alternatives and towards appeals to the court's sympathies, prejudices, and emotions. Once this shift occurred, the parties would become supplicants rather than litigants, and whatever the court's decision in such a context, it would not be the product of adjudication.

Accepting for purposes of argument that a case of the sort just described would be unadjudicable, is the situation altered significantly if we posit a joint action by the wife and children seeking to have the court review and set aside vacation plans already arrived at by their husband-father? That is, does the case become manageable if we assume a unanimity of interest on the part of the wife and children, joined against their self-styled patriarch? Here, the court

13. Fuller employs two other examples which may be helpful: dividing an art collection between two museums on the basis of "Which division is best?" and assigning personnel to a coachless football team on the basis of "The most effective lineup." See Fuller, Adjudication and the Rule of Law, *supra* note 7, at 3-4.

would not be asked to fashion a vacation plan and impose it upon the family, but rather to review a plan already devised by the head of the household. Would this difference render the case adjudicable? The answer depends upon the legal basis of judicial review. For example, were courts to set vacation plans aside only if "irrational," the range of inquiry in our hypothetical case would probably be sufficiently limited to permit the parties to participate meaningfully as litigants in the process of judicial review. To be sure, relatively few cases would end in results favorable to plaintiffs under such an approach. But the fact remains that irrationality as a basis of judicial review and decision probably would suffice to support meaningful, orderly argument.[16] On the other hand, were the courts in such cases to uphold or set aside vacation plans made by heads of households depending on whether the plans met some test of "reasonableness" — e.g., whether the plans were "good for the family" — judicial review of vacation plans would surely retain enough open-endedness to frustrate meaningful participation by the litigants. Implicitly in every case decided on that basis, and more explicitly across a range of cases, the courts would be required to adjudicate solutions to the same intractable problem — "What is a sensible, reasonable family vacation?" — encountered in the four-party case considered earlier.[17]

Of course, cases involving the reasonableness of family vacation plans never actually get into court in our system of law. There are no generally recognized legal rules, absent contract, upon which family members may sue one another over the question of what to do with their leisure time. In effect, our system avoids these potential difficulties by adopting a "no duty" stance with regard to a wide range of intrafamily disputes. Responsibility has thus been delegated to the heads of households to exercise managerial authority in making binding decisions regarding such matters. To be sure, under some circumstances a wife may sue her husband for support; and a parent's supervision of his minor children may be suspended or terminated for abandonment or neglect; but the rules traditionally governing such disputes are relatively specific and limited in a way which avoids open-ended questions such as "What shall we do on our vacation?"

16. Courts have traditionally used similarly narrow bases of review of administrative action for the very same process reason — to reduce the open-endedness of the problems brought before them for decision.... To the extent that courts adopt narrow bases of review, they delegate a major part of the responsibility to the extrajudicial decision-making agencies. To be sure, to the extent that the extrajudicial agencies exercise discretion, "rule of law" problems may arise. But in our system, fairly wide agency discretion has long been recognized as a legitimate necessity....

17. Passing judgment on the reasonableness of conduct implies a relatively particularized standard against which to measure that conduct....

If one searches for a shorthand way of referring to the problems which are unsuited to being solved by adjudication, several possibilities present themselves. A leading writer has referred to them as "polycentric," or "many-centered," suggesting the non-linear way in which the issues in such problems are interrelated.[23] Another useful term might be "open-ended," emphasizing the lack of defined limits upon inquiry and argument. Or, observing that these problems necessarily involve the decisionmaker in the processes of planning and design, they might usefully be referred to as "planning problems," or "design problems." Or finally, returning to the need in adjudication for relatively specific rules of decision, these problems might be described as "requiring the exercise of unlimited discretion on the part of the decisionmaker."

This last way of referring to unadjudicable problems deserves further comment. Much attention has recently been given in law journals to defining "discretion" and to exploring the philosophical implications of its exercise by courts. If the term is employed to refer to the power exercised when any solution, or a wide range of solutions, are permitted by the established rules, then by definition a court must exercise discretion in attempting to solve a polycentric problem. Obviously, the distinction between decision-by-rule and decision-by-discretion is a matter of degree; the less specific and more general the rule, the greater the need for the exercise of discretion. From this, two important points follow: First, there is probably no such thing as a problem — even a classically legal problem — without a certain amount of open-endedness. Thus, it is inevitable, and no doubt desirable, that to some extent courts exercise discretion in deciding legal problems of even the most formalistic variety. What we are concerned with here are problems which tend toward the extreme on the scale of open-ended polycentricity — i.e., cases in which the dominant mode of decision is the exercise of discretion.

And second, even with regard to highly polycentric problems, the point is that adjudication is ill-suited to solving them, not that it is absolutely incapable of doing so. When pressured, courts can react in some fashion or other to the most open-ended problems. The important thing to recognize is that whenever courts yield to such pressures, the parties affected by the decisions are, in proportion to the extent to which the problems are open-ended, denied the opportunity to participate meaningfully in the decision process. Moreover, it must be recognized that this denial of the opportunity to

23. I have borrowed the term "polycentric" from Professor Fuller. See Fuller, *supra* notes 2 and 7. It appears that he borrowed the term from Michael Polanyi. See M. Polanyi, The Logic of Liberty 170-84 (1951). . . .

participate strikes at the very heart of the integrity of adjudication. If it recurs routinely, the judicial system itself may be threatened. When asked, cajoled, and finally forced to try to solve unadjudicable problems, courts will inevitably respond in the only manner possible — they will begin exercising managerial authority and the discretion that goes with it. Attempts will be made to disguise the substitution, to preserve appearances, but the process which evolves should (and no doubt eventually will) be recognized for what it is — not adjudication, but an elaborate, expensive masquerade.

II.   Expanding the Negligence Concept: Retreat from the Rule of Law

If I have succeeded in demonstrating the need for relatively specific rules of decision as prerequisites to adjudicability, then my objective in the analysis which follows ought to be fairly obvious to anyone familiar with the developments in tort law in recent years. Gradually, step-by-step, the traditional limitations upon liability in negligence, which gave sufficient specificity to the negligence concept to allow it to be the subject of adjudication, have been eliminated. With increasing frequency, courts have abandoned traditional doctrines and have embraced the idea of a single, unified, most general principle upon which to determine liability. Many torts scholars and commentators have encouraged and praised these developments. I do not. Consistent with the foregoing analysis of the limits of adjudication, I submit that this judicial expansion and purification of the negligence concept has proceeded to the point where courts are beginning routinely to confront the sorts of open-ended, polycentric problems described above. As a consequence, the integrity of the judicial process in these cases is very much threatened. I do not use the word "threatened" lightly. If anything, it understates the level of my concern. If the developments to which I refer continue unchecked, I doubt seriously that our common law system of negligence-based liability will survive to the end of this century.

In the sections which follow, I shall trace the major elements in the expansion of the negligence concept, beginning with an analysis of the ways in which traditional negligence doctrines have allowed courts to cope with potential difficulties and ending with a description of the role of torts scholarship in encouraging the potentially destructive developments of recent years. Before turning to this task, I should like to emphasize that I have no quarrel with judicial law reform, as such, nor are my objections to what is happening based upon disagreement with the substantive social goals reflected in recent developments. Instead, my concern is directed at the form these recent reforms have taken—i.e., the particular means chosen to achieve the social objectives—and the very real threat to the adjudicative process presented by its being asked to perform tasks which are clearly beyond its capabilities. The simple truth which has escaped attention in recent years is that courts are not capable of solving our society's problems, including problems of risk management, without substantial formal guidance from the law. We torts people will continue to ignore this fact only at our peril.

A. The Role of Traditional Doctrine in Rendering the Negligence Concept Adjudicable

Implicit in the foregoing statements of my thesis is a recognition that judicial implementation of the negligence concept is not necessarily, in and of itself, a bad idea. To be sure, the issue of whether a particular defendant's conduct was "reasonable under the circumstances" is precisely the type of issue which, potentially at least, threatens courts with open-ended, polycentric problems that are beyond their capacity to solve. However, courts have, until the recent acceleration of the expansionary trend referred to above, managed to cope fairly well with the potential difficulties associated with the negligence concept, and have kept the levels of polycentricity in negligence cases within tolerable limits. To better understand the manner in which recent developments and reforms threaten the integrity of the torts process, it is necessary to consider the methods by which, until recently, the negligence concept has been rendered adjudicable.

Two techniques have been developed and used by courts to cope with the potential difficulties posed by the negligence concept. On the one hand, in cases involving the individual conduct of "the man in the street" in his arm's length relations with others in the society, courts have relied heavily upon two institutions which have, as a consequence, come to occupy a centrally important position in this area of the law: the reasonable man test and the lay jury. Given the nontechnical nature of the issues presented in these cases, the moralistic, flesh-and-blood qualities of the reasonable man have provided an adequate vehicle with which to bring a semblance of order to the task of addressing the polycentric question of what modes of conduct individual members of society have a right to expect from one another. And the collective jury verdict, reached in secret and rendered without explanation, is ideally suited to disguising and submerging the analytical difficulties encountered in applying so general a concept as "reasonableness" to the facts of particular cases. Admittedly, this combined technique of couching argument in terms of how a hypothetical reasonable person would or would not have acted, and then turning the ultimate question of liability over to a jury, depends for its success upon its ability to hide from view, rather than to confront and solve, the polycentricity in these cases.[31] Nevertheless, it must be conceded that in the negligence cases in which content is given to the reciprocal duty of reasonable care owed generally by individuals in our society, the difficulties have not proven insurmountable.

However, there are limits to the effectiveness of this sort of judicial sleight of hand. Inevitably, cases arise in which a complicating factor makes it unmanageably awkward to purport to ask how a reasonable person in the defendant's position would or would not have acted. As will be developed in subsequent discussions, these factors fall within three basic categories: (1) the evaluation of a particular defendant's conduct may require an unusually complex, highly technical analysis; (2) the parties may be in a special relationship which must be taken into account by modifying the duties each owes to the other; and (3) practical considerations may compel courts to place limits upon the extent of potential liability for certain types of conduct. Whatever the complicating factor in a given case, the characteristic common to all is that the technique traditionally employed in cases involving the application of the general duty of reasonable care to arm's length transactions between strangers — i.e., obscuring the analytical difficulties by positing a hypothetical reasonable person and letting the jury decide on the basis of its collective intuition — will not work. The presence of the complicating factor and the explicit recognition that it be taken into account make it much more difficult to hide the reality that the court is being asked to plan social relations on a case-by-case basis. Given the polycentric nature of that planning task, meaningful adversary argument would be difficult, if not impossible; and the reliance interests typically at stake are too important to be left to decision by intuition, or by whim.[32]

31. The fact that legal standards tend to be thought of as minimum standards probably helps to reduce the open-endedness of the negligence issue somewhat. But as long as implementation of the negligence concept requires the balancing of the utility and risk associated with defendant's conduct under all the circumstances of each particular case (see United States v. Carroll Towing Co., 159 F.2d 169 (2d Cir. 1947)), the issue retains sufficient polycentricity to necessitate such judicial sleight of hand.

32. Admittedly, this point about the importance of the reliance interests detracts somewhat from the neutrality of my position that denial of the litigants' right to participate is, in and of itself, an unjustifiable perversion of the judicial process. However, I raise it here because it helps to underscore the practical, as well as the theoretical, implications of my thesis to torts lawyers and scholars. If the integrity of adjudication is routinely compromised, those adversely affected will undoubtedly move to replace it with some more honest and efficient mode of resolving disputes.

Therefore, courts have traditionally employed a different technique in this second category of negligence cases. Unable and unwilling to hide the open-endedness procedurally, courts have sought to avoid it substantively by introducing sufficient specificity into the rules governing liability to render the cases adjudicable. Thus, the issue for decision is not whether the defendant's conduct was reasonable under all the circumstances, but whether the requirements of relatively specific, formal rules of decision are satisfied. These rules share the functional characteristic of all common-law rules of liability — that of screening out polycentricity and rendering legal controversies adjudicable.

Although we will be exploring them in greater detail in the next section, it will be helpful to consider briefly a few concrete examples of the ways in which courts have modified the negligence concept to render it adjudicable. Perhaps the best example of a case recognized by courts from the beginning to involve potentially threatening levels of polycentricity is that involving the alleged negligence of a physician rendering treatment. Clearly, the question of whether or not a particular mode of medical treatment meets the general requirement of reasonable care presents a technically complex, open-ended, and unadjudicable planning problem. Equally clearly, the difficulties could not successfully be obscured by positing a "reasonably prudent doctor" and asking the members of the jury to negotiate or intuit their way to a sensible result. Therefore, courts have adopted a rule of liability which eliminates the potential open-endedness in malpractice cases by providing a great deal of specificity. Traditionally, defendant doctors have not been judged on the basis of whether their conduct was "unreasonable," or "inconsistent with the interests of society," but on the basis of whether their treatment failed to conform to the recognized custom of their profession. Thus, the open-ended task of planning reasonable medical care is not attempted in court, but is delegated to the collective managerial authority of the medical profession.

The clearest example of a formal modification of the general duty of reasonable care being prompted by a special relationship between the parties, in the absence of technical complexity, is the traditional judicial reaction to negligence actions brought by one close family member against another. For example, when a young child brings an action against his parents alleging them to have negligently caused him harm in the course of their exercising parental supervision, the court is confronted with the necessity of weighing the special factor of the parties' relationship in reaching a decision. To be sure, if the court were willing to treat the case as one involving the arm's length interaction of strangers, no particular problem would be presented.

But given the parent-child relationship, no such willingness can be expected. In effect, the court is being asked to adjudicate a solution to the problem of what sort of behavior can properly be demanded of parents who must balance the physical well-being of their children against the concomitant need to exert discipline and encourage development. Not surprisingly, courts have traditionally refused to address such a polycentric issue in the course of implementing the negligence concept. However, in contrast to the technique employed in the medical malpractice cases, in intrafamily negligence actions courts have simply refused altogether to attempt to adjudicate solutions to these problems of intrafamily responsibilities—parents have traditionally been granted immunity from liability to their minor children for allegedly negligent conduct. In this way, by adopting a specific rule of decision immunizing parents from negligence-based liability to their children, the task of planning reasonable parental supervision is not attempted in court, but instead is delegated to the managerial authority of individual parents.

. . . What I have sought to accomplish thus far is to present an overview of the law of negligence as it existed prior to the recent developments of concern in this article, and to suggest that much of the formal content of traditional negligence law is as explainable in terms of the necessity of courts avoiding polycentric problems as it is explainable in terms of the desirability of courts furthering the substantive objectives of society. Obviously, judicial avoidance of polycentricity is not the *only* explanation for the parameters of traditional negligence law—presumably, these limitations upon the general negligence concept—e.g., the rules governing the liability of doctors to their patients and parents to their children—would not have been adopted if they had not been perceived by courts to further the interests of society in regulating, and often encouraging, the types of conduct to which they are applied. But I submit that the relative formality of those exceptions was dictated to no less extent by the necessity to avoid trying to adjudicate answers on a case-by-case basis to questions such as "How should doctors practice medicine?" and "How should parents handle their children?" Consistent with the earlier analysis of the limits of adjudication, courts were required to adopt formal exceptions to, and modifications of, the general duty of reasonable care in order to render manageable the negligence concept in a broad range of cases in which the unadjudicability of the issues presented could not be hidden by procedural sleight of hand.

To be sure, not all traditional negligence doctrines serve the function of insulating courts from the potentially destructive open-endedness of helping to plan a rational society in the context of case-by-case adjudication of torts disputes. The rule of charitable immunity, for example, would appear to serve entirely the substantive objective of subsidizing the activities of charitable organizations — there is no technological complexity, special relationship, or need to establish practical limits upon potential liability which differentiates conduct on behalf of charity from other types of conduct. But the charitable immunity rule is unique in this respect. Behind most, if not all, of the other traditional limitations upon the general negligence concept lurk problems of social planning whose potential open-endedness would seriously threaten the integrity of the judicial process had those limitations, or others of equal formality, not been recognized. . . .

NOTES AND QUESTIONS

1. In the next section of his essay, Henderson provides examples of the three categories of cases referred to at p. 118, *supra*, that are particularly ill-suited to resolution through the process of adjudication. The first category consists of cases that involve "unusually complex, highly technical analysis." His main example of unprincipled resort to a reasonableness standard in such cases is product design defect litigation. His second category of cases involves "defining the contours of a special relationship." Here, he discusses three examples of the inadequacy of a reasonableness standard — parental liability for negligent supervision, governmental liability, and land-occupier's liability. Finally, his third category of cases in which a reasonableness standard is undesirable involves the need for "practical limits" on potential liability — cases such as emotional distress and economic loss.

Consider Henderson's arguments, and illustrative categories of cases, in light of the recent developments discussed in the Schwartz essay, pp. 71-79, *supra*. Is the "explosion" of the negligence concept documented by Schwartz entirely at odds with Henderson's thesis about the limits of adjudication? To the extent that it is, do you agree with Henderson's position?

2. Schwartz concluded: "As for the prosperity of negligence, a preliminary assessment is that judges have been strongly impressed by the ideas favoring the negligence principle and have undergone a loss of belief — whether wisely or not — in the host of reasons that have long been relied on to restrain that liability."

Have the courts simply grown indifferent to the concerns expressed by Henderson about limits on the process of adjudication? Do you agree with his warning that continued expansion of the "polycentric tendencies" of tort law is likely to lead to its demise before the end of this century?

3. Why is the determination of reasonable conduct in a negligence case — even in a nontechnical case involving everyday behavior, according to Henderson — invariably "polycentric"? Why does it axiomatically involve "judicial sleight of hand"? Do all negligence cases involve fundamentally the same kind of conflict resolution issue as the planning of a family vacation?

4. Are existing social customs on the appropriate norms of everyday behavior relevant in evaluating Henderson's thesis? Why is it that until recently, according to Henderson, the concerns he expresses about polycentric decision making have been less salient, even when courts have resorted to a generalized reasonableness standard?

5. What precisely is the relationship that Henderson sees between "open-ended problems" and the denial of meaningful participation for the parties? In a product design defect case, for example, or a parental negligence case, does a reasonableness standard deny the parties meaningful participation?

6. Reconsider his two examples of rules of specificity that "render the negligence concept adjudicable" — the medical custom rule and the intrafamily tort immunity. What are the similarities and differences between these two types of rules of specificity? Can you construct your own typology of rules of specificity in the negligence area? For further consideration of Henderson's views, see a section of his essay not included here: Henderson, Expanding the Negligence Concept: Retreat from the Rule of Law, 51 Ind. L.J. 467, 484-521 (1976).

Chapter 4

The Principles of Fault Liability in Action: The Impact of Negligence Doctrine

Most of the writing about the impact of the law of negligence has been addressed to the purpose of the fault principle rather than to its actual effect. On that score, we have already examined two "economic" versions of the role played by negligence doctrine in the early industrial era [1]

Whatever might be predicted about how the rules worked from textual analysis of tort doctrine, one obviously needs data on the operations of the system in order to assess the impact of negligence law. Unfortunately, apart from data on the industrial injury problem —where legislative commissions conducted extensive empirical investigations pursuant to the enactment of workers' compensation acts[2]—there is virtually no reliable information on the social and economic effects of the negligence system through its early maturity.

In recent years considerable attention has been given to the

1. See Gregory, Trespass to Negligence to Absolute Liability, *supra,* pp. 35-42, and Posner, A Theory of Negligence, *supra,* pp. 14-31. In another section of his article, Posner does make an effort to assess the behavioral evidence in support of his efficiency thesis. See Posner, A Theory of Negligence, 1 J. Legal Stud. 29, 73-96 (1972).
2. See W. Dodd, The Administration of Workmen's Compensation 19-21 (1936).

dimensions of the automobile accident problem, including major studies of the extent to which victims are compensated.[3] Apart from these studies, however, there is relatively little systematic analysis of the behavioral and loss-allocation effects of the negligence system.

What might we expect to learn from studies of the impact of tort rules?[4] A preliminary response would be that the outcome depends on how we define "impact." The auto accident and industrial injury studies have yielded aggregate data on the type, extent, and timing of compensation received by injury victims. Such studies contributed to our pool of knowledge about how the system works by providing more precise information on the extent to which the law of negligence actually resulted in a transfer of funds from injurers and insurers to victims. This approach to assessing impact might be called the compensation perspective.

A different perspective would raise questions about the impact of negligence law on primary behavior. Apart from determining the right to compensation on a case-by-case basis, does the rule of liability have a systematic influence on the way the injury-generating activity will be conducted in the future? Aggregate data on compensation cannot provide an answer to this question. It seems probable that the impact of liability rules differs greatly depending on the type of activity involved. Most commentators, for example, would want to distinguish between the potential deterrent effect of liability rules on drivers and on the manufacturers of defective products. Similarly, doctors and homeowners would appear almost certain to differ in their sensitivity to potential liability. In general, then, this perspective on impact raises the question of when liability rules will have an important influence on precautionary behavior.[5]

Still another perspective on the impact issue would focus on the administration of liability rules. This perspective raises the familiar question of whether textual analysis of doctrine is a reliable tool or if, on the other hand, doctrine is used to achieve unarticulated ends. If,

3. See pp. 149-150 *infra*, n.2.
4. The discussion that follows is generally applicable to the purposes served by impact studies of tort liability rules, rather than being limited to the impact of the law of negligence.
5. Thus, a key factor in assessing the comparative merits of fault and strict liability principles is whether the respective systems are likely to have a different impact on precautionary behavior. For a theoretical discussion of this issue, see Calabresi, Optimal Deterrence and Accidents, 84 Yale L. J. 656 (1975). For an early empirical effort to assess the effects, on precautionary behavior, of moving from negligence to a strict liability theory in defective product cases, see Whitford, Strict Products Liability and the Automobile Industry: Much Ado About Nothing, 1968 Wis. L. Rev. 83. On the impact of auto no-fault statutes, see E. Landes, Insurance, Liability, and Accidents: A Theoretical and Empirical Investigation of the Effects of No-fault Accidents, 25 J. L. & Econ. 49 (1982).

for example, the contributory negligence rule has been consistently ignored by juries in cases in which the plaintiff's fault is slight — as has been frequently claimed — then the impact of the doctrine is quite different from that one would discern from exclusive reliance on analysis of appellate court opinions. When we examine a claims-processing system in all its complexity — taking into account, for example, the jury, insurance adjuster, and personal injury litigator — the administrative perspective acquires a distinctly bureaucratic flavor. The participants play specialized roles that may have a unique influence on how they interpret the rules.

The readings in this chapter are addressed to the perspectives I have discussed. The excerpt from Richard Pierce's essay is principally concerned with the effect on primary behavior — the deterrent effect — produced by application of tort principles.[6] H. Laurence Ross, in contrast, explores the contemporary world of the claims adjuster in auto accident cases, focusing on the effects insurance practices have on the outcome of disputes that are formally governed by negligence doctrine. Rather than constituting an exhaustive analysis of the negligence system in action, these readings and accompanying materials are meant to suggest some of the salient characteristics of the actual impact of the law.

Encouraging Safety: The Limits of Tort Law and Government Regulation*

Richard J. Pierce, Jr.

III. Tort Law as an Aid to the Market

Tort law attempts to serve three societal goals. It reduces individual hardship by providing compensation to the victims of some accidents. It reduces the secondary costs of the accidents for which it allows compensation by spreading the costs of such accidents over a larger group. Finally, it assists the market for safety by forcing internalization of some accident costs to entities that are assumed to have the ability to reduce those costs through greater spending on safety. This analysis will focus exclusively on the safety-enhancing

6. Strictly speaking, Pierce's essay is not limited to the impact of the fault principle. However, as he points out, his analysis does in fact focus on fault liability. It should be noted that his analysis draws heavily on the first relatively comprehensive empirical analysis of the products liability system, the Interagency Task Force on Product Liability: Final Report (1978).

*Source: 33 Vand. L. Rev. 1281, 1288-1307 (1980).

goal of tort law, but the implications of the analysis are broad. If tort law does not serve the goal of encouraging spending on safety, it may be that safety enhancement should be abandoned as a goal of tort law. It is much easier to establish and administer a mechanism designed to serve only the goals of compensation and secondary accident cost reduction than it is to attempt to pursue all three goals with the same legal mechanism. . . .

A. Advantages of Tort Law

At least in theory, tort law has all the advantages of the market as a means of encouraging spending on safety. Chief among those advantages is, of course, accommodation of individual tastes for safety risks, and the resulting freedom of each individual to purchase that degree of safety that corresponds to his or her tastes. Tort law, in addition, addresses the externalities problem by forcing individuals and firms with theoretical control over safety to internalize the costs of accidents.

Internalization of accident costs can enhance the operation of the safety market in two related ways. First, forcing individuals and firms with a measure of control over accident costs to absorb those costs provides an incentive to reduce the accident rate, the consequences of accidents, or both. If the costs of accidents are calculated accurately, internalization of those costs to the entity with control over accident costs should produce an optimal level of spending to reduce accident costs. The entity bearing the costs of accidents will have an incentive to keep spending to reduce those costs up to the point at which marginal cost of accident cost avoidance equals marginal cost of accidents. Second, by forcing firms whose products or services are responsible for accident costs to absorb those costs, society forces the prices of goods and services to reflect all costs required to make them available, including costs of accidents. The higher price, in turn, reduces accident costs by inducing consumers to switch from goods and services with high accident costs to functional substitutes with lower accident costs. Failure to internalize all accident costs, then, amounts to a subsidy for high accident cost goods and services, and an indirect subsidy for accidents.

B. Limits of Tort Law

For tort law to assist the market for safety in the manner described, it must accomplish two critical subgoals. First, calculation of the costs of accidents must be accurate. That is, the accident costs internalized to activities must reflect a reasonable approximation of the value society places on avoiding various consequences of accidents. Second, tort law must internalize costs of accidents to entities that are in a position to control those costs. In the first step of this analysis, the second subgoal is assumed to be achieved, or at least achievable. The focus of inquiry is thus entirely on the manner in which tort law calculates the costs of accidents. I will analyze the extent to which tort law actually accomplishes the second subgoal after discussing the manner in which tort law calculates accident costs.

1. CALCULATING THE COSTS OF ACCIDENTS

Rather than attempting an exhaustive survey of the law of damages in tort, this analysis will be confined to an overview of the manner in which tort law values human life — one of the more difficult accident cost valuation problems. Courts often disclaim any attempt to place a value on human life when they determine damages in wrongful death actions. In a functional sense, however, courts must necessarily place an implicit value on life when they determine such damages. If tort law assists the market for safety in the manner hypothesized earlier, the level of damages assessed for a particular consequence of accidents will determine the level of spending to avoid that consequence. The courts are providing price signals to firms positioned to avoid accident costs, indicating that they should spend a particular amount of money to avoid a particular consequence of accidents.

The law of damages for wrongful death is complex. It has as many variations as there are jurisdictions whose laws govern it. For purposes of this analysis, however, it is not necessary to pursue all the subtleties of wrongful death law; it will suffice to develop an overview of the major factors that determine the magnitude of a wrongful death award and the general range of damages awarded for broad categories of lives.

There are two approaches to calculating damages for wrongful death — loss to survivors and loss to estate. The two approaches differ to some extent in concept and in the factors considered in determining damage awards. Many major elements of damages are common to both approaches, however, and the amount of damages awarded does not seem to vary greatly among jurisdictions depending upon the theory of valuation used.

The loss-to-survivors approach has been adopted in a majority of jurisdictions. In these states, the basic function of judge and jury is to determine the amount of money (or equivalent goods and services) that the victim would have provided to his dependents if his life had not been prematurely terminated. The minority loss-to-estate approach requires the judge and jury to determine the amount of money the victim would have earned and left in an estate if his life had not been prematurely terminated. For purposes of this analysis, the characteristics shared by the two approaches are far more important than their distinguishing features.

In most wrongful death actions in which the victim is an adult, the largest element of damages by far is the present value of the future net earnings of the victim. Depending upon the jurisdiction, those earnings are included to the extent they would have contributed to the support of the victim's dependents or would have been passed on to the victim's heirs. By either measure, this makes certain characteristics of the victim extremely important in calculating the cost of premature loss of life.

For people who have already begun a career, the measure of damages is related to age. Other things being equal, a younger victim will have a future earnings stream greater than an older victim, and thus a larger damage award. This valuation may be consistent with prevailing social values. The amount of damages also relates to the future earning power of the victim, with the result that the life of a salaried executive is valued more highly than that of a factory worker. It is at best questionable whether this distinction is consistent with prevailing social values. One must wonder whether society really wants to place no value on the life of a person who has no future earning power or to spend five or ten times as much to protect the lives of highly paid executives as is spent to protect the lives of laborers. Of course, the origin and persistence of this distinction as a basis for valuing life in the tort law context is almost certainly attributable to its consistency with the compensation goal.

Another factor that can greatly influence the valuation of life in the tort system is the existence and characteristics of the dependents of the victim. In most jurisdictions, there are no damages if there are no dependents, and the future earnings component of damages stops accruing whenever, as in the case of a dependent minor child, the cessation of dependency status can be predicted at some future time. Again, the goal of compensation provides a rationale for tying the value of life to the existence and status of the victim's dependents. Viewing tort law as a means of encouraging spending on safety, however, the relationship between the existence of dependents and the implicit valuation of life in tort law does not seem to reflect society's values. Surely society does not want to provide a price signal indicating that the life of a person with no dependents has no value.

Traditionally, so-called "nonmonetary" factors were not considered in calculating damages for wrongful death. In recent years, a distinct trend toward recognition of nonmonetary factors, such as loss of companionship and even mental anguish, has emerged. In the bulk of modern cases involving wrongful death of adult wage earners, however, the present value of expected future support to surviving dependents continues to be a major component of damages, and the amount awarded for nonmonetary factors remains modest in all but a few highly publicized cases.

Some of the irrationalities inherent in tort calculations emerge from an analysis of the manner in which damages are determined, but the true anomalies become starkly apparent when the results of that process are analyzed. Consider the wrongful death of a child. While the adult wage earner's life is assigned a relatively high value in most cases, the life of a child is given little value in tort law. The general approach to determining damages for wrongful death should actually yield a negative value for the life of a child, but judges and juries usually "cheat" in this area and find some basis to assign a positive value to the life of a child. Still, the results of the process imply a very low value for the life of a child. The average award for wrongful death of a child was determined in a recent study to be $28,355.[28] Thus, the signal given a firm is that it should spend up to, but no more than, $28,355 on safety per child's life saved by its expenditures. It is inconceivable that society actually desires to establish a market in safety that assigns such an absurdly low value to the life of a child. This valuation also is absurd relative to other implicit valuations in tort law. Indeed, the average damage award in a personal injury case is $181,401,[29] and the average damage award for wrongful death of an adult male is $240,228.[30] It is unlikely that society really wants to encourage firms to spend six times as much to avoid personal injury to an adult and ten times as much to avoid the death of an adult male as it spends to avoid the death of a child. Nevertheless, by merging the compensation decision with the liability decision, and then selecting compensation as the more important goal, the tort system has precisely this effect.

The argument might be made that the anomalous relative values placed on life versus serious injury, life of a child versus life of an adult wage earner, etc. are of no great importance in determining whether tort law creates a rational and effective market for safety because firms have very limited ability to make decisions on safety that reflect fine distinctions among the potential consequences of accidents. In other words, it is practically impossible for a firm to take

28. Finkelstein, Pickrel & Glasser, The Death of Children: A Nonparametric Statistical Analysis of Compensation for Anguish, 74 Colum. L. Rev. 884, 890 (1974).

29. Interagency Task Force on Product Liability: Final Report II-56 (1978) [hereinafter cited as Final Report].

30. Million Dollar Jury Awards, Natl. L.J., June 18, 1979, at 1, 12-13.

measures that avoid serious injury or death to wage earners without also protecting children. If this view is correct, it follows that irrational differences in the valuation of particular consequences of accidents do not create functional aberrations in the market for safety as long as the aggregate valuation of the consequences of accidents is rational.

There are two reasons why this defense of current tort law cannot be accepted. First, there are many circumstances in which firms can determine their optimum level of spending on safety based upon the specific type of individual whose safety is at stake or the particular type of injury affected by a safety decision. A clear example is the manufacture of children's clothing. The rational children's clothing manufacturer can ignore the tort law signals concerning the relatively high value attached to serious injuries or death of an adult wage earner and base its decisions on expenditures for features such as resistance to fire entirely upon the $28,355 value tort law places on the life of a child. Firms often can choose as well between risks of injury and risks of death. For instance, a toy manufacturer might spend money to redesign a toy so that its edges cannot cut a child, but decline to analyze the toxicity of a toy part that is small enough to ingest. The tort system's relative valuations of injury versus loss of life of a child make this decision rational. Indeed, there are many broad areas in which tort law's bizarre relative valuations of accident costs have a material effect upon safety spending decisions. For instance, manufacturers of airplanes, intercity buses, and school buses confront very different tort-derived incentives to spend on safety because of the wide disparities in the average earning capacities and dependency status of their respective passengers.

The second reason for rejecting the defense of tort law's methods of valuing accidents is even more fundamental. There is a consistent downward bias in tort law valuations of important consequences of accidents, such as loss of life. By failing to include as elements of damages such very real costs as the grief of relatives and friends, tort law understates accident costs and thereby creates insufficient incentives for safety.

2. INTERNALIZING COSTS IN TORT LAW

In order to provide an effective market for safety, tort law must both calculate accident costs and internalize those costs to individuals and entities that can control the magnitude of accident costs either by avoiding accidents altogether or by reducing their consequences. The preceding discussion focused solely on the quantification process. The next step in evaluating the effectiveness of tort law is to analyze the actual cost internalization process. Theoretically, tort law forces internalization of all accident costs considered in the damage calculation process to individuals or entities who, by virtue of a judicial finding of "fault," are believed to be in a position to control accident costs. Empirical evidence demonstrates conclusively that the actual internalization process differs dramatically from theory.

There are many ways in which tort law either fails to internalize accident costs in the first instance or permits those costs to be reexternalized. A major source of tort law's failure to internalize accident costs is simply the victim's failure to make a claim for compensation. In most cases in which the victim bears the accident costs, the victim externalizes those costs through social welfare programs and first party insurance. The possible explanations for the failure to make claims include the difficulty of proving fault, the difficulty of proving causation, the high transaction costs of the tort system, availability of compensation from other sources (first party insurance, social welfare programs, etc.), potential inability to collect from a judgment-proof defendant, the belief that it is wrong to sue someone unless they have done something "bad," and ignorance of the fact that the victim's injury was caused by some other party or that compensation is available from that party. Many of these factors will be discussed in subsequent sections of this Article. I know of no way to isolate the effect of each, but several studies demonstrate that their combined effect is to undermine significantly the tort system's cost internalization function.

Only a small fraction of personal injuries arising from various causes actually yield a claim for compensation. Ten percent of product-related injuries give rise to claims for compensation.[32] The analogous figure for injuries to patients resulting from the therapeutic process is one percent,[33] and, when the tort system was still functioning in the employment context, between six and thirty percent of employment-related injuries resulted in claims for compensation.[34] These figures may tend to overstate the extent of externalization of accident costs attributable to victim failure to file a claim, since high cost accidents are more likely to result in a claim for compensation than low cost accidents. It is apparent, however, that failure to file a claim is a major source of externalization of accident costs in the tort system.

Costs are further externalized by the tendency of many victims to

32. Final Report, at VII-212-13.
33. Bernzweig, Some Comparisons Between the Medical Malpractice and Products Liability Problems in Interagency Task Force on Product Liability: Selected Papers 430-31 (1976).
34. J. Chelius, Workplace Safety and Health: The Role of Workers' Compensation (1977), at 19.

settle for compensation well below the actual costs of an accident. This pattern results from a combination of factors, including the victim's desperate and immediate need for money, the uncertainty of success in pursuing a tort remedy, the cost of processing a tort claim, and, above all, the amount of time required to obtain any compensation through judicial resolution of a contested claim. The victim (or the victim's survivor) often has little choice but to be content with a combination of benefits from external sources, such as social welfare and first party insurance, supplemented by a few thousand dollars in settlement of a disputed tort claim.

Another major source of cost externalization is the difficulty of proving fault. Although tort law has undergone a number of changes in recent decades designed to ease the burden of proving fault, the tort system nevertheless remains based almost exclusively upon fault in some form.[36] The magnitude of externalization attributable directly to the difficulty of proving fault can in part be seen by comparing the number of particular accidents found by an objective research study to be caused by third party violation of a safety rule with the number of similar accidents in which costs were actually shifted to a third party based upon a finding of fault. Comparative data suggest that fault is actually proven in only about ten percent of incidents involving the fault of third parties.[37]

Persuasive anecdotal evidence that the difficulty of proving fault externalizes a high percentage of accident costs is available in the literature on the tort litigation concerning the prescription drug MER/29.[38] Over 5000 people suffered serious injury, including blindness, from using MER/29. Approximately 1500 victims filed tort claims against the manufacturer. The principal factual issue contested in the litigated cases was whether the manufacturer either negligently or intentionally failed to notify consumers and the Food and Drug Administration of test results that the manufacturer knew, or should have known, indicated the potential for serious adverse side effects. Most of the cases were settled based on the results of a few reported cases. In a majority of the reported cases, the manufacturer escaped liability based upon findings either that the drug raised no risks or that the manufacturer had no reason to know of such risks. Yet, subsequent studies and litigation established beyond doubt the

36. The so-called strict liability in tort adopted for product-related injuries is merely a fault-based system in which the method of determining fault differs from that employed in traditional negligence actions....

37. R. Smith, The Occupational Safety and Health Act 66-67 (1976)....

38. For descriptions of the MER/29 incident and resulting litigation, see M. Mintz, By Prescription Only 230-47d (2d ed. 1967); Merrill, Compensation for Prescription Drug Injuries, 59 Va. L. Rev. 1, 22-23, 40-43 (1973); Rheingold, The MER/29 Story — An Instance of Successful Mass Disaster Litigation, 56 Calif. L. Rev. 116, 117-21 (1968).

knowledge and fault of the manufacturer. In one of the later reported civil cases, the manufacturer was found to have directed its employees in knowingly, maliciously, and recklessly failing to disclose serious risks. In addition, the company and several of its employees ultimately were indicted and pleaded nolo contendere to criminal charges of submitting false data to, and withholding data from, the Food and Drug Administration.

The difficulty of proving causation is another major reason that accident costs tend to be externalized. Indeed, causation problems have led to an almost complete breakdown in the tort system as a mechanism for internalizing accident costs in several important areas. Diseases caused in part by the toxic properties of chemicals contained in products or in the workplace rarely form the basis for successful tort claims. The judicial system cannot contend with causation problems in the context of consequences that have long developmental periods and whose etiology suggests the likelihood of joint causation. More generally, the tort system has extreme difficulty coping with statistical indications of causation. There are many circumstances in which a rational decision-maker can go no farther than to conclude, for example, that forty percent of accidents of the type at issue are caused by one factor and forty percent by another. In this large class of accidents, the judicial system typically externalizes accident costs by refusing recovery to the victim who, in turn, externalizes the bulk of the costs through first party insurance or social welfare programs.

Of those accident costs internalized initially through the tort system, the vast majority are reexternalized through liability insurance. In theory, liability insurance assists tort law in achieving its secondary loss minimization goal, while compromising only slightly the safety enhancement goal. As long as the cost of insurance is spread in proportion to the varying risks created by particular activities and firms, the availability of liability insurance should not frustrate the goal of encouraging safety. The problem in practice is that insurance costs reflect only crudely, if at all, variations in risks of accidents among firms and activities.

The recent interagency study of product liability insurance provides extensive data demonstrating the high degree of accident cost externalization produced by liability insurance. Only a small fraction of product liability insurance is made available at a premium calculated on the basis of the risks associated with the particular insured.[44] Indeed, a substantial portion of liability insurance is made available only through comprehensive all-risk policies that provide no basis for determining the premium associated with various risks.

44. Only very large companies are able to purchase insurance at premiums that

Although most insurance companies maintain that premiums reflect differences in the risks of accidents, most firms that purchase liability insurance believe there is no relationship between the reduction of product-related accident risks and the liability insurance premium they must incur. Moreover, studies have been unable to detect a correlation between accident cost avoidance measures and liability insurance premiums except in the case of very large firms and a few common products. Thus, when the liability insurance mechanism is added to the tort system, tort liability appears in most instances to internalize costs to such a large group (all purchasers of products liability insurance or, in some cases, all members of a large industry) that the effect is reexternalization. As a result, the incentive for safety theoretically created by the tort system is all but eliminated.

The explanation for the high degree of cost reexternalization lies in the actuarial techniques necessary to relate insurance premium costs to accident costs. "Loss-rating" an insurance policy requires considerable historical data on the cost of claims arising from a particular firm or activity. The tort system produces accident cost data very slowly because of the low claim rate relative to the accident rate and the slow progress of tort litigation through the judicial system. Moreover, historical data on accident costs as measured by the tort system are poor predicters of the future accident costs of a firm or activity. The rules for determining liability and damages in fields such as product liability law are so complex, and the results of litigation so unpredictable, that litigation results are actuarially useless until a great many cases have been concluded. In terms of both liability and, perhaps even more importantly, the magnitude of the award, actuaries perceive so little relationship between the results of past tort litigation and factors that can form the basis for predictions concerning future awards that an enormous amount of historical data is required to loss-rate a policy. Yet the paucity of claims and the slow pace of tort litigation retard development of an adequate data base. As a result, loss-rating is possible for only very large companies or for broad activities, such as an entire manufacturing industry.

Many aspects of the tort system thus combine to externalize accident costs: inadequate valuation of the consequences of many accidents, failure to make a claim, inability to prove fault, inability to

---

are "loss-rated," that is, determined with specific reference to the risks associated with the particular firm, Final Report, at V-12. Approximately another ten percent of product liability insurance coverage is available at premiums calculated with reference to specific product lines. This tends to be available only for a limited number of common, low-risk products. Id. at V-10, 11. The basis for calculating the premiums for most product liability coverage is obscure and appears to bear only a remote relationship to specific risks. Id. at V-9-12.

prove cause, and liability insurance. When the interrelationships of these powerful externalizing forces are considered, it becomes clear that tort law actually serves the goal of creating a market for safety very poorly indeed. For a system whose transaction costs are approximately equal to the total amount of compensation provided, tort law must be considered an extraordinarily inefficient and ineffective method by which to obtain a rational level and pattern of spending on safety.

C. Future Effectiveness of Tort Law

It is difficult to be sanguine about the future of tort law as an efficient and effective means of encouraging safety. Indeed, there are good reasons to expect that its current appalling inefficiency and ineffectiveness will become more pronounced over time. Tort law is becoming vastly more complicated with the emergence of comparative negligence. This increased complexity will have two effects. It will increase the transaction costs of the tort system, and it will confound the actuarial process by introducing additional sources of predictive uncertainty. The first will reduce the efficiency of the system, while the second will increase the degree of reexternalization through liability insurance. New social welfare programs now under serious consideration, such as national health insurance, will externalize an even greater proportion of accident costs, thus further reducing the effectiveness of tort law as a means of encouraging safety.

D. The Utility of Incremental Changes in Tort Law

Most changes in tort law now under consideration, such as changes in statutes of limitations or tinkering with rules of liability or damages, would have virtually no effect on the problem of inadequate safety incentives. Minor palliatives cannot touch the endemic inadequacies in the tort system. It is possible to conceive, however, of more drastic changes in tort law that, at least in theory, could improve its effectiveness while retaining the present institutional structure. For example, liability insurance could be severely limited or abolished, the basis for recovery could be broadened substantially to approximate a no-fault methodology, and damages could be calculated so that the consequences of accidents are translated into costs that reflect more accurately societal values. In theory, this combination of changes would eliminate the defects in the tort system that cause it to be ineffective as a mechanism for encouraging safety. Unfortunately, there are many reasons to believe that such a total revamping of tort law would fall far short of its theoretical promise, and that further, it would create a whole new set of collateral problems.

One reason that such dramatic changes might not succeed is that individual decisionmakers tend to emphasize the short-term consequences of their decisions and to deemphasize the long-term consequences, a phenomenon known as the "Faust effect." The existence of this "effect" has long been recognized by students of accident law. It explains the tendency of individuals to discount at an irrational level many safety risks whose consequences are not likely to be manifested until some time after exposure to the risk. There is growing evidence that firms are also materially affected by this tendency. As the cost of product liability insurance has increased in recent years, many firms have "gone bare" — that is, they have simply stopped insuring. Thus, rather than responding to increased accident costs by attempting to reduce those costs, as tort theory anticipates, these firms have chosen to avoid all current costs of accidents and to expose themselves to staggering potential future costs. The data also suggest an explanation for this phenomenon. The "going bare" syndrome is widespread among, and limited to, small and medium-sized firms. Many of these firms could not possibly cover a major damage award or a cluster of large awards resulting from a particular activity or product. Given the mortality rate for such firms and the protection of personal assets of firm owners afforded by the corporate form and bankruptcy laws, it may be perfectly rational for them to ignore the potential future costs of accidents. In any event, a large proportion of small and medium-sized firms play the role of Faust to the extent that they will not respond to speculative future tort liability by making large current expenditures on accident cost avoidance. Indeed, the same study that showed a high percentage of small and medium-sized firms "going bare" found that, although insurance costs and tort awards are increasing, very few small and medium-sized firms have taken measures to increase the safety of their products.[57]

The limited cognitive ability of decisionmakers within firms also suggests that the potential advantages of revamping tort law would not be fully realized. For increased exposure to potential tort liability to produce a corresponding increase in accident cost avoidance expenditures, it is necessary to assume that individual firms have sufficient knowledge of the hazardous characteristics of their products and activities to be aware of the risks they are incurring and to act accordingly. Again, particularly for small and medium-sized firms, this assumption is not valid. For instance, a small chemical firm has

57. Final Report, at IV-4.

only limited toxicological expertise. If the firm cannot predict future costs, it surely cannot be expected to take measures to avoid or reduce those costs.

Finally, causation problems will continue to undermine the practical advantages of tort law revision. Even if "fault" is eliminated as a criterion, the courts will still face the difficult task of determining causation in each case. This creates two significant problems. First, individualized determinations of causation would continue to produce high transaction costs, high uncertainty in predicting future tort costs, and delay in handling claims. Each of these would impair the efficiency and effectiveness of the revised tort system. Second, decentralized individual determinations of cause would not internalize accident costs to the entity with the greatest ability to control accident costs. Professor Calabresi has demonstrated persuasively that there is a poor correlation between judicial determinations of fault and identification of parties in the best position to control the costs of accidents.[58] This poor correlation is attributable to three factors. First, many parties who are found to be at fault lack the information or cognitive capabilities to predict accident costs. Therefore, they cannot control future accident costs. Second, the fault that is often the basis for determining liability is simply an instance of routine individual carelessness or inattention, the occurrence and frequency of which cannot be affected by expectations of liability. Third, tort litigation frequently does not even bring before the court the party who is in the best position to control the costs of accidents. This third factor obviously is equally true of causation, and there are reasons analogous to the first and second factors that suggest a low correlation between judicial determinations of causation and identification of the entity best positioned to control the costs of various types of accidents.[62] Moreover, decentralized individual determinations of cause still could not cope with the recurring problem of statistical cause and joint cause alluded to earlier.

---

58. G. Calabresi, The Cost of Accidents (1970), at 244-65.

62. Consider, for example, the manner in which costs might be allocated for typical motorcycle accidents. The largest class of motorcycle accidents result from failure of the operator of an automobile to yield the right-of-way to a motorcycle. The fault-based system assigns the costs of these accidents to individual automobile operators who, in turn, externalize them to all automobile operators through liability insurance. Even without externalization through insurance, placing the costs of these accidents on the automobile operators involved is unlikely to have any effect on the incidence of such accidents. In-depth studies of the automobile operators involved in such accidents demonstrate that they simply do not see the motorcycle. See They Have Eyes to See, Cycle World, Oct. 1979, at 21. Obviously, no deterrent can be effective in encouraging automobile operators to yield the right-of-way to something they do not see. Instructing the court to ignore fault and to focus on causation in its classic sense would not be likely to improve the results. The court probably still would find that the

Even if modifying tort law would not produce a truly effective market for safety, the changes suggested might produce enough improvement to make them worth undertaking were it not for a number of collateral problems that could also be expected to result from such a revamping of tort law. Taking the most obvious disadvantage first, prohibition of or stringent restrictions on liability insurance would substantially sacrifice the tort law goal of reducing the secondary costs of accidents. Very high dislocation costs could attend the elimination of liability insurance as a cost-spreading device. Yet, the reexternalization effect of insurance is one of the main evils of the present system that the proposed changes are designed to correct.

The other potential disadvantages of tort law revision are less obvious but, in a sense, are more fundamental. Because many products and activities that are dangerous are also beneficial, there is a distinct possibility that forcing complete internalization of accident costs to those entities that can best control accident costs would *not* produce optimum allocation of resources in important segments of the economy. Consider, for example, a hypothetical prescription drug. Assume the drug is only used to treat a serious condition that is impervious to any other form of treatment. The drug is effective for some people, but it has fatal side effects for others. The net effect of the drug is to save the lives of three people for every one it takes. Assume also that the modified tort system values each life at $500,000. Under the modified tort system, the manufacturer of the drug almost certainly would be identified as the party with the best opportunity to control the costs of accidents associated with the drug, so the costs of the loss of life associated with the drug would be internalized to the manufacturer. In theory, this internalization should produce an optimal allocation of resources, but in practice the effect probably would be to force off the market a drug that saves three lives for every one it takes—a result that would be hard to defend under any concept of optimal resource allocation.

With full internalization of the accident costs of the drug, the cost of the drug would be approximately $166,667 for each patient.[64] At

---

automobile operator's conduct "caused" the accident. Even if the court found that the motorcycle operator's conduct "caused" the accident, allocating costs of such accidents to motorcyclists would be unlikely to reduce the incidence or costs of such accidents. The motorcyclist will not modify his conduct to avoid accidents of this type for several reasons. First, he can externalize most of the costs of accidents through a combination of insurance and social welfare benefits. Second, and more fundamentally, the motorcyclist is unlikely to be aware that lack of visibility of motorcycles to automobile operators creates a large risk of accidents. . . .

64. I am assuming that the costs of manufacturing the drug are negligible compared with the accident costs the manufacturer is required to bear.

this price, very few individuals could afford to purchase the drug. Even though society has chosen to value each life affected by the drug at $500,000, it is unlikely that any potential lender would place even one-third that value on most individuals' future income stream as collateral. Because the manufacturer is unable to internalize the beneficial externalities associated with the drug and is forced by the tort system to internalize its accident costs, society's resources are seriously misallocated. This misallocation could only be avoided either by forcing internalization of a lower proportion of accident costs or by providing a subsidy to account for the drug's beneficial externalities.

Even the present system, with its only partial cost internalization, may result in a serious misallocation of resources when the activity in question produces substantial beneficial externalities. One manifestation of this phenomenon is the extraordinarily high cost of malpractice insurance for surgeons and anesthesiologists that has temporarily jeopardized the continued availability of surgery in some jurisdictions. Many more misallocations could be expected if tort law were reformed in a manner that forced greater internalization of accident costs, since there are beneficial externalities associated with most activities.

At present, tort law attempts, through its rules for determining fault, to avoid misallocation of resources that results from the combination of full internalization of accident costs and large beneficial externalities. Judge Hand's formula for determining whether conduct is negligent[66] and the Comment k exception to product liability[67] should produce a finding of no liability, and hence, no internalization of accident costs in circumstances when existence of large beneficial externalities makes full internalization of accident costs undesirable. Here again, however, theory and fact diverge. Even assuming that the legal rules for liability focused the attention of the decisionmakers on the right question,[68] it is unlikely that individual judges and juries could determine whether a product or service creates substantial beneficial externalities. Moreover, decentralized decisionmaking cannot deal with the common situation in

---

66. "[I]f the probability be called P; the injury, L; and the burden, B; liability depends upon whether B is less than L multiplied by P...." United States v. Carroll Towing Co., 159 F.2d 169, 173 (2d Cir. 1947).

67. "There are some products which, in the present state of human knowledge, are quite incapable of being made safe for their intended and ordinary use. These are especially common in the field of drugs.... Such a product, properly prepared, and accompanied by proper directions and warning, is not defective, nor is it *unreasonably* dangerous." Restatement (Second) of Torts §402A, Comment k (1965) (emphasis in original).

68. Judge Hand's formula requires simply a cost-benefit analysis. Thus, it does

which the existence of beneficial externalities requires a reduction of the amount of accident costs that are internalized to an activity, rather than complete avoidance of accident cost internalization. In any event, elimination of fault as a criterion for tort compensation would require creation of some new means of dealing with this potentially significant problem.

Another related reason for skepticism as to the desirability of modifying tort law to obtain full internalization of accident costs lies in the potential foreign trade effects of such a change. It is, of course, axiomatic in comparative advantage theory that all nations benefit from free international trade. Significant differences among nations in the degree of internalization of the costs of products, however, can distort the operation of comparative advantage theory. If the United States forces internalization of a much higher percentage of accident costs associated with its products than do other countries, United States exports may decrease while its imports increase even for products in which the United States has an initial comparative cost advantage. With a system that produces full internalization of accident costs, this distortive effect on foreign trade could become substantial. Even with the partial internalization of the current tort system, product liability insurance rates of fifteen percent of total manufacturing costs have been reported for some products.[70]

In summary, it is not clear that a major overhaul of tort liability and damage rules would create a more effective market for safety. In fact, as long as the present institutional structure of tort decisionmaking is retained, it is likely that such a revision would fall well short of its theoretically attainable goals and would cause significant collateral problems. A major source of the inefficiency and ineffectiveness of tort law — decentralized decisionmaking in individual situations — would remain. . . .

NOTES AND QUESTIONS

1. In assessing the safety incentives of tort law, Pierce is highly critical of the rules used in calculating the cost of accidents. He suggests that these costs ought to reflect "a reasonable approximation

---

ask the right question: whether total societal costs associated with a safety precaution are greater or less than total societal benefits. Unfortunately, in practice courts tend to focus only on the immediate burdens of safety precautions on the parties before the court and to ignore broader burdens on society. This has the same effect as ignoring beneficial externalities associated with activities. Comment k does not even ask the right question. It suggests no need to inquire into the accident costs or the beneficial externalities associated with a product that is "unavoidably unsafe."

70. Final Report, at VI-27.

of the values society places on avoiding various consequences of accidents." Reconsider his discussion of wrongful death awards, at pp. 127-130. Do you agree with this criticism? Is his argument equally applicable to cases of damages in nonfatal cases? Is the concept of "societal value attached to human life" intelligible? As Note 6, below, indicates, Pierce would rely on average valuations drawn from empirical studies of risk-taking behavior in situations such as driving and the workplace—studies which, he candidly reports, yield valuations of life ranging from $166,000 to $2,600,000. Are such studies likely to yield a more satisfying approximation of the value of human life than current tort litigation techniques?

2. Pierce discusses a number of ways in which the tort system "externalizes" the cost of accidents by failing to compensate the victims of injury-related activities. Is it necessarily the case that injury costs are externalized by leaving them on accident victims? Does it depend on how "activities" are defined? Does it turn on whether the victims receive benefits from collateral sources?

3. Drawing on data from the Interagency Task Force on Product Liability: Final Report, Pierce indicates that even those accident costs initially internalized by the tort system are frequently "reexternalized" by the rating practices of liability insurers. Is this finding likely to have relevance for other major categories of tort cases, such as auto accidents, medical malpractice, and household injuries?

4. Other findings from the Task Force report, such as the propensity of smaller firms to operate without insurance and the lack of technological sophistication of such enterprises, leave Pierce deeply skeptical about the potential allocative efficiency of the tort system. With respect to each of his arguments, is the products liability area likely to raise distinctive issues about the efficacy of tort law?

5. Why does the tort system fail to take account of the "beneficial externalities" associated with products like prescription drugs? Is the problem one of doctrinal deficiency or institutional incapacity? Why does it matter whether the courts are sensitive to the social value of injury-causing products?

6. Following his critique of the tort system, Pierce analyzes direct regulation of safety and concludes that standard setting, either by cost-benefit analysis or feasibility criteria, is a similarly flawed approach. See Pierce, Encouraging Safety: The Limits of Tort Law and Government Regulation, 33 Vand. L. Rev. 1281, 1308-1319. He then proposes a system that would feature a single federal agency in charge of both "safety enhancement and compensation." Id. at 1319-1330. The agency would award compensation for virtually all unintended injuries "through generic formulas similar to those used for

workers' compensation." It would be funded by assessments against injury-causing firms, industries, and activities, on the basis of aggregate data collected in processing claims for compensation.

The cost internalization goal, however, would be treated as distinct from the compensation goal. Thus, while aggregate claims data would be used to identify cost-generating activities, they would not be used to determine actual cost assessments. Rather, "a generic set of accident consequence valuations would be used to determine the aggregate accident costs associated with any industry or activity." These generic valuations would, in turn, be based on "average market values of life," which would be established by assessing empirical studies of risk-taking behavior in various socioeconomic settings.

Does such a system seem likely to achieve the goals of compensation and cost-minimization better than the tort system? For an earlier proposal of a somewhat similar mechanism for replacing the tort system, see Franklin, Replacing the Negligence Lottery: Compensation and Selective Reimbursement, 53 Va. L. Rev. 774 (1967). These issues are considered in detail in Chapter Seven, in the context of evaluating auto no-fault and social insurance schemes.

Settled Out of Court: The Social Process of Insurance Claims Adjustment*

H. Laurence Ross

The Tort Law in Action

In the insured claim, it is the adjuster's task to evaluate the case according to the criteria of formal law, and to negotiate a settlement that will be justified in the light of these criteria and avoid the expensive formal procedure of courtroom trial.

The formal law of torts specifies that someone injured in an automobile accident may recover from a driver if he can show, by the preponderance of evidence, that the driver violated his duty to conduct the vehicle in the manner of an ordinarily prudent person. The driver, however, need pay nothing if he in turn can show by the preponderance of evidence that the claimant also violated a similar duty. Various qualifications apply, depending on the jurisdiction. For example, a governmental or charitable organization may be excused

*Source: 233-243 (1970).

from paying claims, or a husband may not be able to recover from his wife, or a guest from his host. In some exceptional states payment may be reduced rather than eliminated where the claimant's negligent behavior has contributed to the accident.* The formal law prescribes a recovery sufficient to make the claimant "whole," repaying in cash for everything he has lost in the accident (regardless of whether or not some other source such as health insurance or sick leave has also compensated for the accident-related losses), and for pain, suffering and inconvenience in addition to more tangible losses.

The formal criteria might lead to the expectation that relatively few people injured in an automobile accident would receive reparation. Most drivers may be thought to be ordinarily prudent people, and even where one is not, formal law embodies the difficulty of affirmative proof of unreasonable behavior. Moreover, to the extent that numbers of negligent drivers are on the highway, an equivalent number of negligent claimants might be expected, who ought to recover nothing. On these assumptions one would expect most claimants to be denied completely, the balance recovering something more than their economic losses. In contrast, the actual picture of recoveries shows that most people injured in traffic accidents are paid, and those who are seriously injured are paid in the large majority of cases. The amount of recoveries fits the formal model only for small claims; where injuries are serious, most claimants fail to recover even their out-of-pocket losses.

The reason the distribution predicted by knowledge of the formal law does not fit the observed distribution of claims settlements is that other factors influence the settlement process. Some of these have been described in this book. Among them are the attitudes and values of the involved personnel, organizational pressures, and negotiation pressures. They exert a direct effect on the enormous majority of bodily claims. As Fleming James indicates:

> The settlement practices of insurance companies constitute another factor which has a great impact on the actual operation of tort law today. The vast majority of accident claims never get into any stage of litigation; only an infinitesimal proportion of them ever come to trial. The "law" that directly governs the disposition of most tort claims, then, consists in these practices. The legal rules affect most cases only to the extent that they are reflected in the process of settlement.

The personalities—attitudes and opinions—of the personnel are perhaps the least significant of the factors mentioned. Generally speaking, adjusters approach their work with conventional business values. Other things equal, they will seek low, conservative settle-

*Comparative negligence has now replaced contributory negligence in the majority of states.

ments, although a sense of fairness makes them disinclined to settle for less than net out-of-pocket losses in a case that is deemed to warrant any settlement at all. The goal of paying no more and no less than these tangible losses is often achieved in routine cases settled directly with the claimant. This is a settlement that many adjusters would characterize as ideal. However, many settlements are made for amounts quite different from the ideal, reflecting pressures and constraints of the employee role and the negotiating situation. Personal dispositions may affect the style with which an adjuster responds to external demands, but they seem to be relatively unimportant in determining the outcome of claims.

Organizational pressure would seem to be a more important factor than personality in affecting the outcome of claims. Pressures from the supervisory structure can even lead adjusters to violate some of the most important company rules, such as those forbidding nuisance payments. Perhaps unexpectedly, the most insistent of organizational pressures is not to keep payments low, but to close files quickly. The closing of files represents for adjusters something of the same kind of central goal as the attainment of good grades represents for the college student, or number of placements for an employment counselor, or a high clearance rate for policemen. As explained... elsewhere, the chief effect of this pressure on the behavior of claims men is to increase the number and raise the level of payments. This effect is unexpected and unrecognized by many claims department executives, who are insulated from the front lines by organizational distance, but it is understandable as a means to alleviate specific and recurring pressures experienced by adjusters from their supervisors. The pressure to close files quickly also causes adjusters to simplify their procedures of investigation, as well as their thinking in evaluation. Although the textbooks and manuals propose elaborate and time-consuming routines, the case load prescribes short cuts and approximations. There is a strong parallel here with the behavior of police detectives noted by Skolnick, who deliberately overlook many reported crimes and accept numbers of admittedly false confessions in order to raise the rate of crimes cleared by arrest. Skolnick comments:

> The behavior of the detectives involved should not be seen as an instance of corruption or even of inefficiency. On the contrary, their actions are to be interpreted as an unanticipated consequence of their superiors' development of a method for controlling their efficiency. The response of the detective to the clearance rate is easily understandable. It stems from a sociological tendency manifesting itself in all work organizations: the worker always tries to perform *according to his most concrete and specific understanding of the control system*. That is, in general, workers try to please those supervising *routine activities*.

Another important factor affecting settlement outcomes, particularly with represented claimants, is the medium of negotiation. Negotiation is a social process with a strong implicit rule structure and a repertory of tactics different from those available in litigation. In the case at hand, the most effective tactics threaten recourse to the expense of formal trial, and these threats can be nailed down with commitments. Bodily injury claims negotiators are in roughly the same position as negotiators for two nations disputing a border city, where all involved know that each party can obliterate a major interior city of the other. In such a situation there is strong pressure for compromise, as opposed to an all-or-none disposition. It does not matter much that the formal law prescribes the latter.

As a consequence of these and other pressures, the tort law in action is differentiated from the formal law by its greater simplicity, liberality, and inequity. The concepts of the formal tort law are quite complex: definitions of both damages and negligence suggest the need for case-by-case consideration. The rule of contributory negligence as a bar to recovery makes the formal law appear close-fisted, though it may be lavish in the recovery that it grants a "blameless" victim of a "negligent" driver. Above all, the formal tort law — like the bulk of Anglo-American law — is equitable in its insistence that cases similar in facts be treated in a similar fashion. The law in action departs from the formal law on these three main dimensions.

In order to process successfully vast numbers of cases, organizations tend to take on the characteristics of "bureaucracy" in the sociological sense of the term: operation on the basis of rules, government by a clear hierarchy, the maintenance of files, etc. Such an organizational form produces competence and efficiency in applying general rules to particular cases, but it is not well suited to making complex and individualized decisions. One form of response of bureaucracies to such demands involves a type of breakdown. There will be long delays, hewing to complicated and minute procedures, and a confusion of means with ends. A common and perhaps more constructive response is to simplify the task. This was the tack taken by the claims men I studied. Phone calls and letters replaced personal visits; only a few witnesses, rather than all possible, would be interviewed; and the law of negligence was made to lean heavily on the much simpler traffic law.

Traffic laws are simple rules, deliberately so because their purpose is to provide a universal and comprehensible set of guidelines for safe and efficient transportation. Negligence law is complex, its purpose being to decide after the fact whether a driver was unreasonably careless. However, all levels of the insurance company claims department will accept the former rules as generally adequate for the latter purpose. The underlying reason for this is the difficulty if not impossibility of investigating and defending a more complex decision concerning negligence in the context of a mass operation. In the routine case, the stakes are not high enough to warrant the effort, and the effort is not made. The information that a given insured violated a specific traffic law and was subsequently involved in an accident will suffice to allocate fault. No attempt is made to analyze why this took place or how. The legal concepts of negligence and fault in action contain no more substance than the simple and mechanical procedures noted here provide.

The law of damages is also simplified in action. Although the measurement of special damages appears rather straightforward even in formal doctrine, some further simplification occurs in action when, for instance, life table calculations are used to compute future earnings. More important, the measurement of pain, suffering, and inconvenience is thoroughly routinized in the ordinary claim. The adjuster generally pays little attention to the claimant's privately experienced discomforts and agonies; I do not recall ever having read recitals of these matters in the statements, which are the key documents in the settlement process and in which all matters considered relevant to the disposition of a claim are recorded. The calculation of general damages is for the most part a matter of multiplying the medical bills by a tacitly but generally accepted arbitrary constant. This practice is justified by claims men on the theory that pain and suffering are very likely to be a function of the amount of medical treatment experienced. There is of course a grain of truth in this theory, but it also contains several sources of error. Types of injury vary considerably in the degree of pain and suffering, the necessity for treatment, and the fees charged for treatment; and the correlations between these elements are low. I believe that the more important reason for the use of the formula is again that all levels of the claims department find it acceptable in justifying payment over and beyond special damages. The formula provides a conventional measurement for phenomena that are so difficult to evaluate as to be almost unmeasurable. It provides a rule by which a rule-oriented organization can proceed, though the rule is never formalized. This simplification also meets the comparable needs of plaintiffs' attorneys and is acceptable to them as well. Because of the mutual acceptability of the formula, attorneys will try to capitalize on it by adding to the use and cost of medical treatment, a procedure known as "building" the file, and adjusters will argue concerning the reasonableness of many items that purport to be medical expenses and thus part of the base to which the formula is applied. The procedure is still far less complicated — and less sensitive — than that envisaged in the formal law. Thus again it appears that, relative to the formal law, the law in action is simple and mechanical. Although more individual consideration occurs in larger cases, the principle of simplification governs to a great degree the entire range of settled claims.

The tort law in action is more liberal than the formal law. The formal law of negligence appears to be very stingy from the victim's point of view; this appearance is not surprising considering the law's development as a means of relieving nineteenth-century industry of charges imposed for accidental injuries by the earlier strict liability doctrine. The doctrine of contributory negligence is of course the main block to recovery in the formal tort law, and it is this doctrine that is most strongly attenuated in action.

The principal evidence of this attenuation is in the large number of claims on which some payment is made. Insurance company procedures create a file for nearly every accident victim involved with an insured car. Any reasonable estimate of the number of cases in which the insured is not negligent plus the number in which the claimant is contributorily negligent suggests that well under half of all claims deserve payment by formal standards.... Contrary to formal expectations the majority of claims are paid, and where serious injuries are involved virtually all claimants recover something from someone else's liability insurance. Similar findings have been reported in other studies. It is true that in larger claims particularly, the payments may not equal the economic loss experienced, but they may still exceed the level of payment required by the formal law with its rule of contributory negligence.

In small claims, a fair number of denials are successfully made. The adjuster rationalizes his actions on the basis of formal law and the company is shielded from reprisals by [means of] high processing costs for the claimant relative to the amount at stake. The adjuster closes his files by denial when he feels the formal law warrants this and also that the claimant will take his case no farther. When he believes that the formal law favors the claimant, and thus finds himself ethically obliged, or when he believes the claimant is determined to press the claim, a payment can be made of considerable magnitude relative to the economic loss involved, although collateral sources — e.g., Blue Cross and sick pay — are usually deducted from negotiated settlements.

In claims based on large losses, the claimant's threat to litigate becomes more credible, and denial thus becomes more difficult. However, the adjuster uses the uncertainty of the formal process as a tool to secure a discount from the full formal value of the claim. Although processing costs may be disregarded, most claimants seem to prefer a definite settlement for a lower amount of money to the gamble of trial for a higher amount of money. The company — like a casino, which is able to translate a large number of gambles into mathematical certainty — is indifferent between these outcomes and can demand a concession for the definite settlement.

The claimant determined to press a claim that would most likely be thrown out of court and the company determined to obtain a discount on a claim that would most likely prevail are unforeseen in the formal law, but it is in predicaments like this that the law in action develops. The result may correspond to no theory of formal law, but it is none the less comprehensible. The resultant law in action, on the whole, is more liberal than is the formal law. More claims are paid, particularly where the loss is serious, than might be predicted on the basis of the latter. However, the ratio of payment to loss declines as the size of the loss increases.

The tort law in action may also be termed inequitable. It is responsive to a wide variety of influences that are not defined as legitimate by common standards of equity. The interviews and observations I conducted convinced me that the negotiated settlement rewards the sophisticated claimant and penalizes the inexperienced, the naive, the simple, and the indifferent. Translating these terms into social statuses, I believe that the settlement produces relatively more for the affluent, the educated, the white, and the city-dweller. It penalizes the poor, the uneducated, the Negro, and the countryman. It is also responsive to such matters as the appearances and personalities of the parties and the witnesses to the accident. Above all, it rewards the man with an attorney, despite the adjuster's honestly held belief that the unrepresented claimant will fare as well. Apart from the discrimination embodied in allowing recovery of different levels of lost income, these differences are unjustified in formal law, yet their effect on negotiated settlements is considerable.

Although this research was based for the most part on experience in a single, narrow, area of law, I believe that the distinctions noted here between the formal law and the law in action may be more generally applicable. Wherever law or any other body of rules is applied on a day-to-day basis by a bureaucracy, pressures similar to those observed here may be expected to be present and to produce similar results. Simplification is the essence of mass procedures, and one would expect to find a deemphasis upon sensitivity, individualization, and subtlety in such situations, regardless of the complexity of the philosophy underlying the procedure. Where every man has his day in court, where each is judged according to his ability, where the whole man is being treated, an examination of the machinery in action can be predicted to yield evidence of routinization, categorization, and regimentation. Liberality or something akin to it may also be expected when rules are applied by a bureaucracy, depending on the extent to which sheer volume is emphasized by the processor. The bureaucratic employee under these circumstances seeks a trouble-free and expeditious resolution of disputes, and this may lead more frequently than previously thought to a liberal treatment of the case. Finally, inequity in the sense of applying formally inapplicable criteria is also likely to mark a wide variety of situations in which bureaucracies apply rules. Cases that are alike according to the formal rules may be for many reasons dissimilar when regarded as material to be processed. Factors ranging from the bureaucrat's idiosyncratic whim to strong and systematic organizational pressures may be expected to affect both the process and the outcome wherever the formal law or other rule is put into action. . . .

NOTES AND QUESTIONS

1. Ross's findings are based on interviews of claims adjusters and their supervisors at three large insurance companies that write automobile coverage. He supplemented this information by analyzing more than 2,000 claims files at one of the companies and by interviewing seventeen plaintiff's attorneys. Settled Out of Court examines in considerable detail the world of the claims adjuster: professional norms and ethics, investigative and negotiating techniques, and general social and political attitudes and values. As the preceding excerpt suggests, Ross, a sociologist, is interested in the adjuster both as an employee of an organization with its own distinctive norms, and as an agent in a system concerned with promoting broader social objectives—the resolution of personal injury claims.

2. Beginning in 1932 with the Columbia Report, a number of independently-conducted empirical studies have reported similar patterns of compensation for automobile victims: using economic loss as the measuring-stick, small claims tend to be vastly overcompensated while large claims are systematically undercompensated. The imbalance between loss and reparation steadily increases as one moves towards either end of the scale. The following illustrative data are reported in Bombaugh, The Department of Transportation's Auto Insurance Study and Auto Accident Compensation Reform, 71 Colum. L. Rev. 207, 214, Table 3 (1971). The information is compiled from Department of Transportation data on total benefits received— including but not limited to tort payments—by seriously injured

Total economic loss	% Receiving more than loss	Average excess	% Receiving less than loss	Average deficiency
$ 1-499	100%	$ 1,175	—	$ —
500-999	92	1,322	8%	108
1,000-1,499	81	2,131	19	280
1,500-2,499	77	2,674	23	495
2,500-4,999	65	4,131	35	1,386
5,000-9,999	53	4,531	47	3,064
10,000-24,999	32	7,279	68	10,328
25,000 and over	4	23,830	96	63,756

victims who received at least some benefits. Moreover, a stubborn percentage of cases involving rather substantial loss continues to be entirely uncompensated, even with the recent dramatic growth in alternative systems of reparation (various forms of social and private accident insurance).

The disparity between loss and reparation is explained by a number of factors. A major reason for the overcompensation of minor claims is the economic incentive for insurers to dispose quickly of nuisance claims involving small losses. Critical to the undercompensation of large claims is the inability of seriously injured claimants to tolerate a long period of delay in receiving some monetary assistance. As might be expected, these findings on patterns of compensation for auto injury victims have generated substantial criticism of the fault system. The major empirical studies of the compensation problem are U.S. Department of Transportation, Motor Vehicle Crash Losses and Their Compensation in the United States (1971); U.S. Department of Transportation, Economic Consequences of Automobile Accident Injuries (1970); Conard, Morgan, Pratt, Voltz, & Bombaugh, Automobile Accident Costs and Payments (1964); Morris & Paul, The Financial Impact of Automobile Accidents, 110 U. Pa. L. Rev. 913 (1962); Franklin, Chanin, & Mark, Accidents, Money and the Law: A Study of the Economics of Personal Injury Litigation, 61 Colum. L. Rev. 1 (1961); and Columbia University Council for Research in the Social Sciences, Report by the Commission to Study Compensation for Automobile Accidents (1932). A useful summary of the data reported in the Department of Transportation studies can be found in the Bombaugh article, cited above.

3. Is it adequate to dichotomize between the formal law and the law in action, as Ross does? Is it not more likely that adjusters discount formal law on an experiential basis? If juries systematically ignore trial court instructions on contributory negligence in certain kinds

of cases, that would seem to be a more salient datum than the formal law for adjusters involved in developing a negotiating position. Thus, "the law in action" takes on an additional dimension, perhaps more critical to adjusters than their reading of "formal law."

4. Ross says that "the most insistent of organizational pressures [on the claims adjuster] is not to keep payments low, but to close files quickly." Why? He suggests that this phenomenon is analogous to the goal of good grades for a student, placements for an employment counselor, and clearances for a police officer. What, exactly, is the dominant theme that links these apparently diverse activities with the rapid closing of claim files?

5. Would you expect the negotiating process to be influenced by the respective size of the personal injury bar and the insurance community? What would be the likely impact of a plaintiffs' bar dominated by a limited number of attorneys? Would the degree of specialization of the plaintiffs' bar be likely to influence the process?

6. Do Ross's findings have any implications for analysis, from an economic efficiency perspective, of the handling of auto accident cases under the negligence system?

Chapter 5

The Search for a Comprehensive Theory of Tort Liability: An Economic Perspective

Every tort case in which harm is established raises an issue of loss allocation: whether the loss should be left on the victim or shifted to the injurer, an insurer, or some other third party. Moving from the discrete case to *types* of injury situations, questions of proper loss allocation become even more salient. Viewing auto accidents, product injuries and malpractice cases as categories, and confronting the aggregate cost of injuries associated with each, we are impelled to ask whether there is a "best" way of distributing the loss. Because questions of risk distribution and loss allocation are central to an economic perspective on law, it comes as no surprise that tort scholars and reformers have turned to the discipline with some regularity in search of a better way of resolving injury problems. Indeed, writing in 1967, Walter Blum and Harry Kalven suggested that:

> It would be a worthwhile task to write the intellectual history of economic ideas in tort liability theory, beginning perhaps with Holmes's remark that "The state might conceivably make itself a mutual insurance company against accidents and distribute the burden

of its citizens' mishaps among all its members." Holmes, The Common Law 96 (1881). In rough profile, the ferment begins with the debate over workmen's compensation legislation at the turn of the century, when it is argued that the costs of industry should be placed on industry. A decade or so later Laski, Smith, and Douglas seek to rationalize vicarious liability rules by analogy to workmen's compensation. The point changes somewhat, the emphasis being placed on the wide distribution of losses through use of the market mechanism and liability insurance, and the phrase "enterprise liability" is exploited. After the passage of another decade or two, tort scholars, in particular James, Morris, Ehrenzweig, and Green, attempt to adapt the agency analysis to tort liability rules. Again the emphasis changes slightly, and the concern is with the customary patterns of carrying insurance and relative accessibility to insurance. The quest is for the "superior risk bearer." Finally, in the current decade the stimulus to use of economics is found mainly in the auto compensation discussion.[1]

An essay by William O. Douglas, Vicarious Liability and Administration of Risk,[2] provides a good example of the early efforts to bring economic analysis to bear on the tort system. Like the similarly disposed proponents of workers' compensation legislation, Douglas's effort was directed at a single set of liability rules that raised a discrete issue. His inquiry was aimed at determining whether respondeat superior made sense from an economic perspective, just as a decade earlier debate had centered on whether a strict liability system for industrial injuries was economically warranted.

Beginning in the post-World War II period the mode of analysis shifted, reflecting the major impact that the growth of liability insurance had on tort scholarship and, gradually, on tort law as well. Probably the most influential commentator in this period was Fleming James.[3] James analyzed virtually every aspect of tort doctrine, with a paramount concern for economic considerations. He argued that the development of accident insurance created a mechanism for wide distribution and increased prevention of losses attributable to products of the mechanical age. As a consequence, James asserted, tort doctrine fashioned to allocate losses between individually responsible actors was obsolete, and ought to be modified whenever possible to maximize compensation of injury victims.[4]

While James and his contemporaries thought in system-wide terms about the economic consequences of liability insurance, only in

1. Blum & Kalven, The Empty Cabinet of Dr. Calabresi: Auto Accidents and General Deterrence, 34 U. Chi. L. Rev. 239, 245 n.14 (1967).

2. 38 Yale L.J. 584, 720 (1929).

3. James's overall contribution to tort law is best reflected in Volume 2 of the treatise, F. Harper & F. James, The Law of Torts (1956).

4. See, e.g., James, Accident Liability Reconsidered: The Impact of Liability Insurance, 57 Yale L.J. 549 (1948).

more recent years have scholars brought formal economic theory directly to bear on tort doctrine. An important article by economist Ronald Coase raised the fundamental question of whether the content of rules of tort liability really matters from the perspective of economic efficiency. As Coase put it:

> The question is commonly thought of as one in which A inflicts harm on B and what has to be decided is: how should we restrain A? But this is wrong. We are dealing with a problem of a reciprocal nature. To avoid the harm to B would inflict harm on A. The real question that has to be decided is: should A be allowed to harm B or should B be allowed to harm A?... [An] example is afforded by the problem of straying cattle which destroy crops on neighboring land. If it is inevitable that some cattle will stray, an increase in the supply of meat can only be obtained at the expense of a decrease in the supply of crops. The nature of the choice is clear: meat or crops.[5]

Coase went on to argue that if there are no transaction costs, what matters is that the rule of liability be clear; but it does not matter whether the cattle owner is liable or not. If he is liable he will only invest more in fencing when doing so is cheaper than paying damages. If he is not liable, the farmer will bribe him to invest in fencing when doing so costs the farmer less than he would incur in crop damage. Whatever the liability rule, the choice between fencing and crop damage will result in precisely the same amount of resources being invested in the elimination of harm—although, of course, the distributional consequences (who bears the loss) will differ.

While Coase's theorem created a stir, the vigorous intellectual debate over the economic justification for competing liability rules during the succeeding decade cannot be adequately explained without reference to the dynamics of the judicial and political processes. As early as 1944, in a frequently cited concurring opinion in a defective product case, Justice Traynor wrote:

> ...I believe the manufacturer's negligence should no longer be singled out as the basis of a plaintiff's right to recover in cases like the present one.... Even if there is no negligence...public policy demands that responsibility be fixed wherever it will most effectively reduce the hazards to life and health inherent in defective products that reach the market.... The cost of an injury and the loss of time or health may be an overwhelming misfortune to the person injured, and a needless one, for the risk of injury can be insured by the manufacturer and distributed among the public as a cost of doing business.[6]

While the process is not yet complete, the courts have effected a

---

5. Coase, The Problem of Social Cost, 3 J.L. & Econ. 1, 2 (1960).
6. Escola v. Coca Cola Bottling Co. of Fresno, 24 Cal. 2d 453, 461-462, 150 P.2d 436 (1944).

veritable revolution in products liability law during the last decade, substituting strict liability in tort for a liability system based on the fault principle.[7] At the same time, dissatisfaction with the fault system as a method of dealing with automobile accidents triggered intense debate in both the academic community and the political arena over no-fault auto compensation plans.[8]

With the two major areas of liability for unintended harm in a state of flux, comprehensive reexamination of the merits of the fault principle was virtually inevitable. A leading influence among scholars taking an economic perspective has been Guido Calabresi, whose book, The Costs of Accidents, provides a comprehensive and systematic economic analysis of the tort system. The initial reading in this chapter consists of excerpts from the book that are meant to provide an understanding of his framework of analysis. The next two readings deal with applications of an economic perspective to the two critical areas of accident law just mentioned: Walter Blum and Harry Kalven explore the auto accident problem in an article criticizing Calabresi's economic analysis, and Calabresi and Jon Hirschoff elaborate an economic framework for defective product law. Finally, Richard Posner and Steven Shavell redirect our attention to the central theme of evaluating the comparative merits of strict liability and fault. Posner argues that from the perspective of economic efficiency the case for strict liability has not been made. Shavell explores the consequences of considering injurer-victim activity levels in determining the respective efficiency of strict liability and negligence rules.

The Costs of Accidents*

Guido Calabresi

Some myths will make our analysis difficult if not cleared up. The first is that our society wants to avoid accidents at all costs; the second is that there is an inexorable economic law that dictates the "right" way to allocate accident losses; the third is that when critics and courts talk about distributing the risk of accidents they have a specific goal or subgoal in mind;...

7. The initial stages are described in Prosser, The Assault Upon the Citadel, 69 Yale L.J. 1099 (1960) and The Fall of the Citadel, 50 Minn. L. Rev. 791 (1966).

8. See the introduction to Chapter Seven, infra.

*Source: 17-21, 26-29, 68-75, 135-138, 139-141, 143-152, 160-161 (1970).

Avoid Accidents at All Costs

Our society is not committed to preserving life at any cost. In its broadest sense, the rather unpleasant notion that we are willing to destroy lives should be obvious. Wars are fought. The University of Mississippi is integrated at the risk of losing lives. But what is more pertinent to the study of accident law, though perhaps equally obvious, is that lives are spent not only when the quid pro quo is some great moral principle, but also when it is a matter of convenience. Ventures are undertaken that, statistically at least, are certain to cost lives. Thus we build a tunnel under Mont Blanc because it is essential to the Common Market and cuts down the traveling time from Rome to Paris, though we know that about one man per kilometer of tunnel will die. We take planes and cars rather than safer, slower means of travel. And perhaps most telling, we use relatively safe equipment rather than the safest imaginable because — and it is not a bad reason — the safest costs too much. It should be apparent that while some of these accident-causing activities also result in diminution of accidents — the Mont Blanc tunnel may well save more lives by diminishing traffic fatalities than it took to build it — this explanation does not come close to justifying most accident-causing activities. Railroad grade crossings are used because they are cheap, not because they save more lives than they take.

Economic Laws Give Absolute Answers

Since we are not committed to preserving life at any cost, the question is the more complex one of how far we want to go to save lives and reduce accident costs. This leads us to the second myth: that economic theory can answer the question. Just as economic theory cannot decide for us whether we want to save the life of a trapped miner, so it cannot tell us how far we want to go to save lives and reduce accident costs. Economic theory can suggest one approach — the market — for making the decision. But decisions balancing lives against money or convenience cannot be purely monetary ones, so the market method is never the only one used. The decision to build the Mont Blanc tunnel is not based solely on whether the revenue received from tolls will pay for the construction costs, including compensation of the killed and maimed. Neither is the decision to permit prostitution based solely on whether it can pay its way. Such pure free enterprise decisions have never been acceptable and have been, in fact, rejected by even the most orthodox of classical economists, who did, however, feel it necessary to explain the rejection through the use of such terms as external social costs and benefits, concepts which are not self-defining and are in fact as narrow or as broad as any society cares to make them.

The issue, whether or not expressed in terms of hidden social costs or hidden social savings theories, is how often a decision for or against an activity should be made outside the market. Such decisions operate on the one hand to create subsidies for some activities that could not survive in the marketplace, and on the other to bar some activities that could more than pay their way. The frequency with which decisions to ignore the market are made tells something about the nature of society — welfare, laissez faire, or mixed. It is clear, however, that in virtually all societies such decisions to overrule the market are made, but are made only sometimes.

In accident law too, the decision to take lives in exchange for money or convenience is sometimes made politically or collectively without a balancing of the money value of the lives taken against the money price of the convenience, and sometimes made through the market on the basis of such a value. The reasons for choosing one way rather than the other are not entirely reasons of principle. Great moral issues lend themselves to political determination and must be decided in whatever political way a society chooses. But whether to use rotary mowers instead of reel mowers and what method to use for making steel are questions not easily answered collectively. For one thing, they occur too frequently. Every choice of product and use involves, tacitly or otherwise, a decision regarding safety and expense. The dramatic cases can be resolved politically. We ban the general sale of fireworks regardless of the ability or willingness of the manufacturer to pay for all of the injuries resulting from their use. But we cannot deal with every issue involved in every activity through the political process. In most cases, the marketplace serves as the rough testing ground. A manufacturer is usually free to employ a process that occasionally kills or maims if he is able to show that consumers want his product badly enough to enable him to compensate the injured. Economists would say that, except in some areas where collective decisions are needed, this is the best method for deciding whether the activity is worth having. But the tautologous nature of this statement makes it clear that ultimately, we collectively, and not economics, are the boss.

In other words, although the market can help us to decide how far we wish to go to avoid accidents, it cannot solve the whole problem for us. And when we overrule the market and ban an accident-causing activity that can pay its way or subsidize an activity that cannot, we are not violating absolute laws. We are making the same type of choice between accidents and accident-causing activities that the market makes, but we are choosing, for perfectly valid reasons, to make it in a different way. We are preferring a collective approach or method (e.g., because it enables consideration of nonmoney costs which the market cannot deal with, or because in the particular instance it is cheaper) to a market approach, even though the market might allow for individual differences in tastes and desires that the collective decision might tend to ignore.

Risk Distribution Is Self-Explanatory

The third myth involves the meaning of risk distribution. It has often been suggested that distributing the risk of accidents requires drivers rather than pedestrians to pay for automobile accidents, employers rather than employees to pay for work accidents, and so forth. Yet advocates of such systems of loss allocation often fail to explain or justify this and assume that the term *risk distribution* is self-explanatory. Actually, they may be using the term to mean three quite different things. The first possible meaning is the accomplishment of the broadest possible spreading of losses, both over people and over time. The second is the placing of losses on those classes of people or activities that are best able to pay, usually the "wealthiest," regardless of whether this involves spreading. The third is the placing of losses on those activities that, in some undefined sense, engender them.

Unfortunately, these meanings, while they represent valid methods for achieving valid aims, are not always consistent with one another. They are, moreover, supported by quite different ethical and economic postulates — postulates that are probably not accepted equally by anyone, and certainly not equally accepted by everyone. The first and second meanings of risk distribution represent two different methods for achieving a common subgoal which may loosely be called compensation. (I shall sometimes use this term, but more often will call the aim "secondary accident cost avoidance.") The first meaning of risk distribution I shall call the "risk spreading" method; the second I shall call the "deep pocket" method. The third meaning of risk distribution has very little in common with the first two except that it has been confused with them. It represents one method for achieving a different subgoal of accident law: the reduction of the immediate costs of accidents. In my locution, it represents a particular approach to achieving "primary accident cost avoidance." I call it the general deterrence or market approach. . . .

[Next, Calabresi turns directly to consideration of the goals of a system of accident law.]

Reduction of Accident Costs

Apart from the requirements of justice, I take it as axiomatic that the principal function of accident law is to reduce the sum of the costs of accidents and the costs of avoiding accidents. (Such incidental benefits as providing a respectable livelihood for a large number of judges, lawyers, and insurance agents are at best beneficent side effects.) This cost, or loss, reduction goal can be divided into three subgoals.

The first is reduction of the number and severity of accidents. This "primary" reduction of accident costs can be attempted in two basic ways. We can seek to forbid specific acts or activities thought to cause accidents, or we can make activities more expensive and thereby less attractive to the extent of the accident costs they cause. These two methods of primary reduction of accident costs are not clearly separable; a number of difficulties of definition will become apparent as we consider them in detail. But the distinction between them is useful because from it flow two very different approaches toward primary reduction of accident costs, the "general deterrence" or market method and the "specific deterrence" or collective method.

The second cost reduction subgoal is concerned with reducing neither the number of accidents nor their degree of severity. It concentrates instead on reducing the societal costs resulting from accidents. I shall attempt to show that the notion that one of the principal functions of accident law is the compensation of victims is really a rather misleading, though occasionally useful, way of stating this "secondary" accident cost reduction goal. The fact that I have termed this compensation notion secondary should in no way be taken as belittling its importance. There is no doubt that the way we provide for accident victims *after* the accident is crucially important and that the real societal costs of accidents can be reduced as significantly here as by taking measures to avoid accidents in the first place. This cost reduction subgoal is secondary only in the sense that it does not come into play until after earlier primary measures to reduce accident costs have failed.

The secondary cost reduction goal can be accomplished through...two methods...both of which usually involve a shifting of accident losses: the risk (or loss) spreading method and the deep pocket method.

The third subgoal of accident cost reduction is rather Pickwickian but very important nonetheless. It involves reducing the costs of administering our treatment of accidents. It may be termed "tertiary" because its aim is to reduce the costs of achieving primary and secondary cost reduction. But in a very real sense this "efficiency" goal comes first. It tells us to question constantly whether an attempt to reduce accident costs, either by reducing accidents themselves or by reducing their secondary effects, costs more than it saves. By forcing us to ask this, it serves as a kind of general balance wheel to the cost reduction goal.

These, then, are the principal subgoals into which the goal of accident cost reduction can be divided—primary accident cost reduction, which includes the general deterrence or market method and the specific deterrence or collective method; secondary accident cost reduction, which includes the risk spreading and the deep pocket methods; and the tertiary or efficiency cost reduction.

. . . It should be noted in advance that these subgoals are not fully consistent with each other. For instance, a perfect system of secondary cost reduction is, as we shall see, inconsistent with the goals of reducing primary accident costs. We cannot have more than a certain amount of reduction in one category without forgoing some of the reduction in the other, just as we cannot reduce all accident costs beyond a certain point without incurring costs in *achieving* the reduction that are greater than the reduction is worth. Our aim must be to find the best combination of primary, secondary, and tertiary cost reduction taking into account what must be given up in order to achieve that reduction. . . .

[Here, Calabresi expands on the notion of primary accident cost avoidance through elaboration of the general deterrence approach, which he has introduced above.]

. . . [T]he primary way in which a society may seek to reduce accident costs is to discourage activities that are "accident prone" and substitute safer activities as well as safer ways of engaging in the same activities. But such a statement suggests neither the degree to which we wish to discourage such activities nor the means for doing so. As we have seen, we certainly do not wish to avoid accident costs at all costs by forbidding all accident-prone activities. Most activities can be carried out safely enough or be sufficiently reduced in frequency so that there is a point at which their worth outweighs the costs of the accidents they cause. Specific prohibition or deterrence of most activities would cost society more than it would save in accident costs prevented. We want the fact that activities cause accidents to influence our choices among activities and among ways of doing them. But we want to limit this influence to a degree that is justified by the cost of these accidents. The obvious question is, how do we do this?

There are two basic approaches to making these difficult "decisions for accidents," and our society has always used both, though not always to the same degree. The first, which I have termed the specific deterrence or collective approach, will be discussed later. At present it suffices to say that it involves deciding collectively the degree to which we want any given activity, who should participate in it, and how we want it done. These decisions may or may not be made solely on the basis of the accident costs the activity causes. The collective decisions are enforced by penalties on those who violate them.

The other approach, and the one I wish to discuss first, involves attempting instead to decide what the accident costs of activities are and letting the *market* determine the degree to which, and the ways in which, activities are desired given such costs. Similarly, it involves giving people freedom to choose whether they would rather engage in the activity and pay the costs of doing so, including accident costs, or, given the accident costs, engage in safer activities that might otherwise have seemed less desirable. I call this approach general, or market, deterrence.

The crucial thing about the general deterrence approach to accidents is that it does not involve an a priori collective decision as to the correct number of accidents. General deterrence implies that accident costs would be treated as one of the many costs we face whenever we do anything. Since we cannot have everything we want, individually or as a society, whenever we choose one thing we give up others. General deterrence attempts to force individuals to consider accident costs in choosing among activities. The problem is getting the best combination of choices available. The general deterrence approach would let the free market or price system tally the choices.

Theoretical Basis

The theoretical basis of general deterrence is not hard to find. The problem posed is simply the old one of allocation of resources which for years has been studied in the branch of economics called welfare economics; the free market solution is the one traditionally given by welfare economics. This solution presupposes certain postulates. The most important of these, and the only one we need consider now, is the notion that no one knows what is best for individuals better than they themselves do. If people want television sets, society should produce television sets; if they want licorice drops, then licorice drops should be made. The proportion of television sets to licorice drops, as well as the way in which each is made, should also be left up to individual choices because, according to the postulate, as long as individuals are adequately informed about the alternatives and as long as the cost to society of giving them what they want is reflected in the cost to the individual, the individual can decide better than anyone else what he wants. Thus the function of the prices of various goods must be to reflect the relative costs to society of producing them, and if prices perform this function properly, the buyer will cast an informed vote in making his purchases; thus the best combination of choices available will be achieved.

The general deterrence approach treats accident costs as it does any other costs of goods and activities — such as the metal, or the time it takes, to make cars. If all activities reflect the accident costs they "cause," each individual will be able to choose for himself whether an activity is worth the accident costs it "causes." The sum of these choices is, ex hypothesis, the best combination available and will determine the degree to which accident-prone activities are engaged in (if at all), how they are engaged in, and who will engage in them.[2] Failure to include accident costs in the prices of activities will, according to the theory, cause people to choose more accident-prone activities than they would if the prices of these activities made them pay for these accident costs, resulting in more accident costs than we want. Forbidding accident-prone activities *despite* the fact that they can "pay" their costs would, in theory, bring about an equally bad result from the resource allocation point of view. Either way, the postulate that individuals know best for themselves would be violated.

A hypothetical example may help clarify this. In Athens, accident costs are in some way or other charged to the activity that engenders them. Sparta is a society in which all accident costs are borne by the state and come out of general taxes. C. J. Taney, a businessman in Athens, has one car and is considering buying a used car in addition. The cost of owning the second car would come to about $200 a year, plus an addition to his insurance bill of another $200. Alternatively, the cost of train fares, the taxis he would occasionally need to take, and the other expenses incurred to make up for not having a second car come to about $250. Contrasting the $400 expense of owning a second car with the $250 expense of riding in trains and taxis, he decides to forgo the car.

If Taney lived in Sparta, on the other hand, he would have to pay

___

2. The sum of individual choices will not necessarily be the best combination available, however, if the activities' other costs are not reflected in their prices. Thus if the petroleum industry were subsidized, we might have too much driving as against walking, even though both driving and walking bore their proper share of the costs of accidents. And some economists would contend that once one cost is not reflected properly, the reflection of other costs may even worsen the overall result in terms of proper resource allocation. . . .

a certain sum in taxes as his share of Sparta's general accident program. Short of moving out of Sparta, he could not avoid this cost whatever he did. As a result, the comparative costs in Sparta would be $200 per year for the car as contrasted with $250 for train and taxi fares. Chances are Taney would buy the car. In purchasing a second car in Sparta, he is not made to pay the full $400 that it costs society. In fact, he must pay *part* of that cost whether or not he buys one. He will, therefore, buy a car. If he had to carry the full burden of a second car, he would use trains and taxis, spending the money saved on something else — television, or perhaps a rowboat.

For the theory to make some sense there is no need to postulate a world made up of economic men who consciously consider the relative costs of each different good and the relative pleasure derived from each. If the cost of all automobile accidents were suddenly to be paid out of a general social insurance fund, the expense of owning a car would be a good deal lower than it is now since people would no longer need to worry about buying insurance. The result would be that some people would buy more cars. Perhaps they would be teenagers who can afford $100 for an old jalopy but who cannot afford — or whose fathers cannot afford — the insurance. Or they might be people who could only afford a second car so long as no added insurance was involved. In any event, the demand for cars would increase, and so would the number of cars produced. Indeed, the effect on car purchases would be much the same as if the government suddenly chose to pay the cost of the steel used by automobile manufacturers and to raise the money out of general taxes. In each case the objection would be the same. In each, an economist would say, resources are misallocated in that goods are produced that the consumer would not want if he had to pay the full extent of their cost to society, whether in terms of the physical components of the product or in terms of the expense of accidents associated with its production and use.

As I shall show later, I do not believe resource allocation theory in its extreme or pure form can find much acceptance today, especially as applied to accidents. Its inherent limitations, together with those added by its application to accident costs, are simply too great. But this is far from saying that the theory is useless. It has always had, in fact, a remarkable practical appeal, and tenacity. It can even stand substantial modification of its basic ethical postulate — that individuals know what is best for themselves by and large — and still play an important role, albeit a more limited one, in highly welfaristic or socialistic societies. Indeed, it is hard to imagine a society where, somewhere along the line, the market deterrence approach to primary accident cost control would not be significant.

All that is needed for the approach to have some influence is acceptance of the notion that *sometimes* people know best for themselves, even if for no other reason than that the choices involved arise too frequently for adequate collective decisions. To make the reasons for the appeal of general deterrence even clearer, it may be useful to discuss how it operates to reduce accident costs....

How Costs Are Reduced by General Deterrence

The general deterrence approach operates in two ways to reduce accident costs. The first and more obvious one is that it creates incentives to engage in safer activities. Some people who would engage in a relatively dangerous activity at prices that did not reflect its accident costs will shift to a safer activity if accident costs *are* reflected in prices. The degree of the shift will depend on the relative difference in accident costs and on how good a substitute the safer activity is. Whatever the shift, however, it will reduce accident costs, since a safer activity will to some degree have been substituted for a dangerous one.

The second and perhaps more important way general deterrence reduces accident costs is that it encourages us to make activities safer. This is no different from the first if every variation in the way an activity is carried out is considered to be a separate activity, but since that is not how the term activity is used in common language, it may be useful to show how general deterrence operates to cause a given activity to become safer. Taney drives a car. His car causes, on the average, $200 per year in accident costs. If a different kind of brake were used in the car, this would be reduced to $100. The new kind of brake costs the equivalent of $50 per year. If the accident costs Taney causes are paid either by the state out of general taxes or by those who are injured, he has no financial incentive to put in the new brake. But if Taney has to pay, he will certainly put the new brake in. He will thus bear a new cost of $50 per year, but it will be less than the $100 per year in accident costs he will avoid. As a result, the cost of accidents to society will have been reduced by $50.

This example of how general deterrence operates to reduce costs is, of course, highly simplified. It assumes, for instance, that we know that Taney "causes" $200 in accident costs. It also assumes that the government or the victims, if they bear the losses, cannot cause the brakes to be installed as readily as Taney. Indeed, the assumptions are so simple that they lead one to ask, why we do not simply make all Taneys install the new brakes. Why, in short, do we not specifically deter the "dangerous conduct" instead of bothering with so cumbersome a method as general deterrence?

Mentioning a few more of the many complications inherent in the situation may make clearer why general deterrence is worthwhile. Suppose that Marshall, who uses old-style brakes, has only $25 worth of accidents per year. It is not worth our while to force him to install the new brakes. Indeed, if he were made to install new brakes and if we can assume our measurements of costs to be accurate (a matter calling for a good deal of discussion later), forcing Marshall to install new brakes would add an unnecessary $25 to our cost burden. Yet we would still wish to have Taney install the brakes in order to get his $50 saving. It will be expensive, if not impossible, to make collective decisions distinguishing the Taneys from the Marshalls. It will, in fact, be much easier if we let the distinction be made by Taney and Marshall themselves by letting them choose between paying for the accidents and paying for the new brakes.

Another complication may be even more significant. Suppose we do not yet have the safe brakes, and requiring such brakes is therefore impossible. Placing the cost on cars may still bring about general deterrence in the form of a continuous pressure to develop something — such as new brakes — that would avoid the accident costs and would be cheaper to make and sell than paying the accident costs. General deterrence creates a market for this cost-saving substitute and, therefore, an incentive for someone to develop it and bring about a cost reduction. . . .

[Next, Calabresi discusses the criteria for deciding which "activity" is to be assigned the cost of accidents.]

A pure market approach to primary accident cost avoidance would require allocation of accident costs to those acts or activities (or combinations of them) which could avoid the accident costs most cheaply. This is the same as saying that the system would allocate the costs to those acts or activities that an arbitrary initial bearer of accident costs would (in the absence of transaction and information costs) find it most worthwhile to "bribe" in order to obtain that modification of behavior which would lessen accident costs most.[2]

This formulation implies several things. If there were no transaction or information costs associated with paying people to alter their behavior, it would not matter (in terms of market control of accidents) who bore the accident costs initially. Regardless of who was initially liable, there would be bribes or transactions bringing about any change in the behavior of any individual that would cause a greater

2. "Bribe" as used throughout this book implies no moral turpitude or corruption by either party, but rather an open, legitimate inducement.

reduction in accident costs than in pleasure.[3] Since in reality transactions are often terribly expensive, it is often not worthwhile spending both the cost of the transaction and the amount needed to bribe someone else to diminish the accident-causing behavior. As a result, the accident cost is not avoided by society, while another allocation that could eliminate or lessen the transaction cost is available and would result in the avoidance of the accident cost. The aim of the pure market determination of which activity to hold liable is to find this other allocation.

An overly simple example may be in order. Suppose car-pedestrian accidents currently cost $100. Suppose also that if cars had spongy bumpers the total accident costs would only be $10. Suppose finally that spongy bumpers cost $50 more than the present bumpers. Assuming no transaction costs, spongy bumpers would become established regardless of who was held responsible for car-pedestrian accidents. If car manufacturers were liable they would prefer to spend $50 for the new bumpers plus $10 in accident damages, instead of $100 for accident damages. If pedestrians were held responsible and could foresee the costs, they would prefer to bribe the car manufacturers $50 to put in spongy bumpers and bear $10 in damages, rather than bear $100 in damages. Exactly the same result would occur if an arbitrary third party, e.g., television manufacturers, were held liable initially; they too could lessen costs to themselves by bribing car manufacturers to put in spongy bumpers. The result is the same simply because the cost of avoiding the accident is in all instances smaller than the cost of compensating for it. Wherever this is so, and wherever it costs nothing to bribe (and people have the necessary knowledge), the market will seek the cheapest way and avoid the accident.

Now let us alter the example to add transaction costs. Assume that any allocation other than leaving the cost where it falls (i.e., on the pedestrian) entails $5 in administrative costs. Assume also that for pedestrians to bribe anyone is very expensive, e.g., $65. (This is because it is costly to gather pedestrians together to bargain and to handle the problem of would-be-free-loaders.[4]) Assume finally that it

3. See generally R. H. Coase, The Problem of Social Cost, 3 J.L. & Econ. 1 (1960). On these assumptions no misallocations of costs would ever be possible.... In fact, information costs are really part of transaction costs, and hereafter when I use the term transaction costs, I include them.

4. The free-loader is the person who refuses to be inoculated against smallpox because given the fact that almost everyone else is inoculated, the risk of smallpox to him is less than the risk of harm from the inoculation. If enough people are free-loaders it becomes necessary to compel inoculation to avoid smallpox epidemics. The free-loader is also the person who refuses to join a union because the fact that most other workers are union members assures him of the benefits of unionization without the cost. The

would cost television manufacturers $30 to bribe. What would happen in our example?

If car manufacturers were held liable, they would bear $100 in accident costs plus perhaps the $5 allocation cost. They could avoid this in the future by putting in spongy bumpers at $50, paying $10 in damages, and perhaps the same $5 in administrative costs (assuming for the sake of simplicity that these remained constant). Clearly they would install spongy bumpers.

If pedestrians were held liable, they would bear $100 in accident cost. But to get spongy bumpers installed would cost then $50 (bribe) plus $65 (transaction costs), and they would still bear $10 in accident costs. Since $125 is more than $100, a change to spongy bumpers would not seem worth the expense. But the absence of spongy bumpers would in fact entail an unnecessary cost to society of the difference between $100 (accident costs when borne by pedestrians) and $65 (the cost to society when car manufacturers are held liable).

If television manufacturers were held liable, the figures would be $100 plus $5 with no spongy bumpers, compared with $50 (bribe) plus $30 (transaction costs) plus $10 (remaining accident costs) plus perhaps $5 (administrative costs). Since $95 is less than $105, spongy bumpers would probably be installed. But this result would have been achieved in a more expensive, less efficient way than if car manufacturers had been liable, for $30 in unnecessary transaction costs would have been imposed on society.

Clearly then, on the basis of our initial assumptions, it would be best to make automobile manufacturers liable. . . .

The question for a pure market approach is, then, how we should determine who, in practice, is the cheapest cost avoider, i.e., how we should determine who is in the position of the car manufacturer in the example for each category of accidents. In almost every area we can make some rough guesses, based on intuitive notions or on indifferentiated and unanalyzed experiences, as to who is clearly not the cheapest cost avoider and who may be. These could be further refined by controlled experiments, but such experiments are unlikely to be carried out because they cost too much. There are, however, guidelines which can be used for finding out who, in the absence of more information, is likely to be the cheapest cost avoider. If even the guidelines give no satisfactory indications, a market approach can either make a guess, divide the costs equally among the activities not

use of compulsion in these areas suggests that the problem of free-loaders is crucial whenever many people must agree to bear a cost in order to bring about a change favorable to all of them. It would not be crucial if nonpayers could be excluded from the benefits of the change, but such exclusion is often extremely expensive. It is precisely that expense which justifies compulsion. . . .

excluded by the rough guess or the guidelines, or be "indifferent" as to who should bear costs in these extreme cases and allocate them on the basis of approaches and goals other than market reduction of primary accident costs....

The Initial Rough Guess

The general deterrence rough guess must be guided by market considerations. It is essentially a collective guess, but one concerning individuals' market valuations. It will be limited to ruling out as potential loss bearers those activities that could reduce the costs being allocated only at what would *obviously* be too great an expense. The cost of reducing accident costs by reduction in or modification of a given activity will depend both on its market desirability (how much people want it and how many substitutes it has) and on the relation it bears (in some causal sense) to the accident costs under consideration. For example, although the costs of car-pedestrian accidents could probably be reduced substantially by reductions and modifications of pedestrian activity, such cost reduction might be too expensive if pedestrianism is viewed as a fixed activity, i.e., one without ready substitutes. Similarly, placing the costs of car-pedestrian accidents on leather shoes would be silly even though leather shoes have close substitutes, e.g., rubber shoes, because a shift to such substitutes would have virtually no effect on the costs of car-pedestrian accidents.

Thus the general deterrence rough guess must be made with special reference to the relative desirability and uniqueness of activities (as expressed in the market) and to their relation to the costs being allocated. Of course, in practice even a general deterrence rough guess may have reference to specific deterrence criteria. Some activities might be excluded because politically (and regardless of the market) we wished them to be left unaffected and fixed, despite the effect placing part of accident losses on them would have on accident costs.

The rough guess, then, is designed to exclude from consideration as potential loss bearers all those activities that could reduce costs only by causing losses which are clearly much greater, in terms of meeting individuals' desires as expressed in the market, than would result if one achieved the equivalent or greater reduction in accident costs by burdening other activities. Needless to say, all collective judgments as to relative abilities of different activities to achieve primary cost reduction, and as to relative costs at which these could be achieved, are very hard to make and very tenuous. They always involve a guess as to which activities can avoid accidents most easily (at the least expense) by reduction of the activity or by the introduction of safety devices. And even worse, they involve guesses as to what *combinations* of activities can achieve cost reductions most cheaply, for often the optimal reduction in accident costs would be achieved by dividing them among a number of activities. They are not, however, any harder than the equivalent rough guess that must be made under specific deterrence. And at the rough guess stage, where only activities that clearly cannot avoid the accident costs relatively cheaply are excluded, it may not be so hard in practice to make reasonably satisfactory decisions. . . .

A Guideline: Relationship Between Avoidance and Administrative Costs

The first guideline for picking the cheapest cost avoider is to seek the optimal relationship between avoidance costs and administrative costs. This simply means that if finding (or allocating costs to) the cheapest cost avoider is very expensive, it may lower total costs to allocate costs to a slightly more expensive cost avoider. Any cost savings achieved by the seemingly better allocation may not be worth the costs borne to find it. If placing accident costs on drivers according to miles driven results in nearly as much car-pedestrian accident cost avoidance as a charge on drivers according to age and accident involvement, and if the latter costs much more to administer, in practice the cheapest cost avoidance may well be achieved by the first method. . . .

A Guideline: Avoiding Externalization

The second guideline is to seek the maximum degree of internalization of costs consistent with the first guideline. This is a bit of economic jargon for a fairly simple concept. I have said that while we often do not know with certainty which allocation of costs would in theory accomplish the cheapest cost avoidance, in most cases we can rule out a great many allocations as almost certainly being no good. We may not know whether pedestrians or drivers are the cheapest cost avoiders of car-pedestrian accidents, but we may nonetheless be sure that either is better than taxpayers in general or television manufacturers. Therefore we should rule out any allocation that externalizes costs from pedestrians or drivers to taxpayers in general unless this allocation of costs is so much cheaper administratively that administrative savings make up for the lack of accident cost savings. . . .

Externalization occurs in three ways. I call the first externalization due to insufficient subcategorization, the second, externalization due to transfer, and the third, externalization as a result of inadequate knowledge.

Externalization Due to Insufficient Subcategorization

Allocation of car-pedestrian accident costs to driving in general (through a fixed tax on all drivers) might be an example of externalization due to insufficient subcategorization. If it turned out that teenage drivers were responsible for a disproportionate number of car-pedestrian accident costs, the allocation described would result in externalizing some of the cost from this subcategory of driving to the broader category of driving in general. Had the accident costs been allocated to drivers by accident involvement according to age group, the result would be that *all* drivers would bear a portion of the cost, but teen-age drivers would bear a greater share.

A broader example of externalization due to inadequate subcategorization would occur if the cost of car-pedestrian accidents were treated as general costs of living (the broadest category) and paid out of general taxes. If this were the case, accident costs might, in theory, affect whether people lived in America or in Argentina (assuming that these accident costs and the taxes based on them were different in the two countries). But once people decided to live in America, these costs would not affect their decisions to drive or walk. People would be in a position to make the proper choice for or against accidents at the "where shall we live" level but not at the "driving-walking" level. Thus only a very attenuated general deterrence pressure would exist. Of course, car-pedestrian accidents *are* general costs of living in America. But putting the cost on cars or on pedestrians will affect not only the decision to drive or walk (the subcategory) but—if the cost is significant enough—the decision to move to Argentina as well (the category).

Subcategorizing, moreover, is fairly immune from the post hoc ergo propter hoc fallacy, at least after a period of time. Suppose that car accident costs are put on drivers and that drivers of red cars bear more of the costs than drivers of blue cars, not because red cars are inherently more dangerous, not because drivers of red cars tend to drive more dangerously, but because of a coincidence, a statistical quirk. The cost pressure now borne by red cars will cause some drivers to switch to blue cars temporarily. But over time the quirk will disappear and the accident cost records of the two colors will tend to be equalized. If, surprisingly, the quirk persists, not because red cars are more dangerous than blue cars but because people who prefer red cars are more accident prone, some cost pressure in favor of blue cars will also persist. The ultimate equilibrium reached between red and blue car accident costs will depend on the extent to which preferring red cars is in fact linked to dangerous driving. Since there will be some drivers who prefer red cars and do not drive dangerously, the subcategorization will almost certainly not be as good as a further one which found a more direct criterion for identifying accident-prone drivers than driving red cars. But this does not mean that the subcategorization that took place was undesirable. To the extent that driving red cars and dangerous driving were simply connected by coincidence no harm was done, while to the extent that some real, even if subconscious link existed, a roundabout general deterrence pressure would have been achieved.

Since subcategorization is expensive, it will be cheaper at some point to have externalization to a broader category than to sub-categorize indefinitely. That is why the guideline is the greatest internalization possible consistent with the optimal level of adminis-trative costs.

There are three types of cost associated with subcategorization: the cost of gathering the facts necessary for subcategorization, the cost of analyzing the facts gathered and converting them into actuarially significant data, and the cost of assigning accident costs to increasingly smaller subcategories. If these costs are substantial, we might not be willing to spend the money to define some actuarially significant subcategories, even though their definition is possible, or to allocate accident costs on the basis of some of the actuarially significant subcategories we have actually defined. But this is simply another way of saying that sooner or later the point is reached where the cost of further subclassification is greater than the value in primary cost avoidance subclassification is likely to give.

The problem of how far to subcategorize in practice, however, is not an unduly complex one. It is in fact quite similar to the problem faced today by insurance companies when they subclassify for fault-proneness. They find it worth their while to charge higher rates for unmarried male drivers under 25 than for females, married males, or unmarried males over 25. But they do not break this down further and charge different rates for unmarried male drivers of 22 and 7 months as against unmarried male drivers of 22 and 8 months. The expected difference in accident-proneness — even if it could be measured — is not worth the cost of the subclassification.

The fact that the costs of subclassification limit the desirability of such subcategorization suggests that at times it may not be worth categorizing at all. If the reduction in primary accident costs achieved through general deterrence were minimal and the costs of employing that approach — the costs of categorizing — were too great, it might well be that social insurance paid out of general taxes would be the best solution. In effect, this would be placing the cost on the broadest category—living in a given country—of which all other classifications are subcategories. It seems unlikely, however, in view of insurance company actuarial practices, that no subclassification would be worthwhile in those areas where accidents and accident costs are a significant problem.

Externalization Due to Transfer

Allocation of car-pedestrian accident costs to pedestrians is one of many possible examples of externalization due to transfer. If the result of this allocation is that society picks up the tab through social insurance paid out of general taxes because most pedestrians are inadequately covered, what looks like a decision to put the costs on pedestrians rather than drivers actually results in neither bearing the costs. Under these circumstances, who should bear the costs depends on whether drivers or taxpayers are likely to be the cheapest cost avoiders, since the practical effect of allocating costs to pedestrians is to make taxpayers bear the costs.

There are many reasons why externalization due to transfer may occur, some practical and some political. Many of these will be discussed later when we compare how the fault system and the pure market approach would allocate the same costs. Here it is sufficient to note that the search for the cheapest cost avoider requires a comparison of the cost avoidance potential of those who will actually bear the accident costs after transfers, rather than of the initial loss bearers. Wherever one of the posttransfer loss bearers could be ruled out on either rough guess, subcategorization, or other grounds, it follows that the other loss bearer is the cheapest cost avoider.

Externalization Due to Inadequate Knowledge

Externalization due to inadequate knowledge would occur if pedestrians to whom car-pedestrian accident costs were allocated could not, because of inadequate knowledge or for psychological reasons, accurately foresee the risk of bearing accident costs involved in walking. We are assuming that pedestrians would be the cheapest cost avoiders if they could accurately convert into money the risk they take by walking. But if they cannot, because of inadequate knowledge, putting the cost on them would not affect their behavior and would have as little effect on accident control as scattering the cost would. It follows here too that whatever division between drivers and pedestrians were desirable in theory, allocation to drivers would give the cheapest cost avoidance in practice, assuming, of course, that they had adequate knowledge.

Avoiding Externalization: An Example

It may not be readily apparent why, when we do not know how to divide car-pedestrian accident costs between pedestrians and cars, it is better, from a general deterrence point of view, for cars to bear all the costs than for cars to bear part and for the rest to be externalized and removed from both cars and pedestrians.

An example may help explain this. Let us make the basic assumption that a rough guess has excluded all activities other than walking and driving as cheapest cost avoiders of car-pedestrian accidents. Let us also assume that the cheapest way of reducing car-pedestrian accident costs would be to affect both cars and walking somewhat, but that we do not know how much we should try to affect each. We do know, however, that together they cost society a certain amount. We can therefore say that from a resource allocation or general deterrence point of view we are always better off if we reduce or alter the combined activities (jointly or severally) up to the point where people would rather pay for the accident costs than bear the costs of a further reduction or alteration. Up to that point, the change "costs" people less than the accidents avoided and so is worthwhile. This is so, moreover, even if the change is entirely at the expense of one activity and even if a cheaper change could be accomplished *in theory* by affecting both. This last premise does not deny that the original change "cost" people less than it saved them; all it shows is that a theoretically better change was possible. But under our basic assumption, this theoretically better change is not available in practice. The situation we are examining is one where whatever part of the accident costs is not put on cars is removed from both cars and pedestrians and borne in a way that affects neither. Instead of the theoretically better combined effect on both activities, the result of dividing the costs is no change in walking and some in driving, when ex hypothesis a still greater change in driving would save more than it would cost.

A Guideline: The Best Briber

The third guideline for picking the cheapest cost avoider is rather different from the first two. It is to allocate accident costs in such a way as to maximize the likelihood that errors in allocation will be corrected in the market. This criterion assumes that despite transaction costs, a tendency exists for the market to find the cheapest cost avoider and influence him by bribes. It therefore urges us, to the extent we are unsure of who the cheapest cost avoider is, to charge accident costs to that loss bearer who can enter into transactions most cheaply. This means that if the initial loss bearer chosen is not in fact the cheapest cost avoider, we have minimized the obstacle transaction costs impose on the market's finding and influencing the behavior of the cheapest cost avoider. Obviously this criterion does not suggest picking a party that clearly is not the cheapest cost avoider simply because he can bribe easily. It suggests that to the extent we are unsure of our choice among possible cheapest cost avoiders, the best briber in the group is our best bet.

In practice, finding the best briber is somewhat more complicated than might appear. The requirement that this be the activity that can most cheaply enter into transactions with other potential cost causers hides within it several other requirements.

The first has to do with awareness of the risk. No matter how cheaply an activity can enter into transactions, it is not the best briber if those who engage in the activity are not sufficiently aware of the risks of accident costs involved. Without this awareness they would not know enough to try to enter into transactions to reduce their cost burden, and allocation of the costs to them would therefore not result in the market seeking out the cheapest cost avoider.

The second requirement involves the ease with which different activities can discover whom to bribe. In effect this simply means that one of the costs of entering into transactions is the cost of learning whom it is most advantageous to transact with. The use of the best briber guideline implies that we do not know collectively who the cheapest cost avoider is, since if we did we would have allocated the costs to him in the beginning. It also implies that we believe that market trial and error offers the best way of locating the cheapest cost avoider. It is not true, however, that such trial and error techniques are equally cheap for all the activities we might consider charging. Accordingly, we should charge that activity which can minimize all the costs of entering into transactions, including these information costs.

Finally, the cheapest way of entering into transactions may, in some situations, involve coercion of some potential free-loaders. Coercion in our society is costly, but this does not mean that it always costs more than it is worth. The best briber may therefore be the activity that can enter into transactions with the least use of coercion, or, if coercion is cheaper than other devices, which can call forth at the least cost that degree of coercion needed to bring along the would-be free-loaders and establish the transaction.

In other words, the loss bearer who can enter into transactions most cheaply must be chosen with *all* the cost elements involved in entering into transactions in mind, and these include not only the most obvious transaction costs, but also costs of risk, information, and even coercion where it is the cheapest device available.

Allocating costs to the best briber assumes that when the two other guidelines are insufficient, the cheapest cost avoider is more likely to be identified by the market than through a collective decision. This assumption is based on the usual reasons for preferring the market: market decisions automatically involve a great number of experiments by individual parties, changes in conditions do not require new collective decisions, mistakes will affect only the individual businessman, and so forth. Not all of these reasons, however, always apply. For example, if transactions can only be entered into by coercing nearly everyone involved in an activity to join in the bargain, the advantages of experimentation and flexibility do not exist. Where this is the case, burdening the best coercer results in something closely analogous to a societal determination of the cheapest cost avoider, except that the determination will be made by the burdened party rather than by the forum we would normally use to make such a societal decision. In these situations, where the myriad of individual choices usually contemplated in market decisions is unavailable, we may well decide that a societal decision made on an experimental basis (for society can also experiment to a limited extent) would be more likely to determine the cheapest cost avoider than the market.

The Hard Case

All this suggests that while the guidelines I have discussed will often indicate which activities should be charged with accident costs, there will be some areas in which they will be insufficient. In such areas the general deterrence approach can operate in three ways. It can make a guess about which activity is likely to be the cheapest cost avoider and then test it experimentally; it can divide costs among all the activities the choice has narrowed down to; or it can allocate losses in accordance with guidelines derived from approaches other than the market. . . .

Forum and Method

All this leads us to what is perhaps the most important single requirement for picking the cheapest cost avoider. A forum and method must be chosen that are best suited to take the previous criteria into account and to examine which party can most cheaply modify its behavior so as to avoid accidents. In other words, we must entrust the choice of cheapest cost avoider to a forum which is capable of (1) ruling out all those activities that by a kind of rough guess we would readily agree cannot be the cheapest cost avoiders of a category of accidents; (2) considering which allocation leads to maximum internalization at any given administrative cost level; (3) ruling out allocations that cost more to bring about than they are worth; (4) identifying the cheapest briber among loss bearers; (5) making the best intuitive guess of the activity likely to be the cheapest cost avoider (to the extent previous guidelines do not settle the issue) and testing that guess through controlled experiments or statistical record-keeping; and (6) doing all this without introducing other, extraneous factors.

Since in practice we will never want pure general deterrence, it is not worthwhile discussing at length which forum and method are most likely to accomplish it. The basic issue resolves itself into two questions: (1) Can the cheapest cost avoider be found more easily through case-by-case decisions of who could avoid costs most cheaply in each accident or by deciding directly which insurance categories or activities could avoid various categories of accidents most cheaply? (2) What body is likely to make each of these types of decisions best? My own conclusions are that if finding the cheapest cost avoider is our aim, case-by-case decisions are not desirable, in which case a body like the jury is very unlikely to be suitable for selecting the cheapest cost avoiders. . . .

NOTES AND QUESTIONS

1. Calabresi makes the point that both collectively and individually we undertake a wide variety of activities, despite the statistical certainty that a substantial injury toll will result. We do not, in other words, consider human life of unlimited value. Yet, in some situations we appear to behave otherwise. In the mine disaster or mountaineering rescue effort, for instance, we rarely calculate the cost of rescue so long as a real possibility of success exists. Why the difference?

2. Where, precisely, does the concern about postaccident compensation of injury victims fit into Calabresi's analytical scheme? Is there a tension between compensation and general deterrence? Between risk spreading and general deterrence? Are there situations where risk-spreading and general deterrence objectives support the same liability rules?

3. What are the income distribution implications of the general deterrence theory? Suppose transaction costs preclude much precision in subcategorization—suppose, for example, insurance companies' premium charges are assigned to drivers according to gross age-discrimination categories. *Which* drivers under age 25 are going to be coerced into substitute activities? Will it be the "worst" youthful drivers or some other discernible class? Even if premiums do accurately reflect individual safety records, will the "worst" drivers necessarily be most strongly deterred from driving? Do you see any political issues here?

4. In the first chapter, we examined Richard Posner's effort to demonstrate the congruence between considerations of economic efficiency and the law of negligence. Would a strict liability system, designed to implement the general deterrence theory, serve economic efficiency goals better than the negligence system? The issue is joined in Posner, Strict Liability: A Comment, at pp. 214-222, *infra*.

5. The Cost of Accidents is so rich and elaborate that it is not easily excerpted. I have chosen to emphasize what I regard as Calabresi's most important contribution: the systematic presentation of general deterrence theory as a means of optimizing accident costs. Even here, a substantial amount of detail was omitted—only because of space limitations—including his treatment of the important question of *what* constitutes the cost of an accident. The latter is a highly complex issue since we do not have a "demand" side of a market for accident victims—i.e., we cannot know the "price" victims would actually charge to be victimized.

For certain items, Calabresi points out, we can make a fairly accurate estimate by resorting to other markets; for example, property loss, medical expense, and some aspects of lost income. On the other hand, pain and suffering provides the clearest example of a cost that is virtually impossible to monetize through resort to a market. Throughout, we face a collateral issue: who is to make the required "collective" judgment—juries on a case-by-case basis, a legislative body through a scheduled approach, or some other institutional actor? See generally The Costs of Accidents, pp. 198-235.

In addition, Calabresi discusses at length the so-called specific deterrence approach, by which he means enacting safety regulations as a method of controlling accident costs; and he presents an extended analysis of the shortcomings of the fault system as an efficient method for allocating the costs of accidents. An interesting review of the book, describing the theoretical framework and attempting to apply it to the problem of controlling air pollution is Michelman, Book Review, 80 Yale L.J. 647 (1971).

The excerpt included in this book should convey a sense of the analytical framework that general deterrence theory provides for determining questions of cost allocation. However, there is no substitute for a more concrete consideration of applications of the theory. The following two excerpts serve that purpose by exploring general deterrence in what are arguably the two most critical current areas of accident law: defective products and auto accidents. Consider first Blum and Kalven's rejoinder to Calabresi, focusing on the auto accident problem.

The Empty Cabinet of Dr. Calabresi: Auto Accidents and General Deterrence*

Walter J. Blum & Harry Kalven, Jr.

...Calabresi...sets out a purpose he wishes to achieve in allocating the costs of auto accidents to society, and he proposes to do so by utilizing what he thinks are the possibilities for general deterrence which can be exploited by placing liability costs on motorists. Although in theory we today might have either too much or too little general deterrence pressure, Calabresi proceeds on the assumption that we have too little because no part of losses in non-fault accidents is now charged against motorists. Thus he assumes that moving toward optimization of costs calls for reducing the number of auto accidents.

An extended illustration of how liability law can be made to serve the objective of general deterrence is needed at this point. Whatever the economist's phrasing, what is being discussed is human behavior and ways of changing it. To put the problem in a formal way, for liability law the choice is between placing liability for a loss on Group A or leaving the loss on Group B upon whom it initially falls. In general deterrence terms, there is only one argument for imposing liability on Group A: we should do so if the behavior of Group A and of Group B will be different than when we leave the loss where it falls, and if this difference in behavior will reduce the net loss to society.

The tracing of such behavioral consequences can be quite complex. To use again an illustration from an earlier essay [Public Law Perspectives on a Private Law Problem — Automobile Compensation Plans (1965)], we will assume that Group A are manufacturers of a watch with a radium dial that will cause distinctive skin damage

*Source: 34 U. Chi. L. Rev. 239, 246-259, 261-263, 264-266 (1967).

to some users. The policy issue is who is to bear the cost of the skin damage — the manufacturers or the users, who as a class can be looked upon as Group B. The situation thus posed looks promising for various strategies of reducing the net losses from skin damage. Without working through these exhaustively, attention should be called to the possibilities that a substitute product not having radium on the dial might be developed, that a shield might be designed to protect against skin irritation, or that users might change their habits of wearing the watch continuously so as to reduce the hazards of exposure. Several things should be noted. None of the behavior listed has yet occurred, but is merely a future possibility. Each will represent a net gain in productivity to society so long as the cost of it does not exceed the reduction in losses it can effect. Further, independent of liability law there are strong motivations present to come up with safer products. Economic self-interest suggests that there must already be a race among manufacturers to develop a safer watch, especially when we look to the competition from substitute products. It would thus be a pretty fair prediction that sooner or later one of these possible lines of improvement will materialize, whatever the law does or does not do about the liability problem.

What Calabresi might show here is that the process will go faster — that the motivations toward safety will be deepened — if the law intervenes by placing liability on the manufacturers. And indeed he sketches what could be a plausible case in this situation. By making the manufacturer liable for all such losses, the law forces him to become aware of his recurring experience with the loss. Being an enterpriser he presumably can also calculate the costs of any given "remedy." The result is that he should be in a position to make a calculus of safety versus cost. Moreover, at least in the short run, it will be to his economic advantage to innovate safety measures that, by reducing his liability losses, will reduce the net costs of his operations, and thereby increase his net profit.

Assuming that the strategy of holding the manufacturers liable will induce them to seek out desirable safety measures, are there offsets in the motivation of users to minimize injuries? While they can now shift the loss of skin damage back to the manufacturer, it would seem that on balance the positive impact on manufacturers will be greater than the negative impact on users. The users are not centralized; they are unlikely to have technical expertise; they are less likely to perceive the incidence of damage; and for the individual user, the cost of seeking alternatives must outweigh the advantage to him. Whether the losses are left on users or are shifted off of them is not likely to make a perceptible difference in their behavior.

From the viewpoint of general deterrence there is another

advantage in placing liability on the manufacturer, an advantage which is paradoxical from the perspective of the common law. If liability is placed on the manufacturer by law, the accepted economic analysis is that through the operation of market forces this additional cost on the producer ultimately will be passed on to the users in the form of increased prices. Whichever way the law jumps here, the users of radium dial watches as a class will end up bearing the cost of losses from skin damage; yet there is a gain in having the loss placed on the manufacturer and shifted back to the users. The point is that the individual user is more likely to perceive the increase in his purchase price than to perceive his share of the risk of skin damage. In this sense he is more accurately confronted with the costs of using radium dial watches and gets to cast a more intelligent consumer vote. As a result, any "over consumption" of radium dial watches due to unawareness of the true costs of using them is eliminated.

We have dwelt at some length on this example to give a "feel" for the subtleties of the behavioral analysis on which general deterrence theory rests. In the radium watch situation we think it is likely that a case can be made out for placing liability on the manufacturer. Perhaps a vague perception of such a general deterrence calculus is at the source of the contemporary revolution in products liability law. This is not to say that a case for general enterprise liability to consumers has been established regardless of context. Consider, for example, the commercial airline. Motivation of the airline enterpriser to seek out safety may already be so close to optimum that change in liability law could not be justified by the argument that it would make a difference in behavior.

There is one final characteristic of the radium watch dial type of case that needs to be underscored. It is seen that the choice here is not ultimately between placing the loss on the consumer or relieving him of it; it is rather between placing the loss on him by one method or by another — either by leaving the loss on him initially or by shifting it to the manufacturer via liability rules in the expectation that it will be shifted back to the consumer via market forces in the form of increased prices. In this special context even a slight advantage in general deterrence may be persuasive. The strains on general deterrence analysis, however, may be considerably greater when the choice is whether or not to place the costs on a group that would not otherwise bear them.

. . . We propose here to attempt to think through in some detail where the pursuit of general deterrence in the auto case might lead. In thus going beyond the analysis Calabresi has so far offered on general deterrence, we run the risk of committing some errors in its name.

Since we presumably are talking about a change in the existing law, that law provides the baseline against which any gains in general deterrence have to be measured. The law now places the cost of negligently caused accidents on motorists and does so on the theory that motorists are having accidents a reasonable man would not have had. A proposal to place all costs on motorists on general deterrence grounds must therefore seek its justification in the likelihood that such an allocation of costs will reduce the accidents that even a reasonable man would otherwise have had, and will do so without excessive offsetting costs. To state the matter this way suggests that to establish the general deterrence thesis in respect to auto accidents will be something of an uphill fight.

There are other reasons why the auto field may prove an unfertile one for a general deterrence approach, both of which become apparent when we compare the auto case to the radium dial watch case. That there may have been a valid reason for placing all accident costs on the watch manufacturer does not establish a comparable reason for placing all accident costs on motorists. In very large part the cost savings that were expected to be achieved in the watch situation depended upon two circumstances. First, the manufacturer as an enterpriser is presumably in a position to make an economic calculus both about the probability of accidents from the watches and about the cost of alternative means of reducing them. He can therefore be expected to invest in safety up to the appropriate degree. Second, since as a result of market forces the consumer will in the end inevitably bear the cost of accidents from the watches, it is desirable to place him in a position where he will confront and recognize these costs as directly as possible, and will regulate his purchases accordingly. Neither of these points holds for the auto case. The driving of autos is not basically a business; and, as we shall see, it is far more difficult for the individual driver to make an economic calculus of accident losses and accident risks. Moreover, the decisive fact about auto accidents is that market forces do not inexorably place the costs of these accidents on any group. If the law elects to leave them on victims, they will be left on victims. If the law elects to place them on motorists, they will remain on motorists. There is therefore no point in talking about confronting any group with the costs of auto accidents on a theory that such a confrontation makes explicit to them what they must bear in any event.

Since the costs will not fall on motorists through the operation of market forces but will do so only if the law decides to place them on motorists, it may be useful to conceive of the issue as if it were one of taxation. The question is: Should motorists be taxed to pay for all the losses suffered by auto accident victims? We would agree with

Calabresi that a case for such a tax might be made if it can be shown that once the levy is imposed the behavior of motorists and potential victims will be so altered that there will be a significant improvement in achieving an optimum number of auto accidents for society as a whole.

As far as we can see, there are just three routes through which general deterrence can be expected to operate on auto accidents. It can lead to the discovery of safety devices or techniques. It can induce an improvement in driving habits. It can cause a discriminating reduction in the level of driving and a substitution of safer activities in place of driving. As Calabresi has summarized the prospects: "we may, if we are made to pay for car-caused accidents, drive less, or less at night, or less when we are of accident-prone ages, or with more safety devices than if we are not made to pay for accident costs when we decide to use a car." And he adds: "I call this thesis general deterrence, because it seeks to diminish accident costs not by directly attacking specific occasions of danger, but (like workmen's compensation) by making more expensive those activities which are accident prone and thereby making more attractive their safer substitutes."

It may be true, as James and now Calabresi have argued, that the advent of workmen's compensation did provide a stimulus for discovery of safety measures for coping with the industrial accident. But even if this reading of a complex history is correct, it does not help us much in tracing through why taxing motorists will lead to the discovery of safety measures for coping with the auto accident. The theory must be that motorist-consumer awareness of accident costs will create an increased demand by them for safer cars, thus putting the pressure on manufacturers to increase their level of innovation concerning safety features in autos. This sequence of behavior seems quite unpromising in view of the long history of consumer unwillingness to pay for safety in the purchase of autos. In any event, if one is serious about taking this route, it might make more sense to place the costs on manufacturers of autos directly.

As an aid to analysis, we proceed to test our reactions to an auto compensation plan which imposes strict liability on the manufacturer for all accidents involving its cars. Let us assume that this "plan" would be appropriately qualified to take account of various outrageous accidents, such as those caused by drunken driving of old, secondhand, beat-up cars. The auto case might then be seen as in line with the radium watch case or workmen's compensation—that is, there would be economic pressure put on the manufacturer, and these costs would be passed on to motorist-consumers via the market. Some intractable difficulties remain, nevertheless. It appears likely that a majority of accidents are traceable to the driver and not to the car. Certainly this kind of major change in liability policy ought not be predicated on the futuristic possibility of a driver-proof car. Even when we acknowledge, as we must, that changes in construction and design will have a greater impact on the gravity of accidents than on their incidence, it seems that the possibility of reducing auto accidents in major part falls beyond the reach of this strategy.

Further, it is well to recognize what we are talking about. The objective is to encourage inventiveness, research, discovery. And what are sought are not safer devices simply, but safer devices which are roughly the economic equivalent of those now in use. It is true that placing economic pressure on the manufacturer works in the right direction. But if we are willing to tax on behalf of this objective, we confront the difficulty that there are alternative ways of stimulating such research that might well be more effective dollar for dollar. We might, for example, utilize government subsidies of research laboratories and perhaps a scheme of honorific government prizes. But whatever might be the best technique, once the quest is avowedly for stimulating inventiveness it is no longer clear why motorists alone are the proper group to call upon to pay for the stimulus.

In the end, the strategy seems to come down to this: motorists, who on hypothesis are driving cars that could have been built safer, are to be made to pay for the losses from accidents caused by those cars in the hope of inducing someone else to be more inventive or persistent about designing safer cars.

One final point of perspective might be added. Once a safety discovery has been made and has become economically feasible, the compulsion of an accident compensation plan is not required to bring it into use. The existing law is capable of quite quickly absorbing the change as a matter of the common law calculus of negligence; and if that is thought too slow a process, society can always turn to specific safety legislation.

The second route for general deterrence in the auto case is one that sounds more familiar to the legal ear. It is that we might by law change the conduct of motorists. No one doubts that an enormous reduction in auto accidents would be effected if we could devise some way of altering the habits of motorists. The theory, although Calabresi does not seem to rely on it, must be that by imposing the "liability tax" on those involved in auto accidents without regard to fault, we can make them more sensitive to the connections between their driving behavior and the accidents, and thus induce a change in their habits. Since the law already imposes on them the obligation to drive with reasonable care, the hope here is to induce what might well be called super-care. In brief, the thesis is that economic pressures may be able to mould conduct better than law using criminal fines, license suspensions, and tort liability keyed to negligence. The target at this point in the analysis is not the more effective screening of potential drivers, but rather the interstitial improvement in the behavior of those who are already driving.

At the threshold this approach runs into a major obstacle. It is surely commonplace knowledge that any driver is always risking not simply the safety of others, but equally his own personal safety. Inasmuch as the situation thus already seems to present a very high inducement to safety, it is hard to see what additional incentive to super-care will be added by economic pressure.

If we go on to assume that there may be some people who would react to the change in costs, there are some less obvious difficulties to consider. There is the circumstance that any motorist compensation plan will operate through use of auto insurance. The economic pressure or tax we seek to impose consequently will appear in the form of premiums. In turn this means that the premiums will have to be differentiated so as to show the individual motorist that if he engages in super-care, he will be rewarded by a smaller premium. Just how one does this is not clear. Presumably, since we are not going to introduce the fault system all over again in order to graduate insurance premiums, the allocation will be on the basis of some test such as involvement in accidents. If the motorist understands that this is the way premiums are graded, he may learn the wrong lesson or be discouraged when he realizes that, no matter how careful he is, he will not get his "reward" if he is the victim of another's carelessness.

But beyond this, there is a further sense in which the motorist's fate is linked to the behavior of others. The nature of insurance requires that we deal with classes of persons representing different degrees of risk. Any one motorist is therefore stuck with a kind of guilt by association. The extent to which he gets his premium adjusted downward for his super-care always turns in part on the incidence of accident involvement by strangers.

These difficulties are no surprise. They reflect those characteristics of insurance which critics of the current common law system have pointed to in arguing that, because of the dilution of impact due to insurance, even the fault system does not deter. Further, if some way of making auto insurance a more discriminating mechanism among insured motorists could be devised, there is nothing that would keep us from using it under the existing system of negligence law without waiting upon a compensation plan.

But even if we assume for the sake of argument that adjustment of insurance premiums can have an impact on motorist conduct, the quest for super-care is still left with one last difficulty. The aim of general deterrence strategy, it may bear repeating, is an overall net reduction of costs. Super-care may generate offsetting costs.

From the point of view of society, the simple facts are that people can drive too carefully, and excessive care may produce problems of its own. Since the impact on driving habits very likely will be most evident with respect to speed, let us look briefly at the consequences of a widespread but not universal reduction in speed below what is now under the negligence calculus thought to be a reasonable maximum. There is a distinct possibility that this change may work to increase the number of accidents. It is becoming a commonplace that the slow driver on a throughway is as much of a hazard as his excessively speedy brother, largely because his pattern does not mesh easily with that of most drivers, thus resulting in periodic foul-ups of the traffic flow. Moreover, if super-care causes a significant number of drivers to change habits, there will on the average be a general slowing up of traffic. This can be counted on to set off a chain of cost consequences, such as loss of time of those being transported or the building of additional roads or the altering of existing ones.

Society of course can always change the speed limits when it is persuaded that slower traffic is more desirable. The puzzle is why we would ever use indirect stimuli to induce people to drive slower than the legal limit. The quest for super-care may, it is true, work better on other aspects of motorist conduct than speed, but we think the analysis has been carried far enough to suggest that there are troublesome problems of offsetting costs to be taken into account. We may in our argument be doing no more than repeating a concern the common law has always had against overinhibiting an activity. The point is more widely understood in a different context: the overanxious parent is not the model.

We come to the third route through which general deterrence may be expected to operate: the discriminating reduction in the level of motoring. It is probably accurate to say that this represents Calabresi's best hope for general deterrence in the automobile field. In contrast to stimulating safety discovery or to inducing super-care in driving, there is little doubt but that imposing higher charges on motoring will affect behavior significantly. This is simply to say that we have another illustration of the great axiom of economics that price will affect demand.

Calabresi, as we might anticipate, has a more interesting idea in mind than lessening auto accidents by a blunt reduction in the overall level of motoring. He would seek to reduce the level of driving in a discriminating way by forcing the motorist to attend to the distinctive costs of driving under various definable conditions. If, for example, teen-age driving shows a distinctively higher than average rate of involvement in auto accidents, these costs can be placed on such driving by means of differential insurance premiums. We can then expect that "by making more expensive those activities which are accident prone" we would discourage them. Presumably under this scheme there would be fewer teenagers driving, and consequently costs in the society would be reduced.

This is indeed an attractive prospect. It links legal control to the free market mechanism and thereby achieves its social goals with a minimum of direct restraints on individual freedom and with a minimum of reliance on the political process and majority vote. It accommodates with little friction a wide variety of judgments as to whether the activity remains worthwhile at higher prices. As a matter of affecting behavior it will, we repeat, work.

Insofar as we can follow Calabresi at this point, his thinking runs this way. Under a motorist compensation plan it will be possible for insurance purposes to group motorists into specific categories and to base rates on involvement in accidents regardless of fault. Thus premiums for teenagers will be based on the number of accidents in which teenagers are involved, wholly apart from the number in which they are at fault. This process of dealing with specific subcategories of driving could be extended so long as using smaller breakdowns proved to be feasible.

To turn these points into an argument against the common law system and in favor of liability without fault, an important further step is required. It must be shown that this scheme of accident accounting can be exploited to a greater extent under a strict liability system than under a fault system. It is this prospect that we find unpersuasive. Today the differentials in insurance rates are in large measure based on the incidence of involvement and not of ultimate liability due to fault. Further, there is nothing in the nature of things to prevent the insurance institution under a negligence liability law from more fully utilizing such an accounting in setting its rates. The main subcategories in use today—age, urban/rural, sex—are not wedded to fault; and whatever subcategories might be developed under a motorist compensation plan could just as readily be developed today. Hence, all that would be accomplished along these lines by shifting from fault to strict liability would be to increase the total charge placed on motoring but not to place it any more discriminatingly among motorists.

On our view, the argument stumbles over this initial hurdle; nevertheless, it may be useful to push the analysis a little deeper. Thus far we have been concerned with discriminating among motoring activities solely in terms of seeking to repress those which carry the greater risks of accident—that is, we have been exploring the possibility of maximizing the amount of accident loss reduction for every dollar of "tax" imposed on the motorist. One might, however, misunderstand Calabresi to be saying something further, to be suggesting that there may be another dimension to the discrimination he advocates. Is it possible to locate as targets for repression those categories of motoring which are of lesser value to society? It will be remembered that the objective is not simply to reduce accidents, but rather to reduce the net costs of accidents. If qualitative discrimination could be made to work, it would have the benign consequence of holding down the level of accident-producing activity at what would seem to be the lowest offsetting cost. But this happy prospect quickly evaporates upon analysis. There is no likelihood that the driving categories which have the highest accident potential are those which have the lowest social value, as is sufficiently shown by the case of the urban fire engine or police car. In any event, there is no palatable way of ranking driving activity in terms of its social utility. Is driving on weekends less socially useful than driving to work? Undoubtedly some people would be willing to rank the activity for all of us, but we obviously run afoul here of the basic issue of sumptuary legislation.

We are left then, as we compare behavior under the existing system with behavior under the proposed system, with the prospect of an across-the-board reduction in the level of motoring, and a consequent reduction in the overall number of auto accidents. Under these circumstances, whether or not the change over is desirable turns on weighing the offsetting costs that flow from reducing the general level of the activity. Many are obvious though difficult to trace in any detail. There will be a loss of either work time or leisure time insofar as people shift to slower forms of transportation; there may be an increase in hazard in the more intensive use of some forms of substitute transportation such as car pools or helicopters; there may be increased investment in mass transportation and underuse of investment already committed to auxiliary motoring facilities like garages and parking lots; there may even be a change in driving habits as traffic flows lessen. In brief, this one change will set off a chain reaction of other changes, not all obviously advancing the goal of economizing on resources; and all of these consequences must be taken into account in appraising whether the changeover in liability rules will yield in the end a net reduction in costs to the society.

One of the possible consequences is interesting enough to stop for. In the radium watch example, it will be recalled, we were concerned not only with the conduct of the manufacturer, but also with the conduct of the victim-consumer. Similarly, in the auto case we should look not exclusively at the behavior of motorists, but at the behavior of potential victims (for convenience, pedestrians) as well. Is there any likelihood that changing the behavior of the one will produce any offsetting change in the behavior of the other? More specifically, as we shift all costs off victims in order to encourage super-care in motorists or to reduce the level of motoring, will we be lifting existing restraints on pedestrians, causing them to become more careless or to engage more freely in risky alternatives such as riding motor bikes? We would readily agree that there is a lack of perfect symmetry here. The motorist and the pedestrian are not literally on a see-saw; any legal change on the one that affects his conduct in the desired direction does not necessarily produce an equal change in the wrong direction in the conduct of the other. Nevertheless, in the grand toting up of all pluses and minuses which the general deterrence analysis calls for, we would expect fo find some additional costs due to liberating pedestrians to be more careless....

Calabresi argues that a motorist compensation plan as contrasted to other viable alternatives will move us further in the direction of optimizing accidents. He has, however, been willing to play the game only with limited stakes. The dollar magnitudes he wishes to use under a motorist compensation plan to control driver behavior are determined by the number of dollars that will be needed to compensate victims under the plan. As we shall see, there is no likely relationship between the amount of repressant on motorists required to optimize accidents and the amount of compensation needed to pay victims. We may still have too many auto accidents, and thus still be short of the goal. Or, as we have already indicated, the opposite may well turn out to be the case, leaving us with too few accidents.

This line of thought invites readdressing ourselves to the goal of bringing about the optimum number of auto accidents. If we liberate ourselves for the moment from conventional uses of law in the accident area, how might we conceivably arrange matters so as to come closer to that goal? The answer admittedly takes on a science-fiction flavor.

If we were to assume a kind of omniscience giving us full knowledge relevant to auto accident costs—data we clearly do not now have—we could build a mathematical model for stating the optimization problem in precise quantitative terms. Once we reached this stage, there would be no difficulty in solving the mathematical problem thus posed. To set up the model, our omniscience would have had to provide the answers to the following questions: (1) What factors have a bearing on auto accident costs? (2) How should these factors be priced or translated into dollar terms? (3) What is the price curve for each of the factors—that is, how does its contribution to accident costs vary with increases and decreases in its magnitude? (4)

How do these curves interact on each other? When the computer finally ground to a halt, it would tell us what pattern of factors would give us the optimum allocation of resources for the auto accident problem. The law would thereby be told exactly where it should be going. The legal problem would then be how best to apply pressures so as to bring about this mix.

In order to leave the widest area for individual choice and to achieve our goal in the most efficient, frictionless way, we would want to use the price mechanism as the control wherever possible. This would call for intruding into the market with taxes or subsidies as conditions required: for example, if optimization called for a certain number of autos on the road, we could, by adjusting the price of motoring up or down, get to the desired number, while leaving to each individual the choice of driving or not. In making these moves no consideration would be given to the compensation of victims. Compensation payments would be made under the social security system, and there would be no need to draw any balance between the "prices" the motorists would pay for driving and the size of the fund required for compensation. The final result would be a perfection of general deterrence — a Utopian use of the strategy.

It is worth noting that this fantasy serves among other things to illuminate the meaning of the key phrase, "costs of driving." In our Utopia it is more than possible that the costs of driving will be greater than under any motorist compensation plan. They will, however, be costs of driving in just as valid a sense as they are asserted to be costs of driving under a motorist compensation plan. Since in the auto accident situation costs are instrumental and since there is no way of relying on the market to fix them, they can only be assigned by some authority. For this reason it can never be helpful to talk of placing the costs of driving on driving. . . .

It is time to bring justice back into the discussion. We noted at the outset that Calabresi, finding the idea largely unintelligible, had virtually ruled it out as a goal for the legal system. And in so doing he was echoing the views of fellow economists who would distinguish sharply between justice and economic efficiency as guides to social policy. We stumble here upon what we suspect is a fundamental issue which goes well beyond auto compensation. There are various ways in which the basic query may be put: Is there any meaning "left over" for justice once efficiency goals have been attended to? Can efficiency ever conflict with justice?

Whatever the full range of such questions, they are vividly framed by the controversy over general deterrence and the auto accident. If society is coercively to impose a burden on citizens, we submit that there must be some justification for imposing it on one group rather than another. In this context we mean by justice the avoidance of what will be perceived as an arbitrary imposition of a burden.

The difficulty with general deterrence as a justification for shifting non-fault auto accident losses to motorists is that it is too fragile to carry the weight that would be put on it. Where the burdens are clear, certain, and not trivial, something more than conjecture about possible patterns of behavior is needed as a countervalue. To put the disagreement in a nutshell: when we know as little as we appear to know now about the prophecies of general deterrence, it is unjust to tax motorists on behalf of it.[55]

A more critical difficulty turns on the relative magnitude of the gains and the burdens involved. Let us assume that we know enough to devise a general deterrence strategy and to put it into operation, and that when it is implemented there will at the end of the year be an increase in the gross national product of $1000 as a result of a reduction in the net costs of auto accidents by that amount. Let us assume further that to achieve this social good it is necessary to levy an additional tax of $100 on each motorist. We pick an example as extreme as this in order to raise a key question: Is there not some point at which even an unqualified gain in the efficient allocation of resources, achievable only through this particular route, is not of sufficient importance to justify the burdens which it calls for placing on particular individuals?

Although we recognize that the most rigorous and austere economic analysis might insist that the answer is no, we are quite confident that most people, and especially those in the traditions of law, would say that the answer must be yes. We therefore have a final difficulty with the Calabresi thesis. Even if we are to resolve all doubts in favor of the ability of a general deterrence strategy to bring about a net reduction in the costs of auto accidents, we may still confront a disturbing imbalance between the social gain achieved and the individual burdens imposed. Where the social gain seems small and the individual burdens in the aggregate seem relatively large, we find ourselves thinking of the dangers of reversing Churchill's famous epigram: "Never have so many owed so much to so few." If we were to put our reaction into somewhat less personal terms, it would be that there very likely are hidden values that cannot be translated into economic costs, such as the value of having individuals understand why they are being subjected to a special tax and the value of not departing too lightly from traditional and accepted ways of doing things. . . .

___

55. Put another way, it is unjust not also to tax others who contribute to the accidents.

NOTES AND QUESTIONS

1. Blum and Kalven begin by carefully limiting the terms of the dispute. They want to challenge Calabresi only on the usefulness of general deterrence in devising a system for handling auto accident cases. In limiting their response, they indicate general acceptance of his analysis as applied to defective product cases. This dichotomization is more restrictive than the potential scope of the theory. With the Calabresi-Blum and Kalven exchange in mind, try to assess the usefulness of the general deterrence theory in allocating losses in other major unintentional injury situations. How useful is it, for example, in analyzing the medical malpractice problem? Landowner's liability? Is it relevant to relational torts like defamation?

2. While general deterrence is essentially designed to optimize primary accident costs, Calabresi repeatedly argues that the theory may achieve the best mix of primary, secondary, and tertiary cost considerations. In cataloguing the shortcomings of general deterrence strategy for resolving auto accident cases, do Blum and Kalven adequately deal with this point? How does general deterrence measure up against fault in secondary and tertiary cost terms?

3. Blum and Kalven argue that insurance rating practices — viz. subcategorizations among insureds — are unlikely to change much under a strict liability system. Consequently, they argue, deterrence pressure would probably continue to operate in about the same way as under the fault system. Who has the better of this point? Is it dependent on the impact of a compensation scheme on informal settlement practices? On political considerations?

4. The extent of subcategorization by auto insurers, considered above, raises an issue about effective internalization of accident costs. Reconsider the other major threats to effective internalization discussed by Calabresi: inadequate information to assess accurately the risk of injury, and inability to prevent transfer to an external cost-bearer. Have Blum and Kalven made out the case for retaining the fault system with respect to these considerations? Are they important concerns in auto accident cases?

5. Blum and Kalven point out that the statutory ceiling on loss covered by a compensation plan is established through the political process, without reference to market deterrence considerations. Consequently, there is no particular reason to expect that we will get an appropriate amount of general deterrence. How might Calabresi respond?

6. Auto compensation plans enacted in recent years feature fixed ceilings on recovery and limit pain and suffering. See generally Blum and Kalven, Ceilings, Costs and Compensation in Auto Compensa-

tion Plans, pp. 287-314, *infra,* for an analysis of the current legislative approaches. While the common law system has often been retained above the fixed ceiling, compensation under the plan itself limits reparation, in contrast to the law of negligence. On the other hand, the strict liability system for defective products, which has been established through court decisions, maintains a commitment to the common law approach to damages. How would a comparative analysis of the two non-fault strategies proceed from a general deterrence perspective?

7. In a car-bicycle collision, how would Calabresi have us decide whether the activity to be charged is driving or bicycling? Would he make the decision on a case-by-case or a category-wide basis? What would be Blum and Kalven's response?

8. In analyzing Holmes's The Common Law, a question was raised about the relationship between maximizing individual autonomy of action and adopting a liability system based on the fault principle. See Question 3, p. 14, *supra.* Does the Calabresi-Blum and Kalven debate afford a new perspective on the relationship of liability rules (strict liability versus fault) to individual freedom of choice?

Toward a Test for Strict Liability in Tort*

Guido Calabresi & Jon T. Hirschoff

I. Introduction

. . . Strict liability has never meant that the party held strictly liable is to be a general insurer for the victim no matter how or where the victim comes to grief. General insurance was not the rule in classical instances of strict liability, such as ultrahazardous activities, or in legislatively mandated instances, such as workmen's compensation, and it is not the rule in the recent instances of application such as products liability. The questions which the courts now find themselves asking (and being asked) in the new areas of application, such as products liability, involve the same basic issue as did equally difficult questions faced in traditional areas of strict liability, which were couched in words such as "natural or unnatural use" and "arising out of and in the course of employment." The issue is just where strict liability should stop.

Despite the courts' recognition that strict liability must be

Source: 81 Yale L.J. 1055, 1056-1078, 1082-1084 (1972).

limited, they have seldom been very confident in trying to describe the limits. Indeed, their efforts at answering the questions posed in strict liability cases seem in many cases to degenerate into either meaningless semantic disputes or attempts at balancing the costs of the accident against the costs of avoiding it; yet the latter approach sounds devilishly like the very calculus of negligence, or Learned Hand's test for fault, which strict liability was meant to replace.

Strict liability's limits can, however, be defined in a meaningful way. The questions the courts have been asking are often highly relevant to those limits, and strict liability so limited is very different from the negligence calculus, or Learned Hand's test for fault. Analysis of strict liability's limits together with a suggested test for strict liability will, we believe, give insight into both the negligence calculus and its growing disfavor.

II. The Learned Hand Test Considered

Learned Hand's test for fault defines the defendant's duty of care as a function of three variables: (1) the probability that the accident will occur, (2) the gravity of the injury which will be suffered if the accident does occur, and (3) the burden of precautions adequate to prevent such accidents. If the cost to the defendant of avoiding the accident would have been less than the cost of the accident, discounted by the probability of its occurrence, the defendant's failure to avoid the accident is termed negligence.

For the purpose of the first parts of this discussion, we will assume that the traditional test for fault, as given expression in Learned Hand's formula, was designed to do what Professor Posner says it was designed to do, namely to minimize the sum of accident costs and the costs of accident avoidance. The Learned Hand test would seem to accomplish this objective in theory, because *if it were applied perfectly,* it would put the costs of the accident on the injurer when and only when it was cheaper for him to avoid the accident costs by appropriate safety measures than to pay those costs. *Assuming injurers had the requisite foresight,* this would cause potential injurers to avoid all accidents worth avoiding, i.e., those where avoidance costs less than the accident, and to have only those accidents not worth avoiding.

The application of the traditional rule of contributory negligence would make some difference, but not much. Using the rubric of the test, contributory negligence would exist when the victim, too, could have avoided the accident at a cost lower than the cost generated by the accident. Since under the traditional rule contributory negligence is a complete defense, the cost would remain on the victim despite the negligence of the injurer, *even if avoidance by the injurer would have cost less than avoidance by the victim.* Thus, even in the wonderful, let us freely admit, fantastic world of Professor Posner, in which none of the costs of an accident are borne by third parties other than the injurer and victim, and in which there is perfect foresight, the rule of contributory negligence would prevent the negligence calculus from optimizing primary accident cost reduction. The potential injurer who could avoid a $100 accident at a cost of $5, knowing that the victim could do so at a cost of $50, might well not undertake the $5 safety measure because of his knowledge that the victim will either avoid the accident or be held contributorily negligent. Given adequate foresight, one would expect the accident to be avoided, but at a cost $45 higher than necessary.

A Learned Hand test for injurer liability with the defense of contributory negligence removed, however, would also fail to optimize accident costs, and for exactly the same reason. Under such a rule, there would be instances in which the victim who could avoid an accident more cheaply than could the injurer would fail to do so, because he would know that the injurer would nonetheless be held liable. Thus the *correct* optimizing rule, under the Learned Hand test, would be to have a doctrine of contributory negligence, but to apply it only where the cost of injurer avoidance exceeds the cost of victim avoidance.

Whatever defects the Learned Hand test may have, given the existence of an absolute defense of contributory negligence, it can at least be said that if the test worked, all the accidents worth avoiding would be avoided. If they were occasionally avoided at somewhat greater expense than necessary, that would not be a matter of great consequence. At the same time, it must be recognized that all the costs of all the accidents not worth avoiding would fall on the victim, raising distributional or justice issues. We will, however, postpone consideration of those issues to a later section of this article, and limit our discussion here to primary accident cost reduction.

If we make the assumptions under which the Learned Hand test would work adequately, the fascinating thing is that as good a result in terms of reducing primary accident costs could be achieved by a liability rule which is the exact reverse of the Learned Hand test. Under such a "reverse Learned Hand test," the costs of an accident would be borne by the *injurer* unless accident avoidance on the part of the victim would have cost less than the accident. If a reverse contributory negligence test were added, the victim would bear the accident costs only if the injurer could not also have avoided the accident at less cost than the accident entailed. A reverse Learned

Hand test, in other words, which always made the injurer liable without fault unless the victim were negligent, and even then held the injurer liable if he also were negligent, would do for primary accident cost avoidance just what the actual Learned Hand test with contributory negligence is said to do. The only difference between the tests is distributional. Under the Learned Hand test, the costs of all accidents *not* worth avoiding are borne by victims, whereas under the reverse Learned Hand test they would be borne by injurers.

In focusing on the reverse Learned Hand test, we are not simply playing with mirrors. The point is that a perfect world with perfect foresight is a prerequisite to optimization of primary accident cost reduction under *either* Learned Hand type test, and that given such a world, any number of other devices would also accomplish that goal. To the extent that we are concerned with the practical minimization of accident costs, the choice among these devices will depend not on their *theoretical* ability to optimize accident costs given certain assumptions, but on the degree to which the particular assumptions required by each device actually do obtain.[17] We will suggest a test which we think is much more likely than either Learned Hand type test to accomplish a satisfactory job of primary accident cost optimization. We also think that application of the proposed test requires asking questions which are closely related to those questions courts have always asked in strict liability cases. That is why we believe the proposed test is an appropriate one for defining the limits of strict liability.

III. The Strict Liability Test Defined

When a case comes to judgment under either of the two Learned Hand type tests, a cost-benefit analysis is made by an outside governmental institution (a judge or a jury) as to the relative costs of the accident and of accident avoidance. Liability would be placed on the party initially free of responsibility only if the *decider* found the benefits of avoidance (i.e., not incurring the cost of the accident) to be greater than the costs of such avoidance to that party. The strict liability test we suggest does not require that a governmental institution make such a cost-benefit analysis. It requires of such an institution only a decision as to which of the parties to the accident *is*

17. These assumptions relate, inter alia, to the cost of information to each party, the absence of psychological or other impediments to acting on the basis of available information, the administrative costs of shifting losses, and the extent to which parties actually bear the costs which the particular tests impose upon them. These are, in economists' terms, principally assumptions relating to transaction costs and externalization....

in the best position to make the cost-benefit analysis between accident costs and accident avoidance costs and to act on that decision once it is made. The question for the court reduces to a search for the cheapest cost avoider.[19]

So stated, the strict liability test sounds deceptively simple to apply. Instead of requiring a judgment as to whether an injurer *should* have avoided the accident costs because the costs of avoidance were less than the foreseeable accident costs as the Learned Hand test does, the strict liability test would simply require a decision as to whether the injurer or the victim was in the better position both to judge whether avoidance costs would exceed foreseeable accident costs and to act on that judgment. The issue becomes not *whether* avoidance is worth it, but which of the parties is relatively more likely to find out whether avoidance is worth it. This judgment is by no means an easy one, but we would suggest that in practice it is usually easier to make correctly than is the judgment required under either the Learned Hand test or its reverse.[21] It also implies a lesser degree of governmental intervention than does either of the Hand Type tests.

As a first step toward seeing what is implied in such a strict liability test, we propose to examine how the issues raised by courts in various areas of strict liability relate to the proposed test. We will do this first in an oversimplified context, treating accidents as though they involved only the injurer and the victim. Subsequently, we will examine what is implied for the test in considering accidents as events involving whole categories of victims, injurers and affected third parties.

In strict products liability cases, the first question asked is, "was

19. The cheapest cost avoider has been elsewhere defined as the party "an arbitrary initial bearer of accident costs would (in the absence of transaction and information costs) find it most worthwhile to 'bribe' in order to obtain that modification of behavior which would lessen accident costs most." . . . This definition, unlike the terminology we have been using in this article, includes the costs of accident avoidance within the term "accident costs." It should be clear upon reflection that the most"worthwhile"bribe would be one to the party who is in the best position both to determine what accident cost avoidance measures will result in the minimal sum of avoidance costs and accident costs (i.e., to make the cost-benefit analysis) and to act upon that determination. We do not mean to suggest that the party in the best position to make the cost-benefit analysis is always in the best position to act upon it; where that is not the case, the decision requires weighing comparative advantages.

The imposition of accident costs on the cheapest cost avoider will, of course, have its own set of distributional consequences, and these may well differ from those resulting from applications of the Learned Hand or reverse Learned Hand tests.

21. It is an easier judgment because it looks to questions such as which party is better informed as to risks and alternatives instead of to questions requiring the weighing of accident costs and avoidance costs, both of which must be subjectively determined by the trier of fact.

there a defect?" A defect may be defined to mean simply that something went wrong. All that in turn means, however, is that a safer product might have been designed, and this would mean that there is a defect whenever there is an accident. If, instead, existence of a defect is defined to mean a failure of a product to meet levels deemed customary in the trade, then strict liability would be even less successful in achieving optimal reduction of primary accident costs than is the Learned Hand test and would be far narrower than fault. It is not surprising, therefore, that courts have tended to reject both of these extremes.

The courts have instead tended to determine whether a defect exists by asking a series of secondary questions relating to (a) the adequacy of warning and (b) the use to which the product was put. They have also noted that assumption of risk on the part of the victim might serve either to negate the existence of a defect or to be a defense to it. In fact, the defense of assumption of risk may be viewed as broad enough to encompass adequacy of warning and appropriateness of product use, which are in turn appropriate ways of raising some of the questions implicit in the strict liability test we have offered.

Let us look first to adequacy of warning. Suppose that a product occasionally causes the user's leg to fall off. Failure to warn the potential user that this may happen in .0001 per cent of the cases will normally result in manufacturer liability. But even such a warning is not likely to allow the user to make an intelligent cost-benefit analysis between accident and avoidance costs. Unless the user has reason to believe himself to be in the dangerous category and unless a close substitute exists which at some cost avoids the danger, the user is hardly in a position to evaluate the benefits of the product as against its costs. The producer may seem to be no better suited, but if we move from a static to a dynamic situation, this will not be the case. The producer is in a position to compare the existing accident costs with the costs of avoiding this type of accident by developing either a new product or a test which would serve to identify the risky .0001 per cent. The consumer, in practice, cannot make this comparison. Relatively, the producer is the cheapest cost avoider, the party best suited to make the cost-benefit analysis and to act upon it.

Should a patch test be developed which enables the consumer to identify himself as an especially risky user, the situation may well be changed. The existence of the patch test, sold together with the product and coupled with a warning, may be enough to make the consumer the party best able to avoid the costs of mishap. This will depend in part, but only in part, on the nature of the warning and the adequacy (including ease of use) of the patch test. Even if the warning is unmistakably clear and the patch test 100 per cent accurate, however, the manufacturer may still be in the best position to make the cost-benefit analysis. For the analysis depends not only on the adequacy of the warning and the likelihood that a risky user will be able to identify himself, but also on the availability of alternatives to the product. If the product is a cosmetic with many reasonably close substitutes, identifying and clearly warning the risky group will very likely put the user in the best position to choose. If instead the product is a medicine, the use of which is the only way of saving the user's life, identifying and warning the risky users probably would not suffice to make the users the better choosers. [29] The manufacturer would in those circumstances be best suited to compare the cost of the occasional lost leg with the *cost of further research* designed to give rise to an adequate substitute entailing fewer risks, or equivalent risks but to another definable group.

We do not mean to suggest that these examples resolve the issue, but they should serve to indicate why, when courts ask about adequacy of warning in attempting to determine whether a defect exists, they are often on the right track. The examples also demonstrate why mere clarity of warning or mere percentages of likelihood of harm may not by themselves resolve the issue. For these are only factors going to the basic question of who is in the best position to make the cost-benefit analysis and act upon it, and must be considered together with other factors such as availability of substitutes and the nature of the user's use of the product in order to determine liability.

The relevance of the use to which the product is put has seemed especially troublesome for the courts. The fact that a lawn mower was not designed to protect its driver should he care to drive it on the throughway ought not to be viewed as a design defect making the manufacturer liable either to users or to rescuers. But neither should a

29. This is because the cheapest cost avoider must be able to make the required analysis and act upon it, and the only meaningful action is one which would reduce the risk. Where the product is the only medicine which will save the user's life, it is meaningless to say that the user is in a position to act upon the basis of the analysis.

The cost of action by the manufacturer in such a situation (i.e., research for alternative products) may have an undesirable effect in the long run. Charging the manufacturer may unduly reduce the number or output of drug companies. Whether the long run effect, if it exists, is sufficiently adverse to negate the short run effect depends on the relative ability of the users as against the manufacturers to avoid the accident costs in the long run, that is, on which is the cheapest cost avoider in the long run. In this example it is hard to see what the user could do in the long run. In other situations, however, the long run issue may turn on the relative merits of more output in different industries.

Undesirable long run effects may, of course, be dealt with through governmental subsidies funded by lump sum taxes on the long run cheapest cost avoider; this seems to us to be a better solution by and large than denying liability....

warning that the lawn mower ought not to be used where there are rocks *preclude* manufacturer's liability to passers-by hit by rocks or even to the user himself. Again, the issue is who can best make a cost-benefit analysis and act on it, viewed in realistic terms. Many uses of a product, though forbidden by the producer, are actually not unexpected. Other uses, though not forbidden, are in fact so unusual as to make the user more suited to make the cost-benefit analysis than the manufacturer.

Moreover, the question whether the manufacturer could sufficiently anticipate the use as to be in a good position to make the cost-benefit analysis has little to do with whether society deems the use worth its costs. In other words, it is logically distinct from the question of whether the user was contributorily negligent. Thus a user may have an excellent reason for driving down the throughway on a lawn mower (the benefits of the use outweigh the costs), in which case the collective decider in a negligence/contributory negligence regime ought not to deem his conduct to be contributorily negligent. Yet such a user would in all probability be a better evaluator than the manufacturer of the costs and benefits involved. As a consequence, his strict liability suit against the manufacturer for injuries resulting from such driving would fail. Conversely, the fact that a use of the product is deemed contributorily negligent does not necessarily mean that the manufacturer is not in a better position than the user to evaluate the costs and benefits. To take an example from a different area of strict liability, a worker may negligently use a piece of equipment, but his employer may nonetheless be in a better position to evaluate the relevant costs and benefits. That is, he may know the propensity to negligent use and be better able to evaluate a substitute piece of equipment which cannot readily be negligently used. This explains why contributory negligence has not been an inevitable defense to an action based on strict liability.

We hope that the foregoing discussion of adequacy of warning and appropriateness of use has caused the reader to think that what we have been talking about sounds strangely like assumption of risk, not in its secondary, and technically improper, sense of contributory negligence, but in its original sense. The doctrine of assumption of risk—though grossly misapplied by courts which have not looked realistically to whether the plaintiff in practice had the requisite knowledge and possibility of choice the doctrine implied—is essential to an understanding of a non-fault world. It is, and always has been, a kind of plaintiff's strict liability—the other side of the coin of defendant's strict liability. It may even go to negate defendant's negligence, by expressing a judgment that although the defendant's conduct was not worth its costs (i.e., was negligent), the plaintiff was in a better position than the defendant to evaluate the costs and benefits involved (i.e., the plaintiff assumed the risk). Just as the employer may be in the better position to evaluate the costs and benefits of a piece of equipment given the likelihood of occasional employee negligence (defendant's strict liability), so a spectator at a baseball game may be best suited to evaluate the desirability of sitting in an unscreened bleacher given the likelihood of occasional negligent wild throws by the players during the game which may result in the spectator's being hit on the head (plaintiff's strict liability, or assumption of risk). In both these situations, the conclusion as to whether an accident cost should be shifted depends not on whether a party was negligent, but rather on a judgment as to which party was in a better position to make the cost-benefit analysis irrespective of the other's negligence. In each situation, strict liability (whether defendant's or plaintiff's) is imposed regardless of whether the other party "ought" to have done what he did.

The doctrine of assumption of risk, properly interpreted, not only encompasses the questions the courts are now asking about adequacy of warning and appropriateness of use, but also can be viewed as covering much of the traditional rubric by which the classical forms of strict liability were limited. These forms of liability, whether for animals, ultrahazardous activities, Fletcher v. Rylands situations or even workmen's compensation, were limited in two general ways. The first limit was usually put in terms of whether the injury stemmed from the risk whose presence was the reason for making the activity strictly liable. Had a cow trespassed or had it instead bitten a neighbor; had a tiger mangled somebody, or had it simply chewed grass; had a bomb exploded, or had it just rolled and crushed somebody's foot? The second limit was usually put in terms of whether the victim had done something which, though not necessarily *negligent*, had especially exposed him to the risk. Had the victim engaged in an "unnatural" use of his land; had the victim, a zoologist, gone into the tiger's cage to study the family habits of large cats; had the victim gone where no blasting company could expect humans to be? In setting out these limits, the courts were in effect expressing judgments as to whether the injurer or the victim could better decide the advantages of avoidance as against accident costs. Both limits suggest questions such as who has the greater knowledge of the risk involved and who is better able to choose to avoid that risk by altering behavior should the risk appear too great. In discussing both these limits, moreover, the courts seemed to consider irrelevant the question of whether a third-party decider would approve of the decision made or not, and concentrated instead on who could best make the decision. The issue was not, in other words, whether the owner of the land *ought* to build a reservoir or keep tigers as he did. Neither was it whether the victim acted "reasonably" in engaging in an unnatural use of *his* land or in entering the tiger's cage. Instead it was whether his situation made him better suited than the owner to compare the benefits and the costs of the risk he took.

To say this, though, is to remain at much too simple a level. We have so far assumed simply an injurer and a victim, when in fact each belongs to a category of blasters, factory owners, product users, workers, and so forth. We have assumed that the costs of paying for accidents or avoiding them rest on the individual, and therefore that the cost-benefit decision under a strict liability rule is made at a totally decentralized level. Furthermore, we have ignored the problems which arise when the victim is neither the blaster nor the blastee, but a third party rescuer, neither the lawn mower manufacturer nor the user who rides it on the highway, but a pedestrian who is hit when it goes out of control. Such problems obviously cannot be ignored under either a fault or a strict liability standard. Similarly, we have avoided the problem of who is to decide which category is in the best position to make the cost-benefit analysis and act on it, and how generalized this decision is to be. That is, we have ignored (a) who decides whether blasters are generally better suited than blastees to balance costs and benefits, (b) how many exceptions to this general notion will be permitted, and (c) who will be permitted to find that a given situation is an exception. These problems do not alter the test; they require, however, somewhat more sophistication in its application.

IV.   The Strict Liability Test Refined

A.   *Level and Generality of Application*

The greatest differences among areas of strict liability go precisely to the question of the level of generality at which a decision is made with respect to the category or party best suited to make the appropriate cost-benefit analysis. In blasting and ultrahazardous activities generally, the court-made decision that the blaster is best suited to make the cost-benefit analysis is at a high level of generality. In many jurisdictions the decision contemplates virtually no exceptions so long as the injury arises out of the risk which makes the activity ultrahazardous. The likelihood of foolish behavior by the victim or the unusual sensitivity of some victims are deemed to be best considered by the blaster. Some courts, it is true, have raised the question of whether there would be liability if a blaster blasted in what seemed to be a totally deserted place. The victim, these courts have in effect said, is better suited to gauge the costs of making his presence in such an unusual place known as against the costs of taking whatever risks may be attendant on being in a place unexpectedly. But some judges have in effect reasoned that such an exception, precisely because it would require more individualized judgments, might not be worth making. Perhaps an occasional victim would be better suited to make the cost-benefit analysis, but the administrative cost of dealing with such instances would not be worthwhile, given their presumed rarity.

In strict products liability, instead, the judgment, again court-made, that by and large producers are better suited than users to make the cost-benefit analysis is deemed much less generally applicable, and the manufacturer is allowed to try to show in each specific case that the user was in the best position to make the analysis. The questions asked as to the adequacy of warning and the appropriateness of use, and, in some jurisdictions, the availability of the defense of contributory negligence, suggest how far from certain courts are that the generalized premise that the producer is the cheapest cost avoider will apply to the individual case. As a result, a combination of judge and jury is allowed to find that given the availability of substitutes, the adequacy of warning and the capacity of an individual user to identify himself as being especially risky or especially safe, the general assumption as to who is better suited to compare the risk and benefits will not apply. That such determinations must be made in ways which are much more realistic than were analogous decisions in old assumption of risk cases, is the lesson of cases like *Henningsen* and *Sills*. But this in no way detracts from the judgment that in determining who is better suited to make a cost-benefit analysis in products liability cases, a fair degree of case by case analysis is worthwhile.

Workmen's compensation differs from both ultrahazardous activities and products liability in that the original decision was legislatively made. It also differs in that it tends to divide the decision of who is better suited to evaluate costs and benefits according to the *type of damage* rather than *type of accident*. We are not here concerned with the fact that workmen's compensation schedules are hopelessly out of date, but instead with the very fact that they deal with damages on a scheduled basis. The result of this is that the measure of damages for dignitary losses and even wage losses is that of the ordinary worker doing that job. If a great violinist mangles his hand in a steel mill, causing him extreme suffering and economic loss, that is his burden. One may contrast this with cases involving ultrahazardous activities where, except in very unusual situations, one takes one's victim as one finds him. On the other hand, the fact that a worker is warned that a machine is especially dangerous, or must be used in a given way, will not negate the employer's liability, short of extremes like wanton and wilful behavior by the victim.

Without going into further detail, one can discern a certain rationality in these cases as to the appropriate level of generality of the original liability decision and the exceptions made to it. This does not mean we agree with all of the cases, by any means. But it is not unreasonable to suppose that a violinist is the best evaluator of the relative advantages and costs of working in a steel mill, with regard to the suffering he will feel if he loses his hand, while he is not as likely to be in that position with respect to blasting injuries. Similarly, a user of a product may be well suited to evaluate whether he wishes to use a given product in a given way despite a warning of danger, whereas an employee using that same product on the job would not be so suited. If we add to the foregoing considerations the administrative costs inherent in allowing an attempt to show an exception to the general rule, it is easy to understand the levels of generality which have in fact emerged.

B. Categories of Injurers and Victims

So far we have discussed the problems involved in minimizing primary accident costs as if either the injurer or the victim actually bore the losses which occurred. As has been amply discussed elsewhere, that is clearly not the case. The existence of insurance and of other ways in which a cost is removed from its initial bearer and borne ultimately by others need not be reexamined here. The effect of factors such as insurance on the choice of the party to hold liable under a strict liability test must, however, be made explicit.

It does no good to leave the accident cost on the victim in a products liability case, on the ground that he is in a better position than the injurer to make a cost-benefit analysis, if the victim will not bear the loss in any event. The issue must be whether, given the fact of this "externalization," the *actual* bearer of the loss is better suited to make the analysis than is the injurer (assuming, of course, that the injurer would bear the loss if he were held liable). The point is a simple one and need not be gone into at length. The crucial decision on who is best suited to make the appropriate cost-benefit analysis must be made among the *categories* which actually bear a loss and not among the individuals who only do so initially.[54]

This point is, of course, equally valid for the two Learned Hand

---

54. This does not mean that there should be one liability rule for insured persons

type tests. Sophisticated application of those tests would require that the collective judgment as to whether costs are worth avoiding be made at the level of categories which would end up paying, and not at the level of the single injurer and single victim. The fact that in practice this is almost impossible under existing fault rules is one of the weaknesses of the fault-insurance system as a device for reducing primary accident costs. In theory, however, it should be admitted that one could apply a Learned Hand test at a category level. Whether the language of fault with the stigma it implies would also be appropriate to such a test at a non-individual level may be quite another matter.

C.   The Need for Realism in Applying the Test

It should come as no surprise that considerations of knowledge, alternatives, and category levels are implicit in the search for the cheapest cost avoider. The very fact that these factors *are only implicit* in the test, however, requires us to be extremely practical in gauging their existence in specific situations.

In this regard, it is well to reemphasize the relational nature of the test. It does not matter that there is currently no way in which a manufacturer of a risky medicine can make it safer for users who have no realistic alternative to taking the medicine — even though the user can identify himself as an especially risky party. *Relatively*, the manufacturer is better suited to make the only cost-benefit analysis that matters, which is one between further research and current damages. The problem may be very different if the medicine has reasonably close substitutes which carry different risks for different groups of people. An example might be a birth control pill which carries some risks of thrombosis to a group which can readily identify itself (say, through a blood test), but which has substitutes — either another pill which avoids that risk but is slightly less than 100 per cent effective (and, therefore, carries a risk for another easily self-defining group, those who wish a baby under *no* circumstances and object to abortions even if legal), or other fully effective but cumbersome birth control devices. The existence of close substitutes in this case may make the user best able to conduct the appropriate cost-benefit analysis.

Similarly, the need to establish the relative ability to make a cost-

---

and another for the uninsured. It means instead that in devising a rule appropriate to a particular category, the availability of insurance and other means of externalizing costs should be taken into account. The resulting liability rule would thus reflect the general extent of externalization from the individual to the entire category, though the rule might well be applied to all those within the category, whether insured or not. . . .

benefit analysis requires us to look realistically at the ability of the parties to act upon a perception that they are in risky categories. If there are only two medicines available to combat a serious disease, one involving a .0001 per cent risk of losing a leg, and the other involving a .0001 per cent risk of losing an arm, it is not realistic to suggest that the user is well suited to act upon the findings of a cost-benefit analysis. True, violinists will tend to prefer one medicine and Olympic runners the other, but for most people no meaningful choice is available, and the size of the risk involved is so small, that it seems likely that leaving the loss on the user will result in little incentive to research. It seems to us preferable to make the producer liable and thereby create a situation where there is a meaningful incentive to research, even though this may somewhat increase pharmaceutical costs to people who value only their feet.

Realism is especially necessary when third parties are involved. Then the question is not whether, for example, the category to which the seller belongs or the one to which the user belongs is in the best position to make the cost-benefit analysis; rather, it must be asked which category is in that position relative to the category to which the third-party victim belongs. Sometimes the third party's category is the cheapest cost avoider and then the problem is easy. At other times, however, things are not so simple. If both the manufacturer and the user are in a better position than the third party victim to make the cost-benefit analysis, the strict liability test would require, as a general rule, that the victim should recover, whether he sues the manufacturer or the user. If the victim chose to sue the party other than the cheapest cost avoider, that defendant should be free to join the cheapest cost avoider as a defendant or to sue him subsequently for indemnity. In either case, the strict liability rule would make the cheapest cost avoider liable and optimization of primary accident costs would be achieved, at least if we ignore the administrative costs of joinder or of the indemnification suit. There may well be situations, however, in which the relative abilities of the manufacturer and the user to make the cost-benefit analysis are so clear, and the administrative costs of joinder or indemnification are so great, that we would deny liability if the victim made the "wrong" choice and sued a defendant other than the cheapest cost avoider. For in these cases the victim is in the best position to choose the optimal defendant and should be induced to do so. But courts may in some cases be misled into assuming that where the user is in a better position than the manufacturer to make the cost-benefit analysis, it follows that the manufacturer should not be liable to third parties. This error may be compounded by a tendency to assume that in third party situations the user is in a better position merely because the manufacturer warned him. Instead, the fact that a manufacturer has warned the user to avoid a particular use should serve to bar a third party victim from recovering from the manufacturer only if (a) the warning is so clearly adequate as to settle the issue between manufacturer and user and (b) this fact is sufficiently known to the victim after the accident as to put him in a good position to choose the proper defendant. The point is not so much that the concepts are hard, but rather that they can quite easily be applied erroneously.

In this respect, the history of the doctrine of assumption of risk is instructive. The doctrine asked questions like whether the defendant had the "right" to impose the risk on the plaintiff, which frequently made it circular. An emphasis instead on knowledge and appreciation of the risk and availability of alternatives, equally part of the doctrine, might easily have enabled it to serve to absolve defendants only in those situations where the plaintiff's category was the cheapest cost avoider — where, in other words, the cost-benefit analysis was better left to the plaintiff. Instead, the doctrine came to be applied in cases where knowledge and appreciation of the risk and availability of alternatives were in no realistic sense present for the plaintiff. This may well have been because goals other than primary cost reduction prevailed in those cases, and the circular elements in the language of assumption of risk were emphasized while nonexistent knowledge and appreciation of risk were assumed in order to suit those goals. Thus applied, the doctrine has been much attacked. That it survived at all suggests that the kernel of truth it contains is quite real, not that its application was often correct. Concepts like "the cheapest cost avoider" or "the category best suited to make the cost-benefit analysis" can be as easily misapplied as assumption of risk. This does not, however, mean they are useless. It only means that courts and legal scholars should be assiduous in scrutinizing their use, in criticizing misapplications and in pointing out when they are being employed to serve goals other than those of primary accident cost reduction.

V.   The Learned Hand Test Versus the Strict Liability Test

If the strict liability test is often difficult to apply correctly, and if Learned Hand type tests might, *in theory*, be just as capable of accomplishing optimal primary accident cost reduction, why have such fault-based tests fallen increasingly into disfavor? It is not likely that the answer lies simply in the existence of distribution goals which are better served by the strict liability test. That such goals are relevant we have no doubt, and we shall discuss their relevance later.

But their relevance must be limited, since the two Learned Hand tests themselves accomplish diametrically different distributional results. Thus if the aim of the current trend away from the fault system were simply to favor victims as a category, this could be done as well — indeed better — by shifting from the Learned Hand test to the *reverse* Learned Hand test than by shifting to a strict liability standard. The suspicion must remain that the shift to strict liability is based in part on other grounds.

It has already been noted that the Learned Hand type tests are more "interventionistic," more collective, than is the strict liability test. Under either of the Hand tests, an organ of the state decides whether an action is worthwhile or not, and imposes the costs on the actor if it deems the action *not* worthwhile. It is not hard to see that this involves a greater degree of state involvement than that implied in the strict liability test. The latter implies state intervention only to decide which category can best determine whether an action is worthwhile, and this in turn implies less risk that traditional kinds of collective considerations will come into play. But this difference between the tests, though politically significant, hardly accounts for the decline in popularity of the fault tests. After all, we have also seen an increase in recent years in direct criminal prohibitions aimed at conduct in the accident area deemed not worthwhile. Such prohibitions surely involved greater state intervention than do even the Learned Hand tests. That political preference for laissez faire has spurred the move toward strict liability therefore seems as unlikely as the explanation that the move has been solely influenced by distributional goals. We suspect that the move to strict liability today, no less than similar moves to respondeat superior, ultrahazardous activity liability and workmen's compensation in the past, are based at least in part on a desire to accomplish better primary accident cost reduction.

Earlier we noted that it seems unlikely that either Learned Hand test could effectively be applied in practice at the category level. We questioned whether at the level where it really mattered, that is at the level of who actually pays, the rubric of "fault" is likely to be congenial. And yet it is clear that if the Learned Hand tests *are* to accomplish optimal primary accident cost reduction they must be applied at that level, and not at the arbitrary level of parties to an accident who do not ultimately bear the costs and who are not therefore given any incentive to choose avoidance even where it is worthwhile. The appropriate avoidance decisions *must* be made at a category level, and at that level the Learned Hand tests may seem unjust. Furthermore, the categories which end up bearing the losses as a result of an application of negligence tests on a case by case basis are not likely to be those which would be selected were such tests applied at a category level, nor is this technique likely to be the most efficient way available for selecting the categories which *are* chosen. All this has been discussed at length elsewhere, and need not be gone into further,[74] but it is important to note that the reluctance to apply the Learned Hand test to categories may be a significant underlying explanation for the current disfavor of "negligence" calculus type tests.

There is, however, another set of reasons which may explain the move away from Learned Hand tests. Hard though the strict liability test may be to apply correctly, it is nonetheless easier to apply than is the calculus of fault. We have seen that it may well be difficult to know whether the category to which a seller, user, or third party belongs can best make a cost-benefit analysis of risks involved and act on that analysis. But it is more difficult still to decide correctly not only who can most cheaply act on a cost-benefit analysis, but also what the result of that cost-benefit must be. Yet this is precisely what the Learned Hand type tests require of the governmental deciders if they are to achieve optimal primary accident cost avoidance. None of the significant difficulties involved in the strict liability test are avoided, and to them is added the danger that the governmental deciders will resolve the cost-benefit analysis incorrectly.

One cannot answer, moreover, that the Learned Hand type tests avoid some of the difficulties inherent in the strict liability test by deciding collectively whether or not avoidance is worthwhile, whereas the strict liability test leaves such judgments to the individual categories. This answer is not available because the negligence tests result in compensatory damages rather than prohibitions. Individual categories are, therefore, allowed to decide that avoidance is *not* worthwhile despite a contrary determination by the collectivity (or vice versa).

This may serve to explain the concomitant, seemingly paradoxical rise of collective prohibitions together with the less interventionistic strict liability test, at the expense of negligence type tests. Where a collective determination that an action is *not* worthwhile can be made with a modicum of assurance, prohibitions enforced criminally or through uninsurable fines seem appropriate. Where, instead, there is serious doubt that such a collective determination of utility is likely to be correct, the best solution is an individualistic one. This implies a

---

74. See Costs [of Accidents] at 255-259. To summarize that discussion briefly: case-by-case determination entails substantial administrative costs, tends to focus on unusual rather than recurring causes and on accident avoidance rather than accident cost avoidance, and is a misleading way of compiling those statistics which are meaningful at the category level.

decision limited to selecting the best decider, the cheapest cost avoider, among the relevant categories, and not extending to which particular acts or forbearances are appropriate. Viewed in this light, the rise of criminally enforced prohibitions in some areas, and strict liability in others, rather than being paradoxical, can be viewed as a quite sensible reaction to the same stimulus — that is, to the desire to minimize the sum of accident costs and the costs of avoiding accidents.

VI. Relationship to Other Goals

We have seen that there are a variety of devices which could in theory be used to accomplish primary accident cost reduction. Conceptually, they range from: (a) those in which the decision-maker is highly centralized and makes criminally enforceable determinations of which actions are worthwhile and which are not; through (b) those in which negligence type calculi are employed to make the same decisions at a more decentralized but nonetheless state agency level, enforcing those decisions through compensatory damages; to (c) those in which collective decisions are made only to identify who is the cheapest cost avoider — the category best suited to determine if avoidance of accidents is worth its costs — allowing the chosen category to make the cost-benefit decision itself. We have also seen that these devices in practice imply different likelihoods of success in accomplishing primary cost avoidance. Finally, we have seen that these approaches will each have a different distributional effect. Far from being insignificant, distributional differences may well deter mine the approach chosen. Some discussion of distributional effects and goals is thus essential to an understanding of the two Learned Hand type tests and the strict liability alternative.

In discussing the distributional aspects of liability rules there are two problems which it is well to separate. The first relates to the types of effects that are lumped together in the concept of distribution, and the proper role of each of these effects in the choice of liability rules. The second goes to the quite different question of the appropriate role of juries and courts, as against legislatures, in selecting among liability rules in order to accomplish distributional effects.

That both problems are crucial can be seen through an example. The present Learned Hand test tends to make injurers richer at the expense of victims. The reverse Learned Hand test would have precisely the opposite effect. In choosing between them a society will presumably be influenced not only by which of the two tests is more likely to accomplish optimal primary accident cost reduction, but also, if it has such a preference, by which category it wishes to make wealthier. This choice may be affected by factors such as the initial relative wealth of the categories, but relative wealth is only a part of the choice implied. For one category may be better able to spread losses than the other, or one category may in some sense be viewed as being worthier. Sorting out the relevant effects lumped under the term distribution, therefore, is a necessary task for society in choosing among liability rules. But when that is done another series of questions remains: Which, if any, of the distributional considerations are appropriate to judicial decisions among liability rules, which are appropriate to ad hoc jury determinations, and which can only be properly settled by legislatures?

It should be plain that a full treatment of these questions cannot be attempted in this article. Nevertheless, some indications of relevant distributional considerations and some reflections on the historical role of courts and juries with respect to these can be offered.

For the purposes of this article, we are lumping together as distributional all those effects of liability rules which do not relate to minimizing (a) the sum of accident costs and avoidance costs, and (b) the administrative costs entailed by that minimization. Thus under a society's distributional goals we are including preferences of quite varied types. These preferences may reflect a desire to distribute or fractionize losses, often called spreading. They may reflect a preference for moving toward a given distribution of wealth, such as greater wealth equality, better treatment for higher castes, or better treatment for castes which in the past have been poorly treated. They may instead reflect a desire to further what might be viewed as dynamic efficiency goals — as might occur by favoring the doers, the entrepreneurs in a society. Finally, they may reflect a society's notion, if it has one or if it has many, of rewarding individuals' merits — of recognizing their just deserts.

All of these preferences are in fact relevant in some way to the choice of liability rules. Indeed, all of them, together with the pure efficiency notion reflected in the aim of minimizing the sum of accident and accident avoidance costs, are part of what is at times called justice. They are relevant because there is no a priori reason why a legislature might not choose a liability rule solely because it tends to redistribute income from, say, rich to poor. Whether a legislature would be wise to employ liability rules for this purpose is, of course, another matter. That depends on, among other things, the availability of alternative devices for accomplishing the desired income redistribution and on the effect which this use of a liabiity rule might have on the achievement of other goals whose effectuation is tied to the operation of such rules. But there is no logical reason why a legislature's desires with respect to income equality or caste preference cannot be well served through the choice of one liability rule as against another. Similarly, and in practice even more commonly, a legislature's preference as to spreading, desert, and long run efficiency can effectively be furthered by choosing one liability rule rather than another.

... [W]e do not here need to argue with Professor Posner over whether the particular choice of Learned Hand test made and applied between 1895 and 1905 was based, as many have said, on distributional considerations or was, as he maintains, essentially an efficiency choice. It is perfectly clear *at the very least* that that choice, both when made well before 1895 and as applied for many years, had distributional effects which are very different from those produced by alternative tests which were as, or more, likely to accomplish primary accident cost avoidance. That these different distributional goals seem to be in the ascendancy today may again help to explain the move away from the classical Learned Hand test. They do not, however, suffice to explain why the move has been to strict liability rather than to a reverse Learned Hand test, which would seem to serve the currently dominant distributional goals of spreading and distribution in favor of victims more fully than does the strict liability test.

One more consideration remains in discussing the relationship to the test chosen of goals other than efficiency. Not only does the choice of test have substantial distributive effects, but its application in specific or doubtful cases does also. Thus the issue is not simply whether a society opts for a direct prohibition, a Learned Hand test, a reverse Learned Hand test or a strict liability test. Whatever goals are sought will also be at the mercy of applications of the chosen test. ... The issue is a nice one and reasonable men may differ as to whether distributive considerations should apply (1) at all, or (2) only in cases where primary cost avoidance considerations do not provide a clear outcome, or (3) whether they ought to dominate over efficiency considerations even when the latter would imply a clear result.

As a practical matter, we would suggest that in applications of the traditional Learned Hand test, distributive considerations have very frequently at least played the second role and not infrequently the third. Unlike Posner, we find some support for this point of view in his admirable collection of appellate decisions. Many dubious and some clearly "inefficient" decisions can be thus explained. Without doing a similar study in more recent times, we would suggest that the change in the application of the fault standard since 1905 which has seemed so obvious to so many writers, may well reflect a similar kind of interplay between new distributional goals and the efficiency implications of the traditional Learned Hand test.

This kind of interplay is unlikely to stop merely because a change is made to a strict liability test which combines better primary accident cost avoidance with distributional goals which seem more congenial to the current age. Even within a regime of strict liability, courts and juries deciding which category is the cheapest cost avoider will in unclear cases most likely continue to consider whether some distributional goals are not best served by one decision rather than the other.

Nor would we be surprised if distributional goals will fairly frequently lead to liability results under a strict liability test which are pretty clearly wrong if one considers primary cost avoidance alone. Sometimes this will be the effect of legislative determinations, but at other times it will be the result of decisions by judge and jury — as it has been in the past. To say that this is wrong would be to conclude that once a liability test is chosen the role of the courts is to give effect only to efficiency. It may well be that this conclusion is appropriate, given the nature of courts and the lack of consensus for particular distributional preferences like spreading, greater wealth equality, or compensation of maltreated castes. This conclusion is not, however, a necessary one. Indeed, many years ago, Professor Clarence Morris argued that courts were very well suited to make just this kind of distributional decision, though only when whole *classes* of cases were affected. Similarly, the ability and suitability of the jury to do the same in *individual* cases has been frequently argued.

As a practical matter, introducing such distributional considerations, whether at the legislative or the judicial level, does make application of the strict liability test easier, just as in the past it made application of the Learned Hand test easier. For often a hard issue of whether the victim's category or the injurer's category is best suited to make a cost-benefit analysis between avoidance and compensation becomes easy if one choice serves distributional goals while the other undercuts them. In practice it will also be as hard to tell just what the roles of efficiency and distribution were in making the choice as it is for Professor Posner and us to agree on what the roles of the two sets of goals were in his 1895-1905 cases. Analytical frameworks, and the distinctions made therein, serve to elucidate; they rarely tell us what judges and juries did in individual cases. . . .

NOTES AND QUESTIONS

1. Why would Calabresi allocate liability to the cheapest cost avoider in situations in which rational cost-benefit analysis — as determined through application of the "Learned Hand test" — would lead that party to decide against avoiding the cost?

2. In a case in which the risk of injury is .001 per cent to an unidentifiable victim, if we make the assumption that the manufacturer will treat the residual incidence of risk as de minimis, is there any reason to invoke strict liability on the cheapest cost-avoider rationale? Should a manufacturer be allowed to establish as a defense that no further incentive to engage in safety research exists?

3. Driver falls asleep at the wheel while travelling at a high speed on the freeway. His car crashes into a viaduct and Driver suffers serious internal injuries from the restraining effect of his seat belt—which did, however, secure him from impact with the dashboard. Under Calabresi's test, is Manufacturer strictly liable in tort? Instead of falling asleep, suppose Driver was an epileptic who, for the third time in his life, suffered a fit. Same analysis? Suppose Driver's wife was in the car and suffered severe emotional distress from witnessing her husband's injury—but no physical harm herself. Is Manufacturer strictly liable to her? Would Dealer be strictly liable to Driver under Calabresi's analysis?

4. Under Calabresi's test, could Driver recover from Manufacturer if he were injured when the car was struck by lightning?

5. Aside from cases of injury to pedestrians, why shouldn't the auto manufacturer *always* be responsible for the cost of accidents on the grounds that it could build an accident-proof vehicle that would avoid all injuries?

6. In a case in which an informed consumer is compelled by the higher-risk alternatives to buy a drug dangerous to her but not to users in general, why should those other users pay—through the medium of manufacturer's strict liability—for her idiosyncratic reaction? In resolving this case, are we still principally motivated by primary accident-cost considerations (i.e., economic efficiency goals)?

7. What is the argument for making primary accident-cost decisions at the "category" level rather than on a case-by-case basis? What does Calabresi mean when he says that fault does not operate "at the level of who actually pays"?

8. What is the mechanism for making a determination at the category level? In Calabresi's lawn-mower example—where a passerby or the user is hit by a rock despite the manufacturer's preclusionary warning to the purchaser—is a category-wide decision appropriate? Why and by whom?

9. Does the qualification that the cheapest cost avoider be able to act on the decision, once made, seriously undercut Calabresi's expressed preference for decision making at the "category" level? Who weighs the "comparative advantages" (fn.19) when the question does arise?

10. Why is the Learned Hand test a less adequate risk-distribution device than strict liability in tort? And conversely, why is

the reverse Learned Hand test a better medium for risk distribution than strict liability?

11. Why should a liability theory take account of the distribution of income in society? Or is the appropriate question the converse, that is: why should we be concerned about any goal (viz. economic efficiency) other than just distributional consequences in allocating liability for tortious harm? In this chapter our focus has been almost exclusively on considerations of economic efficiency. In the next, we will concern ourselves with theories premised on moral notions of corrective justice.

Strict Liability: A Comment*

Richard A. Posner

Within the last year there have appeared several major articles that, while otherwise extremely diverse, share a strong preference (in one case implicit) for using the principle of "strict liability" to resolve legal conflicts over resource use. I shall argue in this comment that the authors of these articles fail to make a convincing case for strict liability, primarily because they do not analyze the economic consequences of the principle correctly.

To explicate these consequences I shall use the now familiar example of the railroad engine that emits sparks which damage crops along the railroad's right of way. I shall assume that the costs of transactions between the railroad and the farmers are so high that the liability imposed by the law will not be shifted by negotiations between the parties.

The economic goal of liability rules in such a case is to maximize the joint value of the interfering activities, railroading and farming. To identify the value-maximizing solution requires a comparison of the costs to the railroad of taking steps to reduce spark emissions to various levels, including zero, and the costs to farmers of either tolerating or themselves taking steps to reduce the damage to their property from the sparks. The value-maximizing solution may turn out to involve changes by both parties in their present behavior; for example, the railroad may have to install a good but not perfect spark arrester and the farmer may have to leave an unplanted buffer space between the railroad right of way and his tilled fields. Or, the value-maximizing solution may involve changes by the railroad only, by the farmer only, or by neither party.

*Source: 2 J. Legal Stud. 205-212, 213-215 (1973).

Let us consider what, if any, different effects negligence and strict liability—competing approaches to the design of liability rules—might have in nudging railroad and farmer toward the value-maximizing (efficient) solution, under various assumptions as to what that solution is.

The railroad will be adjudged negligent if the crop damage exceeds the cost to the railroad of avoiding that damage. But the farmer will still not prevail if the cost of the measures *he* might have taken to avoid the damage to his crops is less than the crop damage; this is the rule of contributory negligence.

If the efficient solution requires only that the railroad take some measure to reduce the farmer's crop damage, then the negligence approach leads us toward the efficient solution. Since the railroad is liable for the damage and the damage is greater than the cost to the railroad of preventing it, the railroad will adopt the preventive measure in order to avoid a larger damage judgment. If the efficient solution is either that the railroad do nothing or that both parties do nothing, the negligence standard will again lead to the efficient solution. Not being liable, the railroad will have no incentive to adopt preventive measures; the farmer will have no incentive to take precautions either, since by hypothesis the cost of doing so would exceed the crop damage that he suffers. If the efficient solution requires only the farmer to take precautions, the negligence approach again points in the right direction. The railroad is not liable and does not take precautions. The farmer takes precautions, as we want him to do, because they cost less than the crop damage they prevent.

That leaves only the case where the efficient solution involves avoidance by both parties. Again the negligence standard should lead toward an efficient solution. The farmer will adopt his cost-justified avoidance measure so as not to be barred by the contributory negligence rule and once he has done so the railroad will adopt its cost-justified avoidance measure to avoid liability for the accidents that the farmer's measure does not prevent.

The foregoing discussion must be qualified in one important respect. If the efficient solution requires only the railroad to take precautions but the farmer could take a precaution that, although more costly than the railroad's (otherwise *it* would be the optimum solution), would be less costly than the crop damage, the farmer's failure to adopt the measure will, nonetheless, be deemed contributory negligence. He will therefore adopt it and the railroad will have no incentive to adopt what is in fact the cheaper method of damage prevention.

A principle of strict liability, with no defense of contributory negligence, would produce an efficient solution where that solution was either for the railroad alone to take precautions or for neither party to do so,[6] but not in the other two cases. In the case where the efficient solution is for the farmer alone to take avoidance measures, strict liability would not encourage efficiency, for with the railroad liable for all crop damage the farmer would have no incentive to avoid such damage even if it was cheaper for him to do so; he would be indifferent between the crops and compensation for their destruction. Similarly, in the case where the efficient solution consists of precautions by both railroad and farmer, strict liability would give the farmer no incentive to shoulder his share of the responsibility. But we need only add a defense of contributory negligence in strict liability cases in order to give the farmer an incentive to take precautions where appropriate. There would still be the problem of inefficient solutions where the farmer's precaution, although less costly than his crop damage, was more costly than the railroad's precaution; but this could be remedied by redefining the contributory negligence defense—a step that should be taken in any event.

At least as a first approximation, then, a strict liability standard with a defense of contributory negligence is as efficient as the conventional negligence standard, but not more efficient. This conclusion would appear to hold with even greater force where, as in a products liability case, there is (or can readily be created) a seller-buyer relationship between injurer and victim. Indeed, it can be shown that in that situation an efficient solution is likely to be reached not only under either strict liability (plus contributory negligence) or negligence, but equally with no tort liability at all.

The cost of a possibly dangerous product to the consumer has two elements: the price of the product and an expected accident cost (for a risk-neutral purchaser, the cost of an accident if it occurs multiplied by the probability of occurrence). Regardless of liability, the seller will have an incentive to adopt any cost-justified precaution, because, by lowering the total cost of the product to the buyer, it will enable the seller to increase his profit.[7] Where, however, the buyer can prevent the accident at lower cost than the seller, the buyer

6. In the first case, the railroad would be liable and would have an incentive to adopt the precaution. In the second case, the railroad would still be liable but it would have no incentive to adopt precautions; it would prefer to pay a judgment cost that by hypothesis would be lower than the cost of the precautions.

7. Suppose the price of a product is $10 and the expected accident cost 10¢; then the total cost to the (risk-neutral) consumer is $10.10. If the producer can reduce the expected accident cost to 5¢—say at a cost of 3¢ to himself—then he can increase the price of the product to $10.05, since the cost to the (risk-neutral) consumer remains the same. Thus his profit per unit is increased by 2¢. (In fact, he will be able to increase his total profits even more by raising price less.) The extra profit will eventually be bid away by competition from producers but that is in the nature of competitive advantages.

can be counted on to take the precaution rather than the seller, for by doing so the buyer will minimize the sum of the price of the product (which will include the cost of any precautions taken by the seller) and the expected accident cost.[8]

Although both strict liability and negligence appear to provide efficient solutions to problems of conflicting resource uses, they do not have identical economic effects. The difference comes in cases where the efficient solution is for neither party to the interference to do anything. This is the category of interferences known in negligence law as "unavoidable accidents." They are rarely unavoidable in the literal sense. But frequently the cost either to injurer or to victim of taking measures to prevent an accident exceeds the expected accident cost and in such a case efficiency requires that the accident be permitted to occur. Under a negligence standard, the injurer is not liable; under strict liability, he is. What if any economic difference does this make?

It can be argued that unless an industry is liable for its unavoidable accidents, consumers may be led to substitute the product of the industry for the safer product of another industry. Suppose the only difference between railroads and canals as methods of transportation were that railroads had more unavoidable accidents. If the railroad industry were not liable for those accidents, the price of railroad transportation would be the same as the price of transportation by canal, yet we would want people to use canals rather than railroads because the former were superior in the one respect — safety — in which the two methods differed. In principle, a negligence standard would require the railroad to bear the cost of those accidents. They are not unavoidable. In fact, they could be avoided at zero cost by the substitution of canal for railroad transportation. But perhaps courts are incapable of making interindustry comparisons in applying the negligence standard. Nonetheless the argument affords no basis for preferring strict liability to negligence, since an identical but opposite distortion is created by strict liability. Compare two different tracts of land that are identical in every respect except that one is immediately adjacent to a railroad line and one is well back from any railroad line. If the railroad is strictly liable for crop damage inflicted by engine sparks there will be no incentive to use the tract near the railroad line for fire-insensitive uses and to shift the growing of flammable crops to the tract that is remote from a railroad line, even though such a rearrangement may eliminate all crop damage at zero cost.

8. This is actually a more efficient solution than either negligence or strict liability, since it avoids the problem we noted earlier of the law's economically incorrect definition of contributory negligence.

A related misconception involves the question of the comparative safety level in the long run under strict liability versus negligence liability. The level of safety is unaffected in the short run by which liability rule is chosen. Even if the injurer is strictly liable, he will not try to prevent an accident where the cost of prevention exceeds the accident cost; he will prefer to pay the victim's smaller damages. However, he will have an incentive to invest in research and development efforts designed to develop a cost-justified method of accident prevention, for such a method would lower the cost of complying with a rule of strict liability. It is tempting to conclude that strict liability encourages higher, and in the long run more efficient, levels of safety, but this is incorrect. Rather than creating an incentive to engage in research on safety, a rule of strict liability merely shifts that incentive. Under the negligence standard the cost of unavoidable accidents is borne by the victims of accidents. They can reduce this cost in the long run by financing research into and development of cost-justified measures by which to protect themselves. The victims will not themselves organize for research, but they will provide the market for firms specializing in the development of new safety appliances.

Let us consider some other possible differences, in economic effect, between strict liability and negligence. It might appear that strict liability would reduce the costs of tort litigation, both by simplifying the issues in a trial and thereby reducing its costs and by removing an element of uncertainty and thereby facilitating settlements, which are cheaper than trials. But the matter is more complex than this. By increasing the scope of liability, strict liability enlarges the universe of claims, so even if the fraction of cases that go to trial is smaller the absolute number may be larger. And, by increasing the certainty that the plaintiff will prevail, strict liability encourages him to spend more money on the litigation; conceivably, therefore, the costs of trials might actually increase.

Under strict liability, in effect the railroad (in our example) insures the farmer against the loss of his crops; under negligence liability, the farmer must obtain and pay for insurance himself (or self-insure). Thus, although strict liability, under the name "enterprise liability," has long been defended on the ground that it permits accident losses to be spread more widely, there is little to this argument: the farmer can avoid a concentrated loss by insuring. However, if we were confident that the cost of insuring was lower for the railroad than for the farmer, we might on this ground prefer strict liability.[12]

---

12. The farmer may not want to insure; he may be a risk preferrer. A risk

Strict liability increases the costs of railroading, in our example, and negligence the costs of farming. But the implications for the overall distribution of income and wealth are uncertain, at least in the example, so intertwined were the economic interests of railroads and farmers during the period when the modern system of negligence liability was taking shape. Any increase in the cost of railroading would be borne in significant part by farmers since they were the railroads' principal customers. The intertwining of economic interests is characteristic of many modern tort contexts as well, such as automobile and product accidents. Most victims of automobile accidents are owners of automobiles; victims of defective products are also consumers.

Additional considerations come into play where there is a buyer-seller relationship between victim and injurer; but they relate primarily to the question whether sellers' liability (either strict liability or negligence) has different consequences from no liability (i.e., buyers' liability). There are two reasons for believing that there might be different safety consequences. First, if the buyers of a product are risk preferring, they may be unwilling to pay for a safety improvement even if the cost is less than the expected accident cost that the improvement would eliminate. Under a rule of no liability, the improvement will not be made; under a rule either of strict liability or of negligence liability, the improvement will be made.[13] But the higher level of safety is not optimum in the economic sense, since it is higher than consumers want.

Second, consumers may lack knowledge of product safety. Criticisms of market processes based on the consumer's lack of information are often superficial, because they ignore the fact that competition among sellers generates information about the products sold. There is however a special consideration in the case of safety information: the firm that advertises that its product is safer than a competitor's may plant fears in the minds of potential consumers where none existed before. If a product hazard is small, or perhaps great but for some reason not widely known (e.g., cigarettes, for a long time), consumers may not be aware of it. In these circumstances

---

preferrer is someone who likes to take chances. He will pay $1 for a lottery ticket although the prize is $1000 and his chances of winning only one in 2000. And he may prefer to accept a one one-thousandth chance of a $1000 loss rather than pay $1 to insure against the loss. He will be especially hostile to the idea of paying $1.10 for that insurance, a more realistic example since insurance involves administrative expenses that consume a part of the premium. Hence, if many farmers are risk preferring and do not want insurance, the benefits of strict liability, as perceived by them, may be slight.

13. This assumes that the producer cannot disclaim liability; the effect of a disclaimer is to shift liability to the consumer.

a seller may be reluctant to advertise a safety improvement, because the advertisement will contain an implicit representation that the product is hazardous (otherwise, the improvement would be without value). He must balance the additional sales that he may gain from his rivals by convincing consumers that his product is safer than theirs against the sales that he may lose by disclosing to consumers that the product contains hazards of which they may not have been aware, or may have been only dimly aware. If advertising and marketing a safety improvement are thus discouraged, the incentive to adopt such improvements is reduced. But make the producer liable for the consequences of a hazardous product, and no question of advertising safety improvements to consumers will arise. He will adopt cost-justified precautions not to divert sales from competitors but to minimize liability to injured consumers.

In principle, we need not assume that the only possible sources of information about product safety are the manufacturers of the product. Producers in other industries would stand to gain from exposing an unsafe product, but if their products are not close substitutes for the unsafe product, as is implicit in our designation of them as members of other industries, the gain will be small and the incentive to invest money in investigating the safety of the product and disseminating the results of the investigation slight. Firms could of course try to sell product information directly to consumers; the problem is that because property rights in information are relatively underdeveloped, the supplier of information is frequently unable to recover his investment in obtaining and communicating it.

The information problem just discussed provides an arguable basis for rejecting caveat emptor in hazardous-products cases, but not for replacing negligence with strict liability in such cases, which is the trend of the law. The traditional pockets of strict liability, such as respondeat superior and the liability of blasters and of keepers of vicious animals, can be viewed as special applications of negligence theory. The question whether a general substitution of strict for negligence liability would improve efficiency seems at this stage hopelessly conjectural; the question is at bottom empirical and the empirical work has not been done. Finally, it is interesting to note that in the area of tort law that is in greatest ferment, liability for automobile accidents, the movement appears to be from negligence to no liability![15]

. . . Professor Calabresi proposes that liability be placed on the party to an interaction who is in the better position to "make the cost-

---

15. Most no-fault auto compensation plans involve (1) compulsory accident insurance and (2) exemption from tort liability.

benefit analysis between accident costs and accident avoidance costs
and to act on that decision once it is made." The application of this
rule would lead in many, although not in all, cases to strict liability
without any defense of contributory negligence. For example, suppose that people are frequently injured because the blade of their
rotary mower strikes a stone and that these accidents could be
prevented at least cost by the operator of the mower, who need only
remove the stones in his path. Calabresi suggests that the manufacturer of the mower might nonetheless be liable under his approach.
The injury is an expectable one and the manufacturer is in a better
position than the user to figure out how to minimize the relevant
costs.

To impose liability on the manufacturer in this case, however, is
inefficient: it eliminates the incentive of the operator to adopt a more
economical method of preventing the injury. One could argue,
perhaps, that the incentive created by fear of physical injury is
already so great that adding or subtracting a pecuniary cost will not
affect behavior. But Calabresi does not take this position.

He allows himself an escape hatch. The mower case might be one
where, in his terminology, although the producer is in the better
position to determine the efficient solution he is not in the better
position to implement it, since implementation requires a change in
behavior by the user. But this circumstance, while relevant, is not, for
Calabresi, decisive: where the party in the better position to determine the efficient solution is not the one in the better position to
implement it, "the decision requires weighing comparative
advantages."

I am mystified by his approach. The only reason that Calabresi
offers for not placing liability in every case on the party whose
behavior we want to influence in order to produce the efficient
solution is that identification of that party is often very difficult; but
his approach requires such identification in every case, since it is
always relevant, although never decisive, to inquire whether the
party best able to judge the costs and benefits of alternative courses of
action is also the party whom we want to act upon that judgment.

I can only speculate on the reasons that have led Calabresi into
such an odd corner. He is, of course, strongly committed to the
proposition that the negligence system is incapable of producing
efficient solutions to problems of conflicting resource use. And he
must now believe, perhaps for reasons similar to those presented in
part I of this comment, that strict liability is not sharply distinguishable from negligence so far as the production of efficient solutions to
problems of conflicting resource use is concerned. He has therefore
shifted discussion to a new level, where the inability of either

principle to optimize accident costs is admitted and strict liability defended on another ground altogether: that it is the appropriate method of compelling the party better able to determine the efficient solution to make that determination. Where, however, that party is incapable of acting on the determination — because the solution turns out to require a change in behavior by the other party and transaction costs preclude him from paying that party to make the change — it is very difficult to see what has been accomplished. That is presumably why Calabresi added a second prong to his test, requiring that the party best able to make the cost-benefit analysis also be able to act upon it. But to use the second prong the court (or legislature) must make precisely the determination about which Calabresi is so skeptical when it is made in a negligence case: the determination of which party is in the better position to optimize the costly interaction. . . .

NOTES AND QUESTIONS

1. Posner concludes that the debate over whether a strict liability or negligence system better promotes economic efficiency "is at bottom empirical and the empirical work has not been done." While he is clearly correct, his correlative conclusion that any position on the debate is "hopelessly conjectural" rests on some assumptions about consumer behavior that deserve explicit consideration. Test the empirical assumptions discussed in the following questions against your own experience and observations.

2. Posner challenges Calabresi's argument that a system holding manufacturers strictly liable creates greater incentives for safety research than a negligence system; he responds by arguing that under a negligence system consumers will finance research by providing a market for new firms specializing in the development of safety appliances. Do you agree?

3. Posner considers it a close question whether a strict liability system is more effective than negligence law from a risk-spreading standpoint. He argues that the farmer, who must bear the risk of nonnegligent accidents, can insure his crop as easily as the railroad can take out the requisite coverage under a strict liability system. But is the railroad-farmer example decisive for the major types of contemporary accident situations?

4. Posner argues that the farmer with two tracts of land, one near the tracks and the other far back, will be indifferent as to the use of one or the other under a strict liability system, since compensation

for loss is assumed in either case. Yet he points out that, everything else being equal, we would obviously prefer use of the far-removed tract, which will minimize the cost of accidents. Would the farmer be indifferent? Compare the following assertion by Harold Demsetz:

> If drivers are held liable in automobile-pedestrian accidents, the incentives for pedestrians to be careful about how and where they cross streets will be reduced. The incentives for drivers to be careful will be increased. Indeed, if each pedestrian would be guaranteed *full* compensation for all financial, physical, and psychological costs suffered in an accident, then pedestrians would become indifferent between being struck by an auto and not being struck. [Demsetz, When Does the Rule of Liability Matter?, 1 J. Legal Stud. 13, 26-27 (1972)]

Presumably we could ask people what they regard as full recovery for a particular type of accident. Is Demsetz correct that once we obtained an honest answer, and guaranteed the specified amount as compensation, our respondents would be indifferent about being injured? Is it meaningful to postulate a victim who is indifferent between receiving "full compensation" and suffering serious injury?

5. Posner concedes that unequal access to information about product risks "provides an arguable basis for rejecting caveat emptor in hazardous product cases, but not for replacing negligence with strict liability in such cases...." What is the basis for this distinction?

6. He also considers the litigation cost issue a standoff. While strict liability removes an element of uncertainty, it enlarges both the universe of claims and of potentially winning claims. Does it seem likely that the administrative costs of greater resistance to settlement on the part of injury victims would be about equal to the costs of uncertainty under a fault standard? The element of uncertainty unique to the fault system is, of course, that a decision must be made whether the accident was "unavoidable" — or, more accurately, whether the accident was caused by unreasonable conduct. What kind of litigation costs are involved in getting that question decided? Are the costs likely to be of the same magnitude in a medical malpractice and a defective products case? In other common types of injury situations?

7. Calabresi replies to Posner's criticism of his approach in Optimal Deterrence and Accidents, 84 Yale L. J. 656 (1975). Consider, especially, Posner's assertion that the cheapest cost-avoider rationale, as espoused by Calabresi, does not eliminate the necessity for frequent resort to case-by-case determination of the party best able to make the cost-benefit analysis *and to act on it*. Reviewing Calabresi, at pp. 201-209, *supra*, do you reach the same conclusion? Is it possible to estimate how frequently a court would have to go beyond a category-wide application of the cheapest cost-avoider rule?

8. Posner's comparative analysis of the efficiency thesis, as applied to strict liability and negligence, is succinctly restated in Posner, Economic Analysis of Law 137-142 (2d ed. 1977). In that later treatment, he again contrasts interindustry comparisons between railroads and canals, on the one hand, with railroading and farming, on the other—concluding, as in his present discussion, that strict liability may lead to the efficient solution in the former type of case but that negligence liability is more likely to promote efficiency in the latter. Does his analysis adequately treat the distinction between a liability rule that is sensitive to injurer-victim levels of conduct on a case-by-case basis and a rule that focuses on injurer-victim levels of activity? On this issue, consider the following essay.

Strict Liability versus Negligence*

Steven Shavell

I. Introduction and Discussion

The aim of this article is to compare strict liability and negligence rules on the basis of the incentives they provide to "appropriately" reduce accident losses. It will therefore be both convenient and clarifying to abstract from other issues in respect to which the rules could be evaluated. In particular, there will be no concern with the bearing of risk—for parties will be presumed risk neutral—nor with the size of "administrative costs"—for the legal system will be assumed to operate free of such costs—nor with distributional equity—for the welfare criterion will be taken to be the following aggregate: the benefits derived by parties from engaging in activities less total accident losses less total accident prevention costs. . . .

Accidents will be conceived of as involving two types of parties, "injurers" and "victims," only the latter of which are assumed to suffer direct losses. The category of accidents that will be examined initially are *unilateral* in nature, by which is meant that the actions of injurers but not of victims are assumed to affect the probability or severity of losses. The unilateral case is studied for two reasons. First, it is descriptive of situations in which whatever changes in the behavior of victims that could reasonably be expected to result from changes in liability rules would have only a small influence on

*Source: 9 J. Legal Stud. 1, 1-9, 22-25 (1980).

accident losses.[1] The second reason is pedagogical; it is easier to understand the general *bilateral* case after having studied the unilateral case.

Unilateral Case

This case (as well as the bilateral case) will be considered in each of several situations distinguished by the nature of the relationship between injurers and victims.

Accidents between strangers: In this subcase it is supposed that injurers and victims are strangers, that neither are sellers of a product, and that injurers may choose to engage in an activity which puts victims at risk.

By definition, under the negligence rule all that an injurer needs to do to avoid the possibility of liability is to make sure to exercise due care if he engages in his activity.[2] Consequently *he will not be motivated to consider the effect on accident losses of his choice of whether to engage in his activity or, more generally, of the level at which to engage in his activity;* he will choose his level of activity in accordance only with the personal benefits so derived. But surely any increase in his level of activity will typically raise expected accident losses (holding constant the level of care). Thus he will be led to choose too high a level of activity;[3] the negligence rule is not "efficient."

Consider by way of illustration the problem of pedestrian-automobile accidents (and, as we are now discussing the unilateral case, let us imagine the behavior of pedestrians to be fixed). Suppose that drivers of automobiles find it in their interest to adhere to the standard of due care but that the possibility of accidents is not thereby eliminated. Then, in deciding how much to drive, they will contemplate only the enjoyment they get from doing so. Because (as they exercise due care) they will not be liable for harm suffered by

1. Examples of accidents occurring in such situations and which therefore might be considered unilateral are not hard to imagine. a water main breaks and floods the basement of a home; a plane crashes into a house; a surgeon performs the wrong procedure on an anaesthetized patient. Concededly, even in these examples the victim could have taken *some* protective action (the surgeon's patient could have hired another surgeon to watch over the operation), but, we may plausibly assume, not at a cost nearly low enough to make it worthwhile.

2. It is assumed for ease of exposition that courts have no difficulty in determining if a party did in fact exercise due care; the reader will have no trouble in appropriately modifying the arguments to be made so as to take into account relaxation of such simplifications as this.

3. Specifically, while he will choose to engage in the activity just up to the level at which the personal benefit from a marginal increase would equal zero, it would be best from society's viewpoint for him to engage in the activity only up to the level at which his benefit from a marginal increase would equal the (positive) social marginal cost in terms of accident losses.

pedestrians, drivers will not take into account that going more miles will mean a higher expected number of accidents. Hence, there will be too much driving; an individual will, for example, decide to go for a drive on a mere whim despite the imposition of a positive expected cost to pedestrians.

However, under a rule of strict liability, the situation is different. Because an injurer must pay for losses whenever he is involved in an accident,[4] he will be induced to consider the effect on accident losses of both his level of care *and* his level of activity. His decisions will therefore be efficient. Because drivers will be liable for losses sustained by pedestrians, they will decide not only to exercise due care in driving but also to drive only when the utility gained from it outweighs expected liability payments to pedestrians.

Accidents between sellers and strangers: In this subcase it is assumed that injurers are sellers of a product or service and that they conduct their business in a competitive market. (The assumption of competition allows us to ignore monopoly power, which is for the purposes of this article a logically tangential issue.) Moreover, it is assumed that victims are strangers; they have no market relationship with sellers either as their customers or as their employees.

Under the negligence rule the outcome is inefficient, but the reasoning is slightly different from that of the last subcase. While it is still true that all a seller must do to avoid liability is to take due care, why this results in too high a level of activity has to do with market forces. Because the seller will choose to avoid liability, the price of his product will not reflect the accident losses associated with production. This means that buyers of the product will face too low a price and will purchase too much, which is to say that the seller's level of activity will be too high. Imagine that the drivers are engaged in some business activity — let us say that they are taxi drivers. Then, given that they take due care, the taxi drivers will not have liability expenses, will set rates equal to "production" cost (competition among taxi drivers is assumed), will experience a greater demand than if rates were appropriately higher, and will therefore carry too many fares and cause too many accidents.

Under strict liability, the outcome is efficient, and again the reasoning is a little different from that in the last subcase. Since sellers have to pay for accident losses, they will be led to take the right level of care. And since the product price will reflect accident losses, customers will face the "socially correct" price for the product; purchases will therefore be appropriately lower than what they

---

4. Causal or other reasons for limiting the scope of liability are ignored.

would be if the product price did not reflect accident losses. Taxi drivers will now increase rates by an amount equal to expected accident losses suffered by pedestrians, and the demand for rides in taxis will fall.

Accidents between sellers and customers — or employees: It is presumed here that victims have a market relationship with sellers as either their customers or their employees; and since both situations are essentially the same, it will suffice to discuss only that when victims are customers. In order to understand the role (which is important) of customers' knowledge of risk, three alternative assumptions will be considered: customers know the risk presented by each seller; they do not know the risk presented by each seller but they do know the average seller's risk;[5] they misperceive even this average risk.

Under the negligence rule, the outcome is efficient only if customers correctly perceive risks. As before, when the victims were strangers, sellers will take due care in order to avoid liability, so that the product price will not reflect accident losses. However, now the accident losses are borne by the customers. Thus, the "full" price in the eyes of customers is the market price plus imputed perceived accident losses. Therefore, if risks are correctly perceived, the full price equals the socially correct price, and the quantity purchased will be appropriate. But if risks are not correctly perceived, the quantity purchased will be inappropriate; if customers underestimate risks, what they regard as the full price is less than the true full price and they will buy too much of the product, and conversely if they overestimate risks.[6]

Think, for example, of the risk of food poisoning from eating at restaurants. Under the negligence rule, restaurants will decide to avoid liability by taking appropriate precautions to prepare meals under sanitary conditions. Therefore, the price of meals will not reflect the expected losses due to the (remaining) risk of food poisoning. If customers know this risk, they will correctly consider it in their decisions over the purchase of meals. But if they underesti-

---

5. If sellers are assumed to be identical...and therefore to act identically, the average risk will in fact be the risk presented by each seller. But it will be seen from the discussion of the situation when sellers are not liable that the first and second assumptions are nevertheless different.

6. It may be instructive to mention the parallel situation in regard to employee victims. If employees correctly perceive risks at the workplace, then they will (appropriately) choose to work for a firm only if the "net" wage — the market wage less the expected accident losses they bear — is at least equal to their opportunity elsewhere. But if, say, they underestimate risks, they might choose to work for a firm when the net wage is in fact below their opportunity elsewhere.

mate the risk, they will purchase too many meals; and if they overestimate it, too few.

Under strict liability, the outcome is efficient regardless of whether customers misperceive risks. As in the last subcase, because sellers have to pay for accident losses, they will decide to take appropriate care and will sell the product at a price reflecting accident losses. Thus customers will face the socially correct price and will purchase the correct amount. Their perception of the risk is irrelevant since it will not influence their purchases; as they will be compensated under strict liability for any losses, the likelihood of losses will not matter to them. Restaurant-goers will face a price that reflects expected losses due to food poisoning when meals are prepared under sanitary conditions; they will buy the same — an appropriate — number of meals whether they think the probability of food poisoning is low or high, for they will be compensated for any losses suffered.[7]

When sellers are simply not liable for accident losses, then the outcome is efficient only if customers know the risk presented by each seller. For, given this assumption, because customers will seek to buy products with the lowest full price (market price plus expected accident losses), sellers will be induced to take appropriate care (since this will lower the accident-loss component of the full price). While it is true that if a restaurant took inadequate precautions to prevent food poisoning, it could offer lower-priced meals, it is also true that customers would respond not just to the market price of meals but also to the likelihood of food poisoning — which they are presumed to know. Therefore customers would decide against giving the restaurant their business. Consequently, restaurants will be led to take adequate precautions and to charge accordingly. Moreover, because customers will base purchases on the correctly perceived full price, they will buy the correct amount.

If, however, customers do not know the risk presented by individual sellers, there are two sources of inefficiency when sellers are not liable. The first is that, given the risk of loss, the quantity purchased by customers may not be correct; of course, this will be true if customers misperceive the risk. The second source of inefficiency is that sellers will not be motivated by market forces to appropriately reduce risks. To understand why, consider the situation when customers do correctly perceive the average risk (when they do not correctly perceive this risk, an explanation similar to the one given here could be supplied). That is, assume that customers

7. However, it is worthwhile noticing that if they could not possibly be

know the risk presented by sellers as a group but do not have the ability to "observe" the risk presented by sellers on an individual basis. Then sellers would have no inducement to exercise adequate care. Suppose that restaurant-goers know the risk of food poisoning at restaurants in general and it is, say, inappropriately high. Then if a *particular* restaurant were to take sufficient precautions to lower the risk, customers would not recognize this (except insofar as it eventually affected the average risk—but under the assumption that there are many competing restaurants, this effect would be negligible). Thus the restaurant could not charge a higher price for its meals—customers would have no reason not to go to the cheaper restaurants. In consequence, a situation in which sellers take inadequate care to reduce risks would persist; and similar reasoning shows that a situation in which they take adequate care would not persist. (Notice, however, that since customers are assumed to correctly perceive the average risk, at least they will purchase the correct number of meals—correct, given the high risk.)

Finally, it should be observed that the discussion of liability in the present subcase bears on the role of tort law in a contractual setting. When customers make purchases, they are willingly entering into a kind of contract—in which they agree to a price and pay it, receive goods, and expose themselves to a risk (in the absence of liability). Therefore, our conclusions may be generally expressed by the statement that, when customers' knowledge of risks is perfect, the rule of liability does not matter; the "contractual" arrangement arrived at in the market is appropriate. But when the knowledge is not perfect, there is generally scope for the use of liability, and the relative performance of liability rules depends on the precise nature of the imperfection in knowledge. The force of this point, and the fact that it is not always an obvious one, is perhaps well illustrated by the situation described in the previous paragraph. In that situation, customers did correctly perceive average risk, so that there was "assumption of risk," but this did not lead to a desirable result. The situation was one therefore in which, under our assumptions, courts ought not to allow the defense of assumption of risk to be successfully asserted.

---

compensated for a kind of loss from food poisoning, then misperception of risk certainly would matter. For instance, if there were a risk of death from food poisoning and if restaurant-goers underestimated it, then they would expose themselves to a higher risk of death by eating restaurant meals than they would truly want to bear. Thus, the conclusion of this paragraph that misperception of risk does not matter under strict liability holds only in respect to risks compensable by payment of money damages.

Bilateral Case

In this case, account is taken of the possibility that potential victims as well as injurers may influence the probability or magnitude of accident losses by their choices of both level of care and of level of activity.

Accidents between strangers: Under the negligence rule,[10] the outcome is not efficient. As was true in the unilateral case, since all that an injurer needs to do to avoid liability is to exercise due care, he will choose too high a level of activity. In regard to victims, however, the situation is different. Since a victim bears his accident losses, he will choose an appropriate level of care *and* an appropriate level of his activity, given the (inefficient) behavior of injurers. The drivers will exercise due care but will go too many miles. And the pedestrians, knowing that they must bear accident losses, will exercise due care (in crossing streets and so forth) and they will also reduce the number of miles they walk in accordance with expected accident losses per mile.

Under strict liability with a defense of contributory negligence, the outcome is symmetrical to the last — and again inefficient.[11] Because all that a victim needs to do to avoid bearing accident losses is to take due care, he will have no motive to appropriately reduce *his* level of activity; this is the inefficiency. However, because injurers now bear accident losses, they will take the appropriate amount of care and choose the right level of activity, given the inefficient behavior of victims. Drivers will exercise due care and go the correct number of miles. Pedestrians will also exercise due care but will walk too many miles.

From this discussion it is apparent that the choice between strict liability with a defense of contributory negligence and the negligence rule is a choice between the lesser of two evils. Strict liability with the defense will be superior to the negligence rule when it is more important that injurers be given an incentive through a liability rule to reduce their activity level than that victims be given a similar incentive; that is to say, when it is more important that drivers go fewer miles than that pedestrians walk fewer miles.

Because neither of the familiar liability rules induces efficient behavior, the question arises, *"Is there any conceivable liability rule depending on parties' levels of care and harm done that induces efficient behavior?"* . . . the answer is *"No."* The problem in essence is that for

10. In the present discussion, it will make no difference whether or not the reader thinks of this rule as incorporating the defense of contributory negligence.

11. It is of course clear that under strict liability without the defense the outcome is inefficient, for victims would have no motive to take care.

injurers to be induced to choose the correct level of activity, they must bear all accident losses; and for victims to choose the correct level of their activity, they also must bear all accident losses. Yet it is in the nature of a liability rule that both conditions cannot hold simultaneously; clearly, injurers and victims cannot each bear all accident losses.[12]

Accidents between sellers and strangers: Because the reader will be able to appeal to arguments analogous to those already made and in order to avoid tedious repetition, explanation of the results stated in this and the next subcase will be abbreviated or will be omitted.

Under both the negligence rule and strict liability with a defense of contributory negligence, the outcome is inefficient, as was true in the last subcase. Under the negligence rule, sellers will take appropriate care, but since the product price will not reflect accident losses, too much will be purchased by customers. Also, since victims bear accident losses, they will take appropriate care and choose the right level of activity. Under strict liability with the defense, sellers will take appropriate care and the product price will reflect accident losses, so the right amount will be purchased. Victims will exercise due care but will choose too high a level of activity. In addition, as in the last subcase, there does not exist any liability rule that induces efficient behavior.

Accidents between sellers and customers — or employees: As before it will be enough to discuss here only the situation when victims are customers. If customers have perfect knowledge of the risk presented by each seller, then the outcome is efficient under strict liability with a defense of contributory negligence or the negligence rule or if sellers are not subject to liability at all. For instance, in the latter situation, since customers wish to buy at the lowest full price, sellers will be led to take appropriate care; and since customers will make their purchases with the full price in mind, the quantity they buy will be correct; and since they bear their losses, they will take appropriate care.

There is, however, a qualification that needs to be made concerning the way in which it is imagined that customers influence accident losses. If one assumes that customers influence losses only by their choice of level of care and of the amount purchased, then what was stated in the previous paragraph is correct; and in regard to services and nondurables (such as meals at restaurants) this assump-

12. However, when other means of social control are also employed, it is possible to achieve an efficient outcome. For example, if use of the negligence rule were supplemented by imposition of a tax on the level of injurer activity, an efficient outcome could be achieved.

tion seems entirely natural. But in regard to durable goods, it might well be thought that customers influence accident losses not only by their choice of level of care and of purchases, but also by their decision as to frequency of use per unit purchased. The expected number of accidents that a man will have when using a power lawn mower would seem to be influenced not only by whether he in fact purchases one (rather than, say, a hand mower) and by how carefully he mows his lawn with it, but also by how frequently he chooses to mow his lawn. In order for customers to be led to efficiently decide the frequency of use, they must bear their own accident losses. Thus, in regard to durables, the outcome is efficient under the negligence rule or if sellers are not liable, but the outcome is inefficient under strict liability with a defense of contributory negligence; for then if the man buys a power lawn mower, he will have no motive to appropriately reduce the number of times he mows his lawn.

Now suppose that customers correctly perceive only average risks. Then, subject again to a qualification concerning durables, the results are as follows. The outcome is efficient under strict liability with a defense of contributory negligence or under the negligence rule, but the outcome is not efficient if sellers are not liable, for then they will not take sufficient care. The qualification is that if the sellers produce durables, strict liability with the defense is inefficient, leaving the negligence rule as the only efficient rule.

Last, suppose that customers misperceive risks. Then the outcome is efficient only under strict liability with a defense of contributory negligence; and the qualification to that is that, if sellers produce durables, even strict liability with the defense is inefficient, so that there does not exist a liability rule which is efficient. . . .

[In the following sections of the essay, Shavell employs a formal mathematical model to analyze a set of propositions based on the types of injury situations discussed above.]

V. Concluding Comments

1. A question which is in a sense logically prior to the analysis of this article must be mentioned, namely, *"Why isn't the level of activity usually considered in the formulation of a due care standard?"* After all, the inefficiencies discussed here were viewed in the main as deriving from the fact that in order to avoid being found negligent (or contributorily negligent), parties are not motivated to alter their level of activity.[27] The answer to the question appears to be that the courts

27. Were the level of activity included in the "due care" standard, a party would,

would run into difficulty in trying to employ a standard of due care expanded in scope to include the level of activity. In formulating such a broadened due care standard, courts would, by definition, have to decide on the appropriate level of activity, and their competence to do this is problematic. How would courts decide the number of miles an individual ought to drive or how far or how often a pedestrian ought to walk?[28] How would courts decide the level of output an industry — much less a firm within an industry — ought to produce? To decide such matters, courts would likely have to know much more than would normally have to be known to decide whether care, conventionally interpreted, was adequate.[29]

2. From the logic of the arguments presented here, it can be seen that what is important about the variable "level of activity" is only that it is not included in the due care standard. Any other variable omitted from the standard would also be inappropriately chosen in many of the circumstances in which we said the same of the level of activity. For example, in regard to accidents involving firms and strangers it has been noted that, if the scale of a firm's research in safety technology is not comprehended by the standard of due care, then under the negligence rule the firm would not be expected to invest sufficiently in such research.

3. Commentators on tort law have in recent years frequently pointed to the reciprocal nature of harm, especially in the sense that the victim must be present in order to suffer harm. This has unfortunately engendered a misleading piece of folklore: that the very concept of harm is rendered ambiguous. While it is undeniable that for harm to occur there must be a victim, I can see no sense in which this truism leads to conceptual problems in instrumentalist analysis. Here, under the heading of bilateral accidents, the situation when victims as well as injurers could vary their level of activity (and

---

by definition of due care, have to choose both the level of activity and the level of care appropriately in order to avoid liability; thus the inefficiencies analyzed in this article would be eliminated. However, A. Mitchell Polinsky, Strict Liability versus Negligence in a Market Setting [70 Am. Econ. Rev. 363 (1980)] makes a point of qualification to this. He observes that in the market case it is not enough for the level of activity to be incorporated in the due care standard for each firm within the industry, for then too many firms would enter it; rather, the level of activity would somehow have to be made part of the due care standard for the industry as a whole. He also notes a similar point in respect to the nonmarket case.

28. There might also be evidentiary problems. The courts might find it difficult to learn how many miles an individual drives or a pedestrian walks.

29. On this argument, we would expect that when courts could easily discern what the level of activity ought to be, then it would be incorporated into the standard of due care. One legal doctrine which appears to confirm this is that of "coming to the nuisance," for the doctrine is applied in precisely those situations when the *activity* of coming to the nuisance — which is quite distinct from the level of *care* exercised once one is near the nuisance — may be seen as clearly socially undesirable.

of care) was studied; and one such possibility for victims was a level of activity of zero, which is to say, the "victims" are not around to be harmed. Thus, for example, the result concerning strict liability (with the defense of contributory negligence) versus negligence in regard to accidents between strangers might be expressed by saying that strict liability is preferable if it is more desirable to control whether injurers are present than it is to control whether victims are present; . . .

4. The analysis presented here does appear to help to explain certain features of tort law. A notable example is provided by the so-called pockets of strict liability: for ultrahazardous activities, ownership of wild animals, and so forth. These areas of strict liability seem to have two characteristics. First, they are such that injurer activity has a distinctive aspect (which makes the activity easy for the law to single out) and imposes nonnegligible risks on victims (which make the activity worthwhile controlling). And, second, they are such that victim activity is usually not at all special — on the contrary, it is typically entirely routine in nature, part of what it is to carry on a normal life — and is therefore activity that cannot and ought not be controlled. Consequently, it is appealing to explain the pockets of strict liability by the idea that strict liability is preferable if it is more desirable to control injurers' activity than victims'.

However, there are many features of tort law which the analysis by itself does not seem to satisfactorily explain. And this is not unexpected, for it is in the nature of the formal approach to isolate selected factors of interest by ignoring others; the formal approach aims for a particular kind of insight, not for true balance or comprehensiveness. Two examples will illustrate various limitations in our ability to employ in a direct way the results of this article. The first concerns the trend in decisions in product-liability cases toward expansion of manufacturer's liability. If this trend can be likened to one toward holding manufacturers strictly liable, we may be tempted to explain it as broadly rational given some of our results.

However, realism requires us to look at other, complementary explanations of the trend, such as that strict liability may provide a better means of risk sharing than the negligence rule, or that strict liability may be easier to apply than the negligence rule. Moreover, realism requires us to ask whether there even is an explanation of the trend based on its social rationality — whether in fact the trend might be socially undesirable, say on the ground that the expansion in the scope of liability has led to an excessively costly volume of disputes. Similar questions may be asked in respect to the second example, which concerns the fact that the negligence rule is the dominant form of tort liability in Anglo-American and in Western European legal systems today. Our analysis certainly does not suggest why this should be so, since, at least as often as otherwise, strict liability (with a defense of contributory negligence) is superior to the negligence rule. We are therefore led to ask again about such matters as risk sharing, administrative simplicity, and (especially) the social costs of expansion of the scope of liability.

5. Many of the points made in this article have been discussed before, and doubtless numerous times. For example, the literature on enterprise liability virtually always considers the effect of such liability on product price, and the influence of this on purchases. The contribution made here would therefore seem to lie principally in the attention given to context — to the specifics of the relationship obtaining between injurers and victims — and in the unified way in which the variety of problems is viewed.

NOTES AND QUESTIONS

1. How does Shavell's economic efficiency analysis of the distinction between level of care and level of activity influence your assessment of the Calabresi-Posner debate over strict liability versus negligence? Is the distinction consistent with Calabresi's framework of analysis in accident cases? Does Posner address the Shavell thesis?

2. Can you generalize about the situations in which introducing considerations of injurer-victim levels of activity leads to the conclusion that (a) strict liability better promotes efficiency, (b) negligence liability better promotes efficiency, and (c) neither rule is superior to the other with respect to efficiency considerations? Under what circumstances is the answer dependent on available defenses? Is it helpful to divide the types of cases, as Shavell does, into "unilateral" and "bilateral" injury situations?

3. Why is the level of activity ordinarily not taken into account when a court sets a standard of due care? If it were taken into account, would the negligence formula be tantamount to strict liability?

4. Perhaps a simple numerical example will help to clarify Shavell's thesis. Consider his initial example, a pedestrian-automobile accident case in which the parties are strangers (i.e., by hypothesis, a situation where *ex ante* bargaining between the parties is infeasible). Suppose the following: Value of the activity of going on a drive to an individual = 5. *If* the individual goes on a drive, then expected accident costs as a function of his level and "cost" of care are given below.

Level of care	Cost of care	Accident costs	Total costs
None	0	10	10
Reasonable	2	6	8
High	6	5	11

Under these circumstances, total costs are minimized (at 8) if the individual exercises reasonable care; this will thus be the due care standard under the negligence rule. And the individual will obviously decide to go on a drive if this is the due care standard, for her position will be $5 - 2 = 3$, if she does so, and zero otherwise. But the socially optimal outcome is that she not go on a drive, for the social welfare criterion—benefits minus total costs—is $5 - 8 = -3$ if she goes on a drive and exercises due care, and it is zero if she refrains from driving. Does the example clarify precisely why the negligence rule is problematic from an efficiency standpoint?

Try to employ numerical examples to make some of Shavell's other propositions concrete.

5. The economic efficiency thesis discussed in this chapter has been applied to a wide variety of tort issues. A sample of the literature would include Landes & Posner, An Economic Theory of Intentional Torts, 1 Intl. Law & Econ. Rev. 127 (1981); Landes & Posner, Joint and Multiple Tortfeasors: An Economic Analysis, 9 J. Legal Stud. 517 (1980); Shavell, An Analysis of Causation and the Scope of Liability in the Law of Torts, 9 J. Legal Stud. 463 (1980); Calabresi, Concerning Cause and the Law of Torts, 43 U. Chi. L. Rev. 69 (1975); and Landes & Posner, Salvors, Finders, Good Samaritans and Other Rescuers: An Economic Study of Law and Altruism, 7 J. Legal Stud. 83 (1978).

An instructive essay critical of the economic efficiency thesis, on the grounds that information costs and market imperfections make it unworkable, is Rizzo, Law Amid Flux: The Economics of Negligence and Strict Liability in Tort, 9 J. Legal Stud. 291 (1980).

Chapter 6

The Search for a Comprehensive Theory of Tort Liability: Conceptions of Morality

The opening chapter in this book can be viewed as providing two distinct perspectives on the fault principle. Oliver Wendell Holmes regarded fault liability as an expression of moral principles that had a pervasive influence on nineteenth-century political and social thought. In contrast, Richard Posner articulated a rationale for the law of negligence based upon considerations of economic efficiency.

In the last chapter we returned to the economic perspective, exploring in greater detail the allocative consequences of tort rules based on theories of strict liability and fault. The question was whether economic theory can provide criteria for evaluating a general system of liability rules that allocate losses in tort cases.

Now we turn to the other perspective introduced in the initial chapter—a search for a set of moral principles that can serve as a basis for evaluating liability rules. At the outset, however, it is worth repeating a question raised in the preceding chapter: is a moral conception of liability necessarily distinct from an economic perspective? Perhaps considerations of economic efficiency provide an adequate moral foundation for a liability system. More specifically, could it not be argued that the exclusive concern of a tort system should be to assure that society has neither more nor fewer accidents than its members would "choose" through an ideally operating pricing system?

Whatever the ultimate response to this question, an exclusively economic justification for a system of liability rules will inevitably face challenge from a wide variety of competing moral principles. This point is not lost on the economic theorists themselves. Guido Calabresi, for example, has admitted that while notions of justice attach to efficiency considerations,

> [t]hey also attach to distributional preferences like "favor spreading," "further wealth equality," and "benefit of a particular ethnic group," which go to what people are rather than what they do.... Justice notions attach to other societal preferences which can only with difficulty be explained in terms of either efficiency or wealth distributional preferences designed to make some groups richer because of what they are. These other justice notions, which we are unable to describe in general terms, are, of course, crucial to the choice of liability rules.[1]

Liability rules, in other words, could serve as many ends as there are definitions of justice — constitutional issues aside, rules could systematically discriminate in favor of injury victims on the basis of age, wealth, national origin, or a virtually unlimited variety of other characteristics. The quest for a just theory of liability becomes meaningful, of course, only when we begin to explore moral conceptions that are based on widely shared notions of fairness. The paucity of tort literature exploring principles of corrective justice other than those related to fault liability undoubtedly reflects the difficulty in identifying generally accepted norms that would support a comprehensive alternative liability system.

In recent years, however, scholars have begun to indicate an interest in developing new moral perspectives on the tort system. Without a doubt, the recent intense economic debate about liability rules is partially responsible for provoking the new efforts; indeed, the authors presented in this chapter explicitly assert that economic analysis is an unduly restrictive perspective for deciding what they regard as questions of interpersonal corrective justice. At a more fundamental level, however, the articles presented here — like the selections in an economic vein included in the previous chapter — are almost certainly an expression of the pervasive unrest created by the relentless assault on the fault principle in both the judicial and legislative forums.

George Fletcher suggests the need for a fresh conceptual ap-

---

1. Calabresi & Hirschoff, Toward a Test for Strict Liability in Tort, 81 Yale L.J. 1055, 1080 (1972).

proach to liability rules—an approach that cuts across fault and nonfault liability. As a substitute for those traditional categories, he posits two competing "paradigms": reciprocity and reasonableness. These paradigms, he argues, provide a more accurate perception of the moral foundation of tort law than do the established principles of strict liability and fault. Richard Epstein, on the other hand, is less concerned about reconciling seemingly inconsistent doctrinal themes developed in the case law. Rather, Epstein relies on what he regards as a commonly shared view of individual responsibility, expressed in a theory of causation that has, in fact, played an important—but not necessarily dominant—role in determining liability in tort. Despite their distinctly different approaches, the essays share at least one characteristic: both would focus on the moral claims of the parties to the immediate case rather than on the social utility of the rules of liability as evaluated from an economic perspective.

Fairness and Utility in Tort Theory*

George P. Fletcher

II. The Paradigm of Reciprocity

A. The Victim's Right to Recover

Our first task is to demonstrate the pervasive reliance of the common law on the paradigm of reciprocity. The area that most consistently reveals this paradigm is the one that now most lacks doctrinal unity—namely, the disparate pockets of strict liability. We speak of strict liability or "liability without fault" in cases ranging from crashing airplanes to suffering cattle to graze on another's land. Yet the law of torts has never recognized a general principle underlying these atomistic pockets of liability. The Restatement's standard of ultrahazardous activity speaks only to a subclass of cases. In general, the diverse pockets of strict liability represent cases in which the risk is reasonable and legally immune to injunction. They are therefore all cases of liability without fault in the limited sense in which fault means taking an unreasonable risk. Beyond these characteristics distinguishing strict liability from negligence, there is no consensus of criteria for attaching strict liability to some risks and not to others.

I shall attempt to show that the paradigm of reciprocity accounts

*Source: 85 Harv. L. Rev. 537, 543-560, 569-573 (1972).

for the typical cases of strict liability[24]—crashing airplanes, damage done by wild animals, and the more common cases of blasting, fumigating, and crop dusting. To do this, I shall consider in detail two leading, but seemingly diverse instances of liability for reasonable risk-taking—Rylands v. Fletcher and Vincent v. Lake Erie Transportation Co. The point of focusing on these two cases is to generate a foundation for inducing the claim that unexcused nonreciprocity of risk is the unifying feature of a broad spectrum of cases imposing liability under rubrics of both negligence and strict liability.

In Rylands v. Fletcher the plaintiff, a coal mine operator, had suffered the flooding of his mine by water that the defendant had pumped into a newly-erected reservoir on his own land. The water broke through to an abandoned mine shaft under the defendant's land and thus found its way to the plaintiff's adjoining mine. The engineers and contractors were negligent in not providing stronger supports for the reservoir; yet because they were independent contractors, the defendant was not liable for their negligence. Though the defendant's erecting and maintaining the reservoir was legally permissible, the Exchequer Chamber found for the plaintiff, and the House of Lords affirmed. Blackburn's opinion in the Exchequer Chamber focused on the defendant's bringing on to his land, for his own purposes, "something which, though harmless whilst it remain there, will naturally do mischief if it escape." Lord Cairns, writing in the House of Lords, reasoned that the defendant's activity rendered his use of the land "non-natural"; accordingly, "that which the Defendants were doing they were doing at their own peril."

Neither Blackburn's nor Cairns's account provides an adequate rationale for liability. It may be that a body of water will "naturally do mischief if it escapes," but so may many other things, like water in a pipe, oil in a furnace tank, and fire in a fireplace. It is unlikely that Blackburn would favor liability for the harmful consequences of all these risky practices. Cairns's rationale of non-natural use, for all its metaphysical pretensions, may be closer to the policy issue at stake in the dispute. The fact was that the defendant sought to use his land for a purpose at odds with the use of land then prevailing in the community. He thereby subjected the neighboring miners to a risk to which they were not accustomed and which they would not regard as

24. It is important to distinguish the cases of strict liability discussed here from strict products liability, a necessary element of which is an unreasonably dangerous defect in the product. See Davis v. Wyeth Laboratories, Inc., 399 F.2d 121 (9th Cir. 1968). See generally Traynor, The Ways and Meanings of Defective Products and Strict Liability, 32 Tenn. L. Rev. 363 (1965). Because of the market relationship between the manufacturer and the consumer, loss-shifting in products-liability cases becomes a mechanism of insurance, changing the question of fairness posed by imposing liability. . . .

a tolerable risk entailed by their way of life. Creating a risk different from the prevailing risks in the community might be what Lord Cairns had in mind in speaking of a non-natural use of the land. A better term might have been "abnormal" or "inappropriate" use. Indeed these are the adjectives used in the proposed revision of the Restatement to provide a more faithful rendition of the case law tradition of strict liability.

A seemingly unrelated example of the same case law tradition is Vincent v. Lake Erie Transportation Co., a 1910 decision of the Minnesota Supreme Court. The dispute arose from a ship captain's keeping his vessel lashed to the plaintiff's dock during a two-day storm when it would have been unreasonable, indeed foolhardy, for him to set out to sea. The storm battered the ship against the dock, causing damages assessed at five hundred dollars. The court affirmed a judgment for the plaintiff even though a prior case had recognized a ship captain's right to take shelter from a storm by mooring his vessel to another's dock, even without consent. The court's opinion conceded that keeping the ship at dockside was justified and reasonable, yet it characterized the defendant's damaging the dock as "prudently and advisedly [availing]" himself of the plaintiff's property. Because the incident impressed the court as an implicit transfer of wealth, the defendant was bound to rectify the transfer by compensating the dock owner for his loss.[38]

The rationales of *Rylands* and *Vincent* are obviously not interchangeable. Building a reservoir is not availing oneself of a neighbor's property. And mooring a ship to a wharf is not an abnormal or "non-natural" use of either the ship or the wharf. Yet by stripping the two cases of their rhetoric and by focusing on the risks each defendant took, one can bring the two cases within the same general principle. The critical feature of both cases is that the defendant created a risk of harm to the plaintiff that was of an order different from the risks that the plaintiff imposed on the defendant.

Without the factor of nonreciprocal risk-creation, both cases would have been decided differently. Suppose that Rylands had built his reservoir in textile country, where there were numerous mills, dams, and reservoirs, or suppose that two sailors secured their ships in rough weather to a single buoy. In these situations each party

---

38. This case is not entirely apt for my theory. The existence of a bargaining relationship between the defendant and the plaintiff poses the market adjustment problems raised in note 24 *supra*. See Calabresi, The Decision for Accidents: An Approach to Nonfault Allocation of Costs, 78 Harv. L. Rev. 713, 726 (1965) (arguing the irrelevance of the result in *Vincent* as to *both* the efficient allocation of resources and the welfare of the parties). Accordingly, I treat the case as though the defendant were a type of ship owner who never had to enter into bargains with wharf owners....

would subject the other to a risk, respectively, of inundation and abrasion. Where the risks are reciprocal among the relevant parties, as they would be in these variations of *Rylands* and *Vincent*, a rule of strict liability does no more than substitute one form of risk for another—the risk of liability for the risk of personal loss. Accordingly, it would make little sense to extend strict liability to cases of reciprocal risk-taking, unless one reasoned that in the short run some individuals might suffer more than others and that these losses should be shifted to other members of the community.[40]

Expressing the standard of strict liability as unexcused, nonreciprocal risk-taking provides an account not only of the *Rylands* and *Vincent* decisions, but of strict liability in general. It is apparent, for example, that the uncommon, ultra-hazardous activities pinpointed by the Restatement are readily subsumed under the rationale of nonreciprocal risk-taking. If uncommon activities are those with few participants, they are likely to be activities generating nonreciprocal risks. Similarly, dangerous activities like blasting, fumigating, and crop dusting stand out as distinct, nonreciprocal risks in the community. They represent threats of harm that exceed the level of risk to which all members of the community contribute in roughly equal shares.

The rationale of nonreciprocal risk-taking accounts as well for pockets of strict liability outside the coverage of the Restatement's sections on extra-hazardous activities. For example, an individual is strictly liable for damage done by a wild animal in his charge, but not for damage committed by his domesticated pet. Most people have pets, children, or friends whose presence creates some risk to neighbors and their property. These are risks that offset each other; they are, as a class, reciprocal risks. Yet bringing an unruly horse into the city goes beyond the accepted and shared level of risks in having pets, children, and friends in one's household. If the defendant

---

40. One argument for so shifting losses would be that some individuals have better access to insurance or are in a position (as are manufacturers) to invoke market mechanisms to distribute losses over a large class of individuals. This argument assumes that distributing a loss "creates" utility by shifting units of the loss to those who may bear them with less disutility. The premise is the increasing marginal utility of cumulative losses, which is the inverse of the decreasing marginal utility of the dollar—the premise that underlies progressive income taxation. See Calabresi, Some Thoughts on Risk Distribution and the Law of Torts, 70 Yale L.J. 499, 517-519 (1961); Blum & Kalven, The Uneasy Case for Progressive Taxation, 19 U. Chi. L. Rev. 417, 455-479 (1952). This is an argument of distributive rather than corrective justice, for it turns on the defendant's wealth and status, rather than his conduct. Using the tort system to redistribute negative wealth (accident losses) violates the premise of corrective justice, namely that liability should turn on what the defendant has done, rather than on who he is. See The Nicomachean Ethics of Aristotle, Book V, ch. 4, at 114-115 (Ross transl. World's Classics ed. 1954). What is at stake is keeping the institution of taxation distinct from the institution of tort litigation.

creates a risk that exceeds those to which he is reciprocally subject, it seems fair to hold him liable for the results of his aberrant indulgence. Similarly, according to the latest version of the Restatement, airplane owners and pilots are strictly liable for ground damage, but not for mid-air collisions. Risk of ground damage is nonreciprocal; homeowners do not create risks to airplanes flying overhead. The risks of mid-air collisions, on the other hand, are generated reciprocally by all those who fly the air lanes. Accordingly, the threshold of liability for damage resulting from mid-air collisions is higher than mere involvement in the activity of flying. To be liable for collision damage to another flyer, the pilot must fly negligently or the owner must maintain the plane negligently; they must generate abnormal risks of collision to the other planes aflight.

Negligently and intentionally caused harm also lend themselves to analysis as nonreciprocal risks. As a general matter, principles of negligence liability apply in the context of activities, like motoring and sporting ventures, in which the participants all normally create and expose themselves to the same order of risk.[43] These are all pockets of reciprocal risk-taking. Sometimes the risks are grave, as among motorists; sometimes they are minimal, as among ballplayers. Whatever the magnitude of risk, each participant contributes as much to the community of risk as he suffers from exposure to other participants. To establish liability for harm resulting from these activities, one must show that the harm derives from a specific risk negligently engendered in the course of the activity. Yet a negligent risk, an "unreasonable" risk, is but one that unduly exceeds the bounds of reciprocity. Thus, negligently created risks are nonreciprocal relative to the risks generated by the drivers and ballplayers who engage in the same activity in the customary way.

If a victim also creates a risk that unduly exceeds the reciprocal norm, we say that he is contributorily negligent and deny recovery. The paradigm of reciprocity accounts for the denial of recovery when the victim imposes excessive risks on the defendant, for the effect of contributory negligence is to render the risks again reciprocal, and the defendant's risk-taking does not subject the victim to a relative deprivation of security.

Thus, both strict liability and negligence express the rationale of liability for unexcused, nonreciprocal risk-taking. The only difference is that reciprocity in strict liability cases is analyzed relative to the background of innocuous risks in the community, while reciprocity in

43. Negligence is, of course, prominent as well in the analysis of liability of physicians to patients and occupiers of land to persons injured on the premises.... These are cases of injuries in the course of consensual, bargaining relationships and therefore pose special problems. Cf. note 24 *supra*.

the types of negligence cases discussed above is measured against the background of risk generated in specific activities like motoring and skiing. To clarify the kinship of negligence to strict liability, one should distinguish between two different levels of risk-creation, each level associated with a defined community of risks. Keeping domestic pets is a reciprocal risk relative to the community as a whole; driving is a reciprocal risk relative to the community of those driving normally; and driving negligently might be reciprocal relative to the even narrower community of those driving negligently. The paradigm of reciprocity holds that in all communities of reciprocal risks, those who cause damage ought not to be held liable.[46]

To complete our account of the paradigm of reciprocity, we should turn to one of its primary expressions: intentional torts, particularly the torts of battery and assault. Several features of the landlord's behavior in Carnes v. Thompson in lunging at the plaintiff and her husband with a pair of pliers make it stand out from any of the risks that the plaintiff might then have been creating in return. An intentional assault or battery represents a rapid acceleration of risk, directed at a specific victim. These features readily distinguish the intentional blow from the background of risk. Perceiving intentional blows as a form of nonreciprocal risk helps us understand why the defendant's malice or animosity toward the victim eventually became unnecessary to ground intentional torts. The nonreciprocity of risk, and the deprivation of security it represents, render irrelevant the attitudes of the risk-creator.

All of these manifestations of the paradigm of reciprocity — strict liability, negligence and intentional battery — express the same principle of fairness: all individuals in society have the right to roughly the same degree of security from risk. By analogy to John Rawls's first principle of justice, the principle might read: we all have the right to the maximum amount of security compatible with a like security for everyone else. This means that we are subject to harm, without compensation, from background risks, but that no one may suffer harm from additional risks without recourse for damages against the

46. Suppose a motorist runs down a pedestrian on the way to his parked car. Or suppose that an ambulance injures a pedestrian while speeding through the streets to rescue another injured pedestrian. These hypothetical problems pose puzzles at the fringes of the paradigm of reciprocity. The first is the question whether reciprocity must be temporal; the second, whether the interests of the victim or of the class he represents ought to bear on the analysis of reciprocity. These problems require further thought. . . .

Problems in defining communities of risks may account for the attractiveness of the reasonableness paradigm today. The increased complexity and interdependence of modern society renders legal analysis based upon a concept of community that presupposes clear lines of membership, relatively little overlapping, and a fair degree of uniformity in the activities carried on, exceedingly difficult in many cases. . . .

risk-creator. Compensation is a surrogate for the individual's right to the same security as enjoyed by others. But the violation of the right to equal security does not mean that one should be able to enjoin the risk-creating activity or impose criminal penalties against the risk-creator. The interests of society may often require a disproportionate distribution of risk. Yet, according to the paradigm of reciprocity, the interests of the individual require us to grant compensation whenever this disproportionate distribution of risk injures someone subject to more than his fair share of risk.

B.   Excusing Nonreciprocal Risks

If the victim's injury results from a nonreciprocal risk of harm, the paradigm of reciprocity tells us that the victim is entitled to compensation. Should not the defendant then be under a duty to pay? Not always. For the paradigm also holds that nonreciprocal risk-creation may sometimes be excused, and we must inquire further, into the fairness of requiring the defendant to render compensation. We must determine whether there may be factors in a particular situation which would excuse this defendant from paying compensation.

Though the King's Bench favored liability in its 1616 decision of Weaver v. Ward, it digressed to list some hypothetical examples where directly causing harm would be excused and therefore exempt from liability. One kind of excuse would be the defendant being physically compelled to act, as if someone took his hand and struck a third person. Another kind would be the defendant's accidentally causing harm, as when the plaintiff suddenly appeared in the path of his musket fire. The rationale for denying liability in these cases, as the court put it, is that the defendant acted "utterly without...fault."

If a man trespasses against another, why should it matter whether he acts with "fault" or not? What the King's Bench must have been saying is that if a man injures another without fault on his part, there is no rational and fair basis for charging the costs of the accident to him rather than to an arbitrary third person. The inquiry about fault and excusability is an inquiry about rationally singling out the party immediately causing harm as the bearer of liability. Absent an excuse, the trespassory, risk-creating act provides a sufficient basis for imputing liability. Finding that the act is excused, however, is tantamount to perceiving that the act is not a factor fairly distinguishing the trespassing party from all other possible candidates for liability.

It is important to note that the inquiry whether the act sets the actor apart and makes him a fit candidate for liability was originally a non-instrumentalist inquiry. The King's Bench in 1616 did not ask: what good will follow from holding that physical compulsion and unavoidable accident constitute good excuses? The question was rather: How should we perceive an act done under compulsion? Is it the same as no act at all? Or does it set the actor off from his fellow men? Thus, excusing is not an assessment of consequences, but a perception of moral equivalence. It is a judgment that an act causing harm ought to be treated as no act at all.

The hypotheticals of Weaver v. Ward correspond to the Aristotelian excusing categories of compulsion and unavoidable ignorance. Each of these has spawned a line of cases denying liability in cases of inordinate risk-creation. The excuse of compulsion has found expression in the emergency doctrine, which excuses excessive risks created in cases in which the defendant is caught in an unexpected, personally dangerous situation. In Cordas v. Peerless Transportation Co., for example, it was thought excusable for a cab driver to jump from his moving cab in order to escape from a threatening gunman on the running board. In view of the crowd of pedestrians nearby, the driver clearly took a risk that generated a net danger to human life. It was thus an unreasonable, excessive, and unjustified risk. Yet the overwhelmingly coercive circumstances meant that he, personally, was excused from fleeing the moving cab.[60] An example of unavoidable ignorance excusing risk-creation is Smith v. Lampe, in which the defendant honked his horn in an effort to warn a tug that seemed to be heading toward shore in a dense fog. As it happened, the honking coincided with a signal that the tug captain expected would assist him in making port. Accordingly the captain steered his tug toward the honking rather than away from it. That the defendant did not know of the prearranged signal excused his contributing to the tug's going aground. Under the facts of the case, the honking surely created an unreasonable risk of harm. If instantaneous injunctions were possible, one would no doubt wish to enjoin the honking as an excessive, illegal risk. Yet the defendant's ignorance of that risk was also excusable. Under the circumstances he could not fairly have been expected to inform himself of all possible interpretations of honking in a dense fog.

As expanded in these cases, the excuses of compulsion and unavoidable ignorance added dimension to the hypotheticals put in

60. The rhetoric of reasonableness obscures the difference between assessing the risk and excusing the defendant on the ground that pressures were too great to permit the right decision. . . . Yet it is clear that the emergency doctrine functions as a personal excuse, for the defense is applicable even if the actor made the wrong choice, i.e., took an objectively unreasonable risk. . . .

Weaver v. Ward. In *Cordas* and *Smith* we have to ask: What can we fairly expect of the defendant under the circumstances? Can we ask of a man that he remain in a car with a gun pointed at him? Can we require that a man inform himself of all local customs before honking his horn? Thus the question of rationally singling out a party to bear liability becomes a question of what we can fairly demand of an individual under unusual circumstances. Assessing the excusability of ignorance or of yielding to compulsion can be an instrumentalist inquiry. As we increase or decrease our demands, we accordingly stimulate future behavior. Thus, setting the level of excusability could function as a level of social control. Yet one can also think of excuses as expressions of compassion for human failings in times of stress — expressions that are thought proper regardless of the impact on other potential risk-creators.

Despite this tension between thinking of excusing conditions in an instrumentalist or non-instrumentalist way, we can formulate two significant claims about the role of excuses in cases decided under the paradigm of reciprocity. First, excusing the risk-creator does not, in principle, undercut the victim's right to recover. In most cases, it is operationally irrelevant to posit a right to recovery when the victim cannot in fact recover from the excused risk-creator. Yet it may be important to distinguish between victims of reciprocal, background risks and victims of nonreciprocal risks. The latter class of victims — those who have been deprived of their equal share of security from risk — might have a claim of priority in a social insurance scheme. Further, for a variety of reasons, one might wish in certain classes of cases to deny the availability of particular excuses, such as insanity in general or immaturity for teenage drivers. Insanity has always been a disfavored excuse; even the King's Bench in Weaver v. Ward rejected lunacy as a defense. However, it is important to perceive that to reject the excuse is not to provide a rationale for recovery. It is not being injured by an insane man that grounds a right to recovery, but being injured by a nonreciprocal risk — as in every other case applying the paradigm of reciprocity. Rejecting the excuse merely permits the independently established, but previously unenforceable right to prevail.

Secondly, an even more significant claim is that these excuses — compulsion and unavoidable ignorance — are available in all cases in which the right to recovery springs from being subjected to a nonreciprocal risk of harm. We have already pointed out the applicability of these excuses in negligence cases like *Cordas* and Smith v. Lampe. What is surprising is to find them applicable in cases of strict liability as well; strict liability is usually thought of as an area where courts are insensitive to questions of fairness to defendants.

Admittedly, the excuses of compulsion and unavoidable ignorance do not often arise in strict liability cases, for men who engage in activities like blasting, fumigating, and crop dusting typically do so voluntarily and with knowledge of the risks characteristic of the activity. Yet there have been cases in which strict liability for keeping a vicious dog was denied on the ground that the defendant did not know, and had no reason to know, that his pet was dangerous. And doctrines of proximate cause provide a rubric for considering the excuse of unavoidable ignorance under another name. In Madsen v. East Jordan Irrigation Co., for example, the defendant's blasting operations frightened the mother minks on the plaintiff's farm, causing them to kill 230 of their offspring. The Utah Supreme Court affirmed a demurrer to the complaint. In the court's judgment, the reaction of the mother minks "was not within the realm of matters to be anticipated." This is precisely the factual judgment that would warrant saying that the company's ignorance of this possible result was excused, yet the rubric of proximate cause provided a doctrinally acceptable heading for dismissing the complaint.

It is hard to find a case of strict liability raising the issue of compulsion as an excuse. Yet if a pilot could flee a dangerous situation only by taking off in his plane, as the cab driver in *Cordas* escaped danger by leaping from his moving cab, would there be rational grounds for distinguishing damage caused by the airplane crash from damage caused by Cordas's cab? One would think not. Both are cases of nonreciprocal risk-taking, and both are cases in which unusual circumstances render it unfair to expect the defendant to avoid the risk he creates. . . .

Recognizing the pervasiveness of nonreciprocity as a standard of liability, as limited by the availability of excuses, should provide a new perspective on tort doctrine and demonstrate that strict liability and negligence as applied in the cases discussed above are not contrary theories of liability. Rather, strict liability and negligence appear to be complementary expressions of the same paradigm of liability.

III.   The Paradigm of Reasonableness

Until the mid-nineteenth century, the paradigm of reciprocity dominated the law of personal injury. It accounted for cases of strict liability and of intentional torts and for the distinction implicit in the common law writ system between background risks and risks directly violating the interests of others. In the course of the nineteenth century, however, the concepts underlying the paradigm of reciprocity gradually assumed new contours. A new paradigm emerged, which challenged all traditional ideas of tort theory. The new paradigm challenged the assumption that the issue of liability could be decided on grounds of fairness to both victim and defendant without considering the impact of the decisions on the society at large. It further challenged the assumption that the victim's right to recovery was distinguishable from the defendant's duty to pay. In short, the new paradigm of reasonableness represented a new style of thinking about tort disputes.

The core of this revolutionary change was a shift in the meaning of the word "fault." At its origins in the common law of torts, the concept of fault served to unify the medley of excuses available to defendants who would otherwise be liable in trespass for directly causing harm. As the new paradigm emerged, fault came to be an inquiry about the context and the reasonableness of the defendant's risk-creating conduct. Recasting fault from an inquiry about excuses into an inquiry about the reasonableness of risk-taking laid the foundation for the new paradigm of liability. It provided the medium for tying the determination of liability to maximization of social utility, and it led to the conceptual connection between the issue of fault and the victim's right to recover. The essence of the shift is that the claim of faultlessness ceased being an excuse and became a justification. The significance of this transformation is difficult to appreciate today, for the concepts of excuse and justification have themselves become obscure in our moral and legal thinking. To clarify the conceptual metamorphosis of the fault concept, I must pause to explicate the difference between justifying and excusing conduct.

The difference between justifying and excusing conditions is most readily seen in the case of intentional conduct, particularly intentional crimes. Typical cases of justified intentional conduct are self-defense and the use of force to effect an arrest. These justificatory claims assess the reasonableness of using force under the circumstances. The questions asked in seeking to justify an intentional battery as self-defense relate to the social costs and the social benefits of using force and to the wrongfulness of the initial aggressor's conduct in attacking the defendant. The resolution of this cost-benefit analysis speaks to the legal permissibility and sometimes to the commendability of the *act* of using force under the circumstances. Excuses, in contrast, focus not on the costs and benefits of the *act*, but on the degree of the *actor's* choice in engaging in it. Insanity and duress are raised as excuses even to concededly wrongful acts. To resolve a claim of insanity, we are led to inquire about the *actor's* personality, his capacities under stress and the pressures under which he was acting. Finding that the *actor* is excused by reason of insanity is not to say that the *act* was right or even permissible, but merely that the actor's freedom of choice was so impaired that he cannot be held accountable for his wrongful deed.

Justifying and excusing claims bear different relationships to the rule of liability. To justify conduct is to say that in the future, conduct under similar circumstances will not be regarded as wrongful or illegal. Excusing conduct, however, leaves intact the imperative not to engage in the excused act. Acquitting a man by reason of insanity does not change the norm prohibiting murder. Rather, it represents a judgment that a particular person, acting under particular pressures at a particular time, cannot be held accountable for violating that norm. The difference between changing the rule and finding in a particular case that it does not apply is best captured by asking whether in finding for the defendant the court recognizes a right to engage in the activity. To justify conduct as self-defense is to recognize a right to use force, but to excuse homicide under duress is not to acknowledge a right to kill. It is rather to recognize that an actor cannot be fairly blamed for having succumbed to pressures requiring him to kill.

The distinction between justifying and excusing conduct applies with equal coherence in analyzing risk-creating behavior. Questions about the excusability of risk-creation focus on the actor's personal circumstances and his capacity to avoid the risk. Could he have resisted the intimidations of a gunman in his car? Could he have found out about the risks latent in his conduct? Questions about justification, on the other hand, look solely to the risk, abstracted from the personality of the risk-creator. What are the benefits of the risk? What are the costs? Does the risk maximize utility? As the inquiry shifts from excusing to justifying risks, the actor and his traits become irrelevant. At the level of justification, the only relevant question is whether the risk, on balance, is socially desirable. Excusing a risk, as a personal judgment about the actor, leaves the right of the victim intact; but justifying a risk recognizes the defendant's right to run that risk vis-à-vis the victim. If the risk is justified in this sense, the victim could hardly have a claim against the risk-creator. The right of the risk-creator supplants the right of the victim to recover.

That the fault requirement shifted its orientation from excusing to justifying risks had the following consequences: (1) fault became a judgment about the risk, rather than about the responsibility of the individual who created the risk; (2) fault was no longer a question of fairness to the individual, but an inquiry about the relative costs and benefits of particular risks; (3) fault became a condition for recognizing the right of the victim to recover. These three postures of the fault requirement diverged radically from the paradigm of reciprocity. Together, they provided the foundation for the paradigm of reasonableness, a way of thinking that was to become a powerful ideological force in tort thinking of the late nineteenth and twentieth centuries.[81]

The reasonable man became a central, almost indispensable figure in the paradigm of reasonableness. By asking what a reasonable man would do under the circumstances, judges could assay the issues both of justifying and excusing risks. Reasonable men, presumably, seek to maximize utility; therefore, to ask what a reasonable man would do is to inquire into the justifiability of the risk. If the risk-running might be excused, say by reason of the emergency doctrine or a particular defect like blindness or immaturity, the jury instruction might specify the excusing condition as one of the "circumstances" under which the conduct of the reasonable man is to be assessed. If the court wished to include or exclude a teenage driver's immaturity as a possible excusing condition, it could define the relevant "circumstances" accordingly. Because the "reasonable man" test so adeptly encompasses both issues of justification and excuse, it is not surprising that the paradigm of reasonableness has led to the blurring of that distinction in tort theory....

V. The Interplay of Substance and Style

The conflict between the paradigm of reasonableness and the paradigm of reciprocity is, in the end, a struggle between two strategies for justifying the distribution of burdens in a legal system. The strategy of utility proceeds on the assumption that burdens are fairly imposed if the distribution optimizes the interests of the community as a whole. The paradigm of reciprocity, on the other hand, is based on a strategy of waiver. It takes as its starting point the personal rights of individuals in society to enjoy roughly the same degree of security, and appeals to the conduct of the victims themselves to determine the scope of the right to equal security. By interpreting the risk-creating activities of the defendant and of the victim as reciprocal and thus offsetting, courts may tie the denial of

---

81. The impact of the paradigm is not so much that negligence emerged as a rationale of liability, for many cases of negligence are compatible with the paradigm of reciprocity....The ideological change was the conversion of each tort dispute into a medium for furthering social goals. See Prosser's discussion of "social engineering," Prosser 14-16. This reorientation of the process led eventually to the blurring of the issues of corrective justice and distributive justice....

liability to the victim to his own waiver of a degree of security in favor of the pursuit of an activity of higher risk.

These two paradigms, and their accompanying strategies for distributing burdens, overlap in every case in which an activity endangers outsiders not participating in the creation of the risk. Where the courts deny liability, say, for leaving a golf club where a child might pick it up and swing it, they must decide whether to appeal either to the paradigm of reciprocity and argue that the risk is an ordinary, reciprocal risk of group living, or to the paradigm of reasonableness and argue that the activity is socially beneficent and warrants encouragement. They must decide, in short, whether to focus on the parties and their relationship or on the society and its needs. In these cases where the paradigms overlap, both ways of thinking may yield the same result. Yet the rhetoric of these decisions creates a pattern that influences reasoning in cases in which the paradigms diverge.

The major divergence is the set of cases in which a socially useful activity imposes nonreciprocal risks on those around it. These are the cases of motoring, airplane overflights, air pollution, oil spillage, sonic booms — in short, the recurrent threats of modern life. In resolving conflict between those who benefit from these activities and those who suffer from them, the courts must decide how much weight to give to the net social value of the activity. In Boomer v. Atlantic Cement Co., the New York Court of Appeals reflected the paradigm of reciprocity by defining the issue of holding a cement company liable for air pollution as a question of the "rights of the parties," rather than the "promotion of the general public welfare." Similarly, in its recent debate over the liability of airplane owners and operators for damage to ground structures, the American Law Institute faced the same conflict. It too opted for the paradigm of reciprocity.

A variation on this conflict of paradigms emerges when a bystander, injured by a motorist, sues the manufacturer of the vehicle on the theory that a defect in the vehicle caused the accident. In these cases, the ultimate issue is whether the motoring public as a whole should pay a higher price for automobiles in order to compensate manufacturers for their liability costs to pedestrians. The rationale for putting the costs on the motoring public is that motoring, as a whole, imposes a nonreciprocal risk on pedestrians and other bystanders. In addressing itself to this issue in Elmore v. American Motors Corp., the California Supreme Court stressed the inability of bystanders to protect themselves against the risk of defective automobiles. Though it grouped pedestrians together with other drivers in extending strict products liability, the Elmore opinion appears to be more oriented to questions of risk and of who subjects whom to an excessive risk than it is to the reasonableness and utility of motoring. Thus, this opinion, too, hints at a reawakening of sensitivity to the paradigm of reciprocity.

On the whole, however, the paradigm of reasonableness still holds sway over the thinking of American courts. The reasonable man is too popular a figure to be abandoned. The use of litigation to pursue social goals is well entrenched. Yet the appeal to the paradigm might well be more one of style than of substance.

In assessing the reasonableness of risks, lawyers ask many seemingly precise questions: What are the consequences of the risk, its social costs and social benefits? What specific risks are included in the "ambit of the risk"? One can speak of formulae, like the Learned Hand formula, and argue in detail about questions of costs, benefits and trade-offs. This style of thinking is attractive to the legal mind. Its tracings in proximate cause cases are the formulae for defining the scope of the risk. Thus *Palsgraf* enthrones the "eye of reasonable vigilance" to rule over "the orbit of the duty." And the standard of "foreseeability" has become the dominant test of proximate cause. With close examination one sees that these formulae are merely tautological constructs designed to support an aura of utilitarian precision. Only if remote consequences are defined out of existence can one total up the benefits and the costs of all (known) consequences. The test of "foreseeability" permits balancing by restrictively defining the contours of the scales. Unforeseeable risks cannot be counted as part of the costs and benefits of the risk; for, after all, they are unforeseeable and therefore unknowable. There may be much work to be done in explaining why this composite mode of thought—the idiom of balancing, orbits of risk and foreseeability—has captured the contemporary legal mind. But there is little doubt that it has, and this fashionable style of thought buttresses the substantive claims of the paradigm of reasonableness.

The paradigm of reciprocity, on the other hand, for all its substantive and moral appeal, puts questions that are hardly likely to engage the contemporary legal mind: When is a risk so excessive that it counts as a nonreciprocal risk? When are two risks of the same category and thus reciprocally offsetting? It is easy to assert that risks of owning a dog offset those of barbecuing in one's backyard, but what if the matter should be disputed? There are at least two kinds of difficulties that arise in assessing the relationship among risks. The first is that of protecting minorities. Does everyone have to engage in crop dusting for the risk to be reciprocal, or just half the community? A tempting solution to the problem is to say that as to someone not engaged in the activity, the risks are per se nonreciprocal. But the gains of this simplifying stroke are undercut by the assumption necessarily implicit in the concept of reciprocity that risks are fungible with others of the same "kind." Yet how does one determine when risks are counterpoised as species of the same genus? If one man owns a dog, and his neighbor a cat, the risks presumably offset each other. But if one man drives a car, and the other rides a bicycle? Or if one plays baseball in the street and the other hunts quail in the woods behind his house? No two people do exactly the same things. To classify risks as reciprocal risks, one must perceive their unifying features. Thus, risks of owning domestic animals may be thought to be of the same kind. And, theoretically one might argue with equal vigor that all sporting activities requiring the projection of objects through the air create risks of the same order, whether the objects be baseballs, arrows, or bullets. Determining the appropriate level of abstraction is patently a matter of judgment; yet the judgments require use of metaphors and images — a way of thinking that hardly commends itself as precise and scientific.

In proximate cause disputes the analogue to this style of thinking is the now rejected emphasis on the directness and immediacy of causal links, as well expressed in the *Polemis* case and Judge Andrews's dissent in *Palsgraf*. As Hart and Honoré have recognized, we rely on causal imagery in solving problems of causal connection in ordinary, nonlegal discourse. Why, then, does the standard of "direct causation" strike many today as arbitrary and irrational? Why does metaphoric thinking command so little respect among lawyers? Why not agree with Judge Andrews that the issue of proximate cause is akin to assessing when a stream merges with waters of another source?

Metaphors and causal imagery may represent a mode of thought that appears insufficiently rational in an era dominated by technological processes. Yet why should the rhetoric of reasonableness and foreseeability appeal to lawyers as a more scientific or precise way of thinking? The answer might lie in the scientific image associated with passing through several stages of argument before reaching a conclusion. The paradigm of reasonableness requires several stages of analysis: defining the risk, assessing its consequences, balancing costs and benefits. The paradigm of reciprocity requires a single conclusion, based on perceptions of similarities, of excessiveness, and of directness. If an argument requires several steps, it basks in the respectability of precision and rationality. Yet associating rationality with multistaged argumentation may be but a spectacular lawyerly fallacy — akin to the social scientists' fallacy of misplaced concreteness (thinking that numbers make a claim more accurate).

Whether or not multistaged argumentation is more rational than a perception of directness or excessiveness, one cannot but be impressed with the interplay of substantive and stylistic criteria in the conflict between the two paradigms of tort liability. Protecting innocent victims from socially useful risks is one issue. The relative rationality of defining risks and balancing consequences is quite another. That there are these two levels of tension helps explain the ongoing vitality of both paradigms of tort liability.

The courts face the choice. Should they surrender the individual to the demands of maximizing utility? Or should they continue to protect individual interests in the face of community needs? To do the latter, courts and lawyers may well have to perceive the link between achieving their substantive goals and explicating their value choices in a simpler, sometimes metaphoric style of reasoning.

NOTES AND QUESTIONS

1. Does the distinction between reciprocal and nonreciprocal risks provide a satisfying basis for formulating liability rules? Suppose that in Rylands v. Fletcher the defendant mill owner did impose a nonreciprocal risk on the plaintiff mining company. So what? Why should we have a different rule — liability based on fault — if both defendant and plaintiff are in the mining business? Why, in other words, should the victim who potentially imposed a similar risk on his injurer be treated differently, once he is in fact injured, from the victim who did not?

2. What does Fletcher mean by instrumentalist and noninstrumentalist thinking? Is Calabresi's general deterrence theory instrumentalist or noninstrumentalist?

3. Does Fletcher succeed in demonstrating "that the paradigm of reciprocity accounts for the typical cases of strict liability"? He accounts for the distinction between a pilot's strict liability to land occupants and negligence to other flyers. But how would he explain the absence of strict liability to passengers in the other plane?

4. Why is there no strict liability to the pilot's own passengers? This raises a broader question about the applicability of the reciprocity theory to various kinds of bargaining relationships — perhaps most importantly, strict liability for defective products. In the latter area, Fletcher says that the market relationship between the parties creates "a mechanism of insurance, changing the question of fairness posed by imposing liability" (see p. 240, *supra*, n.24). Is this consistent with his general view that the tort system should be an instru ment of corrective rather than distributive justice (see p. 242,

supra, n.40)? More specifically, why does he treat the insurance mechanism as raising special questions in the products liability area, but not with respect to motoring, aviation, and so on?

5. How do we decide whether activities are reciprocal? While Fletcher acknowledges the problem, does he give it sufficient weight? He says, for example, that the risks imposed by owners of cats and dogs "presumably offset each other." Why? Do the risks of cats and active three-year-old children offset each other? Cats and power lawn mowers? Is his injunction to think metaphorically helpful in deciding these cases?

6. What about the non-risk-creator in a world of reciprocal risks? Assume a negligence standard is applicable to motorists because driving imposes reciprocal risks. Would Fletcher impose strict liability on a motorist for an injury to a pedestrian who does not own a car? Would a dog owner be held to a standard of due care when his pet bit a fellow dog owner, but to a strict liability standard when his pet's victim did not own a pet?

7. More generally, would Fletcher opt for decisions about whether an activity was reciprocal at the "category level" — to use Calabresi's terminology — or on a case-by-case basis? Does his aversion to instrumentalism suggest an answer to this question?

8. Fletcher's thesis is discussed and criticized in Calabresi, Toward a Test for Strict Liability in Torts, 81 Yale L.J. 1055, 1078-1082 (1972); Posner, Strict Liability: A Comment, 2 J. Legal Stud. 205, 215-217 (1973); and Schwartz, The Vitality of Negligence and the Ethics of Strict Liability, 15 Ga. L. Rev. 963, 977-1005 (1981) (also evaluating Richard Epstein's strict liability theory, which follows).

9. For an earlier exposition of the distinction between reciprocal and nonreciprocal risks, see Vold, Aircraft Operator's Liability for Ground Damage and Passenger Injury, 13 Neb. B. Bull. 373, 380-382 (1935).

A Theory of Strict Liability*

Richard A. Epstein

Torts is at once one of the simplest and one of the most complex areas of the law. It is simple because it concerns itself with fact patterns that can be understood and appreciated without the benefit of formal legal instruction. Almost everyone has some opinions, often

Source: 2 J. Legal Stud. 151, 160-169, 172-185, 189-191, 197-202, 203-204 (1973).

strong even if unformed, about his rights and responsibilities towards his fellow man; and almost everyone has had occasion in contexts apart from the judicial process to apply his beliefs to the question of responsibility for some mishap that has come to pass. Indeed, the language of the law of tort, in sharp contrast, say, to that of civil procedure, reveals at every turn its origins in ordinary thought.

But the simplicity of torts based upon its use of ordinary language is deceptive. Even if ordinary language contains most of the concepts that bear on questions of personal responsibility, it often uses them in loose, inexact, and ambiguous ways: witness, for example, the confusion that surrounds the use of "malice." While an intuitive appreciation of the persistent features of ordinary language may help decide easy cases, more is required for the solution of those difficult cases where the use of ordinary language pulls in different directions at the same time. There is need for a systematic inquiry which refines, but which does not abandon, the shared impressions of everyday life. The task is to develop a normative theory of torts that takes into account common sense notions of individual responsibility....

II. An Analysis of Causation

...Under the orthodox view of negligence, the question of causation is resolved by a two-step process. The first part of the inquiry concerns the "cause in fact" of the plaintiff's injury. The usual test to determine whether or not the plaintiff's injury was in fact caused by the negligence of the defendant is to ask whether, "but for the negligence of the defendant, the plaintiff would not have been injured." But this complex proposition is not in any sense the semantic equivalent of the assertion that the defendant caused the injury to the plaintiff. The former expression is in counterfactual form and requires an examination of what *would have* been the case if things had been otherwise. The second expression simply asks in direct indicative form what in fact *did* happen. The change in mood suggests the difference between the two concepts.

The "but for" test does not provide a satisfactory account of the concept of causation if the words "in fact" are taken seriously. *A* carelessly sets his alarm one hour early. When he wakes up the next morning he has ample time before work and decides to take an early morning drive in the country. While on the road he is spotted by *B*, an old college roommate, who becomes so excited that he runs off the road and hurts *C*. But for the negligence of *A*, *C* would never have been injured, because *B* doubtless would have continued along his uneventful way. Nonetheless, it is common ground that *A*, even if negligent, is in no way responsible for the injury to *C*, caused by *B*.

Its affinity for absurd hypotheticals should suggest that the "but for" test should be abandoned as even a tentative account of the concept of causation. But there has been no such abandonment. Instead it has been argued that the "but for" test provides a "philosophical" test for the concept of causation which shows that the "consequences" of any act (or at least any negligent act) extend indefinitely into the future. But there is no merit, philosophic or otherwise, to an account of any concept which cannot handle the simplest of cases, and only a mistaken view of philosophic inquiry demands an acceptance of an account of causation that conflicts so utterly with ordinary usage.

Once the "philosophical" account of causation was accepted, it could not be applied in legal contexts without modification because of the unacceptable results that it required. The concept of "cause in law" or "proximate" cause became necessary to confine the concept within acceptable limits. In the earlier literature there was an attempt to work out in great detail specifications of the kinds of events and acts which would serve to break the causal connection between the conduct of the defendant and the harm suffered by the plaintiff. That inquiry is indeed a necessary one in some cases, although it need not be tied to the concept of "but for" causation. In recent years, the inquiry has been continued and refined by Hart and Honoré in their classic work, Causation in the Law. Hart and Honoré do not accept the "but for" account of causation, but instead define causation in a manner which recognizes the kinds of intervening acts and events that are to be taken into account before it can be shown that the conduct of the defendant was the cause of the plaintiff's harm; thus they argue that "an act is the cause of harm if it is an intervention in the course of affairs which is sufficient to produce the harm without the cooperation of the voluntary acts of others or abnormal conjunctions of events." This definition, and its careful explication, however, have been rejected for the most part in the legal literature on the ground that they require courts to confront "the never-ending and insoluble problems of causation," "together with the subtleties of novus actus interveniens." In its stead, the question of proximate cause has been said to reduce itself to the question whether the conduct of the defendant is a "substantial factor" contributing to the loss of the plaintiff, or whether the harm suffered was "reasonably foreseeable." But these formulations of the test of proximate cause do not give much guidance for the solution of particular cases. One might think that this would be treated as a defect in an account of a concept like causation, but in large measure it has been thought to be its strength. Once it is decided that there is no hard content to the term causation, the courts are free to decide particular lawsuits in accordance with the principles of "social policy" under the guise of the proximate-cause doctrine.

But it is false to argue that systems of law that use the principles of causation to decide cases must stand in opposition to those systems that use principles of social policy to achieve that same end. As Hart and Honoré have pointed out, the major premise of most legal systems (until perhaps the recent past) is that causation provides, *as a matter of policy*, the reason to decide cases in one way rather than the other. Moreover, they properly observe that:

> It is fatally easy and has become increasingly common to make the transition from the exhilarating discovery that complex words like "cause" cannot be simply defined and have no "one true meaning" to the mistaken conclusion that they have no meaning worth bothering about at all, but are used as a mere disguise for arbitrary decision or judicial policy. This is blinding error, and legal language and reasoning will never develop while it persists.

But for all their force these remarks have not received general acceptance. Indeed, once it was agreed that the term "proximate cause" gave the courts room to engage in creative decisions of social policy, the next step was not hard to take. If the term "proximate cause" only masks the underlying policy considerations, then academic literature, which need not even pay lip service to precedent, should cast it aside to deal with the policy considerations in their own terms. Thus, in The Costs of Accidents Guido Calabresi uses the tools of economic analysis to develop a comprehensive theory that will provide an adequate framework to test and develop the substantive rules of tort liability. The author makes clear that he does not think the concept of causation plays any part in the development of his theory. He describes "cause" as a "weasel" word and claims that he "does not propose to consider the question of what, if anything, we mean when we say that specific activities 'cause,' in some metaphysical sense, a given accident; in fact, when we identify an act or activity as a 'cause,' we may be expressing any number of ideas." But the term cannot be banished from the lexicon on the ground that it is "metaphysical." The concept is dominant in the law because it is dominant in the language that people, including lawyers, use to describe conduct and to determine responsibility. The importance of the concept is revealed when Calabresi discusses at length the question of "what-is-a-cost-of-what" in two chapters that address themselves to the question of "which activities cause which accident costs." The concept may not be strictly necessary to the development of some theory of tort if the goal of the system is the minimization of the costs of accidents. But its presence reminds us that a system of law which tries to banish it from use may not respond to ordinary views on individual blame and accountability.

This last point is brought home by an examination of another skeptical account of causation. In The Problem of Social Cost, Professor Coase argues that the concept of causation, as he understands it, does not permit the solution of individual legal disputes. Although he does not work from the "but for" paradigm, he does adopt a model of causation that treats as a cause of a given harm any *joint condition* necessary to its creation. Since the acts of both parties are "necessary" it follows that the concept of causation provides, in this analysis, no grounds to prefer either person to another. The problem is "reciprocal" in both causal and economic terms. In effect, Coase argues that the harms in question resulted because two persons each wished to make inconsistent uses of a common resource:

> The question is commonly thought of as one in which A inflicts harm on B and what has to be decided is: how should we restrain A? But this is wrong. We are dealing with a problem of a reciprocal nature. To avoid the harm to B would inflict harm on A. The real question that has to be decided is: should A be allowed to harm B or should B be allowed to harm A? The problem is to avoid the more serious harm. I instanced in my previous article the case of a confectioner the noise and vibrations from whose machinery disturbed a doctor in his work. To avoid harming the doctor would inflict harm on the confectioner. The problem posed by this case was essentially whether it was worth while, as a result of restricting the methods of production which could be used by the confectioner, to secure more doctoring at the cost of a reduced supply of confectionery products. Another example is afforded by the problem of straying cattle which destroy crops on neighbouring land. It is inevitable that some cattle will stray, an increase in the supply of meat can only be obtained at the expense of a decrease in the supply of crops. The nature of the choice is clear: meat or crops. What answer should be given is, of course, not clear unless we know the value of what is obtained as well as the value of what is sacrificed to obtain it. To give another example, Professor George J. Stigler instances the contamination of a stream. If we assume that the harmful effect of the pollution is that it kills the fish, the question to be decided is: is the value of the fish lost greater or less than the value of the product which the contamination of the stream makes possible.

In the first portion of this paragraph, Professor Coase argues that the question is reciprocal because "to avoid the harm to A would be to inflict harm upon B." The real question is "should A be allowed to harm B or should B be allowed to harm A." But that image of reciprocity is not carried through in the concrete description of particular cases used to support the general proposition. The first case concerns a "confectioner the noise and vibrations from whose machinery *disturbed* a doctor"; the second, "straying cattle...*destroy* crops on neighboring land"; in the third, "the harmful effect of the pollution...*kills* the fish." Coase describes each situation by the use of sentences that differentiate between the role of the *subject* of each of these propositions and the role of the *object*. There is no question but that the confectioner harmed the doctor; the cattle the crops; and the contaminants, the fish. The problem only takes on a *guise* of reciprocity when the party harmed seeks his remedy in court. To use but the first example, the doctor wishes to call in aid the court to "harm" the confectioner, in the sense that he wishes to restrain him from acting to harm his practice. But he is justified in so doing because of the harm the confectioner either has inflicted or will inflict upon him. It would be a grave mistake to say that *before* the invocation of judicial remedies the grounds of dispute disclosed reciprocal harm. The confectioner did not seek to enjoin the doctor from the practice of medicine, because that practice did not and could not harm the confectioner. The notion of causal reciprocity should not be confused with the notion of redress for harm caused.[42]

Both Calabresi and Coase, then, share the belief that the concept of causation should not, because it cannot, play any role in the determination of liability for harms that have occurred. The pages that follow are designed to show that the concept of causation, as it applies to cases of physical injury, can be analyzed in a manner that both renders it internally coherent and relevant to the ultimate question who shall bear the loss.

There will be no attempt to give a single semantic equivalent to the concept of causation. Instead, the paper will consider in succession each of four distinct paradigm cases covered by the proposition "*A* caused *B* harm." These paradigms are not the only way in which we can talk about torts cases. They do, however, provide modes of description which best capture the ordinary use of causal language. Briefly put, they are based upon notions of force, fright, compulsion and dangerous conditions. The first of them will be the simplest to analyze. Each of the subsequent paradigms will introduce further problems to be resolved before the judgment on the causal issue can be made. Nonetheless, despite the internal differences, it can, I

---

42. The importance of reciprocity to questions of responsibility is developed in George P. Fletcher, Fairness and Utility in Tort Theory, 85 Harv. L. Rev. 537 (1972). Fletcher argues that the principles of corrective justice require the law to impose liability for harm only where the defendant has exposed the plaintiff to a "nonreciprocal risk of injury," at least where the defendant is not otherwise excused. But Fletcher does not tell us how to determine whether two risks are reciprocal. Moreover, even if that determination could be made, its relevance is questionable once the harm has come to pass. Even if two risks were reciprocal, it does not follow that neither party should have his action when injured.

believe, be demonstrated that each of these paradigms, when understood, exhibits the features that render it relevant to the question of legal responsibility.

Force. We begin with the simplest instance of causation: the application of force to a person or thing. In a physical sense, the consequences of the application of force may be quite varied. In some cases the object acted upon will move; in others it will be transformed; in still others it will be damaged. It is this last case that will be of exclusive concern here, because it is accepted without question that the minimum condition of tort liability is damage to the person or property of the plaintiff.

The identification of causation with force does not of itself complete the first instance of the proposition "*A* caused harm to *B*." It is still necessary to show that the force in question was applied by human and not natural agencies, and thus to tie the concept of force to that of human volition. The term "volition" is a primitive in the language whose function is to mark off the class of human acts from the class of events; to distinguish between "I raised my arm," and "my arm went up." But even if the term cannot be defined, its function can be made clear by some simple examples. In the old case of Smith v. Stone, the defendant was carried on to the plaintiff's land by a band of armed men. The court held that the plaintiff could not recover in trespass, because it was "the trespasse of the party that carried the defendant upon the land, and not the trespasse of the defendant." True, the physical requirement of entrance was satisfied in the case, but the defendant's movement was in no sense an "action" because, if anything, it was contrary to his will.

Only if some concept of volition is accepted into the language will there be a means to distinguish this case from one in which the defendant *entered* upon the land. In another early case, it was noted that "if a man by force take my hand and strike you," I could not be held liable in trespass because my hand was only the instrument of some other person who, in fact, caused the harm. These two examples should be sufficient to show that we cannot do without the term "volition," even if it cannot be defined. But one need not apologize for its use, because there is no alternative system for the description of human conduct or the assignment of responsibility that can do without the term, including those which turn on negligence, either in its moral or economic interpretation, when they ask what the defendant "could have" done. The concept of "volition" is thus crucial in those theories as well, even if it (along with the notion of force) can never be dispositive on questions of legal responsibility.

The combination of force and volition is expressed in the simple transitive sentence, *A* hit *B*. It is true that this proposition as stated is consistent with the assertion that *A* did not harm *B*. But in many contexts the implication of harm follows fairly from the assertion, as anyone hit by a car will admit. Where the issue is in doubt, the verb can be changed, even as the form of the proposition remains constant, to bring the element of harm more sharply into relief. Thus instead of "*A* hit *B*," another proposition of the requisite form could be "*A* pummeled *B*," or "*A* beat *B*." But since the specifics of the harm go only to the measure of damages and not to the issue of liability, the proposition "*A* hit *B*" will serve as the model of the class of propositions to be considered.

The grammatical structure of the proposition "*A* hit *B*" is crucial to analysis of the problem of causation because it describes a situation both where the parties are *linked* to each other and where their respective roles are still *differentiated*. When causation is defined in this manner, the roles of the parties, contrary to Coase, are not reciprocal. The proposition that "*A* hit *B*" cannot be treated as synonymous with the proposition that "*B* hit *A*." Each of these propositions is complete without reference to either further acts, whether or not voluntary, or to natural events, whether or not abnormal. Questions of intervention are not present, and hence there are no problems about the coordination of multiple actions or events to determine responsibility for a single harm. But it may well be necessary as a matter of fact to assess the role of those forces that are the *instruments* of the defendant. Take a simple case where *A* drives his car into *B*. It could be argued that *A*'s act extended no further than the depression of the gas pedal or, perhaps, *A*'s movement of his leg muscles. But the constant and inveterate use of the English language militates against the restriction of an act to the physical movements of *A*'s body. "*A* drove his car into *B*" is a true description of the event; we might explain its significance away, but we can never deny it in good faith. Reference to those subsequent mechanical complications does not falsify that description. The use of the simple transitive proposition confirms the judgment that these subsequent mechanical occurrences are but the *means*, and nothing more, which *A* used to move his car.

Finally, the proposition of the form "*A* hit *B*" does not depend upon the two-part theory of causation developed by the law of negligence. No question of "but for" is ever raised, much less answered. It may well be that "but for the blow of the plaintiff the harm never would have occurred"; but it is not the "but for" test which establishes the causal preeminence of the application of force by the defendant to the person or property of the plaintiff. Since, moreover, the "but for" test was not used to establish cause in fact, there is no further issue to be discussed under the guise of proximate cause; the false opposition between cause in fact and proximate cause thus disappears.

Once this simple causal paradigm is accepted, its relationship to the question of responsibility for the harm so caused must be clarified. Briefly put, the argument is that proof of the proposition *A* hit *B* should be sufficient to establish a prima facie case of liability.[48] I do not argue that proof of causation is equivalent to a conclusive demonstration of responsibility. Both the modern and classical systems of law are based upon the development of prima facie cases and defenses thereto. They differ not in their use of presumptions but in the elements needed to create the initial presumption in favor of the plaintiff. The doctrine of strict liability holds that proof that the defendant caused harm creates that presumption because proof of the nonreciprocal source of the harm is sufficient to upset the balance where one person must win and the other must lose. There is no room to consider, as part of the prima facie case, allegations that the defendant intended to harm the plaintiff, or could have avoided the harm he caused by the use of reasonable care. The choice is plaintiff or defendant, and the analysis of causation is the tool which, prima facie, fastens responsibility upon the defendant. Indeed for most persons, the difficult question is often not whether these causal assertions create the presumption, but whether there are in fact any means to distinguish between causation and responsibility, so close is the connection between what a man does and what he is answerable for. . . .

Fright and Shock. The structure of the prima facie case for assault — the historical companion to trespass to the person — parallels the paradigm for the prima facie case of the tort of trespass, and illustrates the means by which the concept of causation can be extended in a principled manner. The case in assault is *A* frightened *B.* That paradigm indicates, as in trespass, that *A* and *B* do not have symmetrical roles. There is the same close connection between the conduct of the defendant and the harm of the plaintiff. There is, however, a difference between the cases of assault and those of trespass. In trespass actions the plaintiff's conduct is not in issue in the prima facie case. But the *reactions* of the plaintiff must be taken into account before the prima facie case of assault can be completed. Still, the roles of the parties are not identical. The reactions of the plaintiff do not rise to the level of acts because they are in no sense volitional.

Nonetheless, the paradigm does raise some troublesome issues.

48. The argument depends upon "a deep sense of common law morality that one who hurts another should compensate him." . . .

Suppose, for example, the defendant frightened the plaintiff when he raised his hand to mop the sweat off his face at a time when the plaintiff was standing about fifty yards away. Do facts such as these disclose a prima facie case of assault? Our first response to the allegation does not address the issue of substantive law at all. Rather, it says that the harm suffered by the plaintiff is so trivial that it is inappropriate to use, at public expense, the legal machinery to resolve the case. Such a rule, of course, applies with full force both to theories of strict liability and to those of negligence and intent, and does not help choose between theories when both are applicable.

But the case can be made more difficult by assuming that the plaintiff has suffered serious injuries as a result of his fright. If anyone could be frightened by that kind of conduct, however, most likely he could not have survived long enough in life's hustle and bustle to be injured by the defendant. Thus in a sense, the initial statement of fact turns out to be simply unbelievable even where it is assumed for the sake of argument. In cases like these the defendant should be able to deny the allegation contained in the prima facie case, and be able to claim with some truth that the plaintiff had induced his own fright.[65]

But even after these odd cases are put to one side, the paradigm of assault does raise problems of proof that are not present in trespass cases since the allegation "A frightened B," unlike the allegation "A hit B," can be proved in the given case only after the responses of B are taken into account. Courvoisier v. Raymond puts the issue well, even though it is the *defendant* who raises the issue of assault as an affirmative defense. The plaintiff was a plainclothesman who was sent to investigate at the scene of a riot in a small frontier town; the defendant was the owner of a store which had already been robbed several times during the course of the evening. When the defendant saw the plaintiff, he thought that he intended to rob the store and shot him. Under a theory of strict liability, the statement of the prima facie case is evident: the defendant shot the plaintiff. The only difficult question concerns the existence of a defense which takes the form, the plaintiff assaulted the defendant. That question is a question of fact, and the jury found in effect that the plaintiff did not

---

65. The position in the text is not an altogether happy one even if sound. In order to escape the problem, it is possible to argue that the plaintiff should not be allowed to recover, even if frightened, because he was extrasensitive. This position, however, itself has difficulties because it is inconsistent with the position, which I defend in part III, that the defendant must take his victim as he finds him. Nonetheless it is possible to recognize the defense in assault cases only, on the ground that in these cases the causal relationships can never be established with the clarity appropriate to physical injury cases. Thus it is the difficulties with the causal question that invite the recognition of the defense. Consistent with that position, it should be possible to limit the use of this defense to cases where there is no "substantial" ground for fright at all, because only there is the causal question difficult.

frighten the defendant into shooting him. Rather, the defendant either made the judgment to shoot the plaintiff in light of all that he knew about the situation or was frightened by the activities of third persons. One could, perhaps, quarrel with that determination, but at least 'the answer put is to the right question, a question that does not arise where physical invasions are in issue.

The result in *Courvoisier* was much less satisfactory when the case was taken on appeal. The court reverted to the traditional models that predicate responsibility on negligence or intent, and the choice of theories again affected the outcome of the case. The court held that the defendant should be given an opportunity to prove in justification of his act that he acted reasonably and in apparent self-defense given the riot, even though he intended to hurt the plaintiff. . . . [I]t allowed the defendant to shift his problems to the plaintiff.

The arguments for strict liability carry over from cases of trespass to cases of assault. Negligence and intent should be immaterial to the prima facie case of assault, and for the same reasons as with trespass. Nonetheless, the law in fright cases has followed the pattern of the physical injury cases and at a minimum has insisted that the defendant show either negligence or intent. Indeed, in many cases even the basic rules of negligence are hedged about with further limitations. Although the cases exhibit no consistent pattern, it has been held that the plaintiff is allowed to recover for his harm only if there was a physical trespass to the plaintiff, or, in the alternative, a threat of physical injury. In other cases, there is the strong suggestion that a person can recover in fright cases where he is not subject to threat of physical injury only if he can show that some member of his immediate family was in danger of physical harm.

It is true that all of these elements could well be material as a matter of evidence in a fright case. It may well be that a person is more apt to be shocked if he is in danger of physical injury, or if a member of his immediate family is in such danger. But they are only matters of evidence. The crucial question is that of causation and if a defendant frightens or shocks a plaintiff, the recovery should, prima facie, be allowed even if none of the further conditions sometimes placed on recovery are satisfied.

Compulsion. The concept of causation is not limited to cases of the form "*A* hit *B*" or "*A* frightened *B*." There are other relationships that exhibit more complex grammatical forms to which it also applies. Indeed, the proposition "*A* hit *B*" represents only a special case of a more complex relationship, capable of indefinite extension, which for three persons takes the form "*A* compelled *B* to hit *C*."[71]

71. The most famous decided case of this form is Scott v. Shepherd, 2 Wm. Black, 892, 96 Eng. Rep. 525; 3 Wilson 403, 95 Eng. Rep. 1124 (1773). There four persons were

Cases of this form are more difficult to treat than simple trespass cases, because the verb "compel" is not a simple transitive verb. It is rather an instance of a small class of verbs which are "hypertransitive" or "causative" in nature. The logical object of "compel" is not a person (or thing) as it is in the case of the proposition *A* hit *B* (or *B*'s car), but an embedded (and transformed) proposition — *B* to hit *C* — which itself sets out a causal relationship between two persons.

In the discussion of the proposition "*A* hit *B*," it was noted that *A* and *B* assumed different positions in the proposition because of the different roles which they played. In the analysis of this more complex proposition and its relationship to the question of responsibility, there is the same interaction between nonreciprocity and causation as in the simple cases already analyzed. In order to unpack these relationships, consider the case from the standpoint of the injured party, *C*. If the proposition "*A* compelled *B* to hit *C*" is true, then it follows that "*B* hit *C*." The last proposition can be analyzed in accordance with the notions of causation based upon force and volition that have already been developed. Given that paradigm, it follows that *C* has a prima facie case against *B*. *B* cannot escape liability by showing that he did not hit *C*, for a demonstration that he acted under compulsion is not the same as a demonstration that he did not act at all: Smith v. Stone is a different case from Vincent v. Lake Erie.* Nor, if the observations about the defense of "necessity" made earlier are sound, can *B* plead as a defense that he was compelled by *A* to hit *C*. Even if this conduct were reasonable, it does not follow that *B* need not pay. Nor is this result unfair: Vincent v. Lake Erie holds a person in *B*'s position liable for the harm he inflicts in cases of necessity even though the defendant has neither a defense nor an action over. *B* will have an action over against *A* after he has paid *C*, on the theory that *A* compelled him (to his loss) to hit *C*.

The analysis is not yet complete, because *C* is not limited to an action against *B*. He can bring in the alternative an action against *A*. That action, however, could not rely on trespassory theories of causation. *A* did not hit *C*; *B* did. But the roles of *A* and *C* are still both linked, and differentiated, because *A* compelled *B* to hit *C*; *C* did not compel *B* to hit *A*. Coase's requirement of nonreciprocal conduct can be met here as well as in trespass cases, even after the intermediate

---

involved in the chain of causation. Shepherd (the defendant) compelled Ryals to compel Willis to strike Scott. In principle the argument could be extended indefinitely but there quickly comes a point where the truth, not the coherence, of the proposition comes into doubt. [The case involved an explosive instrumentality that was thrown into a marketplace, and thence from one stand to another until it finally exploded, injuring the plaintiff.]

*For a discussion of Vincent v. Lake Erie, see p. 241, *supra*.

act of B is taken into account. That act, done under the compulsion of A, does not sever the causal connection, even if it changes the specific theory of relief in question. B in effect drops out of the picture in the action between A and C once it is shown that he has acted under compulsion.

The changes in causal theory have their effect on questions of proof. Proof of compulsion upon B is crucial if C's action against A is to succeed. The inquiry on that issue, moreover, is more complex than those required under either of the two paradigms of causation already considered. In trespass cases, no conduct of the plaintiff had to be taken into account to complete the prima facie case. In assault cases, only the reactions of the plaintiff to the act of the defendant were material. Thus neither of these paradigm cases required the examination of an intermediate act.

In particular, two points must be observed. First, the question whether B was negligent under the circumstances is, at best, evidence on the question of compulsion. It may well be that a reasonable man would have acted differently under all the circumstances, including his peril. But this actor B may not be that man, and it is his conduct, not that of some legal construct, that is the subject of inquiry: where B was compelled by A, the prima facie case is made out, even if B was negligent. Second, it is not strictly material whether B intended to harm C, because he could have been compelled to act as he did whether or not that harm was intended. Nonetheless, where harm was intended by B, it must be determined that B did not use the act of A as a cloak or excuse to further his own private interests.

One further problem remains. Suppose C is able to bring actions against both A and B. He will not be entitled to a double recovery for the single harm, so it will be necessary to decide whether A or B will be saddled with the ultimate loss. Here again the causal paradigm permits us to link and differentiate the roles of the parties to the suit. A compelled B to hit C; B did not compel A to hit C. Hence it follows that, prima facie, B should prevail over A.

When all of these distinct actions are considered together, the results of this discussion can be reduced to quite simple terms — C over B, B over A, and hence C over A. Since the relationship is transitive, C must be preferred prima facie to A in any action between them. The equities seem correct, because C did nothing at all; B hit C; and A compelled B to so act.

The argument developed in trespass and extended to assault applies with equal force here, once the expanded, nonreciprocal notion of causation is accepted. In each two party situation, one person must win and the other lose, while the rights and duties of third parties need not be taken into account until raised in suits in which they participate. With this kind of scheme, the question of "who is responsible" must be settled between the parties to the lawsuit. And again, it is the notion of causation that prima facie provides the answer.

Causation and Dangerous Conditions. The forms of causation thus far developed are the easiest to comprehend and accept. But an analysis of causation is seriously incomplete if made only in terms of force, fright, and compulsion. Both ordinary thought and legal theory also use a causal paradigm which covers cases involving the creation of dangerous conditions that result in harm to either person or property.

This paradigm shares many of the characteristics of the three paradigms already considered. Although it includes both cases where the dangerous condition is created by human acts and those where it is the result of natural events, the defendant's responsibility depends on a showing that *he* created the dangerous condition in question. The concept of volition thus remains necessary to mark off the class of human acts from the class of natural events. Moreover, the arguments on the question of responsibility parallel those already developed. *A* created the dangerous condition that resulted in harm to *B; B* did not create the dangerous condition that resulted in harm to *A.* The initial balance between the parties is upset, here as before, in a manner which links the parties to each other as it differentiates their roles.

But there are significant differences between this paradigm and those that have come before. First, it makes use of the expression, "result in." While it could be objected that this term defines causation in terms of itself, that is not the case. The term "result in" is intended to cover only those cases of causation — force, fright and compulsion — already developed in previous sections of this paper. In each individual case, it can, and must, be replaced with a description of the particular act or event which is the immediate cause of the harm, where the term "immediate" is used in its literal sense. The creation of a dangerous condition, without more, does not cause harm in the narrow sense of the term. Some further act or event of the kinds already considered must be identified before the causal analysis is completed, and the term "results in" calls attention to that fact. In effect, therefore, this paradigm, unlike those that preceded it, will require a detailed examination of these subsequent acts and events under a wide range of circumstances and conditions.

Second, this paradigm applies only to dangerous conditions. It is possible to divide the most common instances of dangerous conditions into three classes. The first includes things that are "inherently" dangerous, of which stored explosives are the most common example. They are inherently dangerous because they retain their *potential* energy in full, even if they are stored or handled with the highest possible care. A small application of force, or small change in conditions, like temperature and humidity, can release or otherwise set in motion large forces that can cause harm in the narrow sense of that term. The potential for danger remains great even if its probability is low.

The second kind of dangerous condition is created when a person places a thing — not dangerous in itself — in a dangerous position. Instances of this form of dangerous condition are of two sorts. The first class presupposes the recognition of rights of way: highways, footpaths, and the like. Thus, A leaves a roller skate in a walkway such that someone can slip and fall, should he step on it. Or B leaves his truck on the highway where it blocks or obstructs the road to oncoming traffic.

Other situations in this class involve any unstable position where the application of a small force will permit the release of some greater force. Here again the term "unstable" is to be taken in its narrow physical sense. C places a large rock in an unstable position on top of a steep hillside where a light rain or the brush of a hand could send it tumbling to the base of the hill. D drops a vase, or places it on the edge of a table where it can be easily pulled to the ground by the force of gravity. Vincent v. Lake Erie, taken in its own terms, is a case of this sort: in the words of the court, "those in charge of the vessel deliberately and by their direct efforts held her in such a position that damage to the dock resulted." The damage "resulted" not from gravity but "because of the wind and waves striking her starboard quarter with such force that she was constantly being lifted and thrown against the dock."

The third kind of dangerous situation concerns products or other things dangerous because defective. Thus, E fashions a chair that cannot support the weight of a 150 lb. man because its legs are insecurely fastened to the seat; F manufactures a rifle with a weak barrel that can shatter when it is fired; or G constructs a lathe with inadequate screws to hold the wood in place when the lathe is in operation. In each of these cases, the person who made the product has created a dangerous condition that causes harm when subjected to the stress that it was designed to receive when used in its intended manner. It is this concept of dangerous because defective that is crucial to the formulation of products liability rules (even when strict liability principles are not adopted), and the term here is used only in that standard sense.

The use of this paradigm requires us to distinguish between these kinds of dangerous condition on the one hand and "mere" conditions on the other. If all conditions, and not only dangerous ones, were given causal status, then in almost every case the conduct of both the plaintiff and the defendant would both be the "cause" of the harm in question, as a few examples help make plain. H leaves her carving knife in her kitchen drawer. A thief steals the knife and uses it to wound I. Has H caused I harm in any sense of the term? J leaves his car parked on the street. During the night a cyclone picks the car up and carries it along for a half mile until it falls on top of K. Has J caused K harm? The answer to these questions is no. Unlike the cases of dangerous conditions above, neither H nor J could be sued on a theory which alleges that they created a dangerous condition that resulted in harm. It might be possible to show on the strength of other facts not present that these acts were dangerous when performed. But they are not dangerous as described, for in none of these cases did the prospective defendants make a store of energy which was released by the act of a third party or by natural events. It is also possible to state cases that are quite close to this line. The term "dangerous" has a residual vagueness that makes it difficult to apply in some instances. But unless one is prepared to argue that these situations could not be distinguished from the three classes set out above, then it must be accepted that there is some content to the term. Indeed, it seems idle to treat the concept as though it were immaterial, since it pervades the entire fabric of the law of tort. The important question concerns its place in the scheme of liability.

The analysis of this last paradigm is not completed by proof that causal significance attaches only to dangerous conditions. It is also necessary to consider the kinds of acts and events that operate upon the condition so created to complete the causal chain. To consider the question of intermediate acts first, it is best to divide them into the three categories in which they are analyzed by Hart and Honoré: accidental, negligent, and deliberate.

Accidental acts cause little difficulty. On all views of the law, they do not break the causal connection between the plaintiff's injury and the defendant's conduct, whether performed by the plaintiff or a third party. Indeed, it they did not complete the causal link, then in effect no dangerous conditions could ever rise to causal significance. There could, for example, be no recovery in the simplest cases of products liability, because the very use of the defendant's product would serve on causal grounds to defeat an action for injuries sustained.

Again, the acts of either the plaintiff or a third party do not break the causal connection between the defendant's conduct and the plaintiff's harm, even if negligently performed. Negligence in this context means, as ever, the failure to take reasonable steps that could have prevented or avoided the harm in question. Since the forces attributable to the plaintiff or the third party operate on the dangerous condition created by the defendant, proof that either the plaintiff or a third party failed to exercise reasonable care does not deny the causal allegations contained in the prima facie case; it remains true that the dangerous condition created by the defendant resulted in the harm to the plaintiff. Force and dangerous conditions are still the only issues material to the causation question.

To make the discussion concrete, consider again the case where *A* slips and falls on a roller skate placed by *B* on the walkway. Even if it could be shown that *A* could have avoided the harm if he had looked where he stepped, it is still the case that he slipped and fell upon the skate: only the act that created the dangerous condition and that which was the immediate cause of the harm need be taken into account to complete the causal description of the events in question. The requisites of this paradigm of causation — the slip and the fall — are met whether or not *A* was careless.

A's carelessness might be regarded as sufficient to support the defense of contributory negligence. The acceptance of contributory negligence as a defense is natural in a system that presupposes that the plaintiff must allege negligence in order to complete his prima facie case. But let the defendant's negligence be regarded as immaterial to the prima facie case, and it is then difficult to see why the plaintiff's negligence should raise a valid affirmative defense.... If notions of efficient resource allocation do not provide the proper measure of the defendant's conduct, [a reference to the Learned Hand negligence test, discussed in an omitted section] they should not be introduced by the back door in the judgment of the plaintiff's conduct.

By like reasoning, if the act requirement is crucial in the statement of the prima facie case, it should be crucial as well in the analysis of any possible defenses. The plaintiff's act, reference to his want of precautions apart, does not, for the reasons just discussed in conjunction with the accidental conduct of the plaintiff, provide the basis for an affirmative defense. Hence the case for the defendant must rest upon his ability to demonstrate that the plaintiff owes him a duty at common law to take reasonable steps for self-protection, a question that is discussed at length in the last section of this article. But even if such a duty is recognized, the point is that the allegation of carelessness by the plaintiff does not affect the judgment that the conduct of the defendant was, under the paradigm of dangerous conditions, the cause of the harm in question.

It remains only to examine the causal connection between the dangerous condition created by the defendant and the harm to the plaintiff in the most difficult case, where the intermediate actor deliberately inflicted the harm in question. In Causation in the Law, Hart and Honoré argue that it is not possible to establish causal antecedents to a deliberate act designed to inflict harm. On their view, one could never hold responsible a person who creates a dangerous condition of which the intermediate actor takes advantage out of his own desire to inflict the harm. "The general principle of the traditional doctrine is that *the free, deliberate and informed act or omission of a human being, intended to produce the consequence which is in fact produced, negatives causal connexion.*" In support of this "common sense" position, they argue that "voluntary acts" (deliberate acts where neither mistake nor coercion is present) enjoy a special status because "precautions against such acts are specially difficult, since a man who is bent on harm will usually find some way of doing it."

The case appears to be overstated. It does not follow, because a man bent upon harm *usually* can find some way of doing it, that one must *never* seek to go behind a deliberate infliction of harm. There are many cases where the harm, even if deliberate, could be inflicted only because of the dangerous condition created by the defendant. For example, assume that the defendant has placed a boulder perilously close to the edge of a ravine. One day when the plaintiff is in the ravine—it matters not why—X, his bitter enemy, sees him from the side of the ravine and, bent upon his destruction, tips the boulder over the side of the ravine where it falls upon the plaintiff, severely injuring him. X, even if bent upon destruction, took advantage of the dangerous condition created by the defendant, especially if X had no alternative means at his disposal to execute his plans. If alternative means were available, the defendant should be required to prove the fact as an affirmative defense to the cause of action. Such proof does not deny the causal allegations contained in the prima facie case, but only shows that they do not, in the circumstances, support the claim to relief. The issues of causation and responsibility should be kept distinct. The relationship between them is not clarified by the invocation of a per se rule that states that the causal connection is severed wherever a third party seizes upon the dangerous situation so created in order to deliberately inflict harm. The intent of X should be of no concern in the action between the plaintiff and the defendant. Its role, if any, is to insure that the defendant should have an action over against X if he should be able to find him.

Nonetheless, the cases of the deliberate infliction of harm by an intervening action do raise particularly difficult problems of proof, because there will be many situations where the third party will not seize upon the dangerous *aspects* of the situation created by the defendant. For example, assume that the defendant leaves a vase precariously perched on the edge of a high shelf. *Y* picks up that vase and throws it upon the head of the plaintiff who was sitting in a position where he could have been struck by the vase if it had fallen. Here the defendant is not liable because there is no causal connection between his conduct and the plaintiff's harm. *Y* could have caused the same destruction even if that vase had been placed in a safe and stable position in the middle of the shelf. The dangerous potential in the antecedent situation did not "result in" harm to the plaintiff. In cases like these Hart and Honoré are correct, but it is improper to generalize from them to the broad proposition that it is never proper in a causal sense to go behind the deliberate act of a third person.

Thus far we have considered the effects that intervening acts have on the causal connection between the dangerous condition created by the defendant and the harm suffered by the plaintiff. A similar analysis applies when we consider the effect of intervening events. In Causation in the Law, Hart and Honoré divide forces of nature essentially into "big" and "little" forces. In their view, the little forces never break the chain of causation; when operative they serve only to complete it. That position has received general acceptance, and for the same reason that accidental acts never serve to negate the causal connection. If these forces of nature broke the causal connection then the concept of causation would have to be restricted to cases of trespass, assault, and compulsion; dangerous conditions would have no role in causal analysis.

But the other portion of their argument, which holds that vis major or other "abnormal events" serve to break the causal connection, does not appear to be correct in all circumstances. Here the argument is the same as in the case of intervening acts designed to inflict deliberate harm. In some cases forces of nature, no matter how great, can operate only upon the antecedent dangerous conditions created by the defendant. For example, if a huge storm pushes the boulder off the edge of a cliff when a gentle rain could have had the same effect, it is hard to see why the storm should break the causal connection that would otherwise have been completed by the breeze. Here the large force, like the small one, only places the boulder in a position where it could be pulled downward by the force of gravity. The storm did not hurl the boulder onto the plaintiff. Again, the gale winds in *Vincent* did not break the causal connection (and no one even suggested it did) when the defendant continued to hold its ship firm in a position when the winds would dash it against the dock.

Nonetheless, the distinction between large forces and small ones does have importance, because the larger the force, the greater the probability that the defendant did not create a dangerous condition upon which the force acted, and the easier to accept the assertion that the force of nature accomplished all of its destruction on its own without operating upon a dangerous condition created by defendant. For example, if the defendant leaves his automobile atop a hill with its brakes released and its wheels away from the curb, the position of the car, although dangerous, would be quite immaterial if a cyclone lifted the car and carried it a great distance until it landed upon the plaintiff's house. Here the proof of those events shows, as with the case of deliberate harms, that the antecedent dangerous condition bore no causal relationship to the harm.

The theory of causation just developed — that of dangerous conditions — must in all its aspects be distinguished carefully from the "but for" analysis of causation rejected earlier. When a "but for" theory of causation is adopted, the proposition in question takes the form, "but for the negligence (or act) of the defendant, the harm to the plaintiff would never have occurred." That proposition is, to repeat, counterfactual in form, and thus differs linguistically from the assertion, just made, of the form, "The dangerous conditions created by the defendant resulted in harm to the plaintiff," where the proposition remains in the indicative mood throughout, with its emphasis upon what the defendant *did*. The verb "resulted in" covers only the specific kinds of causes discussed in the previous paradigms. Its use does not suggest that the consequences of a given act may extended indefinitely....

III.   The Problem of the Good Samaritan

The first two portions of this paper have compared the common law rules of negligence with those of strict liability in cases where the defendant has harmed the plaintiff's person or property. If that analysis is sound, then the rules of liability should be based upon the harm in fact caused and not upon any subsequent determination of the reasonableness of the defendant's conduct. The question of liability is thereby severed from both general cost-benefit analysis of the defendant's conduct and a moral examination of his individual worth. In the cases of affirmative action, the rules of strict liability avoid both the unfairness and the complications created when negligence, in either its economic or moral sense, is accepted as the basis of the tort law.

The purpose of this section is to show that these conclusions are capable of extension to areas in which the law has traditionally not allowed recovery. The theories of strict liability explain and justify, as the rules of reasonableness cannot, the common law's refusal to extend liability in tort to cases where the defendant has not harmed the plaintiff by his affirmative action. The problem arises in its starkest form in the case of the good Samaritan. *A* finds himself in a perilous situation which was not created by *B*, as when *A* is overwhelmed by cramps while swimming alone in a surging sea. *B*, moreover, is in a position where he could, without any danger of injury to himself, come to *A*'s assistance with some simple and well-nigh costless steps such as throwing a rope to the plaintiff. The traditional common law position has been that there is no cause of action against *B* solely because *B*, in effect, permitted *A* to drown.

It is important to note the manner in which such cases should be decided under a negligence system. In the verbal formulation of the law of negligence, little attention is paid to the distinction between those cases in which the defendant acted and those cases in which he did not act, failed to act, or omitted to act. "Negligence is the *omission* to do something which a reasonable man guided upon those considerations which ordinarily regulate the conduct of human affairs, would do, or doing something which a prudent and reasonable man would not do." The distinction between acts and omissions is of no consequence to the economic analysis of negligence contained in cases like *Carroll Towing*, for there the emphasis is placed in part upon those precautions which a defendant should have taken (but did not take) in order to prevent those instrumentalities which he owns (here the boat in the harbor) from causing harm to other persons.

Thus, if one considers the low costs of prevention to *B* of rescuing *A*, and the serious, if not deadly, harm that *A* will suffer if *B* chooses not to rescue him, there is no reason why the *Caroll Towing* formula or the general rules of negligence should not require, under pain of liability, the defendant to come to the aid of the plaintiff. Nonetheless, the good Samaritan problem receives a special treatment even under the modern law of torts. The reasons for the special position of this problem are clear once the theories of strict liability are systematically applied. Under these rules, the act requirement has to be satisfied in order to show that the defendant in a given lawsuit caused harm to the plaintiff. Once that is done, the private predicament of the defendant, his ability to take precautions against the given risk, and the general economic rationality of his conduct are all beside the point. Only the issue of causation, of what *the defendant did*, is material to the statement of the prima facie case. The theory is not utilitarian. It looks not to the consequences of alternate course of conduct but to what was done. When that theory with its justification is applied to the problem of the good Samaritan, it follows in the case just put that *A* should not be able to recover from *B* for his injuries. No matter how the facts are manipulated, it is not possible to argue that *B* caused *A* harm in any of the senses of causation which were developed in the earlier portions of this article when he failed to render assistance to *A* in his time of need. In typical negligence cases, all the talk of avoidance and reasonable care may shift attention from the causation requirement, which the general "but for" test distorts beyond recognition. But its importance is revealed by its absence in the good Samaritan cases where the presence of all those elements immaterial to tortious liability cannot, even in combination, persuade judges who accept the negligence theory to apply it in the decisive case....

The common law position on the good Samaritan question does not appeal to our highest sense of benevolence and charity, and it is not at all surprising that there have been many proposals for its alteration or abolition. Let us here examine but one of these proposals. After concluding that the then (1908) current position of the law led to intolerable results, James Barr Ames argued that the appropriate rule should be that:

> One who fails to interfere to save another from impending death or great bodily harm, when he might do so with little or no inconvenience to himself, and the death or great bodily harm follows as a consequence of his inaction, shall be punished criminally and shall make compensation to the party injured or to his widow and children in case of death.

Even this solution, however, does not satisfy the *Carroll Towing* formula. The general use of the cost-benefit analysis required under the economic interpretation of negligence does not permit a person to act on the assumption that he may as of right attach special weight and importance to his own welfare. Under Ames's good Samaritan rule, a defendant in cases of affirmative acts would be required to take only those steps that can be done "with little or no inconvenience." But if the distinction between causing harm and not preventing harm is to be disregarded, why should the difference in standards between the two cases survive the reform of the law? The only explanation is that the two situations are regarded at bottom as raising totally different issues, even for those who insist upon the immateriality of this distinction. Even those who argue, as Ames does, that the law is utilitarian must in the end find some special place for the claims of egoism which are an inseparable byproduct of the belief that individual autonomy — individual liberty — is a good in itself not explainable in terms of its purported social worth. It is one thing to *allow* people to act as they please in the belief that the "invisible hand" will provide the happy congruence of the individual and the social good. Such a theory, however, at bottom must regard individual autonomy as but a means to some social end. It takes a great deal more to assert that men are *entitled* to act as they choose (within the limits of strict liability) even though it is certain that there will be cases where individual welfare will be in conflict with the social good. Only then is it clear that even freedom has its costs: costs revealed in the acceptance of the good Samaritan doctrine.

But are the alternatives more attractive? Once one decides that as a matter of statutory or common law duty, an individual is required under some circumstances to act at his own cost for the exclusive benefit of another, then it is very hard to set out in a principled manner the limits of social interference with individual liberty. Suppose one claims, as Ames does, that his proposed rule applies only in the "obvious" cases where everyone (or almost everyone) would admit that the duty was appropriate: to the case of the man upon the bridge who refuses to throw a rope to a stranger drowning in the waters below. Even if the rule starts out with such modest ambitions, it is difficult to confine it to those limits. Take a simple case first. X as a representative of a private charity asks you for $10 in order to save the life of some starving child in a country ravaged by war. There are other donors available but the number of needy children exceeds that number. The money means "nothing" to you. Are you under a legal obligation to give the $10? Or to lend it interest-free? Does $10 amount to a substantial cost or inconvenience within the meaning of Ames's rule? It is true that the relationship between the gift to charity and the survival of an unidentified child is not so apparent as is the relationship between the man upon the bridge and the swimmer caught in the swirling seas. But lest the physical imagery govern, it is clear in both cases that someone will die as a consequence of your inaction in both cases. Is there a duty to give, or is the contribution a matter of charity?

Consider yet another example where services, not cash, are in issue. Ames insists that his rule would not require the only surgeon in India capable of saving the life of a person with a given affliction to travel across the subcontinent to perform an operation, presumably because the inconvenience and cost would be substantial. But how would he treat the case if some third person were willing to pay him for all of his efforts? If the payment is sufficient to induce the surgeon to act, then there is no need for the good Samaritan doctrine at all. But if it is not, then it is again necessary to compare the costs of the physician with the benefits to his prospective patient. It is hard to know whether Ames would require the forced exchange under these circumstances. But it is at least arguable that under his theory forced exchanges should be required, since the payment might reduce the surgeon's net inconvenience to the point where it was trivial.

Once forced exchanges, regardless of the levels of payment, are accepted, it will no longer be possible to delineate the sphere of activities in which contracts (or charity) will be required in order to procure desired benefits and the sphere of activity in which those benefits can be procured as of right. Where tests of "reasonableness" — stated with such confidence, and applied with such difficulty — dominate the law of tort, it becomes impossible to tell where liberty ends and obligation begins; where contract ends, and tort begins. In each case, it will be possible for some judge or jury to decide that there was something else which the defendant should have done, and he will decide that on the strength of some cost-benefit formula that is difficult indeed to apply. These remarks are conclusive, I think, against the adoption of Ames's rule by judicial innovation, and they bear heavily on the desirability of the abandonment of the good Samaritan rule by legislation as well. It is not surprising that the law has, in the midst of all the clamor for reform, remained unmoved in the end, given the inability to form alternatives to the current position.

But the defense of the common law rule on the good Samaritan does not rest solely upon a criticism of its alternatives. Strong arguments can be advanced to show that the common law position on the good Samaritan problem is in the end consistent with both moral and economic principles.

The history of Western ethics has been marked by the development of two lines of belief. One line of moral thought emphasizes the importance of freedom of the will. It is the intention (or motive) that determines the worth of the act; and no act can be moral unless it is performed free from external compulsion. Hence the expansion of the scope of positive law could only reduce the moral worth of human action. Even if positive law could insure conformity to the appropriate external standards of conduct, it, like other forms of external constraints, destroys the moral worth of the act. Hence the elimination of the positive law becomes a minimum condition for moral conduct, even if it means that persons entitled to benefits (in accordance with some theory of entitlements respected but not enforced) will not receive them if their fellow men are immoral.

On the other hand there are those theories that concern themselves not with the freedom of the will, but with the external effects of individual behavior. There is no room for error, because each act which does not further the stated goals (usually, of the maximization of welfare) is in terms of these theories a bad act. Thus a system of laws must either require the individual to act, regardless of motive, in the socially desired manner, or create incentives for him to so behave. Acceptance of this kind of theory has as its corollary the acceptance, if necessary, of an elaborate system of legal rules to insure compliance with the stated goals of maximization even if individual liberty (which now only counts as a kind of satisfaction) is sacrificed in the effort.

At a common sense level, neither of these views is accepted in its pure form. The strength of each theory lays bare the weaknesses of the other. Preoccupation with the moral freedom of a given actor ignores the effects of his conduct upon other persons. Undue emphasis upon the conformity to external standards of behavior entails a loss of liberty. Hence, most systems of conventional morality try to distinguish between those circumstances in which a person should be compelled to act for the benefit of his fellow man, and those cases where he should be allowed to do so only if prompted by the appropriate motives. To put the point in other terms, the distinction is taken between that conduct which is required and that which, so to speak, is beyond the call of duty. If that distinction is accepted as part of a common morality, then the argument in favor of the good Samaritan rule is that it, better than any possible alternatives, serves to mark off the first class of activities from the second. Compensation for harm caused can be demanded in accordance with the principles of strict liability. Failure to aid those in need can invoke at most moral censure on the ground that the person so accused did not voluntarily conform his conduct to some "universal"principle of justice. The rules of causation, which create liability in the first case, deny it in the second. It may well be that the conduct of individuals who do not aid fellow men is under some circumstances outrageous, but it does not follow that a legal system that does not enforce a duty to aid is outrageous as well.

The defense of the good Samaritan rule in economic terms takes the same qualified form. The cost-benefit analysis has in recent literature been regarded as the best means for the solution of all problems of social organization in those cases where market transactions are infeasible. On that view, the basic principles of economics become a most powerful instrument for the achievement of social justice. But there is another strand of economic thought — more skeptical in its conclusions — which emphasizes the limitations of economic theory for the solution of legal problems.

Most economics textbooks accept that the premises of economic theory do not permit so-called interpersonal comparisons of utility.

Thus Kenneth Arrow states: "The viewpoint will be taken here that interpersonal comparison of utilities has no meaning and, in fact, that there is no meaning relevant to welfare comparisons in the measurability of individual utility." In effect, all attempts to compare costs and benefits between different persons require in the end some noneconomic assumption to measure trade-offs in utility between them. Where no noneconomic assumptions are made, it follows that, in strict theory, an economist can make utility comparisons between alternative social arrangements only under a very restricted set of conditions. One social arrangement can be pronounced superior to a second alternative only if (1) it can be shown that everybody is at least as well off under the first alternative as he is under the second, and (2) at least one person is better off under the first system than he is under the second. If these conditions are respected, then no strictly economic judgment can be made between alternative social states where one person under the allegedly preferred state is worse off than he is under the next best alternative. Yet it is precisely that kind of situation that is involved whenever there is a legal dispute. In economic terms, the resolution of every dispute requires a trade-off between the parties, for no one has yet found a way in which both parties could win a lawsuit. In order to decide the case of the good Samaritan, therefore, we must make the very kind of interpersonal comparisons of utility which economic theory cannot make in its own terms. . . .

The arguments made here suggest that the first task of the law of torts is to define the boundaries of individual liberty. To this question the rules of strict liability based upon the twin notions of causation and volition provide a better answer than the alternative theories based upon the notion of negligence, whether explicated in moral or economic terms. In effect, the principles of strict liability say that the liberty of one person ends when he causes harm to another. Until that point he is free to act as he chooses, and need not take into account the welfare of others.

But the law of tort does not end with the recognition of individual liberty. Once a man causes harm to another, he has brought himself within the boundaries of the law of tort. It does not follow, however, that he will be held liable in each and every case in which it can be shown that he caused harm, for it may still be possible for him to escape liability, not by an insistence upon his freedom of action, but upon a specific showing that his conduct was either excused or justified. Thus far in this paper we have only made occasional and unsystematic references to the problems raised by both pleas of excuses and justification. Their systematic explication remains crucial to the further development of the law of tort. That task, however, is large enough to deserve special attention of its own.

NOTES AND QUESTIONS

1. Epstein claims to be principally concerned with spelling out "a normative theory of torts." What is the conception of justice that underlies his theory?

2. Why does he single out the Good Samaritan problem for such detailed treatment? Dean Ames took the position that the law should recognize a limited duty of rescue (see p. 277, *supra*) in a classic essay, Law and Morals, 22 Harv. L. Rev. 97 (1908). For a recent exposition of a limited duty of "easy rescue," see Weinrib, The Case for a Duty to Rescue, 90 Yale L. J. 247 (1980), criticizing in detail Epstein's views and discussing at some length the traditional common-law distinction between nonfeasance and misfeasance that served as the foundation for the no-duty position.

3. Does Epstein's theory afford a satisfying framework for handling passive behavior that causes harm? How would he decide a case in which a garage mechanic simply ignored instructions from a customer to fix the brakes on her car, "causing" subsequent harm to the unwitting auto owner? Would the mechanic be liable? Would a landowner be liable to an injured guest if he allowed his front sidewalk to deteriorate to the point where a portion of the walkway became tantamount to a concealed trap?

4. Epstein is critical of both Ronald Coase and George Fletcher, two authors who also dealt at length with the concept of reciprocity. How do his definitions of reciprocity and nonreciprocity differ from theirs? Is reciprocity central to his theory?

5. To what extent is Epstein's theory inconsistent with the economic efficiency goals discussed in the previous chapter?

6. Suppose surgical treatment for a duodenal ulcer involves a five per cent risk of damage to the spleen, even when done with the utmost care. Surgeon operates and the harm is realized. Under Epstein's theory is Surgeon liable to Patient? Would Epstein reach the same result whatever the risk of harm? Suppose Patient sought to base liability on Surgeon's failure to inform her of the risk in advance of treatment. Would Epstein's scheme hold Surgeon liable for the failure to obtain Patient's consent? The medical cases raise a more general question of how Epstein's theory of strict liability applies to injury situations in which the parties had a preexisting contractual

relationship. His views on the intersection of tort and contract are explored in Epstein, Medical Malpractice: The Case for Contract, 1976 A.B.F. Research J. 87.

7. Driver is seriously injured by postcollision impact with the steering wheel in his car. He was wearing a standard shoulder-strap seat belt, but the collision occurred with such extraordinary force that it would have taken an air bag or some other costly and still-experimental cushioning device to protect him from injury. In Driver's suit against Manufacturer for injury resulting from the design of the auto, what would be the outcome under Epstein's theory? On product-related injuries generally, see R. Epstein, Modern Products Liability Law (1980).

8. In the landmark case of Palsgraf v. Long Island Railroad Co., 248 N.Y. 339, 162 N.E. 99 (1928), plaintiff was injured when efforts to assist a passenger boarding a moving train dislodged a package he was carrying. The package exploded with such force when it hit the ground that a scale standing on the platform — at some distance from the explosion — shattered, injuring the plaintiff. Chief Judge Cardozo, for the court majority, held that no duty was owed to the plaintiff because she was an unforseeable victim. How would Epstein respond?

9. In a subsequent article, Epstein refined his theory of strict liability by discussing a set of effective and ineffective defenses. See Epstein, Defenses and Subsequent Pleas in a System of Strict Liability, 3 J. Legal Stud. 165 (1974). The three effective defenses that he would recognize are causal defenses, assumption of risk, and plaintiff's trespass.

Under "causal defenses" he would include plaintiff's conduct that falls within the four paradigms discussed in the first article. Thus, for example, he incorporates into his system traditional notions of self-defense: since "B hit A" falls within his first paradigm, it can serve as a defense to the claim "A hit B." Similarly, when "B created a dangerous condition" that resulted in an "A hit B" outcome, B's conduct would establish a defense. Recognizing that the assignment of causal priorities can be exceedingly difficult, Epstein relies on a system of presumptions and counter-presumptions — which can be established by subsequent pleas — to deal with more complex situations in which both A and B contribute to an outcome involving single or multiple injuries.

His discussion of assumed risk and trespass introduces the notion of noncausal defenses, without retreating from his strict liability approach. He indicates how both defenses have come to incorporate elements of "reasonableness" that he would eliminate, consistent with his preference for assigning legal responsibility for the consequences of action voluntarily taken, irrespective of utilitarian considerations. Summing up, he suggests that:

> ... the law of strict liability creates a prima facie case that rests on causal notions alone, subject to a series of defenses, replies, and the like, which are designed to reduce the gap between notions of causation and those of responsibility. On the other hand, the law of negligence tries to state many of the necessary qualifications upon the causal principle by adding the element of "reasonableness" to the prima facie case. These two distinct methods of qualifying causal principles work to create a convergence between the two systems, but, even so, it is quite clear that the two systems will yield different results in certain contexts, as the treatment of the defenses of infancy, insanity, compulsion, and best efforts clearly reveals. [These latter defenses are ineffective under Epstein's strict liability theory.] [Id., at p. 213]

For a detailed treatment of the application of his theory to the field of intentional torts, see Epstein, Intentional Harms, 4 J. Legal Stud. 391 (1975). Epstein also engages in an extended treatment of nuisance law, with some concessions to the impact of administrative and transaction costs on liability rules, in Epstein, Nuisance Law: Corrective Justice and Its Utilitarian Constraints, 8 J. Legal Stud. 49 (1979).

10. For an interesting exchange on Epstein's views, examining a wide variety of issues raised by his position, see Borgo, Causal Paradigms in Tort Law, 8 J. Legal Stud. 419 (1979); Posner, Epstein's Tort Theory: A Critique, 8 J. Legal Stud. 457 (1979); and Epstein, Causation and Corrective Justice: A Reply to Two Critics, 8 J. Legal Stud. 477 (1979).

Chapter 7

Merging Theory with Realpolitik: Perspectives on No-Fault Compensation Schemes

If the defective products area is the leading contemporary illustration of the capacity for continuing innovation in court-made tort law, the auto accident problem might well be singled out as the most notable demonstration of the limits of judicial creativity. Currently, courts apply the fault principles embodied in negligence doctrine to auto accident cases, just as similar rules were applied to horse-and-buggy cases a century ago.[1] Even the boldest of appellate judges would be loath to promote a court-fashioned strict liability system for compensating auto accident victims. Nor does one detect much enthusiasm for abandoning fault principles in other areas of tort law, such as professional malpractice or landowners' and occupiers' liability.

As a consequence, critics of the fault system — most notably reformers concerned about auto accident liability — resorted to the

---

1. The most important qualification to this statement is the recent movement to replace contributory with comparative negligence. However salutary that action may be, it constitutes a refinement rather than a rejection of the fault principle. Moreover, that reform has been effected largely through legislation rather than judicial action.

approach taken sixty years earlier with such great success in the case of the industrial injury problem. They took their case to the legislative forum. The ensuing debate over so-called no-fault auto compensation plans was given considerable impetus by the prodigious scholarly and lobbying efforts of two academics, Robert Keeton and Jeffrey O'Connell.[2] Their book, Basic Protection for the Traffic Victim: A Blueprint for Reforming Automobile Insurance (1965), set out a comprehensive legislative scheme that would have replaced much of the tort system with "basic protection" against economic loss for virtually all auto injury victims

The Basic Protection Plan became the focus of political debate in Massachusetts, where — although a different approach was ultimately taken — the first no-fault auto compensation legislation was passed in 1970. Twenty-five states enacted no-fault plans within five years. While the movement lost its momentum in 1975, in the political arena serious doubts have nonetheless been registered in recent times about the continuing efficacy of the tort liability system.[3]

The first essay in this section provides a singular perspective on auto compensation schemes. Eschewing any attempt to convey the staggering diversity of detail included in the existing plans, Blum and Kalven instead isolate the major issues of costs, awards, and compulsion that must be addressed in any compensation scheme. The authors outline the general configurations of these plans and analyze the theoretical underpinnings of the various approaches.

An auto compensation plan, of course, like a workers' compensation statute, is an exercise in incrementalism — a piecemeal approach to compensating for the social and economic loss caused by accidental injuries. Such plans inevitably raise the question whether the fault principle should *ever* serve as a limitation on an injury victim's right to compensation.[4] It seems appropriate, then, that the second essay in this section — and the final essay in the book — should direct our attention to a comprehensive alternative to fault liability: a compensation system unfettered by reliance on tortious conduct, keyed to disabling injury rather than to wrongful acts. James Henderson's essay reviews the theoretical and political bases of support for the

---

2. Needless to say, the no-fault movement gained momentum because of a variety of factors, in addition to academic efforts on its behalf. Rising auto liability insurance rates, congestion in the courts, and disenchantment with the claims-processing system all contributed to the growing sentiment for reform.

3. Less ambitious legislative efforts have been directed at achieving a wide variety of changes in areas such as products liability and medical malpractice. See generally M. Franklin & R. Rabin, Cases and Materials on Tort Law and Alternatives (3d ed. 1983), ch. 2 (medical malpractice) and ch. 7 (products liability).

4. The classic rendition is Smith, Sequel to Workmen's Compensation, 27 Harv. L. Rev. 235 (1913).

New Zealand social insurance system. It affords us a final opportunity to explore recurring themes — the tensions between compensation and deterrence, fault and nonfault recovery, compulsion and freedom of choice.

Ceilings, Costs, and Compulsion in Auto Compensation Legislation*

Walter J. Blum & Harry Kalven, Jr.

The following characteristics are present in all or almost all [nofault auto compensation] plans:

(i) Speaking very loosely, the heart of a plan is a package that, perhaps reflecting the layman's two questions, contains a double prescription. To the extent applicable, the prescription advises a person how he will be treated in each of two roles: one if he is an auto accident victim; the other if he is the "cause" of an auto accident injury to another. In each case, unlike at common law, the answer seems to be ready and uncomplicated. It is on the surface a non-fault answer. As victim, a person can within limits claim reparations on the simple fact of the accident, regardless of whether his conduct, or that of any other, was flawed. As actor, a person may be thought of as immune within limits from a claim against himself due to his actions. Thus the package is a "no-fault" package in the sense that fault has ceased to be a primary operative fact, either from the point of view of the victim or the actor.

(ii) There are two points to make about what might be called the "jurisdiction" of the package. First, the jurisdiction is arrestingly limited to auto accident; financing is solely from motorists, not from public revenues, and not, it should be noted, from all those who might be beneficiaries. Second, all plans have in common the aspiration of furnishing the arrangement for handling a large majority of auto accident events and auto accident claims. They thus can be looked upon as replacements for the preponderant part of the common law's business in the auto accident world.

(iii) The key mechanism of any plan is the use of insurance to create a fund into which a person contributes as motorist and against which he, and others, claim as victims. Participation in the fund is compulsory; it is in effect a condition to the use of an automobile. In all plans advanced to date, the insurance underwriting has been left

*Source: 1973 Utah L. Rev. 341, 343-355, 356-357, 359-370, 376-377.

to private industry; the state has not intervened to compete or to take over as a monopolist.

(iv) Every plan defines fairly precisely the measure of *unconditional reparations* (not conditional on fault) that will be provided an auto accident victim. In setting the measure of unconditional reparations, no plan regards itself as foreclosed by the standards of common law damages.

(v) In distributing unconditional reparations, all plans avoid the common law dilemma of estimating the extent of future losses for the purpose of providing a once and forever lump sum award. They do so by mandating prompt payment of losses periodically.

(vi) There remain three further characteristics which are perhaps derivative of what has already been noted. Victims who are carrying auto insurance will in all likelihood be making their claim for unconditional reparations with their own insurance company — that is, the insurer to which they have been paying premiums. Moreover, under the package arrangement, a pedestrian involved in an auto accident will be able to get unconditional reparations though his own conduct was flawed at the time; this will be true even though he is not a car owner and therefore has not contributed to the fund. Finally, a motorist who is required to contribute to the fund will be able to get unconditional reparations even though no other human agency is involved in the accident — for example, when he drives his car into a tree while driving alone.

Beyond these commonalities, plans can be grouped into broad sub-categories in several ways. One grouping is between those plans that aspire to only minimal unconditional reparations and those plans that aspire to substantial unconditional reparation of victims. This difference, which for many purposes might be ignored, will become crucial at later stages in the discussion. Another grouping is between those plans that explicitly abolish tort liability in specified areas and those plans that affect tort liability only in the sense that provision of unconditional reparations makes such liability superfluous.[8]

8. The term "add-on," which is becoming salient in discussion today, reflects this second distinction. Where the plan does not explicitly eliminate any part of the tort system, it can be said that a system of unconditional reparations has been "added-on" to the tort system (or it can be said that the reparations insurance has been "added on" to the liability insurance). The choice of the term is unfortunate. It suggests double recovery in the sense that the victim can recover both unconditional reparations *and* tort damages for the same loss; the fact is that very few of the "add-on" plans result in such double recovery. First, absent double recovery, the unconditional reparations distributed under either type plan equally siphon off business from the tort system. Second, as will later be developed in the text, the "non-add-on" plans also leave the tort system open to some extent. The functional question should not be whether the plan is "add-on" or something else, but what business in fact is left by the plan to the

This summary has been drawn in quick strokes that involve marginal inaccuracies. It was done so advisedly in order to catch a profile. We turn for the remainder of the Article to points which concern not the commonalities, but the differences possible among plans.

Such discussion proves to be treacherous to organize. We have adopted an unexpected tactic of organization. It is to center quite arbitrarily on two topics — *awards* and *costs*; and by pursuing these in some depth to produce an agenda for discussing the many issues that interrelate with them.

3

A principal concern of any plan is how much the accident victim should be awarded for his accident experience. All plans offering substantial unconditional reparations to victims for personal injuries have had to deal one way or another with three specific operational questions: (i) Is there any top *limit* on the unconditional reparations the plan will pay the victims? (ii) Is there at the bottom, so to speak, any *minimal* loss for which the plan will not make reparations? (iii) To what extent are the unconditional reparations to be the *exclusive* source of compensation — or is the common law tort action to some extent to be preserved?

Whatever the variety of answers given to the three questions, there is one overriding observation to make about the responses. No plan has ever attempted to provide full common law damages as unconditional reparations to all victims. Numerous reasons for this have surfaced in the literature about plans: a desire, for reasons of administrative efficiency, to keep damage items as objective as

---

tort system. It is this question that we explore in the text in our discussion of ceilings, gaps, and treatment of pain and suffering.

Our stance is that nothing significant turns on whether "add-on" arrangements are classified as "plans." For more than a decade first party provisions, such as the medical payments clause and the uninsured motorist clause, have been tacked on to liability insurance policies. There are innumerable gradations possible in moving from the tort-insurance system towards a plan, and it seems sterile to argue over when the movement is far enough to qualify for the term "plan."

A somewhat comparable set of observations may be made about the term "no-fault." It has proved remarkably effective as a matter of rhetoric, but it, too, is an unfortunate choice. The confusion engendered by the term covers much the same ground as in the case of the term "add-on." From one point of view, "no-fault" means only that reparation is unconditional. From another point of view, it means abandoning fault as relevant by explicitly eliminating the tort remedy. Since all plans to some extent preserve a tort remedy, there is, if the usage is taken seriously, no instance of a "pure" no-fault arrangement.

possible; a criticism of some items of common law damages as unsound even for the common law; a distaste for the exploitation felt to be involved in the publicized million dollar awards; and a practical conviction that it would be wholly impolitic to have the new arrangements under the plan be *that* expensive. Behind such reasons we sense a point of principle. The upshot of a plan is to effect a shift from a redress perspective to an insurance perspective. As a result, one is liberated from being controlled by the common law damage answers, and even from being much guided by them.

For purposes of a plan it is proper to look elsewhere to set the award levels. The puzzle is where to look. There is an unexamined choice of basic assumptions underlying most discussions of award levels. To overstate the polarity: Are the award levels to be set on the assumption that there is a more or less fixed aggregate pool to be distributed as unconditional reparations to the victims, *or* on the assumption that the size of the pool is not a given, but is to be determined by notions of what the award levels *ought* to be? It is our impression that in almost all discussions it is implicit that there is a more or less determined limit to the pool, and that this sense of limit is perhaps the controlling factor in determining the award structure.

One does not have to look far for an explanation. A chief point of rhetoric in the advocacy of plans has been that they will offer a better product, dollar for dollar, than the motorist is now buying; in brief, under a plan, a motorist's total insurance premiums will not increase, but will in all likelihood decrease. It follows that the maximum size of the pool to be distributed in unconditional awards has to be set by the size of the "pool" that is generated under the common law tort-insurance system. Whatever the need to acknowledge the political imperatives, an anomaly lurks here. The award potential under a plan is being largely determined by a factor which is irrelevant to the aspirations of a plan. The aggregate amount the common law "collects" for distribution to victims is crucially affected by the fact that the law is not intended to pay all victims, but only those who qualify under common law liability rules. A principal point of every plan in mandating unconditional reparations is to reject those common law criteria of eligibility for compensation. Yet in effect the outcome is to permit these rejected criteria to limit how much a plan will do for victims. This almost automatic acceptance of the size of the common law "pool" as a limitation may be a key clue in explaining why the discussion of awards under plans has been so little concerned with theory. Once it is assumed that the size of the pool is already determined, many genuine issues about award levels are readily short-circuited.

4

Plans, particularly high-ceiling plans, have been designed as if to meet the problem of insolvency: the losses of victims are like claims that exceed the total assets of the estate or "pool" to be distributed. One solution has been to refuse recognition to certain claims or losses hitherto accepted as valid. Excluding from the unconditional reparations any claims based on pain and suffering is, we suspect, largely a strategy for dealing with the "insolvency" problem—although, as will be seen later, it admits of other rationales.

But the point we wish to build on here is the response of plans *even to items of strict economic loss.* Whatever the case for pain and suffering as loss, the case for recognition of loss of earnings is more sturdy and stubborn. If we assume for the moment that the rationale for limiting compensation for loss of earnings is the sheer insufficiency of the pool to meet such loss in full, there are three principal ways to "balance the budget." A plan can employ a floor, a ceiling or upper limit, or a percentage scale-down of claims. Purely as a matter of arithmetic, any of these methods will serve to make the fund go around. While traces of floors and scale-down arrangements can be found in proposed plans, the dominant strategy has been to impose an upper limit or ceiling.

This preference for a ceiling yields the anomalous result that the more serious the economic loss, the greater the likelihood that it will *not* be paid in full by the unconditional reparations of the plan. Assume a $4,000 ceiling on unconditional reparations for economic loss: all losses below $4,000 will be paid in full; a loss of $6,000 will be compensated two-thirds; a loss of $8,000 will be compensated one-half, and so on. If instead the preference were for a floor, the result would be that the larger the claim, the greater the percentage of loss paid. If a pro rata scaling down were the preferred alternative, the result would be that all claims, whatever their size, would bear the same fraction of uncompensated loss. But it should be noted that under neither the floor nor the scale-down approach would *any* victim recover one hundred percent of his economic loss.

We find it a considerable puzzle that the floor and scale-down alternatives have not proved more popular to plan designers. Use of the floor would serve to eliminate a large fraction of the total number of claims being processed under the common law tort-insurance system; it would yield great internal economies in administration and have a direct bearing on the nuisance claim phenomena; it is, moreover, given its wide use in collision insurance, a device very familiar to the motoring public. Use of the scale-down alternative would have the deep appeal of treating all claimants evenhandedly.

The puzzle cuts deeper. For generations, a grievance urged against the common law has been that it so often dealt harshly with the seriously injured victim of an auto accident. Surely a much voiced aspiration of plans has been to do better by him. An empirical finding which has been widely publicized by advocates of plans appears to show that the common law tends on average to grossly overpay small claims, while grossly underpaying large ones. Whatever the aspirations of plans, the achievement is, at best, to correct the overpayment for small losses, while continuing to underpay large losses — once the "budget is balanced" through ceilings.

It may be helpful to consider why those who design plans nevertheless have found the choice of a ceiling so attractive. Undoubtedly there has been a strong desire to be able to say that the vast majority of auto accident victims recover their losses in full — a claim which, as noted, is precluded by use of either the floor or the scale-down. There is further the desire to be able to say that if there is a bias in the plan, the bias runs in favor of the poor.

Use of a floor may present some distinctive drawbacks of its own. It precludes saying that *all* victims will now receive at least *some* compensation. It may also invite insurance industry opposition because it could cut so deeply into the volume of business.

5

This discussion of award levels for economic losses is obviously incomplete. We have been writing as though the unconditional reparations under a plan were to be the exclusive source of compensation. In the historic analogues this was the case. Workmen's compensation, the grandfather of all compensation proposals, and the Columbia Plan of 1930, the first auto plan, were both total replacements of the tort system. Another overriding observation about contemporary auto plans is that virtually never are the unconditional reparations designed as the exclusive source of compensation — virtually all plans keep a tort remedy open to some extent.

The full story about reparations for economic losses then is that it may include unconditional reparations under a plan in combination with some redress under the tort system. Does this combination mitigate the bias against serious harms in the handling of economic losses?

The situations on which to focus are those in which economic losses exceed the limit specified in the plan, whatever that limit may be. The question concerns the fate of these excess economic losses. Assume for present purposes that the plan imposes a relatively high ceiling on awards so that in the vast majority of cases economic losses are compensated in full by the unconditional reparations. Assume also that the part of the common law tort remedy that is preserved will serve for many victims to take care of their economic losses that exceed the unconditional reparations ceiling. A puzzle nevertheless resides in this combination treatment of large economic losses.

The total scheme still appears to discriminate in favor of less seriously injured victims. It seems a fair assumption that large economic losses are associated with more serious auto accidents. Whatever the arguments for compensating victims without regard to fault, these arguments would seem to be stronger in cases where the accident is more serious. The excess economic losses of some victims will not be recoverable because their claims will be ineligible under the liability criterion of the common law. The outcome then of combining the tort remedy and the unconditional reparations of the plan is still that economic losses of the less seriously injured victims will be paid under *all* circumstances, while the economic losses of *some* of the more seriously injured victims will be paid only in part.

For the plan with a high ceiling there are further embarrassments in preserving the tort action. Such a plan is designed to replace the tort system altogether in all but the small minority of very serious cases. The arguments made on its behalf have heavily stressed the inadequacies of the existing tort system. These arguments reduce to the complaints that only victims "lucky enough" to be hit by a negligent driver may recover, and that the system carries an undue invitation to fraud. But it stands to reason that high economic loss correlates to the more serious injury. The use of a ceiling on economic loss leaves a higher portion of that loss beyond the coverage of unconditional reparations, the more serious the injury. Thus, the more serious his injury, the more the victim is left to the mercies of the common law tort system, which will be as imperfect as before. It is implausible that the fault criterion for reparation becomes less arbitrary and the invitation to fraud less potent as the injury becomes more serious.

Whether or not the tort remedy is kept open above some level, the use of a ceiling on unconditional reparations involves the plan in discriminating against the more seriously injured victims. This inconsistency might be met in at least two ways: (i) by questioning the justice of paying in full the high economic losses of the more affluent; (ii) by relying on the use of voluntary insurance to cover the excess economic loss.

6

The justice question is worthy in its own right and has more than one strand. In contemporary society there seems to be a deep-seated uneasiness about high incomes, and undoubtedly some of this carries over to economic losses that reflect high incomes. People whose incomes are considerably higher than the median are likely, if injured, to suffer economic losses beyond the ceiling of a plan. One need only reflect for a moment on the $200,000 a year athlete who is temporarily disabled as a result of an auto accident. A year's disablement results in an economic loss ninety-five percent of which may well be above the limit for a plan, but which may also be twenty times the economic loss for the laborer who suffers comparable injury. This example is admittedly extreme, but is used only to dramatize the strains on any award system that may be generated by the unequal distribution of earned income in society.

At common law the tort system never experienced any qualms in redressing full economic loss regardless of disparities in income levels. It would be unheard of for a defendant to argue that his damages should be reduced because the plaintiff's income was unseemingly high! Tort law, engaged in corrective justice, was able to leave matters of distributive justice for other branches of the law to deal with—if at all.

Calling into question the justice of the earned income distribution in society raises a point so powerful that it becomes difficult to know what to do with it. In this context, setting the ceiling on awards under a plan is inescapably perceived as a normative judgment. In a fashion reminiscent of earlier literature on tax justice, the ceiling suggests a distinction between two levels of income. The first level is that which is "normal"—that is, expected to be used in usual consumption patterns; the second level is that which is "surplus." In taxation this distinction was employed to justify taxing the surplus income at higher rates; in designing compensation plans the distinction can be used analogously to justify not providing unconditional reparations for economic losses above the ceiling.

Notions of surplus income, whatever their plausibility, cannot be decisive for the handling of all high economic losses in the special case of auto accidents. The stumbling block is the serious disability injury. People with middle bracket incomes surely can suffer injuries producing very high aggregate economic losses. To revert to our athlete example again, a journeyman worker with only one-twentieth of the athlete's income may, if disabled for life, suffer an equally large aggregate economic loss. Indeed, the predominant experience with high awards under the present tort system has not been with injuries to the high income earner, but with serious injuries to the man whose income is not high enough to be regarded as surplus. Designers of high ceiling plans presumably would like to take care of this dominant case of severe economic loss, even when for distributive justice reasons they may not wish to cover losses reflecting merely high earned income.

There would seem to be a practical method for separating the treatment of the two situations. All that need be done is to state the award ceiling not in a single aggregate amount, but rather as a limit on loss of earnings incurred in a given time interval; no limit would otherwise be imposed on the total loss that may be covered by reparations. What is striking here is that a detail of plan design — the ceiling format — turns out to implicate a serious and interesting policy question concerning distributive justice.

7

The other route to justifying limitations on awards for economic loss, under plans with high ceilings, is to rely on the opportunity for the motoring public to voluntarily buy insurance to cover any above-ceiling economic loss. Put this way the analysis may again contain an implicit notion of surplus earned income. The thought seems to be that the high earner, if he is concerned about protecting his earning power in full from accident loss, can afford to take out insurance to cover himself. And if he does not, there is no reason why society should have any great interest in second-guessing his judgment.

This approach runs into serious difficulties too, once account is taken of the sources of high economic loss. The dominant case, as pointed out, will be that of the middle income victim. As to him the suggestion that he can make himself whole by voluntary insurance calls into question the social achievement of the plan.

It calls into question something further — the basic commitment that the plan be *compulsory* on the motoring public. Consider first the situation of the man with a large earned income. A plan with a high ceiling explicitly accepts and relies on his judgment as to what to do about the possibility of excess economic loss — which may well be the major part of his loss. If we give him the choice of being a voluntary insurer (or a self insurer) of so major a part of his loss, should he not be accorded the same choice with respect to the whole of his loss?

Is the compulsion different if we focus attention on the accident victim whose income is near the median? A high ceiling plan (that is well designed) will be *compelling* him to insure against *substantially all* of his economic loss from accident. Granting that most people in the median income range would find such insurance a sensible buy, is this a sufficient basis for compelling those who do not see it that way to buy the insurance? Some, once stimulated to think about first party accident insurance, may prefer to buy some more general form of protection, rather than one confined so provincially to auto accidents alone. Others may not wish to insure at all because they have different risk preferences, as is so often apparent in the case of life insurance. For these people, and others, there is a puzzle about the policy behind the compulsion.

However the matter of compulsion may stand as to those with median incomes, is there any way of at least permitting those with high incomes, as to whom the case for compulsion is weakest, to have a choice? The theoretical merit of drawing such a distinction among income levels need not detain us. There is no way to put it into practice. It is not feasible to isolate those who will be permitted to opt out. We here confront, in the unexpected context of an auto plan, the well-known and formidable difficulties of introducing into the law "a means test" — difficulties that have become so familiar under social security and welfare measures.

8

The discussion of award levels for economic loss is still incomplete. We have been directing attention to plans that aspire to unconditional reparations up to substantial amounts. At the outset in our profile of plans we noted that one category of plans had a different aspiration, not calling for substantial reparation. This difference introduces a new note into the discussion. One of the most intense points in debate over plans concerns this difference. The question is: *At what level* of economic loss is the unconditional reparation under the plan to stop and the conditional reparation under the common law to begin? On the surface the debate appears to be over a mechanical detail of little theoretic import — should the award limit under the plan be $500, $1,000, $5,000 or $10,000? But beneath the surface there is posed a fundamental policy choice.

Data providing a rough estimate of the distribution of economic losses in auto accidents illustrate the ramifications that underlie this choice.[19]

19. This table is our best estimate compiled from figures in two Department of Transportation studies: U.S. Dept. of Transp., Motor Vehicle Crash Losses and Their Compensation in the United States (1971); U.S. Dept. of Transp., Economic Consequences of Automobile Injuries (1970)....

Economic loss	Aggregate economic loss		Persons	
	Dollars (millions)	Percent	Number (thousands)	Percent
$ 1–99	$ 891	15%	3,833	90%
1,000–4,999	714	12	294	7
5,000–9,999	397	6	60	2
10,000–24,999	517	9	31	1
25,000 and up	3,447	60	45	1
Totals	$5,966	102*	4,263	101*

(*over 100% due to rounding)

There is no need to settle on a definition of a serious loss in order to acknowledge two key relationships. First, the larger the economic loss, the less frequent its incidence. The gravest economic losses occur in only a very small minority of instances. Second, turning to dollar aggregates, a substantial fraction of *all* economic loss suffered by all victims falls upon the relatively few who are seriously injured. If a choice must be made, there is a tough issue of locating the principal social problem. Is it more important to take care of the vast majority of auto accident victims — under which premise any scheme which disposes of say 85 to 95 percent of such claims is the solution? Or is it more important to concentrate resources on the minority of seriously harmed victims?

Against this backdrop, polar responses have emerged in the popular debate. On one view unconditional reparations under the plan are seen as the heart of the matter; and whether or not the tort system is kept open at any level is pretty much a minor strategy or a footnote. Predictably, high ceilings are advocated. On the opposing view the tort system, with its traditional merits, continues to be seen as the heart of the matter; unconditional reparations under the plan function simply as a way of disposing expeditiously of losses from less serious injuries. Again predictably, low ceilings are advocated. The tort system remains as the channel for what is seen as the central job — the handling of seriously injured auto accident victims.

Under either high or low ceilings there is an embarrassment. With the high ceiling alternative it proves awkward, as we have seen, to explain why the tort system is left alive at all, and there arises an apparently ineradicable discrimination against victims having the most serious injuries. With the low ceiling alternative it proves awkward to explain the need for introducing a plan at all.

Evaluation of low ceiling plans is dampened because they have been put forward largely by the trial bar. The function of the low ceiling has been viewed with deep suspicion since it preserves the symbol of a plan, while leaving as much of the tort system, and therefore the business of the trial bar, as undisturbed as possible.

It is not, however, altogether implausible that a low ceiling plan would be proposed on its merits. Several lines of argument could be advanced for such a plan. Certain characteristics of small claims make it advisable to exclude them from the tort fault system. It is widely thought that they are unduly expensive to process. The expectation is that internal economies from paying small claims unconditionally under a plan will result in substantial savings. Indeed, it is hoped that these savings will make it possible to pay all small claims for economic loss, whether or not compensable at common law, without any increase in overall insurance costs to motorists. On this approach, it might be noted, pressure to employ a ceiling does not, as it did with the high ceiling plan, come from what we have called the fixed fund or the "insolvency" dilemma.

Another concern, especially prominent in the literature, has been with the overpayment of small claims because of their nuisance value. This, it is often said, injects a major injustice into the distribution of damages under common law settlement practices. It is argued that the simplicity of unconditional reparations under a plan will vastly reduce the nuisance value of small claims and their exploitative potential.

If support for the low ceiling plan is predicated either upon the diseconomy or nuisance of processing small claims, why not eliminate small claims from the tort system altogether? Doing so would certainly remove these evils and with the maximum savings to society. If the tactic is to set the ceiling so as to just catch the small claim, leaving everything else to the common law, the purported goals might be better achieved by dropping the plan altogether and, as the alternative, merely setting a floor for redress under the tort system.

The logic plays differently if the assumption as to the purpose of the low ceiling is changed. Such a ceiling may be explained on the ground that a plan will have done enough if unconditional reparations are made in full for the range of auto accident claims that will be experienced by the vast majority of the public. A major part of the rationale here presumably derives from distaste over asking financially poor victims to handle these losses themselves. But if so, this sharply differs from most proposals for assisting the poor. It would avoid having the poor manage the injury losses individually by insisting that the motoring poor (like other motorists) pay in advance for insurance to cover such losses. The puzzle that arises keys once again to the fact that the plan is compulsory. Consequently there is the old problem of forcing people by law to do what is good for them. In this version, the lower the ceiling, the more the "official advice" is concentrated on the poor.

Additional questions about the fit of the sumptuary principle readily come to mind. Is there really *sufficient* justification for being sumptuary on behalf of the motoring poor? Might they not rationally prefer to bear the loss themselves; or, if they elect to insure, might they not choose to cover the unlikely but serious loss rather than the more likely but less serious loss? Can there, moreover, be *any* justification for applying the sumptuary principle to the small losses of the more affluent? Or are they included only because we cannot design any political way to leave them out while insisting upon helping the poor?

It thus appears that compulsion raises difficulties for both high and low ceiling plans. In neither case is it possible to devise ways of screening out those who may not be the object of the coercion. With a high ceiling, it appears that to reach the objective — to force the middle classes to be prudent enough to insure substantially all their losses — it becomes necessary to compel the upper income people to insure. With a low ceiling, everyone is compelled to insure in order to reach the objective of forcing the poor to be prudent enough to insure their typical losses. . . .

10

It has been another overriding characteristic of compensation legislation, dating back to workmen's compensation, to refuse to acknowledge pain and suffering as an item compensable by unconditional reparations. There has been intermittent criticism of pain and suffering as an item of damages at common law, but such criticism has never crystallized into reform. Today pain and suffering remains a vigorous component of personal injury damages.

Some proponents of plans have disapproved in principle of awards for pain and suffering and have seen the plan as an occasion for making a change they would like to have effected at common law. One who staunchly supports such damages under the corrective justice of the tort system might nevertheless be persuaded that there is no justification for including pain and suffering in a scheme of reparations that is wholly divorced from notions of either fault or indignation at being harmed, and that carries no echo of punitive damages.

Other factors very likely play a more important role in explaining the almost universal exclusion of pain and suffering from unconditional reparations. Pain and suffering, if perceived as loss at all, is somehow not of the same nature as other loss. Motorists are not likely to want to pay premiums to insure themselves against experiencing pain and suffering—but if pain and suffering were included in unconditional reparations, the plan would be asking people to do precisely that. The most decisive reasons for its elimination may well be purely practical. If so unbounded an item were to be included in reparations, it would frustrate major objectives of plans—simplifying the processing of claims and reducing premium charges.

At the moment, a great contrast exists between how the courts and how the legislatures are responding to the phenomenon of pain and suffering. As the legislative momentum towards plans grows, there is an increase in the area of law in which pain and suffering will no longer be recognized as loss. At the same time, the courts, pursuing vigorously the common law principles of growth, have been reaching altogether new levels of intensity in acknowledging the awful reality of the intangible concomitants of accidents.

This ambivalence is spotlighted by the way plans treat the right to recover for pain and suffering in a common law action. Since no plan provides unconditional reparations for pain and suffering, a choice must be made whether the victim is to be left free to pursue such loss at common law. This choice is the heart of what is at stake in the dispute today between plans that explicitly eliminate tort liability and the so-called "add-on" plans which do not. Without a threshold below which there is no tort action for pain and suffering, it will be very difficult to keep premium costs down and to control nuisance claims. But any threshold formula seems odd. Pain and suffering will be recognized only when fault is present; but even when fault is present in a valid common law claim, pain and suffering will be recognized only when it is relatively large. Perhaps this result can be explained by a perception familiar to students of the common law tort system. Non-economic awards for graver injuries are rarely for "pain and suffering"; rather they are an acknowledgement of the indignity of the injury. . . .

12

The second axis along which we wish to array policy issues is that of costs. . . .

The relevant question about costs is not whether a given plan will cost motorists more than the existing tort-insurance system costs them, but rather who should pay for whatever the plan does cost.

The common law is no more trustworthy as a guide for the sharing of costs under a plan than it was for setting the levels for unconditional reparations. As with awards, the question again is: If the common law is not a guide, what should be?

In starting our pursuit of this cost question, it will be helpful to employ again the distinction between beneficiaries who are contributors to the pool and beneficiaries who are non-contributors. The distinction becomes architectonic for the issue to be explored.

We focus first on the handling of costs arising from the claims of non-contributors. There can be little question that not requiring contributions to the pool from those who do not own cars, or whose immediate families do not own cars, reflects a practical necessity rather than a normative judgment that they ought not be asked. The plan presumably would make them pay if it could. All auto plans are tied to ownership and licensing of the auto as the mechanism for the collection of insurance premiums. Since anyone in the community might be the victim of an auto accident, there is no way in advance of isolating a class for purposes of seeking a contribution; and if a person does not own a car, there is no practicable way to charge him for insurance coverage.

This explains why the non-car-owning group is not forced to contribute under a plan, but it does not explain why they are allowed to recover unconditional reparations. In theory, at least, it would have been possible not to extend such reparations to them, and to keep the tort action alive for this group of victims. The attractiveness of the social objective of having *all* auto accident victims recover was clearly felt strongly enough to create what might be called reparation without taxation. There were undoubtedly other reasons for the decisions as well. To keep the tort action alive even for this group alone would defeat another objective of plans — that of eliminating the tort action for all claims below a certain level. Perhaps still more compelling was the desire to avoid the practical difficulties that would be occasioned by having to determine whether a given claimant at the time of the accident was a contributor or a non-contributor, and to avoid as well the important pragmatic consequences of that determination for awards in some cases.

When exploring why contributors are made to pay for the unconditional reparations coverage of non-contributors, it is important to discard the perspectives of a strict first party insurance arrangement. If a plan is to take out of the tort system the claims of non-contributors as well as those of contributors, an important choice is presented. Since no one would urge that non-contributors should be excluded from the reparations pool when their common law rights are being erased, and since there is no practical way of having them contribute to the pool, another source must be used to enlarge the pool on their behalf. There are only two practical possibilities: either the general public pays through taxes or the motorists pay. All plans to date have placed the burden on motorists. At common law a good deal of this burden was already on motorists through the operation of the liability rules and third party liability insurance. The plans call for using a form of "third party" insurance to fund the losses of *all* non-contributor victims.

It is at this point that the design of the contemporary auto plan touches the old-fashioned issue of costs that was so central to the workmen's compensation controversy and its aftermath a half century ago. That question was seen starkly as: Why, apart from fault as a justification, should *A* be made to pay for a loss suffered by *B*? One answer, borrowed from the idiom of the economist, is that activities should bear their own costs in a rational market society. Otherwise resources will be misallocated, and there will be a loss of efficiency in the special economic sense that consumer choices will be less perfectly represented in the way resources are allocated. A half century ago the cry was that the blood of the workman should be reflected in the cost of the product. The contemporary analogy is that the blood of the auto accident victim should be reflected in the cost of motoring.

It is doubtful that this premise is a vital part of the case for auto plans today. Reference is often made to it, but it is never discussed in any depth and there is never a sense that the case stands or falls with the premise. Nevertheless, it is worth noting that the premise does not bear scrutiny when applied to auto accidents. Insofar as the economist's idiom is understood to mean that accidents — for the purpose of an efficient allocation of resources — are a cost of motoring, it is misunderstood. There appears to be no way to isolate the role and contribution of owning and operating an auto in producing auto accidents from the role and contribution of other activities. The incidence of accidents is significantly affected by many factors, including population density, road design, pedestrianism, mass transportation, and so on. Motoring of course is a contributing factor to auto accidents, but there is no way of telling how much of the accident cost should be charged to it in order to advance the objective of efficiency in resource allocation.

The history of workmen's compensation proves instructive on another point. While popular controversy centered on the slogan that industrial accidents were a cost of employment, the constitutional controversy over the due process of charging the employer for all industrial accidents was framed not in terms of who should bear the loss, but rather in terms of "a bargain." The "bargain" was struck by the law between employer and employee. At common law, in the event of an industrial accident, the employee could sometimes recover and sometimes not; correlatively, the employer was sometimes liable and sometimes not. The essence of the "bargain" imposed on both sides by the statute was to make the employer liable in all cases, but for a lesser amount, and to give the employee a lesser amount, but provide recovery in all cases. The quid pro quo for the employee was some recovery in those cases where he would have been altogether ineligible at common law.

One might draw an analogy to this sort of "bargain" in the contemporary auto plan. The non-contributors are like the employees and the contributors are in a sense like the employers. Once again the trade is of contingent common law rights for reduced but certain rights under the plan, and of contingent common law obligations for broader but reduced obligations under the plan.

As far as we can tell, no one today seeks to justify charging contributors for the losses of non-contributors by using the "bargain" theory. It may well be that no justification is thought to be called for. Or it may be that today the bargain metaphor has worn thin: it has become apparent that it only verbally circumvents the cost issue. Consider workmen's compensation again. It was a "bargain" only in terms of trading the *prior* rights and obligations created at common law. If the legislature had been deciding how to handle the industrial accident de novo, without the common law background, it would have been meaningless to speak of its legislation as a "bargain." All the statute did in coercively imposing the "bargain" was to impose its formula for allocating costs between employers and employees.

In the case of auto plans, the "bargain" imposed by the legislature results in a complicated allocation of costs between contributors and non-contributors. The complicating factor is that non-contributors fall into two groups: those who had valid claims at common law and those who did not. The cost of reparations for the former is left where the common law placed it — on motorists (who are the contributors). It is highly probable that a good part of the cost of covering those non-contributors who would not have had valid claims at common law — and hence represent a new reparations burden — is being borne by those non-contributors who would have had valid claims at common law.

13

Contributors as a universe and non-contributors as a universe represent quite different risk rating problems. While as we have seen there is something of a problem in the handling of the non-contributor class, it is distinctly a problem involving the minority of victims. The major domain of a plan today is the handling of contributor victims. In our society the number of cars has so vastly increased relative to population that most people will be either car owners or immediate members of car owners' families. The upshot is that there will be a great overlap between contributors and victims: all contributors will be potential victims, and most victims will in fact be contributors. It is this distinctive set of facts which makes it possible today to utilize first party insurance as the dominant technique in plans for handling the auto accident problem.

It is true that first party insurance is the oldest type of insurance. Yet when one starts from the tort perspective, as have almost all discussions of auto plans, the introduction of first party insurance requires a major and almost startling switch in viewpoint. The feature of first party insurance that has received the most explicit attention is the possibility of greater ease in dealing with one's own insurer after an auto accident rather than with another's insurer. But the more significant difference, we submit, concerns the criteria for allocating costs among the insureds; that is, to the setting of insurance premiums fairly among contributors. It is this intramural allocation of premiums that we view as the new central issue of costs posed by contemporary plans.

It may be helpful to reflect for a moment on an old-fashioned and familiar instance of first party insurance — fire insurance on a dwelling-place. The risk that the home-owning insured presents is the risk of his dwelling catching fire — that is, the risk of his being in a position to make a claim against the insurance pool. This risk varies from building to building; the relevant variables include such matters as value of the structure, susceptibility to catching fire, and resistance to the spread of fire. Every fire insurance arrangement takes such factors into account, and everyone understands that fire insurance premiums reflect these variables. It would be regarded as remarkable indeed if fire insurance premiums were homogenized so that each homeowner paid the same total premium for protection of his dwelling from loss by fire.

Is there any difference as we move from fire insurance to the first party insurance component of auto plans? The variables of course are quite different. Moreover, they tend to invite premium differentials that would be impolitic to utilize. To illustrate: key factors would often include the size of the motorist's immediate family — the larger the family, the greater the risk presented to the pool; the seating capacity of the car — the larger the capacity, the greater the risk; the make of the car — the less sturdy the car, the greater the risk; the location in which the car is customarily driven — the more dense the population in the area, the greater the risk; the motorist's age and the ages of those in his immediate family — the younger they are, the greater the risk of economic loss from disabling injury. If these factors combine, as will often be the case, the relatively young motorist, with a large family, living in a concentrated urban area, and driving a lightly constructed car would be called upon by actuarial estimates to pay the highest premium rate. There would no doubt be a marked popular sense that such discrimination is "improper." This feeling of impropriety would in no small part arise from the contrary expectations generated by experience under the existing liability insurance regime for bodily injury, and especially from the fact that this first party insurance is compulsory.

These considerations invite another general observation about contemporary plans. Plans are in most respects silent about the criteria for setting premium rates among motorists. The implication from the silence is that the legislators are happy to leave to the discretion of insurers and insurance commissioners the thorny problems of compelling premium differentials among the first party insured. The absence of explicit legislative attention to such questions strongly suggests that the answer, when it comes, will lie in the direction of homogenizing risks as much as possible. The result will be to introduce a hidden element of subsidization from one group of motorists to another — with the beneficiaries of the subsidy being by and large the urban, less well-to-do motorists with large families.

Another factor affecting the risks presented by first party insureds is the level of earned income. The higher the level of earned income, the greater the economic loss from injury. If there were no ceiling on awards, there likely would be great pressure on plans to differentiate premiums so as to charge more to high income earners. Without such differentiation, there might be a distributive justice problem — one in which, this time, the less well-to-do contributors would be subsidizing the more well-to-do. A ceiling blunts this problem, but does not altogether eliminate it. There remains at least a modest collision between two objectives of a plan: (i) to handle most auto accident claims by unconditional reparations, the ceiling must be set high; (ii) to avoid the perplexities of distributive justice, the ceiling must be set low. The higher the ceiling, the more likely it will be that many contributors will be *forced* to insure beyond the economic loss they would ever suffer.

14

The intramural allocation of costs fairly among contributors has at least one other source of complication. The criterion for fairness on premium allocation has been taken thus far to be the risk of the contributor claiming against the poor. It was on this basis that we said that a person, for example, with a larger family or a lighter car belonged to a higher risk category. It was also on this basis that we could ignore as irrelevant, for the purposes of fair allocation, the role of the contributor in *causing* accidents. We now examine whether it is proper under all circumstances to ignore this factor.

Let us take up again the situation of one who owns a lightly constructed car. There can be no doubt that viewed as a claimant, he represents to the pool a higher risk of a claim than does the owner of a heavier made car. His position may seem analogous to that, arising under fire insurance, of the owner of a frame house in a neighborhood of brick houses. Likewise, the owner of a heavier made car may seem analogous, for relative risk rating purposes, to the owner of the brick house. But the analogies are misleading. The important difference is that the risk of fire damage to the frame house is not increased by the fact that the neighboring houses are brick. Most auto accidents involve collisions between cars. The "extra" risk of personal injury to occupants of the light car is largely traceable to the fact that others are driving heavier cars. It must be asked whether this circumstance creates a new equity issue for the allocation of premiums among car owners.

Certainly where insurance is compulsory, it is troublesome to ignore this equity altogether. The effort to acknowledge it, however, leads to an unexpected result. The point that the owner of the light car represents a greater risk to the pool and should therefore pay a higher premium is exactly counter-balanced by another point. The owner of a heavier car creates for the pool a risk that others involved in accidents with his car will make larger claims against the pool. The two risks are reciprocals. The fair allocation of premiums would seem to call for charging neither the owner of the light car nor the owner of the heavier car more. If each pays the same premium, the distinctive risks that each contributes to the pool will, paradoxically, have been taken fully into account.

The most spectacular instance of this reciprocal relationship is presented by the passenger car-heavy truck dichotomy. Statistics show that in car/truck accidents the ratio of personal injury loss is roughly 10/90. For this reason, under the current liability insurance system, truck owners pay substantially higher premium rates than do passenger car owners. If a shift to pure first party ratings were made under a plan, the relative ratings would be reversed. The occupants in a truck are less likely to be hurt seriously in a collision than are the occupants of a car. Again the fair allocation of premiums would call simply for letting these factors offset each other and charging the same premium rate for both trucks and cars. It is difficult indeed to see a justification on any principle relevant to first party insurance for charging the trucks higher rates. Some plans would nonetheless do so. Such a response seems due more to the logic of politics than to the logic of first party insurance.

15

There is another component of plans affecting costs and awards. It is the accommodation of the plan to the fact that there are in the society *other* sources of reparation for personal injury accident losses, such as disability coverage under social security, private accident insurance, private medical insurance, workmen's compensation coverage, employment fringe benefits, life insurance, and so on. Today the aggregate reparations furnished by these other sources for personal injury losses from auto accidents (the impact of auto plans apart) probably exceed reparations from the tort system itself in coverage. The relative importance of these other sources has been steadily increasing. In another decade, even without an assist from auto plans, it is likely that these other sources would have taken over the great bulk of what is now perceived as the auto accident compensation problem. From one perspective, the role of an auto plan is not so much to replace tort law as simply to add one more regime of reparations to complement these other sources. And in the designing of a plan, the relationship between unconditional reparations under the plan and these other sources may present the single most important practical problem.

Accommodating other sources of reparation is, of course, not a new issue for the law. At common law it appears in the form of the collateral source rule. The dominant common law answer, whatever the complexity of the technical profile, is clear: the injured plaintiff can recover both from the tort-feasor and from other available sources. In brief, the presence of other sources is collateral and irrelevant to the setting of tort damages. There are various explanations for what seems at first an unreasonable outcome. As between the plaintiff and the defendant, it would be the greater injustice to give the windfall to the tort-feasor, who had in no sense contributed to financing the collateral source. It is, moreover, counterproductive as deterrence strategy to relieve him of the sanction in full damages. Further, subrogating the collateral source to the tort awards, which would prevent the double recovery, is often not available as a matter of doctrine. And not infrequently, a double recovery is justified as a rough offset against such inadequacies of common law damages as the non-allowance of lawyer's fees. Finally, there would be formidable administrative and practical problems posed if, in order to set damages properly in the tort action, all collateral sources had first to be detected and then measured.

There is no reason for paying any deference to the common law collateral source rule in making unconditional reparations. Fault is no longer relevant; there is no windfall to the defendant and, indeed, there is no "defendant." Perhaps more decisive, a plan that adopted a full collateral source rule would in effect compel people to insure against a loss that is otherwise already covered for them. Even if they would then be allowed double recovery, there are no grounds on principle for *compelling* them to insure the same determinate risk twice.

A plan, unlike the common law, can utilize several routes to avoid double recovery. The plan can readily be made primary to another source. The plan then will always pay first; steps must be taken to ensure that the other source, if double recovery is to be avoided, will deduct the amount of such reparations in computing its obligation to the victim. Such a move may bring both good news and bad news to the other source. It will be relieved of part or all of its obligation, but it will incur new administrative burdens. Presumably it will be called upon to adjust its premiums to reflect the fact the reparations under the auto plan are primary, and it will have to take care to coordinate its payouts in its secondary role.

The major alternative is for the auto plan to be made secondary to another source. Here the situation is reversed; the plan will be called upon to pay only losses left unsatisfied after recourse to the other source. The administrative burdens will now fall upon the plan to coordinate its payouts and adjust its premiums.

It should be apparent that many combinations are possible, with the auto plan in varying proportions being made primary to some sources and secondary to others. Plans show great variety in the degree of attention paid explicitly to this question of coordinating regimes. The legislation may make the auto plan benefits primary, it may make them secondary, or in some situations it may leave the priority to be determined by contract.

The coordination of regimes has importance not merely for the question of double recovery by the victim, but equally for the question of properly allocating the costs of auto accidents. Under what circumstances, if any, should the unconditional reparations of an auto plan be made the *primary* source (and thus bear a larger share) of reparations for losses falling within the plan? It is not clear that there is a single compelling solution, and to a large extent the matter can only be left to political forces to resolve. There are, however, some factors that might well be taken into account in reaching a solution. Because the plan is the latest upon the scene, it may be easier to tailor the plan than to alter the provisions of existing regimes. There may be a difference between capabilities of the plan and the other regimes for detecting whether other sources are present in the case of a particular claimant. And there may be some force to the notion that the costs of motoring should, insofar as possible, not be externalized, but should be borne by those who have some causal relation to the auto accident.

A special incentive may exist for the auto plan to avoid being the primary source. If the plan were always primary, the necessary premium charges would have to be larger. This discloses a major fact about the situation today. Auto plans have become politically more feasible because there is so vast an amount of reparations already available for auto accidents from other sources. The size of the pool needed for unconditional reparations thus can be substantially smaller, with lower average premium charges as a consequence.

Once it is decided the plan is not to be primary, there is a new twist to the problem of allocating costs among contributors fairly. A new variable is introduced, affecting the relative risk that contributors will make claims against the pool. All, part, or none of the possible claim may, for a given contributor, be offset by other sources. As a risk to the pool, the man with another source of reparation that is primary to the plan is analogous to the man who is a bachelor with no immediate family.

There is an important tension here. Insofar as the plan adjusts rates in order to reflect this differential in risk, its design and administration become more complicated. Insofar as the plan homogenizes differences in risk, its patterns for sharing the burden become unfair. In the extreme case, some participants would be compelled to pay premiums to buy first party insurance on which there is no possibility they can collect reparations.

Because of the combinations of regimes under which a person may come, it often would be wholly impractical to adjust premiums in order to reflect the availability of other primary reparations sources. This may account for why a few plans at times leave open the possibility of recovering both under the plan and from sources not coordinated with the plan. Perhaps the only other practical solution under these circumstances is to offer deductibles in the plan, calling for a corresponding reduction in premiums. To keep the matter simple, these deductibles would be flat dollar amounts, and would not be conditioned on showing that there are in fact other primary sources of reparation.

The upshot is quite remarkable. In the course of solving the problem of integrating and coordinating other reparation regimes with an auto plan, the compulsory aspect of the plan is at least in part erased. And to this degree, out of respect for fairness among contributors, the sumptuary aspirations of a plan have to be sacrificed. In effect, a motorist is given a basis for a preemptory partial opt-out; his reasons for claiming the deductible become irrelevant. Once a plan has gone this far, the fundamental question is again raised: Why should not the first party component be put on a purely voluntary basis?

16

It must have been obvious well before this stage of the discussion that virtually all issues we look at in connection with auto plans, whether involving awards or costs, have been directly shaped by the condition that the plans are compulsory. At this point, it will be profitable to explore whether that condition can be relaxed, and what may happen if it is.

Once again we have need for the distinction between contributors and non-contributors. It is one thing to leave it to the motorist's own judgment whether he will take care of himself and his immediate family; it is quite another to leave it to his discretion whether he will take care of someone else's loss. Obviously, he cannot opt-out of the insurance pool for non-contributor victims without increasing the burden on other motorists. If there is to be a plan covering victims who are non-contributors, it must therefore prohibit motorists from opting-out of this segment.

The matter stands quite differently when we consider awards to contributors — that is, the first party insurance aspect of a plan. So long as a motorist contributes his share to cover non-contributor victims, no one else will be affected if he elects to opt-out for himself and immediate family, both as claimant and as contributor. Once he will agree in advance that neither he nor members of his immediate family will, if injured, make a claim against the fund, there is no anomaly in erasing his obligation to the fund. Under the tort system it would be unthinkable to immunize a man from liability for auto accidents upon his promise in advance not to make a claim if he or his family is injured. The contrast reflects the profound difference between the perspectives of first party insurance and those of corrective justice, even as moderated by third party liability insurance.

From a first party insurance perspective, the contribution exacted in the form of premiums from any participant is set to reflect the actuarial estimate of his claim against the insurance fund; if rates are properly set, the participant will in effect have pre-paid his own claim. If he agrees not to make a claim, he erases the need to contribute. No other contributor to the pool is worse off, or better off, as a result of his action. Further, no matter how many motorists elect to opt-out, the feasibility of first party insurance for the remainder is not spoiled — provided that the group remaining in the pool does not become so very small as to thwart actuarial estimates. Under a "third party" perspective, in contrast, the contribution of an individual motorist is set to reflect the likelihood that others will make a claim against the fund as a result of the motorist's activities. There is little relationship between this likelihood and the likelihood of the motorist himself or his family making a claim against the fund. His promise not to make a claim is irrelevant to his third party obligations so long as he continues to drive a car.

We risk oversimplifying the problem of the contributor opting-out by treating it as if the choice involved only himself. It remains to be seen whether the analysis changes if we now include the fact that the motorist's choice will often affect not only him, but also members of his immediate family.

There is nothing odd in a man buying, say, health and accident insurance for himself and his family, or in effect "opting-out" by electing not to buy such insurance. We are not disturbed by his power to dispose of the "rights" of others in his family. In the auto compensation version of the problem, however, opting out has a double significance. The motorist cannot simply refuse to buy insurance; he must also be able to waive the rights his family might otherwise enjoy. The family is not merely deprived of unconditional reparations under the plan, but it also may be barred by the plan from utilizing the tort system up to the ceiling level. At first blush such an arrangement seems to raise questions about whether motorists should be allowed to dispose of rights of others without explicit waivers. But on reflection, it makes sense to treat the immediate members of the family — those in a common household — as being, collectively, the first party insurer. As such they have available, in common, the money they would have spent for the first party insurance had the motorist not opted-out. The dichotomy between contributors and non-contributors, although thus complicated, nevertheless survives. In this setting, the functional definition of a contributor is one on whose behalf the motorist may be permitted to opt-out from the first party insurance component of a plan.

If then it might be practicable to make the first party component wholly voluntary, what explains the strong consensus to keep it compulsory? It is worth restating that the main objective of all high ceiling plans is to substitute the unconditional reparations of the plan for the expensive, erratic, and "unfair" conditional reparations of the tort system. This objective combines, it should be stressed, two aspirations: (1) within limits; to abolish the tort system and (2) to engineer a first party insurance scheme among motorists. The fact is that all plans have combined the two aspirations in a single package.

The question of compulsion makes one aware that these two aspirations of a plan can be viewed as independent of each other. Assume that the one step has been taken and that the tort system has been abolished in auto accidents for losses to motorists and their immediate families, on the ground that it is such a very poor way to manage things. The second step then has to be confronted. For the society that has given up the tort redress, there is a choice in the design of the insurance arrangement: the society can compel insurance or it can give the motorists freedom of choice. Either way there is a challenge. If the compulsion alternative is adopted, the question is why apply the sumptuary principle only to misfortunes involving auto accidents. If the voluntary alternative is adopted, the question is whether there is any achievement in merely abolishing the tort remedy.

It may be tempting to read the almost universal consensus for compulsion as a strong endorsement of the sumptuary principle. An auto plan may be seen as a half loaf of social insurance, which is better than none. But before embracing this conclusion, two other explanations for the consensus should be considered. The decision may reflect nothing more than respect for the practical administrative difficulties that may arise if a compulsory "third party" insurance scheme to protect non-contributors is put in tandem with only a voluntary first party scheme to protect contributors and their immediate families. Or the decision may reflect the realpolitik of the situation. The insurance industry surely would have been monolithically opposed to a proposal that would eliminate the need for the bulk of liability insurance and that did not require first party insurance. And the public rhetoric would have been destroyed if it could be said that all a plan did was to eliminate the tort system from a large part of the auto accident arena. . . .

19

The underlying theme of this Article has been that auto compensation legislation has been proliferated and elaborated to the point where it is now creating its own jurisprudence. Throughout we have recognized that the auto plan is a new institutional concept. Something new has been brought in to replace something old. At the heart of every plan is the replacement of conditional redress keyed to corrective justice, by unconditional reparations keyed to insurance. One might have thought that a change so conceived would have been able to break sharply with the common law and its legacy of traditions, expectations, and concepts. The most interesting impression with which we are left is that the common law, *even in the case of the most ambitious plans,* still makes its presence felt. Once again Maitland's aphorism is corroborated: auto plans, too, might be said to be ruled from the grave.

On at least three issues the bond is close. The most obvious instance, made explicit in the public rhetoric, is tying the cost of the new arrangement to the cost of the old. Almost universally the baseline for assessing the cost of a plan to the motorist is provided by the cost to him of the common law tort-insurance system. Use of the common law as a baseline is exemplified again in justifying, with respect to non-contributors, the limitations on reparations. This time the reference is not to what the common law costs, but to what the common law affords as redress. The justification may be seen in terms of "a bargain" in which old common law rights are traded for new unconditional reparation rights—a justification which would be without foundation in the absence of any common law rights. Further, we would hazard the guess that it is this same sense of a trade-off of the old for the new which explains why the *compulsion* of the first party insurance component of plans has received so little attention. In general one would not have anticipated that society was so ready to take for granted the propriety of compelling first party insurance. The sumptuary principle, we suggest, was tranquilly accepted in the auto plan instance because the first party insurance was not viewed as simply first party insurance. It was viewed rather as the replacement of an older system which itself is "compulsory" — that is, the common law liability system, whether or not accompanied by compulsory third party liability insurance.

On at least three other issues it has proved surprisingly difficult to replace the common law with unconditional reparations. While they may in fact reflect nothing more than political diplomacy and compromise, on analysis these survivals of tort law present stubborn difficulties. For varying but overlapping reasons, plans have not attempted to bring within unconditional reparations three aspects of loss: pain and suffering, full economic loss, and auto property damage. In each instance, because the item will not be brought within the plan, there is posed the difficult policy choice of whether to eliminate redress of the particular loss entirely or to allow conditional redress under the tort system. The answer in general has been that it is better to continue to do corrective justice via the tort system than to ignore such items of loss altogether.

On three other issues distinct traces of the common law remain discernible. The designers of plans have been reluctant to carry out fully for all motorists the logic of rating risks for first party insurance. The drastic change in moving from rates set under a third party liability insurance principle to rates set under a first party insurance principle has on occasion involved too sharp a break with expectations. This conflict between old expectations and new logic is seen most dramatically in the efforts under plans to work out the relative rates for trucks and cars. Similarly, traces of common law thinking crop up in the problem of integrating other regimes of reparation with that furnished by the auto plan. Discussion of this whole matter remains almost unintelligible unless placed against the backdrop of the common law collateral source rule. A final example arises with respect to subrogation and reimbursement. It is not uncommon for plans to permit the insurer who initially pays the unconditional reparations to recover from the insurer of a motorist who, judged by the common law criteria of liability, was at fault.

NOTES AND QUESTIONS

1. Do the authors make a convincing argument that there are anomalies involved in having a ceiling on the economic loss compensable under a no-fault plan? Why does their discussion of the issue of awards under plans focus on ceilings?

2. Why does their discussion of the costs of plans focus on "intramural" costs — the allocation of costs among insured individuals?

3. Is the compulsory aspect of an auto compensation scheme distinctive, or is it similar to the involuntary element in most modern welfare schemes? Are the ideological issues any different, for example, when considering the Social Security retirement income system? Would it be feasible to set up an auto compensation plan without relying on compulsion?

4. A partial escape from the compulsory element is provided in those plans allowing a deductible. Blum and Kalven refer to the deductible as a "preemptory partial opt-out," and suggest that such a device raises the broader question of why first party insurance should be compulsory. Can you suggest an answer? Is a deductible — especially a fairly sizable one — inconsistent with resort to compulsion?

5. A common basis for supporting compulsion is that the insured would be opting out of coverage for his family as well as

himself. Blum and Kalven argue, in response, that "as such they have available, in common, the money they would have spent for the first party insurance had the motorist not opted-out." The head of the household makes similar decisions that bind the family in other first-party situations, such as fire and casualty insurance. Are the arguments against compulsion convincing?

6. In the concluding section, Blum and Kalven observe that "something new has been brought in to replace something old. At the heart of every plan is the replacement of conditional redress keyed to corrective justice, by unconditional reparations keyed to insurance." Is it accurate to say that the old system is "keyed to corrective justice," rather than to insurance?

7. Does the attractiveness of a no-fault plan vis-à-vis the fault system depend on whether the tort system is retained above the no-fault ceilings? Does it turn on the dollar figure assigned as the operative ceiling on economic loss? More generally, what conditions, if any, would you regard as essential to establish a preference for a compensation plan over the fault system?

8. Blum and Kalven suggest that a partisan supporter of the tort system might nevertheless stipulate that there is no justification for pain and suffering under a no-fault scheme. Why? Are damages for pain and suffering inconsistent with a no-fault plan, or merely impolitic?

9. This essay is the last in a series of contributions written by Blum and Kalven during the decade when theoretical and political debate about auto compensation plans reached an unprecedented level of intensity. Their earlier works are Public Law Perspectives on a Private Law Problem (1965), The Empty Cabinet of Dr. Calabresi: Auto Accidents and General Deterrence, 34 U. Chi. L. Rev. 239 (1967), and A Stopgap Plan for Compensating Auto Accident Victims, 1968 Ins. L.J. 661. By the mid-1970s, some twenty-five states had enacted a form of no-fault legislation. Since then, the movement has virtually ground to a halt — no new comprehensive legislation has been enacted since 1975. Is there anything in the Blum and Kalven essay that is suggestive about why the movement has faltered?

10. Looking to the future, Blum and Kalven observe:

> There can be little doubt that the mood of society now favors legal intervention to shift accident losses off individual victims by one means or another. We think it likely that the auto accident has been singled out for legislative action not because auto accident victims have any special appeal as victims, but because of the high visibility of the auto accident problem and especially because of certain structural features of the auto accident world that make it feasible to rely heavily on first party insurance to compensate victims. These features include: the access to licensing as a way of enforcing the compulsory insurance; the

existence, albeit in another form, of an insurance pool financed by motorists who are thoroughly accustomed to paying insurance premiums; the large overlap between actors who pay premiums and victims who receive reparations; the appeal of having first party insurance protect the motorist as a victim while erasing his legal obligations to others; and, finally, the ease of tracing the injury to the operation of an auto. The question for the next decade is whether some or all of these features, which seem to be special to the auto world, still prove to be limiting conditions on extending the auto plan strategy to other kinds of accidents. [1973 Utah L. Rev. 341, 379, n. 42]

On this note, consider the following essay, reviewing G. Palmer, Compensation for Incapacity (1979), a study of the New Zealand social insurance system.

The New Zealand Accident Compensation Reform*

James A. Henderson, Jr.

I. The Substance of the New Zealand Reforms

The Accident Compensation Act of 1972 in its original form abolished rights to recover in tort and substituted rights to receive no-fault compensation for personal injury or death suffered by earners and motor vehicle accident victims. For the first group, worker's compensation was extended to include employees and the self-employed on a twenty-four-hour basis without a work-connection requirement. For the second group, a statute resembling the automobile no-fault schemes implemented in a number of jurisdictions in this country was enacted. A year later, coverage under the Act, together with the accompanying bar to recovery in tort, was extended to all persons, including nonearners, suffering personal injury or death by accident. The consequence of the expansion was that the Act virtually eliminated liability in tort. Claimants tortiously injured other than "by accident" may bring common law actions; but the phrase "by accident" has been interpreted broadly enough to approach what Palmer describes as "the complete abolition of common law rights."

Variable levies on employers and flat-rate levies on the self-employed fund the coverage for earners; variable levies on motor vehicles fund the motor vehicle compensation system; and appropriations by Parliament fund the supplemental scheme covering nonearners. In cases of overlapping coverage, the motor vehicle coverage

*Source: 48 U. Chi. L. Rev. 781, 782-801 (1981).

is primary. Illnesses not caused by accident are excluded, thus creating the difficulty of distinguishing between an "accident" and an "illness." Willfully self-inflicted injuries also are excluded, as is death due to suicide unless the suicide was caused by a state of mind that was the result of a compensable accident. The Act does not cover property damage.

Under the system, compensation is available for medical, rehabilitation, and funeral expenses; lost earnings and impairment of earning capacity; some pecuniary losses other than medical expenses and lost earnings; nonpecuniary losses such as pain and suffering; loss of bodily function; and payments for support of dependents in death cases. Medical expenses include reasonable expenses for medical treatment and hospital care not paid for under social security, ambulance expenses, nursing care expenses, dental expenses, and expenses for artificial limbs. Full costs of rehabilitation are provided for, including a full-time personal attendant when necessary. Reasonable funeral expenses are covered.

Compensation for lost earnings and reduced earning capacity is equally generous. Earners and the self-employed are paid eighty percent of their lost earnings up to a fairly high weekly limit. Except for certain persons, earnings are not imputed to nonearners. Thus, a housewife accidentally incapacitated cannot recover lost earnings that were not actually received on a regular basis prior to the accident. Nonearners are allowed to receive all other elements of compensation, however, including payments for loss of bodily functions.

The New Zealand compensation system generally avoids lump-sum payments. Medical expenses are paid when incurred and payments for lost earnings are made periodically. Lump-sum payments are authorized only in exceptional circumstances. The only significant exception is for some nonpecuniary losses, where large lump-sum payments are expressly called for by the Act. Widows, minor children, and other dependents of persons killed accidentally are paid stated percentages of the amount the decedent would have received had he survived and been totally incapacitated. Lump sums also are paid to surviving widows and minor children according to a schedule.

Coverage under the Act extends to New Zealand residents who are injured by accident outside the country if the accident occurs within twelve months after departure and if the claimant is either an earner continuing to earn in New Zealand or a self-employed person temporarily absent on business. Such persons presumably are free to pursue tort claims overseas in addition to recovering compensation in New Zealand. Members of the armed services also are covered while abroad, as are government employees assigned overseas. It is interesting that nonearners who are not government employees are not covered while out of the country—a member of the New Zealand Olympic hockey team injured in overseas competition, for example, probably would be forced to seek recovery elsewhere than the compensation system. Visitors to New Zealand are covered by the system while in the country and are barred from bringing tort actions for accidental injuries.

The New Zealand system is administered by an Accident Compensation Commission comprised of three members, one of whom must be a lawyer. Administration of the system reflects something of a "catch-as-catch-can" quality. The primary agent for levies is the Department of Inland Revenue, but levies on motor vehicles are collected by the Post Office as part of the annual vehicle licensing operation. Applications for compensation are filed with the State Insurance Office, which serves as the Commission's sole disbursal agent except for a specialized company that handles seamen's claims. The State Insurance Office has no authority to decline claims. Instead, claims that are not granted are referred to a Commission Officer. Claimants denied at this level are entitled to a hearing before a Commissioner or hearing officer, with the right to appeal to an Independent Appeal Authority. From there, a claimant may obtain judicial review by the Court of Appeal and then by the Supreme Court. Palmer reports that the number of applications for review has increased rapidly since the Act was first implemented, as has the involvement of lawyers in compensation cases.

The relationship between the compensation system and the common law tort system presents interesting questions. As a general rule, tort actions are barred only in connection with accidental injuries for which compensation is payable. Thus, because compensation may not be recovered for property damage, actions at law will lie when property is tortiously damaged or destroyed. Coverage under the Act and the barring of tort claims are not coextensive, however. Strangely, the 1973 amendments, which are designed to extend the Act's coverage, take away the right to proceed in tort in some situations that the extended coverage does not reach. To prevent injustice, the drafters provided a curious solution: the amendments empower the Compensation Commission to make ex gratia payments to persons who suffer injury by accident but who are not covered by the Act. Also, by making the Commission's determination conclusive, the Act avoids a situation where a claimant "falls between the stools" procedurally, that is, where the Commission first denies a claim on the ground that no statutory coverage exists, and a court then denies tort recovery because coverage does exist.

The New Zealand compensation system is a funded, as opposed

to a pay-as-you-go, system. An amount of money is collected and set aside each year that should be sufficient to pay all future claims arising from injuries suffered during the year of collection. The amount necessary to fund the system in this manner is calculated each year by estimating the value of all future claims arising out of accidents occurring that year and reducing that estimate to present value at a conservative rate of interest. If the claims predictions are accurate and the discount rate employed approximates the actual rate of return received, there will be just enough left from the monies collected in any given year to pay the last claim for compensation. The cost estimates under the system seem fairly accurate, although Palmer says this is not certain. The claims rate has risen somewhat more rapidly than had been anticipated, perhaps due to increasing public awareness of the system.

Palmer is admirably candid in assessing the first four years' experience under a new system in which he obviously and passionately believes. He admits, for example, that there "has been a tendency for people to claim for some rather curious matters." His narrative reveals that abuses have occurred in some industries in which employers are required to pay one hundred percent of the employees' wages for the first week of incapacity arising out of work-related injuries. Moreover, he describes the administration of the system as "too often. . .characterized by an abundance of caution, a stubborn inflexibility, and an undue sensitivity to public criticism." Notwithstanding these flaws, however, the author insists that few of the problems relate to the fundamental principles of the system. He concludes:

> Against the difficulties encountered must be matched the achievements of the new scheme. There is much less room for argument. . . than there was under the common law. Everyone who is incapacitated is paid and paid quickly in most cases. The social problem posed by the uncompensated victim has disappeared. Rather than providing a brake on rehabilitation the new scheme promotes it. The removal of the right to sue has been accompanied by no floods of protests. The common law action for personal injury in New Zealand has been buried and there is no demand for its exhumation.

II. Is The New Zealand System Theoretically Justifiable?

A generally accurate if oversimplified summary of Palmer's answer to this question might be as follows: Of course the New Zealand compensation system is theoretically justifiable, because it solves the important social problem of the uncompensated accident victim. Before 1973, the common law tort system in New Zealand addressed this problem inadequately. The rules governing liability were vague and difficult to apply. The common law system resembled a game of chance: most accident victims recovered nothing, while those who were successful often received too little, too late. To make matters worse, the tort system absorbed an outrageously high percentage of benefits in the form of attorney's fees. The deterrent effect on conduct of exposure to tort liability was diminished by the widespread reliance on liability insurance. By responding to these shortcomings, the New Zealand compensation system provides a fair and efficient solution to a significant social problem. Instead of a relatively small fraction being entitled to compensation, *all* accident victims who suffer personal injury are covered. Benefits in most cases are more generous than under the common law, and are paid more promptly. Rehabilitation is a stated goal and a realized objective. The system's negative impact on allocative efficiency, although regrettable, probably is exaggerated and is in any event acceptable in light of the gains in social welfare.

The primary problem with Palmer's rationale is accepting his first premise, namely, that the failure of the New Zealand common law tort system to compensate everyone who suffered injury was an "important social problem." The common law never was intended as a means of accomplishing such a compensation objective. Even if one accepts the premise that every injured victim should be compensated, the insistence of the New Zealand system that in order to be compensable the injuries must be suffered "accidentally" is clearly inconsistent with that premise. Furthermore, the system's potential negative effects on allocative efficiency, rather than having been exaggerated, have been underestimated. In the paragraphs that follow, I shall consider each of these points in turn.

A. The Failure to Compensate Some Accident Victims Was Not a Significant Social Problem

One who believes that accident victims who recover little or nothing through the tort system present a significant social problem probably is thinking of the relatively few instances in which serious and permanent injuries cause great financial hardship for the victims and their families. Such cases do occur, and some are tragic. But there was no strong correlation in New Zealand between suffering accidental injury and experiencing financial hardship. Only a small percentage of accident victims encountered significant financial hardships,[48] because of the availability of free medical care and, for many accident

48. Studies of automobile accident cases in the United States, for example, indi-

victims, of other benefits, including public welfare and personal savings. To the unfortunate few who fell into the hardship category, of course, the problems were significant. But it would seem more realistic to view this minority as part of the problem of poverty than as part of the problem of uncompensated accident victims. Given New Zealand's traditional commitment to ambitious welfare programs aimed at helping the poor and the disadvantaged, it may not even have been a significant poverty problem.

Thus, the New Zealand compensation system can be justified on the basis of social welfare principles only if those principles are expanded to include welfare for those not in particular financial need. Indeed, the book reveals that such an expansion of social welfare is precisely what is involved. Although Palmer cites a vivid "hardship" case at the outset to show how the tort system fails those in great need of assistance, the New Zealand compensation system is mainly concerned with delivering benefits to persons who need them only in the sense that they would otherwise be financially inconvenienced.

Palmer admits that this is, in essence, a social welfare system for the middle and upper-middle classes. He describes the concerns voiced in New Zealand over whether the system might divert public attention from the question of adequacy of welfare benefits for the poor; and he addresses the policy questions inherent in having a system that provides benefits to those who do not need them. But the book conveys the impression that the compensation system addressed a pressing and significant social problem in much the same way that an airlift of food and medical supplies alleviates the problems presented by a flood or an earthquake. In fact, such an impression is mistaken. The circumstances the compensation system addresses deserve to be called "significant social problems" only if that label applies to all unexpected disruptions, great or small, in the economic status of individuals.

B.   The Common Law Tort System Never Purported to Address All Unexpected Financial Hardships of Individuals

The book implies that the tort system failed in its efforts to compensate accident victims and therefore deserved to be replaced with a more efficient means of providing compensation. Palmer

---

cate that a small percentage (no more than five percent) of accident victims suffer significant dislocation costs. See 1 U.S. Department of Transportation, Economic Consequences of Automobile Accidents 362, Table 56FS (1970). It seems reasonable to assume that in New Zealand, with its greater public welfare programs, the percentage was no higher, and probably lower.

recognizes that the first part of this statement is wrong—tort law never set out to compensate victims of misfortune. But the impression conveyed by the book is to the contrary.

A mistaken interpretation of the actual objectives of tort law pervades Palmer's thesis, as it did the analysis of the reformers who supported the Act. The reformers understood that the expanded no-fault compensation system could become a reality only if it replaced the tort system, because otherwise the need for new funding would be so great as to render unattractive any expanded commitment to compensation. Thus, there had to be an "utterly devastating" attack on the common law. If the reformers had focused on the true objectives of tort law—the enhancement of social utility and the promotion of shared notions of fairness—the attack would have fallen short. The reformers possessed no empirical data to support conclusions that the tort system had failed to achieve either of these objectives, so the focus of attention had to be shifted to the compensation objective for the attack to succeed. Indeed, once the compensation objective is considered paramount, it is self-evident that a system promising "integrated and comprehensive...compensation that is usually swift and sure" is preferable to one that offers only "[u]ncertain, uncoordinated, and capricious remedies."

Thus, the strategy of reform that led to the Act was to attack the tort system for failing to achieve an objective that it never purported to recognize and then to belittle as tangential and ineffective its efforts to enhance utility and fairness. Palmer uses this same strategy to persuade readers of the desirability of the New Zealand system. Although he includes all of the arguments relevant to the underlying policy issues, his confessed bias causes him to stack the deck at every opportunity.

I, too, have vigorously attacked the common law tort system.[62] Where I differ with Palmer, however, is on how to remedy the shortcomings of the common law. He focuses on compensation rather than utility and fairness, and advocates a complete replacement of the tort system. I urge that we continue to focus on utility and fairness, and that we change only so much of the tort system as needs changing.[63] An example of our different viewpoints is our reactions to the use of a significant proportion of insurance premiums in the tort system to cover insurance company overhead and to compensate

62. See, e.g., Henderson, Expanding the Negligence Concept: Retreat From the Rule of Law, 51 Ind. L.J. 467 (1976); Henderson, Judicial Review of Manufacturers' Conscious Design Choices: The Limits of Adjudication, 73 Colum. L. Rev. 1531 (1973)....

63. See, e.g., Henderson, Manufacturers' Liability for Defective Product Design: A Proposed Statutory Reform, 56 N.C.L. Rev. 625 (1978).

lawyers who handle claims. Palmer views these expenditures as impediments to the compensation objective, and urges that they be eliminated whenever possible. By contrast, I view these expenditures as essential to the utility and fairness objectives, and would seek to reduce them only when they are unnecessarily high.[65]

Although Palmer belittles the ability of tort law to enhance either utility or fairness, he does recognize the legitimacy of both objectives. And although I believe that utility and fairness are sacrificed to too great an extent in the New Zealand scheme, I recognize the legitimacy and necessity of the no-fault idea in more limited contexts.[67] Even with these caveats, however, there is some mutual exclusivity between the objectives of universal compensation and utility and fairness. It is probable that, to a significant extent, the one objective is accomplished only at the expense of the other. The problem with Palmer's treatment of the objectives is not that he has clearly chosen the wrong one to emphasize, but that he has failed to develop the implications of his choice. By adopting the rhetorical strategy that led to political victory in 1972 and 1973—attacking the tort system for its ineffectiveness as a means of accomplishing an objective at which it never was aimed— he assumes away some of the most philosophically interesting aspects of his thesis.

C. The New Zealand System Is an Inadequate Solution to the Problem of Financial Disruptions

I have expressed doubts about the significance of the uncompensated-victim problem and disagreement with attempts to blame the tort system for its ineffectiveness as a compensation mechanism. Here I am willing to assume for the sake of argument that a problem exists and that more than tort liability is required to solve it. My criticism of the New Zealand system in this context is that there is no reason why victims of misfortunes other than accidents should not have equally valid claims to compensation as accident victims. Why, for example, should the working person whose leg must be am-

---

65. Insofar as one views the tort system as performing functions other than insuring against losses, the costs of running the system may be acceptable even if relatively high. In contrast, Palmer's objective is to return the highest possible percentage of premium dollars to claimants. For him, costs may be unacceptable even if relatively low....

67. See Henderson, Book Review, 56 B.U.L. Rev. 830 (1976), in which I reviewed Professor Jeffrey O'Connell's proposals for elective no-fault plans. My problems with his proposal are mostly problems of implementation, not basic principle. I have also written favorably on the prospects for no-fault approaches to medical accidents. See Designated Compensable Event System: A Feasibility Study 53-101 (1979) (study

putated because of cancer be denied benefits because he lost his leg through disease rather than by accident? Diseases such as cancer may often cause more significant disruptions in people's lives than accidents.

One answer offered by some proponents of the New Zealand reform seems truly remarkable: they extended the compensation system to include only accident victims because that is as far as the common law tort system extended. The statement must be considered in connection with another argument advanced earlier by these same reformers in a different context: "The tort system deserves to be replaced because it fails to extend accident compensation far enough." It appears that the tort system's benefits policy is either to be condemned as short sighted or relied upon for support, depending on whether it suits the reformers' purposes.

The real reasons for limiting the New Zealand system to accident victims have little to do with basic principles. An important point in favor of the reforms of 1972 and 1973 was the promise that the total cost of the new system would not exceed the cost of the old; the savings generated by dismantling the tort system were to cover the additional costs of extending benefits to all accident victims. There also may have been a few vague promises of actually reducing total costs; similar promises, rather than an appeal to basic principles, generated much of the support for motor vehicle no-fault legislation in the United States in the early 1970s. No such promises of holding costs constant, or reducing them, would have been possible if harm associated with diseases were included along with accidental injuries, so the line was drawn at accidents. To the stirring reformist rhetoric of "community responsibility" and "comprehensive entitlement" was added the unspoken contradictory phrase, "so long as it does not add to our costs."

Palmer does criticize the New Zealand system for failing to cover diseases and congenital disabilities, and he urges that the system be amended to cover them. Of course, if the 1972 and 1973 reforms are but an initial step toward a more comprehensive and internally consistent system, the present criticisms lose much of their force. But based upon the information in this book, I doubt that coverage will be significantly extended. Nothing is likely to occur that will make the question of added costs any easier to answer; and some of the problems of abuse under the present system probably will become more significant with the passage of time, exacerbating the problem of costs. If the New Zealand system is not expanded, what will have

---

sponsored by the ABA Commn. on Medical Professional Liability). The important feature shared by these plans is their commitment in principle to allocative efficiency.

emerged from the reforms is a system that violates the principle of compensating victims of unexpected misfortune even as it purports to embody that principle. One may wonder whether the critics who spoke of the "false morality" of tort law will be able to appreciate the hypocrisy reflected in the system they helped create.

D. The New Zealand System Is Likely to Have Negative Effects on Allocative Efficiency and Fairness

The tort system's objectives include the enhancement of allocative efficiency and the promotion of shared notions of fairness. The former objective is accomplished by deterring unacceptably risky conduct,[78] the latter by providing private remedies against those who commit wrongs.[79] The tort system does fail to compensate some accident victims who have suffered loss, but it must neglect the compensation objective if it is to accomplish the others. Replacing the tort system with a compensation system may well generate benefits only at the cost of detracting from efficiency and fairness.

The book supports both of my conclusions. Palmer recognizes the problem of the effects on allocative efficiency: "One problem of such loss-spreading programs for all injuries is that incentives for safety may be lost unless care is taken to draw the contributions for payment of the scheme from activities that engender the injury losses." His point about "incentives for safety" requires further examination. Generally, if actors are not required to pay a fair share of the costs of their activities, including the accident costs, they will tend to overengage in those activities whose costs they can most successfully escape from paying. Thus, if everyone were required to pay into a universal accident compensation fund on a flat-rate, per capita basis, those who engaged in comparatively safe activities would pay more than their share of the total accident costs generated by all activities, and those who engaged in relatively risky activities would pay less. The resulting wealth transfers would encourage actors at the margin (those indifferent to which sort of activities to engage in) to switch from safe to risky activities. Not everyone would switch, but enough would to cause the overall accident costs in the society to

---

78. The tort system deters in two basic ways: specifically, by causing actors to modify their conduct in order to escape liability; and generally, by forcing actors to bear the costs of avoiding accidents or insuring against them. Some actors will decide not to engage in activities that have high avoidance or insurance costs. On the subject of specific and general deterrence, see G. Calabresi, The Costs of Accidents (1970).

79. Fairness in tort admittedly is a vague, largely intuitive concept. For a recent effort to render it more intelligible, see Fletcher, Fairness and Utility in Tort Theory, 85 Harv. L. Rev. 537 (1972).

increase over what they would have been if those engaging in relatively safe activities had not been required to subsidize their risk-preferring fellow citizens. Resources would be misallocated to relatively risky activities; the increase in accident costs would constitute social waste.

The solution to this problem of waste, one that to a limited extent was incorporated in the New Zealand scheme, is to require contribution to the compensation fund in proportion to the risk of accidents created by the actor. If the amount contributed is appropriate, the proper balance between safe and risky activities will be achieved. The tort system consciously aims at attaching the appropriate price tags to risky conduct,[83] but there is no reason in theory why a system providing universal compensation could not do the same thing.[84]

Palmer addresses these issues in some of the most interesting sections of the book. The problem is practical: how can the costs be properly allocated among accident-generating activities? The sponsors of the New Zealand system apparently believed they could achieve adequate safety incentives by providing separate funds for earners and motor vehicles supported by independent, variable levies. The annual levies on motor vehicles in 1978, for example, varied from $2.00 to $86.25, depending on the type, size, and estimated risk potential. But the levies reflected relative risks crudely; for example, all privately owned automobiles were assessed at $14.20. Palmer points out that such a flat rate makes no attempt to distinguish among vehicles by factors affecting risks, even such obvious ones as the varying amounts of use automobiles receive. He suggests a fuel tax as a more appropriate method of funding the motor vehicle compensation scheme.[88]

83. Under a negligence system, activities will reflect the costs of avoiding accidents. In theory, if one assumes zero transaction costs, those are the only "accident-related" costs that will be reflected — all actors will act reasonably and escape liability by investing adequately in avoidance measures. Under a strict liability rule, activities will also reflect the expense of insuring against accident costs that cannot be avoided efficiently. To the extent that the tort system achieves the general deterrence objective, it does so more effectively under a strict liability approach. Strict products liability, for example, causes the prices of various commercially supplied products to reflect their relative defect-related accident costs. Palmer never really addresses the role of strict products liability, although he mentions its development.... His attack is on the "negligence system" more than on the "tort system"; when he thinks of a "tort case," he thinks of one like the automobile accident case he uses as an example at the outset....

84. In theory, nothing prevents the separation of the pay-in and the pay-out mechanisms. So long as the pay-in mechanism is related to risk or cost, general deterrence will be achieved regardless of how the pay-out mechanism is designed. For an interesting recent proposal making this point and calling for a government-operated system of cost internalizations (pay ins) and compensation (pay outs), see Pierce, Encouraging Safety: The Limits of Tort Law and Government Regulation, 33 Vand. L. Rev. 1281 (1980).

88. The tort system is entitled to low marks for the way it has handled motor

Despite his fuel tax suggestions, Palmer sees little likelihood of achieving adequate safety incentives under the New Zealand scheme. He sets forth his conclusions as follows:

> In the injury reforms in New Zealand...the economic deterrence issue caused a good deal of debate with wide differences of opinion. ... There is a reasonable consensus of opinion that the effort to rate differentially should be made. Few people actually get down to the administrative problem of designing an actual system of contributions which is based on reliable data, achieves a high degree of internalization of accident costs, is reasonably cheap to administer, and is fair. I began as a firm believer in the validity of the theory; I have ended up as a skeptic as to whether any scheme capable of implementation will achieve much by the way of economic deterrence, at least so long as it is attached to a compensation scheme. Knowledge about accident prevention is, however, in such a primitive state, that anything offering a hope of reducing accidents should be tried.

As these comments indicate, the sources of Palmer's pessimism are lack of information and costs of administration. Our knowledge of which activities generate which costs is inadequate; even given such knowledge, the cost of imposing differential levies reflecting such information would be too great. The tort system spends significant sums trying to achieve more finely tuned cost allocations.[91] One who would dismantle the tort system to eliminate those expenditures will not welcome suggestions that the overhead of the compensation system be increased to achieve more informed cost allocations.

In addition to considering the potential negative effects on allocative efficiency of moving to a compensation system such as the one adopted in New Zealand, such a move must be assessed from the standpoint of shared notions of fairness. A New Zealand-type system can be criticized on several fairness grounds. First, citizens would no longer have some of the traditional methods of vindicating individual rights in our legal system. A person intentionally struck by another, for example, would no longer be entitled to a legal judgment that his right to personal integrity had been violated. Second, the anomalies created by the Act are open to attack. For example, distinctions drawn between illness and accidental injury under the system cause persons similarly disadvantaged to be treated differently. Third, the measures of recovery include a number of arbitrary limits that cause persons

---

vehicle accidents, from the perspective of achieving allocative efficiency. This judgment also applies to those states in this country that have adopted no-fault automobile insurance plans....

91. Tort law may not succeed in achieving finely tuned allocations, however. There are reasons for suspecting that it falls well short of perfection. See generally Morris, Enterprise Liability and the Actuarial Process—The Insignificance of Foresight, 70 Yale L.J. 554 (1961).

dissimilarly disadvantaged to receive essentially the same benefits. Finally, the procedures under the compensation system reflect a willingness to sacrifice the interests of the individual to the greater good.[94]

These criticisms of the New Zealand system do not suggest that the common law tort system achieves nearly perfect fairness. In areas of tort law that have come to be dominated by vague rules and excessive reliance on supposed experts and lay juries, fairness can sometimes be difficult to detect. But the tort system creates the appearance, at least, of trying to reach individualized results that are fair to all concerned. If the necessary reforms of the rules and processes of decision in the tort system were achieved, the appearance might begin to conform more closely to reality. Moving from a properly functioning common law tort system to a system like that in New Zealand might cause many citizens to feel that traditional commitments to fairness had been compromised or even abandoned. Although more victims of misfortune would be receiving benefits under the new regime and in a democracy it may be presumed that the appropriate balance of interests has been struck, I would not be surprised to discover a general feeling in the community that fairness to the individual had been sacrificed in the name of the greatest good for the greatest number.

Has there been such a feeling in New Zealand? Palmer admits that "[t]he administration of the Act . . . has not matched the vision of the original blueprint." But he insists that the system has worked for four years "without much sign of public dissatisfaction." He suggests that many of the difficulties are due to administrative suspicions about claims, and concludes that "[f]ew of the problems relate to the fundamental principles of the scheme." But if significant numbers of persons have experienced frustration in dealing with the New Zealand system, that may be the product of the system itself rather than of overworked or uninspired clerks.

On balance, however, Palmer's conclusion that New Zealanders are happy with the changes made in 1972 and 1973 is convincing. Thus, it probably is true that "[t]he common law action for personal injury in New Zealand has been buried and there is no demand for its exhumation." Although the compensation reforms appear successful in New Zealand, it is doubtful that the tort system would succumb so easily in the United States. Palmer attributes the probable resistance to such a change in this country to what he sees as support for the common law tort system by powerful vested interests. This may be a significant factor, but it is not the only factor; rather, I believe that the

94. The remedies under a tort system are tailor-made to fit individual cases; a compensation system cannot afford such "luxuries." . . .

sentiment favoring the tort system in this country is widely shared by its citizens. Apart from the opposition of trial lawyers, public dissatisfaction on fairness grounds with a proposal to embrace a New Zealand-type system probably would be widespread.

III. Historical Perspective

Some American readers may conclude from this book that, from the initial Royal Commission Report in 1967 to passage of the Accident Compensation Act of 1972, New Zealand experienced a legal and social revolution aimed at the shortcomings and abuses of the common law tort system. Palmer repeatedly employs phrases such as "changing the law to meet new demands," and refers to "big policy changes" and "radical" solutions in characterizing the changes. He quotes New Zealand newspapers as describing the 1972 Act as "breathtaking" and "so revolutionary that interested parties had been stunned into silence." His account of the events leading to passage of the Act conveys a sense of mounting frustration over the failures of the old system coupled with growing excitement over the prospects for the new.

Despite the views of Palmer and the New Zealand press, however, when the reforms of 1972 and 1973 are placed in their proper historical perspective they are neither radical nor revolutionary. This is not to deprecate the New Zealand experience nor to suggest that Palmer has deliberately misled his readers. Technically, the New Zealand reforms are significantly innovative, and Palmer cannot be faulted for expressing his enthusiasm with having observed and participated in an intellectually exciting experience. But judged in relation to the social context of New Zealand in the 1970s, the Accident Compensation Act of 1972 did not represent the momentous social revolution that American readers, imagining the implications of a similar change in this country, are likely to assume it was.

There are several reasons for this conclusion, which are derived from the book. First, there was no public outcry in New Zealand over the deficiencies of the tort system. To the contrary, the reformers readily admitted that there was an almost total absence of public demand for change. One reason for this lack of demand may have been that New Zealand is a sparsely populated, economically prosperous country that has long prided itself on making substantial commitments to public welfare programs. Another is that, except for the automobile-accident area, the tort system had not expanded in New Zealand to the point of taxing the limits of the judicial process.

Indeed, the areas of medical malpractice and products liability, thought by some observers to be in a crisis in the United States, were not a significant problem in New Zealand. The relative paucity of tort cases in New Zealand seems attributable mostly to a lower level of litigiousness, rather than to any deficiencies in the system of tort law.

To be sure, the New Zealand no-fault system for motor vehicle accidents replaced an active area of tort law. But this part of the 1972 reform was hardly a startling innovation. Not only had many jurisdictions in the United States and elsewhere already adopted that particular type of reform, but New Zealand had defeated only narrowly a motor vehicle no-fault system proposal as early as 1928.

If the tort system played a less significant role in New Zealand than it does in the United States, and if there was no public demand for change, why did the change in New Zealand come about? The answer is that a small group of judges and legal academics launched an attack on the tort system, based solely on principle and rhetoric, and saw a bipartisan, uncontroversial reform proposal enacted by a largely indifferent Parliament. No interest groups opposed the measure; Parliament passed it without a single dissenting vote; and there have been few, if any, postenactment repercussions. Thus, except for the motor vehicle no-fault proposal, which has counterparts in this country, the New Zealand reforms abolished a tort system that was far less significant than the American one and replaced it with a welfare scheme that represented relatively modest extensions of existing social welfare programs.

Midway through his description and analysis of the New Zealand experience, Palmer offers the following observation: "In general it is true to say that the larger the change contemplated in a democratic parliamentary system, the more difficult that change will be to achieve." In light of the relative ease with which the changes in New Zealand were accomplished, I can only conclude that they were less significant than Palmer believes.

Conclusion

If reforms such as have been enacted in New Zealand were proposed for implementation in the United States, I would oppose them for several reasons. First, uncompensated accident victims present a relatively low-priority social problem. Second, apart from the magnitude of the costs involved, abolishing tort liability and moving to a universal compensation system for all victims of accidents and illnesses would have serious negative effects on allocative efficiency and shared notions of fairness. Finally, despite my strong criticism of expansionary trends in American tort law, reforms aimed at curbing judicial excess should be given a chance to work before the tort system is scrapped altogether. . . .

NOTES AND QUESTIONS

1. Henderson suggests that the New Zealand tort system may have been replaced despite the fact that lack of compensation was not a significant problem. His assertion raises both definitional and empirical issues. Does he address these issues adequately? Could it be argued that dramatic changes in life-style, at most income levels, are highly disruptive? Is the welfare economist's refusal to make interpersonal comparisons of utility relevant here? If he is correct that only an "unfortunate few" fell into the "hardship category," does it necessarily follow that no significant social problem existed?

2. Assuming that a significant social problem did exist, Henderson castigates the New Zealand reformers for attacking the tort system on the grounds that it failed to compensate all accident victims. He points out that the tort system never purported to cover all victims of injury. Is this a persuasive line of attack? Why can't the tort system be criticized on the grounds that it assigned too little weight to the goal of compensating all accident victims? Were the reformers obliged to defer to traditional objectives of the tort system?

3. In turn, Henderson suggests that the critics of the tort system paid too little attention to the "true objectives of tort law" — deterrence and fairness. What precisely does Henderson regard as the "fairness" goal of the tort system? Why is compensation necessarily regarded as a goal distinct from fairness?

4. On the fairness point, Henderson asserts that "the tort system creates the appearance, at least, of trying to reach individualized results that are fair to all concerned." Do you agree? In this regard, reconsider the data on patterns of reparation in auto accident cases, p. 150, *supra*, and the description of settlement practices in Ross, pp. 142-149, *supra*.

5. Henderson's reference to deterrence, or allocative efficiency, as a primary goal of tort law has been examined in detail earlier. See Chapter Five, especially the Calabresi excerpt. If, as Henderson suggests, a social insurance scheme can be designed to approximate the allocative efficiency of the tort system, why might the New Zealand reformers have abandoned that objective? What trade-offs ordinarily arise in assigning pay-ins to a social insurance fund on the basis of activity costs? Are those trade-offs absent in the tort system?

Reconsider the discussion of allocative efficiency in Pierce, Encouraging Safety: The Limits of Tort Law and Government Regulation, pp. 130-135, *supra*.

6. Henderson accuses the New Zealand reformers of hypocrisy in arguing for a compensation principle more broadly based than that which the tort system provided, while failing to adopt a social insurance scheme that would cover "the victims of misfortunes other than accidents." Is this argument persuasive? Would it similarly undercut no-fault auto schemes? Worker's compensation legislation? All social legislation that provides assistance to discrete classes, rather than universal coverage?

7. Note that the New Zealand plan includes payments for pain and suffering. As we have seen, virtually none of the no-fault auto plans include such coverage. Do the differences between a social insurance scheme that replaces the tort system and a no-fault auto plan warrant the retention of pain and suffering coverage in the former case? Compare the industrial injury context, where replacement of the tort system was undertaken without retention of compensation for pain and suffering.

8. It seems clear that a wide-ranging social insurance scheme along the lines of the New Zealand plan would encounter far more resistance in the United States. What are the principal reasons? Is it primarily a matter of demographic differences? Interest-group politics? Underlying social attitudes? A combination of these and other factors?